"With *The Obliteration Doctrine,* Dr. Steinbock has provided historians and layman readers alike the definitive guide to understanding the atrocities committed by the Israeli government with the assistance of the American empire. The book is very well documented, very readable, with a great amount of supporting evidence for his claims. I highly recommend it."

SCOTT HORTON, Director of the Libertarian Institute, author of *Provoked: How Washington Started the New Cold War with Russia and the Catastrophe in Ukraine*

"The Obliteration Doctrine places the U.S.-Israeli assault on Gaza in historical context, making clear that it is hardly an Israeli project that the United States and Europe are 'complicit' in, but rather a joint project between western governments and Israel to destroy a threat to their hegemony. While it may seem strange to write a book about a genocide that was documented in real time and live streamed to the world, this is a valuable contribution to understanding what happened, how, and why."

DR. FEROZE SIDHWA, Trauma and critical care surgeon, and program director of San Joaquin General Hospital, volunteering extensively in Palestine, including European Hospital in Khan Younis, Gaza, and in Ukraine, Haiti, Zimbabwe, and Burkina Faso

"The great merit of Professor Dan Steinbock's book is that, thanks to its historical, legal and geopolitical approaches, it allows us to grasp the complexity of the absolute tragedy that the Palestinian people are experiencing. By scrupulously studying the theory of the strategy of annihilation claimed to have been used for years by the Israeli army, and the historical and legal nature of the notion of genocide, it is a valuable tool for understanding the ongoing human catastrophe in the Middle East."

EDGAR MORIN, internationally-renowned French philosopher and sociologist of information, polycrisis and comple, and recipient of the French Legion of Honor

THE
OBLITERATION
DOCTRINE

Genocide Prevention

Israel, Gaza and the West

DAN STEINBOCK

Clarity Press, Inc.

ISBN: 978-1-963892-22-2
EBOOK ISBN: 978-1-963892-23-9

In-house editor: Diana G. Collier
Book interior design: Becky Luening

Library of Congress Control Number: 2025936880

Clarity Press, Inc.
2625 Piedmont Rd. NE, Ste. 56
Atlanta, GA 30324, USA
claritypress.com

ACKNOWLEDGEMENTS

For years, my work has centered on economic growth and development in the increasingly multipolar world. If my previous book, *The Fall of Israel* (Clarity Press, 2025), outlined what happens when development is reversed, The Obliteration Doctrine shows how de-development may end in abject devastation. In this story, the central role belongs to a military doctrine, which should have no place in human civilization, and to genocide, which the Genocide Convention was supposed to prevent. *The Obliteration Doctrine* connects the missing dots.

This work has benefited from decades of exchanges with many government leaders, senior officials of government agencies, multinational corporations, international think-tanks, development banks, financial institutions and non-profit organizations around the world. It builds on my past works and affiliations with India, China and America Institute (U.S.); Shanghai Institutes for International Studies (China); EU Center (Singapore); Harvard Cluster Network (U.S.); OECD Development team; Indian Council on Global Relations, German Institute of Development and Sustainability, several UN agencies.

Like *The Fall of Israel*, this book would not have been possible without the incredible support and assiduous sparring of Diana G. Collier, editorial director of Clarity Press. But nor would it have been viable without the support of my wife Donna and her insistence that justice and peace are not just admirable goals, but something you must fight for daily.

I dedicate *The Obliteration Doctrine* to the memory of Raphael Lemkin and his quest for the prevention of genocides, and the innocent victims of genocidal atrocities from Auschwitz to Gaza.

CONTENTS

PART II
THE FAILURE OF GENOCIDE PREVENTION

FIGURES

FOREWORD

When something totally unexpected happens, words have to be found or created to aptly describe the event.

Genocides have happened throughout history. But genocide is inadequate to describe the deliberate mass killing of the Gaza Palestinians by Israel.

The killings in Gaza are unusual in that they are being done in full view of the world over a long period of time without any action being taken to stop them. Indeed, the genocide is approved and aided by the very people who advocate and talk incessantly of human rights and the sanctity of human life.

The United States and the Europeans created the monster that we are seeing today. They may not have known that they created a monster.

The Jews were the oppressed people in Europe. They had been victims of periodic massacres. And millions of them had been murdered by the Nazis.

Surely such people would know the sufferings of the oppressed, the horrors of genocide. But today we are seeing these people, or more accurately their descendants, committing worse acts than what their people had suffered in the past.

The people who created Israel may not know what kind of monster they created. But they cannot excuse themselves or be forgiven for failing to stop the atrocities committed before their very eyes. And worse still, they actually support the genocide through their funds and supply of weapons.

I have read Dan Steinbock's book entitled *The Fall of Israel*. That book was well researched and detailed. *The Obliteration Doctrine,* Steinbock's latest book, seems to be equally well researched. It discusses genocides in history and the origins of the kind of atrocities committed. It also discusses the factors which led to the laws making genocide an international crime.

The condemnation of genocide marked a milestone in the progress of human civilization. Yet it would seem that its condemnation as an international crime has not been effective in banishing genocide. It is still happening.

Dr. Mahathir Bin Mohamad
Former Prime Minister, Malaysia
May 15, 2025

PREFACE

Eight decades after Auschwitz and Treblinka, the conventional wisdom was that such genocidal atrocities could not happen again. After all, people are more informed and educated, more humane and more aware and connected around the globe.

And yet, the horrific did happen again, in Rwanda and the former Yugoslavia, and then in the Gaza Strip. But Gaza was different. In the Rwandan genocide, all hell broke loose in the course of just three months in 1994. In the Bosnian genocide, these mass atrocities took place in just a few days in July 1995. Starting on October 7, 2023, the genocidal atrocities in Gaza were perpetrated over many months, day after day, night after night, and they happened in real time as "the world was watching." Three months later, on January 5, 2024, UN Under-Secretary General for Humanitarian Affairs Martin Griffiths called Gaza "a place of death and despair."[1]

As of writing this in early 2025, over a year later, these genocidal atrocities prevail. As Blinne Ní Ghrálaigh, the Irish adviser to South Africa's legal team, cautioned in The Hague in late January 2024, Gaza is "the first genocide in history where its victims are broadcasting their own destruction in real time in the desperate so far vain hope that the world might do something."[2]

And still, following these eloquent appeals for ceasefire, diplomacy and talks, things went from horrific to worse, with over 51,000 deaths and close to 120,000 injured by official statistics in April 2025, emergency surgeries without anesthesia, a famine, starvation, ecocide—while the world watched and heard, but did little that made any difference.

What made such indifference possible?

The Obliteration Doctrine tackles the deadliest canon of 21st century warfare. It demonstrates the abject devastation that this military doctrine has achieved, how it was done and those who were behind it. The surreal devastation in Gaza reflects a sequence typical of past genocides, but it has occurred far faster, more efficiently and with greater decimation, reflecting a crescendo in the West's long struggle *against* genocide prevention. It also shows how this devastation became possible despite the Genocide Convention that had been created to prevent mass atrocities in the future.

This book shows how the rise of the Obliteration Doctrine and the associated genocide profiteering was facilitated by weapons and financing mainly by the United States, with strategic partners like Germany, the UK, Italy and Canada. In Gaza, Israel pulled the trigger, but the bullets and the guns came from the West. Hence, the complicity of the U.S.-led West in the fatal carnage, presumably to facilitate American efforts to prolong its global hegemony in an era that is marked by the rise of the Global South and an increasingly multipolar world economy.

Encompassing a multitude of abhorrent practices, the mass atrocities associated with the Obliteration Doctrine are typically justified by legal "state of exception" frameworks purporting to provide a license for incessant mass killing. The quest for genocide *prevention* by Raphael Lemkin, the "founder of the Genocide Convention," included elements of "preparatory attacks" and early warning signals. Together with institutional frameworks, these promised to provide a legal foundation for preempting mass atrocities before they could take place. Yet former colonial powers' efforts to undermine genocide prevention overshadowed the drafting of the Convention, precluding these measures.

What's truly stunning about the Obliteration Doctrine is that, while building on ancient military tactics and modern bombardment canons, it was largely perfected some two decades *before* October 7, 2023. Yet, there was no effective intervention during that time period by the international community to preempt the implementation of the lethal doctrine, which its proponents openly pledged to deploy in their "next war."

But this book is not just about Gaza and its historical precursors. Nor is it just about the financial considerations that accompany genocide and the complicity of the West, demonstrating its horrendous political, economic and moral collapse. It also shows how the Obliteration Doctrine combines lethal forms of warfare—including scorched earth destruction, collective punishment and civilian victimization—with massive and indiscriminate area bombing and counterinsurgency operations. What's new about it is the chilling mix of artificial intelligence and genocidal atrocities violating all humanitarian principles related to the conduct of war.

The erasure of Gaza reflects the tragic inability of the Genocide Convention to prevent genocides it was created to preempt. This shortcoming re-emerged in the exclusion of key elements from South Africa's case against Israel at the International Court of Justice. This was coupled with the dilution of the remaining clauses and enforcement erosion that undermined the prevention of genocide, the original goal of the Convention. Instead of preempting new mass atrocities, the goal is now simply to be able to name, condemn and record genocides once they have (over a lengthy process) been confirmed to have taken place.

Obliteration has long figured large in Western colonial and military enterprises, and in the subsequent struggle to deflect and curtail the rising international effort to establish an effective legal prohibition of genocide and recourse in order to forestall such onslaughts. Accordingly, this book addresses not only how the Genocide Convention was shrewdly diluted and tailored by Western powers to erode measures of genocide prevention. More than this, the Convention was hobbled by definitional quicksand as to whether genocide has in fact occurred, which can only be determined after the genocide has in fact occurred. The book also addresses the question how the West's challenge to genocide prevention might be overcome. In the early 21st century, the key role in this effort belongs no longer just to the West, but to the Global South and its rising efforts to litigate and prosecute those responsible for the greatest genocides of our time.

The response of international civil society is more urgent than ever before. The Obliteration Doctrine violates international law, indeed the very foundations of international society and all human life. In the absence of effective countervailing forces, it is setting an atrocious precedent and could provide a brutal template for far worse to come not just in the Middle East, but in Eurasia, Asia or Africa—in effect, no world region is likely to be immune to such catastrophes—for new "final solutions" paving the way to conventional or even nuclear holocausts of entire nations.

It was this concern that led to the haunting questions: *Why has the world been unable to bring an end to genocide? What is being done about it? And what could be done about it?*

PROLOGUE

A s the opening arguments got underway in January 2024, South Africa made its case against Israel at the International Court of Justice (ICJ). Presenting its opening arguments, the legal team charged Israel with genocidal acts, rhetoric and incitement. South Africa's justice minister, Ronald Lamola, acknowledged the brutal horrors committed by Hamas on October 7, but made it very clear that "no attack, no matter how severe" could justify the magnitude of violence that Israel's devastating ground assault imposed on the Palestinians in the Gaza Strip.[1]

South Africa's Genocide Case Against Israel

Recognizing the ongoing Nakba ("Catastrophe") of the Palestinian people, South Africa's legal team saw "Israel's genocidal acts in the context of its 75 years of apartheid." They asked the ICJ judges to impose binding preliminary orders on Israel, including an immediate halt to Israel's military campaign in Gaza.[2]

Ever since the inception of its ground assault in Gaza, Israel had fervently denied all genocide charges. In a video statement released prior to the ICJ proceedings, Prime Minister Netanyahu defended his country's actions, claiming they had nothing to do with genocide. "Israel has no intention of permanently occupying Gaza or displacing its civilian population," he thundered contradicting a slate of statements that his cabinet members had made in the previous weeks. "Israel is fighting Hamas terrorists, not the Palestinian population, and we are doing so in full compliance with international law." The Israeli military was "doing its utmost to minimize civilian casualties."[3] This would be Israel's standard response as its forces continued to level Gaza, displacing, dispossessing and devastating its residents in violation of international law.

In an official statement posted on X/Twitter, the spokesperson for Israel's foreign ministry claimed that South Africa was "functioning as the legal arm of the Hamas terrorist organization," and "utterly distorted the reality in Gaza."[4] Such statements reflected the views of the Netanyahu government's key constituencies and those Israelis who found it incomprehensible that their country could ever be accused of genocidal atrocities. This

1

was not the first time that Israel's right-wing politicians exploited the legacy of the Holocaust for their own purposes. Typical of the rhetoric of former PM Menachem Begin, these statements had increased since the 1980s when Likud politicians initiated concerted efforts to take over most of the occupied territories. During the 1982 Lebanon War and again in the course of the 2023–2025 Gaza War, mounting evidence of genocidal atrocities countered Israeli denials regarding such massacres, including its weaponization of the Holocaust.[5]

Following the public hearings in The Hague, the ICJ concluded that "it is plausible that Israel's acts could amount to genocide." As a result, the Court ordered Israel to "take all measures within its power to prevent genocidal acts, including preventing and punishing incitement to genocide, ensuring aid and services reach Palestinians under siege in Gaza, and preserving evidence of crimes committed in Gaza."[6]

The bottom line: To hopeful Israeli critics, the ICJ statements represented a turning-point in a trajectory that could ultimately declare Israel an internationally isolated pariah state. These views were reinforced by hearings that began in February, thanks to the UN request for a non-binding advisory opinion on the legal consequences of Israel's activities in the occupied Palestinian territories, including in East Jerusalem. Even sober realists were impressed by the Court ordering Israel to take all relevant measures to prevent any acts contrary to the 1948 Genocide Convention. However, the ICJ did *not order* Israel to suspend its military campaign, even though it recognized the catastrophic situation in Gaza.

In other words, the Court's statements were self-contradictory. The question is, *why?*

Exclusion, Dilution, and Erosion

It is instructive to compare South Africa's original request with the actual Court judgement.[7] The dilutions, which are illustrated in Figure P-1 with strikethroughs, effectively weakened the full impact of the original request, by suspending any reference to Palestinians as a people, deleting mentions of paramilitary atrocity acts (by Jewish settlers), of conspiracy and complicity in genocide (by the U.S., Germany, Italy, and the UK through the provision of arms supplies); all specific references to the obliteration of Palestinian infrastructure, living conditions and Palestinian lives and so on. Similarly, regularized submissions of reports to the Court on measures taken are excluded, as well as orders that Israel should suspend military operations and refrain from aggravating the situation.

Figure P-1. South Africa's Request v. Court's Judgement

Summary	Court judgment, Jan 26, 2024 (revised from South Africa original request, Dec 29, 2023)

(3) ~~The Republic of South Africa and the State of Israel shall each, in accordance with their obligations under the Convention on the Prevention and Punishment of the Crime of Genocide, in relation to the Palestinian people, take all reasonable measures within their power to prevent genocide.~~

Prevent genocide and desist from killing, injuring, destroying life and preventing births

(4) The State of Israel shall, in accordance with its obligations under the Convention on the Prevention and Punishment of the Crime of Genocide, in relation to ~~the Palestinian people as a group~~ Palestinians in Gaza ~~protected by the Convention on the Prevention and Punishment of the Crime of Genocide, desist from the commission of any and all acts within the scope of Article II of the convention,~~ take all [~~reasonable~~] measures within ~~their~~ its power to prevent ~~genocide~~ the commission of all acts within the scope of Article II of this convention, in particular:

a. killing members of the group;

b. causing serious bodily or mental harm to the members of the group;

c. deliberately inflicting on the group conditions of life calculated to bring about its physical destruction in whole or in part; and

d. imposing measures intended to prevent births within the group.

The State of Israel shall ensure with immediate effect that its military does not commit any acts described in point [4] above;

Desist from incitement, and punish acts of and encouragement to genocide

(6) The State of Israel shall take all measures within its power, to prevent and punish ~~in relation to Palestinians, ensure that its military, as well as any irregular armed units or individuals which maybe directed, supported or otherwise influenced by it and any organizations and persons which may be subject to its control, direction or influence, do not commit any acts described in (4) and (5) above, or engage in~~ the direct and public incitement to commit genocide in relation to members of the Palestinian group in the Gaza Strip; ~~conspiracy to commit genocide, attempt to commit genocide, or complicity in genocide, and insofar as they do engage therein, that steps are taken towards their punishment pursuant to Articles I, II, III and IV of the Convention on the Prevention and Punishment of the Crime of Genocide.~~

Enable the provision of basic services and humanitarian assistance

(5) The State of Israel shall, ~~pursuant to point (4) (c) above, in relation to Palestinians, desist from, and~~ take ~~all~~ immediate and effective measures within its power to enable the provision of urgently needed basic services and humanitarian assistance to address the adverse conditions of life faced by Palestinians in the Gaza Strip;

~~within its power including the rescinding of relevant orders, of restrictions and/or of prohibitions to prevent:~~
~~a. the expulsion and forced displacement from their homes;~~
~~b. the deprivation of:~~
~~i. access to adequate food and water;~~
~~ii. access to humanitarian assistance, including access to adequate fuel, shelter, clothes, hygiene and sanitation;~~
~~iii. medical supplies and assistance; and~~
~~c. the destruction of Palestinian life in Gaza.~~

Prevent the destruction of and ensure the preservation of evidence

(7) The State of Israel shall take effective measures to prevent the destruction and ensure the preservation of evidence related to allegations of acts within the scope of Article II and Article III of the Convention on the Prevention and Punishment of the Crime of Genocide against members of the Palestinian group in the Gaza Strip; ~~to that end, the State of Israel shall not act to deny or otherwise restrict access by fact-finding missions, international mandates and other bodies to Gaza to assist in ensuring the preservation and retention of said evidence.~~

Submit ongoing reports to the Court on measures taken

(8) The State of Israel shall submit a report to the Court on all measures taken to give effect to this Order within ~~one week~~ one month, as from the date of this Order, ~~and thereafter at such regular intervals as the Court shall order, until a final decision on the case is rendered by the Court.~~

Suspension of military operations

~~(1) The State of Israel shall immediately suspend its military operations in and against Gaza.~~

~~(2) The State of Israel shall ensure that any military or irregular armed units which may be directed, supported or influenced by it, as well as any organisations and persons which may be subject to its control, direction or influence, take no steps in furtherance of the military operations referred to point (1) above.~~

Refrain from aggravating the situation

~~(9) The State of Israel shall refrain from any action and shall ensure that no action is taken which might aggravate or extend the dispute before the Court or make it more difficult to resolve.~~

SOURCES: *The figure draws from these documents: Application of the Convention on the Prevention and Punishment of the Crime of Genocide in the Gaza Strip; (South Africa v. Israel), Provisional Measures, Order of Jan 26, 2024.*

As we shall see, the judicial process that followed the sanitization of South Africa's quest reflected the broader treatment of the Genocide Convention. During its making in the late 1940s, some of its key parts were excluded from the drafts due to the pressures of the Cold War. Furthermore, other parts of the Convention have been shrewdly diluted. Finally, its implementation continues to suffer from severe erosion. As a net consequence, the Court, having accepted the petition, could not be seen as countenancing Israel's Obliteration Doctrine, but neither was it enabling concerted efforts to forestall it or disrupt its effects.

The net effect was predictable. By late February, Human Rights Watch and Amnesty International stated, on the basis of mounting evidence, that Israel had not complied with the ICJ's provisional measures and that Israel's obstruction of the entry and distribution of aid amounted to war crimes.[8] Worse, the disinclination of the Court to demand a fast end to Israel's military campaign contributed to the Netanyahu cabinet's escalation on the ground, which served to pave the way to mass famine and starvation in the Gaza Strip. By late March 2024, the Court tried to tweak its order by ordering that Israel take new emergency measures to ensure basic food supplies to Gaza immediately.[9] But it was too little, too late. By then the Palestinians in Gaza were struggling with the kind of starvation that was at par with the some of the worst mass atrocities of the 20th century.[10] And with the eclipse of the ceasefire in early 2025, still another wave of starvation ensued, thanks to Israel's renewed attacks.

In April 2024, the Court set the schedule for comprehensive submissions of legal opinions by South Africa and Israel. The South African memorial was submitted by the deadline at the end of October 2024. At this very time, senior members of the Netanyahu cabinet and national lawmakers were speaking at an Israeli conference openly advocating the ethnic cleansing and Jewish recolonization of Gaza. Just days later, South Africa filed 750 pages of "overwhelming" proof that Israel was committing genocide in Gaza to the ICJ. In his statement, South African President Cyril Ramaphosa said the document

> contains evidence which shows how the government of Israel has violated the Genocide Convention by promoting the destruction of Palestinians living in Gaza, physically killing [Palestinians] with an assortment of destructive weapons, depriving them access to humanitarian assistance, causing conditions of life which are aimed at their physical destruction, and ignoring and defying several provisional measures of the International Court of Justice, and using starvation as a weapon of war and to further Israel's

aims to depopulate Gaza through mass death and forced displacement of Palestinians.[11]

In parallel, Francesca Albanese, the UN special rapporteur on the situation of human rights in the occupied Palestinian territories, published a report on Israeli "genocide as colonial erasure," which she saw as "part of a long-term intentional, systematic, state-organized forced displacement and replacement of the Palestinians." This trajectory posed a threat to "the very existence of the Palestinian people in Palestine. Member states must intervene now to prevent new atrocities that will further scar human history."[12]

Since the Court set the deadline for the Israeli response at the end of July 2025, this virtually ensured that all measures the Court had urged Israel to implement in January 2024 would be ignored until Israel had effectively leveled Gaza, decimated its infrastructure, displaced and dispossessed Palestinians and finalized Israel's genocidal atrocities in the Strip. Meanwhile, the Israeli military set up bases and installations in the area. In this sense, the Court's actions, tragically and unwittingly, enabled Israel's "Second Nakba" in Gaza.

How could such a travesty be possible in the name of the Genocide Convention that was enacted to *prevent* such mass atrocities? Why was the issue of complicity progressively suppressed from these early proceedings? And why would the international community, particularly the West with its eloquence on human rights and the rules-based international order, opt for such silence and indifference in the face of an expansive corpus of evidence on genocidal atrocities?

PART I

OBLITERATION AND COMPLICITY

CHAPTER 1

OBLITERATION IN GAZA AND BEYOND

In his efforts to comprehend the long history of genocides, Raphael Lemkin, internationally recognized as the "founder of the Genocide Convention," saw colonial conquest as the primary factor in genocide, and in the 1930s he identified its two basic phases as follows:

> Genocide has two phases: one, destruction of the national pattern of the oppressed group; the other, the imposition of the national pattern of the oppressor. This imposition, in turn, may be made upon the oppressed population which is allowed to remain, or upon the territory alone, after removal of the population and the colonization of the area by the oppressor's own nationals.[1]

In the 20th century, genocidal atrocities, in part due to their comprehensive nature, unfolded gradually over time. The rise of Nazism in Germany, Fascism in Italy and militarism in Imperial Japan emerged in parallel with mass-industrialized warfare, assembly-line mass-killing in concentration camps and gas chambers, Hiroshima and Nagasaki. In the early 21st century, these atrocities, though still sequenced, proceed faster, more efficiently and destructively, thanks to post-industrialization, advanced technologies, and far greater lethality. A comprehensive sequence can be compressed into a matter of months, given a ceaseless flow of weaponry to sustain the brutal obliteration. Why build concentration camps if massive bombardments can do the job? Indeed, even though South Africa initiated its legal case against Israel with stunning speed, tens of thousands of Palestinians were already dead by then.

Let's take a look at the results of Israel's military activities in the Gaza Strip since October 7, 2023. How did the process unfold? Did it fulfill the legal criteria of genocide?[2] And how does it compare with genocidal atrocities in history?

9

Information Censure

As the old adage goes, "truth is the first victim of war." During a conflict, the truth is often the first thing to be compromised, as propaganda, disinformation, and biased narratives spread. The atrocities of Gaza were preceded by the demise of data-gathering mechanisms in the Yemeni Civil War. The destruction of the means of information production, including journalists, is central to the Obliteration Doctrine. The function of the "media blackout" is to facilitate the military objectives.[3]

In Israel, all investigative reporting has historically been constrained by the Military Censor, a unit in the IDF Directorate of Military Intelligence tasked with carrying out preventive censorship regarding the publication of information that presumably could affect national security. Before the Gaza atrocities, some 2,240 press articles in Israel used to be censored each year, a tenth in full, most partially. Articles concerning potentially controversial topics must be submitted to the Censor in advance.[4] There is a freedom of information law, but it is sometimes hard to implement. The confidentiality of sources is not protected by statutory law.[5]

In early May 2024, Prime Minister Netanyahu's far-right cabinet voted unanimously to shut Al Jazeera, the global news network. "The incitement channel Al Jazeera will be closed in Israel," Netanyahu posted in Hebrew on X/Twitter.[6] In the wake of October 7, Communications Minister Shlomo Karhi had pushed legislative action to prohibit news outlets he believed to jeopardize national security. Under his guidance, the Israeli government endorsed an emergency provision targeting Al Jazeera.[7] In an Orwellian twist, the Qatari network, seeking to report about genocidal atrocities, was charged with contributing to such mass killings by reporting on them. Karhi had his own political priorities. In January 2024 he had attended the notorious "Settlement Brings Security" conference advocating for Israeli resettlement of the Gaza Strip after the ethnic cleansing of the Palestinians.[8]

The timing of Al Jazeera's closure was carefully orchestrated. As the IDF ordered Palestinians to move out of eastern Rafah warning it was about to use "extreme force" in southern Gaza, the last thing it needed was bad PR. At the time, Rafah, which had a population of about 270,000 before the war in Gaza started, hosted the majority of Gaza's 2.3 million prewar population. Doctors Without Borders estimated that more than 1.5 million people were trapped there. Al Jazeera condemned the decision to close its operations in Israel as a "criminal act." It warned that the suppression of the free press "stands in contravention of international and humanitarian law."[9] Nonetheless, the censure also threatened other major news organizations, including the few remaining Israeli news organizations critical of the war, such as *Haaretz,* which was targeted by the Netanyahu war cabinet.

Standing in contravention of international and humanitarian law, Israel's ongoing suppression of the free press, which the West condemned in rhetoric yet allowed to prevail in substance, was widely seen as an effort to conceal brutal actions in the Gaza Strip. At the time of Israeli authorities raiding Al Jazeera's offices, more than 140 Palestinian journalists had been killed since the beginning of the war on Gaza. And the numbers continued to climb. In 2022, Palestinian reporter Shireen Abu Akleh, renowned across the Arab world, was killed by the Israeli forces in the occupied West Bank while reporting. Her death heralded the ominous future.

By mid-April 2025, the Committee to Protect Journalists (CPJ) reported that almost 180 journalists and media workers were among the more than tens of thousands killed in Gaza, the West Bank, Israel and Lebanon since the war began, making it the deadliest period for journalists since CPJ began gathering data in 1992. According to CPJ, dozens were directly or possibly targeted. It was also investigating almost 180 additional cases of potential killings, arrests and injuries, but many were challenging to document amid these harsh conditions.[10]

Journalists in Gaza faced high risks trying to cover the conflict, including lethal Israeli airstrikes, famine, the displacement of 90 percent of Gaza's population, and the destruction of 80 percent of its buildings. As civilians, they are protected by international law. Deliberately targeting civilians constitutes a war crime. Mounting evidence suggested that many of these killings were net effects of Israel's targeted executions of journalists, preceded by arrests, intimidation and threats.

The censure went far beyond Al Jazeera and other news media networks. Social media is a textbook example. Based in California, Meta is an American multinational technology conglomerate, with annual revenues exceeding $135 billion in 2023. The company owns and operates Facebook, Instagram, Threads, and WhatsApp, among other products and services. After October 7, Meta's policies and practices were silencing voices in support of Palestine and Palestinian human rights on Instagram and Facebook in a wave of heightened censorship of social media. Between October and November 2023 alone, Human Rights Watch (HRW) documented over 1,050 takedowns (only 1 case involved content in support of Israel) and other suppression of content on Instagram and Facebook that had been posted by Palestinians and their supporters, including about human rights abuses. The documented cases featured content originating from over 60 countries around the world, primarily in English, all reflecting peaceful support of Palestine. The censorship of content related to Palestine on Instagram and Facebook was systemic and global.[11]

As the hostilities continued in Gaza, so did the efforts to steer and shape social media content by the interested parties. In January 2024, CyberWell, an Israeli nonprofit with deep ties to the intelligence arm of an Israeli propaganda effort, pushed to censor accounts disputing the false allegation that Hamas had slaughtered dozens of babies during the October 7th attack. President Biden and leading Israeli figures had falsely claimed that Hamas beheaded or burned 40 babies during the assault into Israel. By mid-2024, CyberWell was shown to have been influential in shaping social media content. Claiming to be independent, the group lobbied Meta, X/Twitter, and TikTok to remove social media posts under the banner of fighting hate and antisemitism.[12]

Overall, these trends in both media and social media reflected larger structural forces that critics characterized as the censorship industrial complex; that is, "the shocking and disturbing emergence of state-sponsored censorship in the United States of America."[13] The Twitter Files, state attorneys' general lawsuits, and investigative reporters revealed a large and growing network of government agencies, academic institutions, and nongovernmental organizations that are actively censoring American citizens, often without their knowledge, on a range of issues, including—and perhaps in particular—the genocidal atrocities in Gaza.

Sanctions, Blockade, and Deliberate Famine

Ever since the establishment of the state of Israel and the concomitant catastrophe or *Nakba* of the Palestinian people, Gaza has struggled for survival. Despite its unilateral disengagement from the Strip in 2005, Israel continued to control its airspace, territorial waters and the movement of goods and people in and out of the Strip. However, the withdrawal did pave the way in 2006 to the first Palestinian election in a decade. When Hamas won a clear majority in all occupied Palestinian territories, Israel and the Middle East Quartet—U.S., Russia, the UN and EU—launched economic sanctions against the Palestinian Authority, Hamas's parliamentarians and Palestinian territories.

The blockade was the result of Israel's *deliberate* attempt to push the Gazan economy "to the brink of collapse," according to a U.S. diplomatic cable released by Wikileaks. Behind the façade, Israeli officials repeatedly told American diplomats outright that the embargo sought to damage the Gazan economy. As part of their overall embargo plan against Gaza, Israeli officials have confirmed "on multiple occasions that they intend to keep the Gazan economy on the brink of collapse without quite pushing it over the edge."[14]

With the inception of its blockade in 2007, the Israeli government estimated how many daily calories were needed to prevent or to cause malnutrition in Gaza.[15] Defining Gaza as a "hostile territory," Israel imposed "severe sanctions in the civilian sphere."[16] The net effect was disastrous, as intended. The blockade compounded the already-catastrophic conditions. Shortly before October 7, Palestinian per capita income was 12.9 percent of the Israeli level. That's over 2 percentage points lower than where it was *over two decades ago*. Living standards in the West Bank and Gaza were falling relative to Israeli levels, while those in Gaza were plunging dramatically compared to the West Bank.[17]

The average daily calorie intake critical to survival is estimated at 2,100 kilocalories (kcal) per day. The Israeli "Red Line" document used a higher calculation of 2,279 calories per person, taking into account the presumed domestic food production in Gaza.[18]

Such calculations have a long and dark history in colonial settler societies. After an intense drought and crop failure in the Deccan Plateau in 1876, the Great Southern Indian Famine lasted for two nightmarish years, spreading northward. At the time, Famine Commissioner Sir Richard Temple implemented human experiments, with "strapping fine fellows" starved until they resembled "little more than animated skeletons . . . utterly unfit for any work." Insisting on limited rations, Temple sought to determine the minimum amount of food for survival, to maximize British revenues. In Madras during 1877, he estimated the adequate calorie intake per day to be around 1,627 kcal. It wasn't adequate for work and survival. The excess mortality related to the famine has been estimated at up to 8 million.[19]

In Gaza, Israel's intent was to keep economy "on the brink of collapse" while avoiding a humanitarian crisis.[20] Basically, the Netanyahu cabinet put the Palestinians "on a diet, but not to make them die of hunger." During the 2008–2009 Gaza War, the Strip was subjected to a "*Shoah*" (Hebrew for Holocaust), as Deputy Defense Minister Matan Vilnai warned. The Israelis hoped this would turn Gazans against Hamas. The idea was to "send Gaza decades into the past," said then commanding general Yoav Gallant, who 15 years later was targeted by an International Criminal Court warrant for alleged responsibility "for the war crimes of starvation as a method of warfare and of intentionally directing an attack against the civilian population; and the crimes against humanity of murder, persecution, and other inhumane acts."[21]

In a comparative view, the Gaza blockade had some affinities with the economic sanctions imposed on Venezuela by the U.S. government since August of 2017. In both cases, the greatest impact has not been on the government but on the civilian population. Typically, such sanctions reduce the public's caloric intake, increasing disease and mortality. They exacerbate the economic crisis and make it nearly impossible to stabilize the economy, contributing further to excess deaths, disproportionately harming the poorest and most vulnerable. In both cases, too, the broadening of sanctions has proved even more severe and destructive, inflicting serious harm to human life and health. In Venezuela, as Jeffrey Sachs and Mark Weisbrot have argued, "these sanctions would fit the definition of collective punishment of the civilian population as described in both the Geneva and Hague international conventions, to which the U.S. is a signatory. They are also illegal under international law and treaties that the U.S. has signed, and would appear to violate U.S. law as well."[22] In the case of Gaza, such conclusions would seem to be even more valid, due to the greater severity of the consequences well before October 7, 2023.

In May 2018, the UN Security Council had adopted unanimously resolution 2417 condemning the starving of civilians as a method of warfare and the unlawful denial of humanitarian access to civilian populations.[23] After a decade of decline in famines worldwide, the decision seemed to herald a new era in the struggle against starvation as an instrument of war. In retrospect, it was a fleeting calm before the storm. The UN resolution took place before the Trump-Biden trade and technology battles, new Cold Wars and geopolitical crises that undermined the promise of global recovery, unleashing energy crises, genocidal atrocities, mass starvation and rounds of inflation, one feeding the other.[24]

In the course of the Gaza War in particular, most tenets of UNSC Resolution 2417 were violated. It was the ruthless decisions taken already in 2007 and the West's unwillingness to challenge those choices long before they became operational that set the stage for Israel's genocidal atrocities in Gaza 15 years later, and for the complicity of the U.S.-led West in these massacres.

"Starvation as a Method of War"

By early 2023—months before October 7—Israel's prolonged occupation of Palestinian territory, particularly its longstanding blockade by sea, land and air of the Gaza Strip, had caused widespread food insecurity across the densely-inhabited occupied territory, with four of five Gaza's residents largely dependent on humanitarian aid.[25] Then, just two days after the Hamas offensive of October 7, 2023, Israel blocked the entry of food and water into the Gaza Strip, as it initiated a massive, largely indiscriminate bombardment, with subsequent ground operations, and restricted humanitarian aid, exacerbating food and water shortages. Defense Minister Gallant announced a "complete siege" of the Strip with no electricity, food, or fuel and removing every restriction on Israeli forces so they could "eliminate everything." He was seconded by Energy Minister Israel Katz reiterating that Gaza would not receive a drop of water or a single battery.[26]

By December 2023, over 90 percent of the Gaza population was estimated to face high levels of acute food insecurity, with 40 percent at emergency levels and over 15 percent at catastrophe levels, indicating an extreme lack of food, starvation and exhaustion of coping capacities.[27]

The UN experts cautioned of genocide, warning that Israel was destroying Gaza's food system and using food as a weapon against the Palestinian people. Despite mounting evidence, the head of Israel's Coordination of Government Activities in the Territories (COGAT) for Gaza stated in there was no food shortage in Gaza.[28] The IDF alleged Hamas stole humanitarian aid, killed people seeking humanitarian aid and kept its own supply reserves.[29] Yet, both the U.S. and the UN denied Israeli claims that Hamas caused the famine.[30] It was the first famine peak in Gaza.

In its second warning in March 2024, the IPC ("Integrated Food Security Phase Classification"), the standardized global food security system, reported that the entire population of Gaza was facing high levels of acute food insecurity, with half at catastrophe levels—a 92 percent increase from the previous analysis.[31] Even then, President Biden was furious at allegations Israel was using starvation as a weapon of war, rejecting pleas to use leverage to persuade its ally Israel, the recipient of billions of dollars of U.S. military aid, to allow sufficient humanitarian aid into Gaza.[32]

By June 2024, the IPC reported that the entire Gaza population remained at high risk of famine as long as the conflict continued and humanitarian access remained restricted.[33] Again, Israel disputed the allegations, pointing to a report by Israeli academics who slammed the IPC's "slanted projections."[34] But as these authors acknowledged, their report relied on data by COGAT and was premised on estimated food availability, which effectively set aside the three remaining pillars of food security: "access, utilization, and stability."[35] In other words, even if there is some food around, people may not have physical access to it due to heavy mobility restrictions. Moreover, there may be inadequate economic access to food because jobs are gone, and prices are inflated by up to 300 to 2,000 percent. And even if people can scrape together something to eat, food preparation is overshadowed by displacement, ecological hazards, bombardment and harsh weather conditions. In brief, ivory-tower projections do not always tackle real-life implications. And yet, the Israeli authors concluded that "with the exception of February, food aid delivered to Gaza during January–July 2024 *exceeded* the minimal daily per capita needs of *all* the people in Gaza, meeting humanitarian standards" [my italics, DS]. It was a stunning generalization in light of the actual dire realities in Gaza.[36]

By contrast, the UN's take was quite different. It concluded in September 2024 that through its "total siege,"

> Israel had weaponized the withholding of life-sustaining necessities, including humanitarian assistance, for strategic and political gains, which constituted collective punishment and reprisal against the civilian population, both in direct violation of international humanitarian law…. Israel's use of starvation as a method of war would affect the entire population of the Gaza Strip for decades to come, with particularly negative consequences for children.[37]

As the IPC estimates indicated, the second climax was expected to peak in early 2025. That it did not happen was due to the ceasefire in January 2025. According to initial plans, the second bout of famine was to be facilitated by a controversial plot. Speaking to members of the Knesset Foreign Affairs and Defense Committee in a closed session in September 2024, PM Netanyahu told legislators he was considering the "General's Plan," led by Maj. Gen. (ret.) Giora Eiland, to lay siege to northern Gaza. After serving three decades in the Israeli military, Eiland had participated in peace talks in the 1990s and advised PM Arik Sharon in the 2000s, with further private and public advisory roles in the past two decades. Initially, he had been against the Israeli ground invasion, but changed his tune soon, advancing arguments for collective punishment and total destruction. Since most Gazans stood behind Hamas, Eiland argued that "Gaza women are the mothers, sisters, and spouses of Hamas murderers." Instead of endangering Israeli soldiers, "epidemics in the South [of Gaza] will bring victory closer and will decrease casualties among IDF soldiers."[38]

Israeli public health experts condemned such views, while human rights group B'Tselem called it a "humanitarian catastrophe as policy."[39]

In late 2024, the IPC projected that through spring 2025, Gaza would remain in an emergency state regarding food insecurity. Some 345,000 people would face extreme lack of food, starvation and exhaustion of their livelihoods and almost 900,000 would be in emergency state. Acute malnutrition was expected to worsen across the Strip, driven by seasonal diseases in high-density population settings, and reduced assistance to children and pregnant and breastfeeding women. The risk of famine would persist as long as conflict continued and humanitarian access was restricted, with an elevated risk of epidemic outbreaks and potential catastrophic scenarios. In turn, Israeli attacks on camps, shelters and infrastructure, and renewed evacuation orders increased the likelihood of worst-case scenarios.

What is so stunning, indeed outrageous, about these *past* projections is the fact that they highlight how cognizant the aid workers were of the realities of the manufactured famine that the Israeli and U.S. authorities so blatantly disputed. And yet, in retrospect, the late 2024 IPC scenario failed to capture the actual, brutal realities. When the ceasefire fell apart, the second famine peak ensued and Israel blocked all humanitarian assistance to Palestinians in the Gaza Strip after March 1, 2025. Ignoring the international tsunami of condemnation, the IDF bombed plants severing pipelines and targeting water infrastructure that left Gazans no choice but to drink seawater and ration contaminated supplies.[40] To contain the international outrage, the previously-mentioned Israeli academic study was used to shun ICC charges and UN warnings. Food had flowed into the Strip in sufficient quantities, the academics said, so food scarcity should be attributed to Hamas's iron grip on aid.[41] That the study was not released by an international professional journal but an Israeli policy publication was blamed on antisemitism and anti-Israeli prejudice. As the promoters of the study headlined: "The ICC claimed Gazans were starving. They lied."[42] International headlines were a very different story, but Israel was now under its worst military censorship in years.[43]

By early April 2025, at least 60,000 children in Gaza were at risk of serious health complications due to malnutrition.[44] The acute hunger crisis was part of a purposeful Israeli strategy to undermine all aid and to banish humanitarian groups to cripple Hamas. Civilian deaths were no longer collateral damage, but a deliberate instrument to achieve the Netanyahu cabinet's broader geopolitical objectives. In early May, Israel's continued blockade of food, water and other critical supplies to the besieged and bombarded coastal territory entered its third month. According to the UN's child rights agency (UNICEF), over 9,000 children had been admitted for treatment for acute malnutrition since the start of the year. But the horrifying status quo was rapidly deteriorating, due to the total blockade, which coincided with the onset of the Trump tariff wars monopolizing international headlines. As an occupying power, Israel was obligated under international law to provide critical supplies to Gaza. But instead of ensuring humanitarian assistance, the Netanyahu cabinet violated the Fourth Geneva Convention by greenlighting a new and expanded Gaza operation with a major reservist call-up, while hundreds of thousands of Palestinians suffered from high levels of food insecurity.[45]

Instead of halting the looming catastrophe, the Trump administration, following in the footprints of its predecessor, seemed to collude with the far-right starvation architects of the Israeli campaign. Speaking at Trump's Mar-a-Lago estate, Itamar Ben-Gvir, the Israeli minister for National Security, a champion of ethnic cleansing, stated openly: "I had the honor and privilege of meeting with senior Republican Party officials at Trump's Mar-a-Lago estate. They expressed support for my very clear position on how to act in Gaza and that the food and aid depots should be bombed in order to create military and political pressure to bring our hostages home safely."[46]

To critics, euphemisms like "relocation" and "population transfer" had dark legacies from bygone periods of ethnic cleansing and genocidal atrocities. Yet, such voices were increasingly shunned, repressed, even criminalized by the Trump administration and elsewhere in the West. But what were the historical facts on weaponized starvation?

Weaponized Starvation in Historical Review

In historical review, the Israeli total siege of the densely inhabited Gaza and its 2.3 million Palestinian refugees was hardly unique. It had affinities with the siege of Leningrad and its 3.1 million people. Part of the Nazi *Hungerplan* by SS ideologue Herbert Backe, the grand objective was to forcibly starve around 31 to 45 million Soviets and Eastern Europeans by capturing food stocks and redirecting them to German forces.[47] Along with American eugenics and white racism, it was U.S. treatment of Native Americans that had inspired the hunger policies in Hitler's Germany.[48] The lethal power of hunger weaponization had been taught to a generation of Germans in 1914–19, when the British imposed a blockade against Germany, where it was called the *Hungerblockade*. It aspired to obstruct Germany's ability to import goods and thus starve the German people and military into submission.[49]

In Gaza, the original "Generals' Plan," premised on the blocking of food supplies and epidemics, could not be carried out in full due to international opposition.[50] But even its partial execution drove the Strip to risk of famine in October 2024, with top UN officials describing the situation in northern Gaza as "apocalyptic" because everyone there was "at imminent risk of dying from disease, famine and violence." In a strongly worded letter, U.S. Secretary of State Antony Blinken gave Israel an ultimatum of 30 days to ensure more aid trucks reached Gaza daily. Israel missed the U.S. deadline in early November, according to the UN.[51] Yet, the Biden administration did nothing.[52]

A comprehensive study of food availability in Gaza shows that between October 2023 and April 2024, food trucks entering Gaza remained below pre-war levels. Israeli data offered higher estimates but featured extreme approximation. Following Israel's takeover of crossings in May 2024, UN data likely featured underreporting, while even Israeli data indicated declining deliveries. Typically, trucked-in food's caloric value was lowest just as food was scarcest amid the first famine peak (February-March 2024).[53]

But how serious was the situation in Gaza relative to its precedents? In his *Axis Rule in Occupied Europe* (1944), Raphael Lemkin, the founder of the Genocide Convention, warned that "the Jewish population in the occupied countries is undergoing a process of liquidation (1) by debilitation and starvation, because the Jewish food rations are kept at an especially low level; and (2) by massacres in the ghettos."[54] Lemkin bolstered his case with data from a 1943 report (Figure 1-1).

Figure 1-1. Racial Feeding in Nazi-Occupied Europe

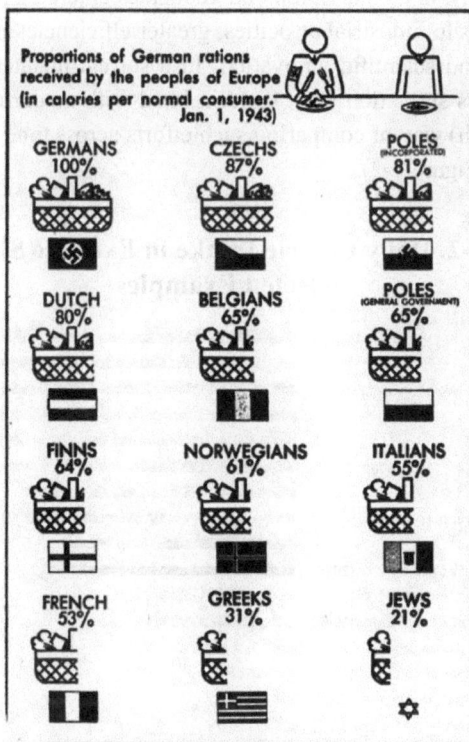

SOURCE: *Starvation Over Europe (Made in Germany), p. 47.*

Set in comparative and historical context, the weaponization of mass starvation has long been associated with imperial and colonial activities as a prelude to genocidal atrocities.[55] In this view, even the Nazi concentration camps can be traced to genocidal atrocities in colonial concentration camps, such as the British camps during the Second Boer War (1899–1902) followed by the Herero and Namaqua genocide (1904–1908) under the German Empire. From the Indian Empire to German South West Africa (now Namibia), famine and starvation have served as a prelude to the final inferno. As far as Lemkin was concerned, starvation was the physical prelude to genocide:

> The most direct and drastic of the techniques of genocide is simply murder. It may be the slow and scientific murder by mass starvation or the swift but no less scientific murder by mass extermination in gas chambers, wholesale executions or exposure to disease and exhaustion.[56]

Historically, mass starvation and genocides entered a new stage in the Nazi era, thanks to industrial atrocities, greater efficiencies in assembly-line mass murder and scientific innovation. In a surreal manner, concentration camps and mass starvation went hand in hand with modernity in the West. One (very rough) way of comparing such efforts across time and place is the calorie count (Figure 1-2).

Figure 1-2. Daily Calorie Intake in Extreme Situations: Selected Examples

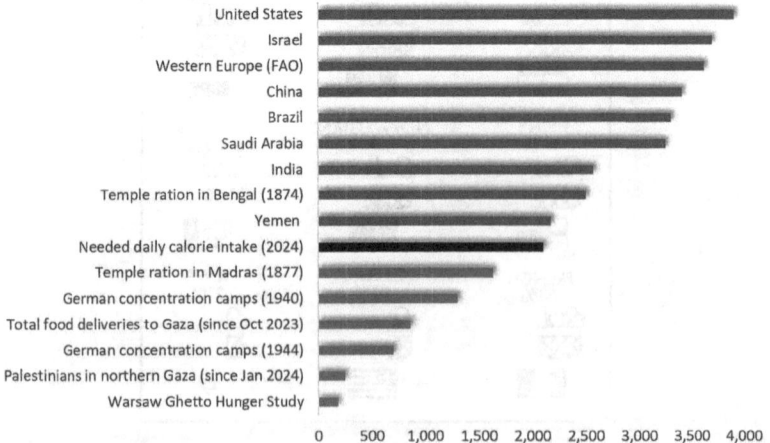

SOURCE: *Food and Agriculture Organization of the United Nations (2023) and other sources; Gaza estimates from Oxfam*

The Nazi siege of Leningrad (St. Petersburg) from fall 1941 to January 1944 was one of the longest and most destructive sieges in history. When German armies prevented food supplies from reaching the city, an estimated half of the city's population of 2.4 million died, mainly as a result of starvation. During the fatal "Hunger Winter" period, the average daily ration was barely 300 calories.[57] An even lower official calorie count was documented in the Warsaw Ghetto hunger study in 1942.[58] Determined to starve the ghetto in just months, the Nazis only permitted a daily intake of 180 calories per prisoner, withholding vaccines and medicine necessary to prevent the spread of disease in the densely-inhabited ghetto. Hence, the thriving black market, which supplied 80 percent of the ghetto's food and a network of 250 soup kitchens.[59] Whatever the ultimate daily intake, it paved the way from starvation to death.

Weaponized mass starvation is the common denominator of settler colonialism, including American Indian Wars, the German Herero and Nama genocide, the Nazi *Hungerplan* all the way to the Yemeni civil war and the genocidal atrocities in Gaza. In this role, it is often associated with ethnic cleansing, as Lemkin noted, "after removal of the population and the colonization of the area by the oppressor's own nationals" (Figure 1-3).

What about Gaza? Measured in terms of total food deliveries into the Strip since October 2023, the calorie intake was about 860 kcal,[60] a third less than in the Nazi camps over eight decades ago. As the German invasion of the Soviet Union failed and the tide of World War II shifted, the Nazi camps deteriorated, with the daily intake shrinking to 700 kcal in 1944. That's almost three times the intake of 245 kcal in northern Gaza in the first half of the year 2024, when the *New York Post* famously headlined that there was no famine in the Strip.[61]

Genocidal Intent and Acts

According to Article 2 of the Genocide Convention, which became effective amid the early Cold War in 1951, the definition of genocide is premised on establishing specific intent. The latter is seen as critical to distinguishing genocide from other international crimes, such as war crimes or crimes against humanity. In the case of the genocidal atrocities in Gaza, the specific intent has been evident, with the course of conflict punctuated by the statements and implicit in the actions of Israel's political, economic and military leaders. In the long view, the frequency, tone and practical effects of the specific intent so manifested has progressively increased over the past 25 years following the crumbling of the peace process, accelerating with the entry of the Messianic far-right into the Netanyahu cabinet in 2022–23 and

Figure 1-3. Weaponization of Starvation:
Selected Historical Examples

Famine stricken people during the famine of 1876 in Bangalore (Wikimedia)

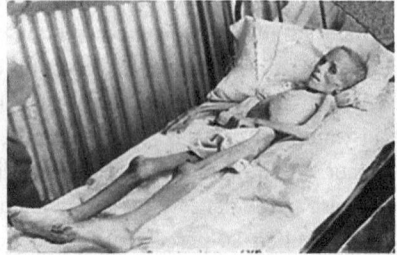

A Boer child in a British concentration camp near Bloemfontein, 1901 (Wikimedia)

Survivors of the Herero genocide, ca. 1907 (Wikimedia)

Bodies of inmates in Dachau (U.S. Holocaust Memorial Museum, Stuart McKeever)

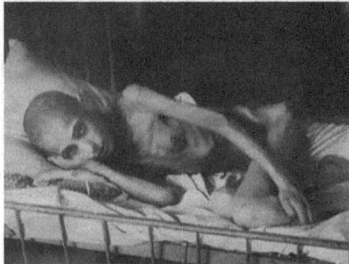

Emaciated child of the Leningrad siege, 1942 (G. Shchukin)

[Left] *Starving children in the Warsaw ghetto* (f)
[Right] *A malnourished child in the Ghetto* (AJC)

The 10-year-old Yazan al-Kafarneh, the Palestinian face for starving children in Gaza

Yazan following his death on March 4, 2024

the consequent proclamations, threats, anti-Arab pogroms and ultimately the ongoing war in Gaza.[62]

A full two decades before the onset of the Gaza War, the international community had a fairly clear idea of the kind of military doctrine that Israel would deploy in the next major war, which was expected to ensue. Despite this awareness of those realities, the international community remained largely ineffective—just as it would in the aftermath of October 7, 2023, when the obliteration principle was fully evoked and deployed against the defenseless civilians of Gaza. As foreseen, the execution proved broad, ruthless and lethal, extending from massive human losses and infrastructural costs, including urbicide, and a war against children and reproduction to cultural genocide and scholasticide, even ecological devastation.

And so, the path was paved to the final solution, the net effects of which are laid out by Article 2 of the Genocide Convention, which defines genocide by certain *acts performed with intent*; that is, any of the following acts intended to destroy, in whole or in part, a national, ethnical, racial or religious group, as such:

(a) *Killing members of the group;*
(b) *Causing serious bodily or mental harm to members of the group;*
(c) *Deliberately inflicting on the group conditions of life calculated to bring about its physical destruction in whole or in part;*
(d) *Imposing measures intended to prevent births within the group;*
(e) *Forcibly transferring children of the group to another group.*[63]

"Killing members of the group"—Human Costs

"Killing members of the group ..."   From the Holocaust to the massacres of the Yazidis by ISIS, recorded genocides feature an almost uniform pattern in which adult men and adolescent boys are singled out for murder in the early stages. In Nazi Germany, mass killings by labor-intensive gunshots morphed to assembly-line mass-killing in gas chambers, which were more effective. In Gaza, October 7 was followed by the Israeli Defense Forces' (IDF) expanded authorization for bombing non-military targets, the loosening of constraints regarding expected civilian casualties—amounting to more than 42,000 by early November 2024—and the use of artificial intelligence (AI) to generate more potential targets than ever before.[64]

"Causing serious bodily or mental harm ..." The second prohibited act comprises a broad variety of *non*-fatal genocidal acts, such as torture and other cruel, inhuman, or degrading treatment or punishment, including the torture and humiliation of male prisoners. When committed with the requisite

intent, the objective is to cause serious bodily or mental harm to members of the target group. In both Gaza and the West Bank, the brutal bullying, lawless harassment, and inhumane treatment are all reminiscent of segregation and suppression of blacks in apartheid-era South Africa. The system of apartheid in the occupied territories, which has dramatically escalated since October 7, has been widely acknowledged—from Israeli human rights groups to the former intelligence chiefs of Mossad and Shin Bet—to pose an existential threat to the future of Israel/Palestine. However, Israeli apartheid goes beyond its South African precedent. Since the late 1970s, the Israeli system has slowly but surely sought to use segregation as an interim instrument to ethnically cleanse the occupied territories through Palestinian displacement, dispossession and, when seen as necessary, abject devastation. In this sense, it is not just apartheid. It is *ultra*-apartheid that shuns classic apartheid yet benefits from the low-cost labor of the underprivileged group while ultimately seeking its dispossession, displacement, devastation or obliteration. This historical shift from a simple apartheid rule, more typical of the 1970s and 1980s, to ultra-apartheid devastation has overshadowed Gaza, with dramatic escalation since October 7.[65]

In any conflict, direct violence accounts for only some of the killed, usually a minority. The subsequent conditions of life—malnutrition, shortages of health services and unsanitary circumstances, that is, *indirect* violence—add significantly to those killed. Projecting the *final* count is challenging. As the conditions progressively deteriorated in Gaza, data integrity suffered as well. By early May 2024, some 30 percent of the deaths in Gaza were *un*identified. Since two of every five buildings in the Gaza Strip had been destroyed in the first quarter of 2024, the number of bodies still buried in the rubble was estimated to exceed 10,000 (or up to twice as high by late summer).[66]

Warfare kills people particularly through indirect violence. According to empirical research, almost 30 million civilian deaths were indirectly attributable to armed conflict globally between 1990 and 2017, *two thirds* of which were due to communicable, maternal, neonatal, and nutritional diseases.[67] Even if the Gaza War were to end immediately, many indirect deaths would ensue in the coming months and years from causes such as reproductive, communicable, and non-communicable diseases and the fallout from the destruction of healthcare infrastructure; severe shortages of food, water, and shelter, exacerbated by the population's inability to flee to safe places; and the loss of funding to UNRWA, the most critical humanitarian organization in the Strip. In recent conflicts, indirect deaths vary around 3–15 times the number of direct deaths. Applying the downside risk of 4:1, it would be expected that direct deaths of up to 48,000 would translate to more than 200,000 total deaths. But the conclusive final count depends on the accuracy of the model deployed.[68]

By July 2024, Israeli strikes on and near hospitals in the Gaza Strip had left healthcare in the Palestinian territory nearing total collapse. These attacks typically involved missile strikes on hospital buildings, the destruction of facilities, shooting of civilians, sieges, and the temporary takeover of hospital buildings. In just nine months, there were at least 136 strikes on 27 hospitals and 12 other medical facilities. The raids on Al-Shifa, the largest medical complex in the Gaza Strip, left it in "complete ruin," and mass graves were later found at the hospital.[69] Although medical personnel and hospitals are specifically protected under international humanitarian law, the attacks claimed significant casualties among doctors, nurses, medics and other civilians. What once was a haven of life to some had been hammered into a death trap of hell to many.

"Bringing about Physical Destruction"— Infrastructural Decimation

Physical destruction in whole or in part . . ." The third prohibited act concerns the creation of deadly circumstances that are prohibitive of a normal lifespan. In Gaza, the IDF spokesperson Daniel Hagari acknowledged early on that the emphasis of the Israeli ground assault "is on damage and not on accuracy." Since October 7, the strategic objective, which the Biden administration tacitly accepted, had been to destroy Gaza's infrastructure—a deliberate destruction of the Palestinian conditions of life, which the Biden administration opposed in rhetoric but effectively permitted in practice. The Palestinians were being pressured to leave Gaza, as stated by the secret memorandum of the Israeli Ministry of Intelligence after October 7.[70] In these operations, Israel was exploiting starvation as a weapon of war.[71]

In the Gaza Strip, the scale, impact and pace of destruction proved overwhelming in a matter of days—far worse than anything seen since the British/American aerial bombing of Dresden or Rotterdam during World War II, when some 25,000 homes were demolished in each city. By contrast, in Gaza *70,000 housing units*—three times more—were destroyed and over 290,000 partially damaged already by April 2024, with more levelled since then. Due to the destructive power of weapons in the early 21st century, calls have increased for a new war-related concept, *domicide* ("domicile" plus "-cide"), to be included among the list of crimes against humanity. Domicide reflects the deliberate and systematic destruction of homes and basic infrastructure in a manner that makes them uninhabitable. The term dates from the 1970s, when it was still used to characterize the destruction of the family cell under any conditions. The current connotation—a massive violation of the right to housing and basic infrastructure in residential areas, now made uninhabitable—originates from a 2022 UN survey involving Syria, Russia, Myanmar and other countries, including Israel.[72]

A demolished home is not just about a physical loss of brick and mortar, which can be replaced, but a deep psychological loss as well. The utter annihilation of Gaza as a lived place seeks to obliterate the past, present and future of the Palestinians. When people lose their home, they lose their stake in the future, as well as their psychological ability to make sense of and be at home in the world. From October 2023 to late May 2024, the number of lost buildings in North Gaza and Gaza City doubled to 70–75 percent of the total. In the south, Deir El-Balah and Khan Younis lost more than half of the total and even Rafah in the Egyptian border suffered almost 40 percent of the total (Figure 1-4).

As the evidence of the intended domicide continued to accumulate, concerns in the Israeli government climbed accordingly. If domicide were to be acknowledged as a crime against humanity; "international legal authorities will no longer be looking to accuse a brigade commander of destroying a neighborhood, but will aim the arrows of prosecution at the leadership of the army or of the state."[73] Despite much speculation on the future of Gaza, the simple reality of domicide suggested that most Gazan residents faced the impossibility of returning home. After the dust would settle, there would be no home to return to, just rubble and ruins.

By late 2024, the UN Development Program (UNDP) developed several scenarios on the costs of the Gaza War. The longest one envisioned a war that would take 10 months or longer, which had already occurred by mid-summer 2024.[74] The nightmare of Gaza has had a catastrophic impact on the Palestinian economy, pushing the territories into a crisis of unprecedented magnitude. The war has resulted in a staggering number of casualties, widespread displacement affecting roughly 1.9 million individuals, and massive destruction of infrastructure in Gaza. Real GDP has plummeted, with the West Bank experiencing a 23 percent contraction in the first half of 2024, and Gaza suffering an 86 percent decline in the same period.[75] This obliteration is historic. In the 21st century, no other armed conflict has caused such a devastating impact on a population in such a short period of time.

Figure 1-4. Progression of Damage to Buildings across the Gaza Strip through 31 October 2024

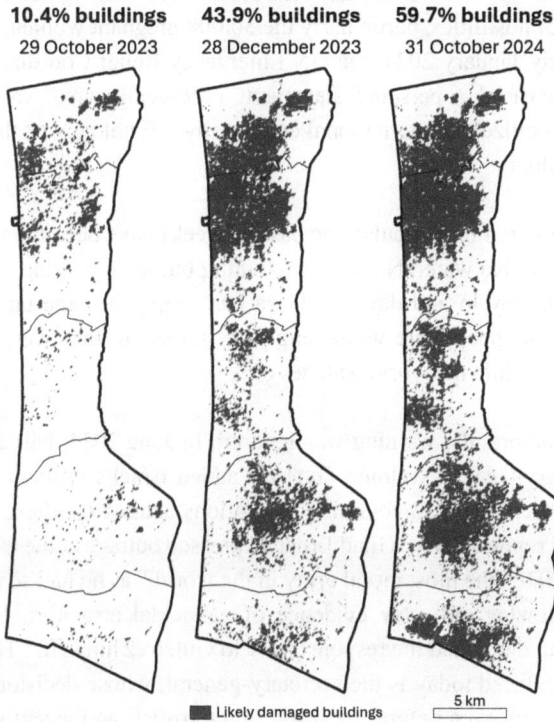

10.4% buildings	43.9% buildings	59.7% buildings
29 October 2023	28 December 2023	31 October 2024

■ Likely damaged buildings   5 km

SOURCE: *Maps based on analysis of Copernicus Sentinel-1 satellite data by Corey Scher and Jamon Van Den Hoek of Oregon State University's Conflict Ecology Lab*

"Measures Preventing Births"— War Against Children and Women

"Preventing births . . ." The fourth prohibited act concerns undertaking measures aimed at preventing reproduction in the protected group, encompassing acts affecting reproduction and intimate relationships, including involuntary sterilization, forced abortion, the prohibition of marriage, and long-term separation of men and women intended to prevent procreation. Building initially on the Holocaust evidence, this condition envisions a fairly long duration, lasting from apartheid and racial acts to mass extinction. Today, the effectiveness of destructive weapons is such that the erasure of a nation can occur faster and more efficiently than by the slow strangulation of birth prevention and development retardation. Nonetheless, in Gaza, the

implementation of this measure was reflected in the deliberate targeting of hospitals, among other such services, with the World Health Organization (WHO) warning that women and newborns were bearing the brunt of the escalation of hostilities, particularly the 50,000 pregnant women.[76]

In early January 2024, the UN Emergency Relief Coordinator, Martin Griffiths, released a personal statement. Foreseeing what was ahead, he hoped to mobilize the international community—if not against the war, then for the children:

> For children in particular, the past 12 weeks have been traumatic: No food. No water. No school. Nothing but the terrifying sounds of war, day in and day out. Gaza has simply become uninhabitable. Its people are witnessing daily threats to their very existence—while the world watches on.[77]

Like before, the warning was ignored. In June 2024, half a year later, UN Secretary-General Antonio Guterres added Israel's military to a global list of offenders that had committed violations against children. In a video, Israel's UN representative Gilad Erdan expressed outrage at the UN decision, calling the IDF "the most moral army in the world," as he had so many times before, following still new evidence of genocidal atrocities. In a surreal move, Erdan derogated the responsibility to Guterrez himself. "The only one who is blacklisted today is the secretary-general, whose decisions since the war started, and even before, are rewarding terrorists and incentivizing them to use children for terror acts .... Shame on him![78]

It was a classic deflection effort. Just a month before, almost 400 bodies had been discovered at Gaza's Nasser and Al-Shifa hospitals, including mostly women and children, with many reportedly showing signs of torture and summary executions, and potential instances of people having been buried alive. At the time, some 63 women, including 37 mothers, were being killed daily and 17,000 Palestinian children were believed to have been orphaned since the war on Gaza began. With the direct bombardment of hospitals and deliberate denial of access to health care facilities by Israeli snipers, the absence of beds and medical resources placed 50,000 pregnant Palestinian women and 20,000 new-born babies at unimaginable risk. Over 180 women per day were giving birth without pain relief, while hundreds of babies had died because of a lack of electricity to power incubators. Consequently, increases in miscarriages were up to 300 percent, while 95 percent of pregnant and breastfeeding women faced severe food poverty.[79]

In the past, Israel had not been featured among the global violators against children. Yet, such brutality was neither unique to nor new in Israel. Violence in the custody of its security and military forces was effectively as old as the Israeli occupation itself, although in its *recorded* form it had intensified amid the Second Intifada, two decades prior to October 7. Between 2000 and 2004, over 1,400 Palestinian children were arrested by Israeli military authorities. Worse, affidavits by Palestinian child detainees suggested that most were subjected to one or more forms of mistreatment during their period of arrest and interrogation, including sexual harassment and physical and psychological threats.[80]

The children of Gaza were the children of the Obliteration Doctrine. All they had seen ever since their birth was violence, war and destruction. The basic conditions of life in the Strip represented textbook risk factors for lasting mental harm, as manifested by symptoms of severe emotional distress and trauma, including fear, anxiety, disordered eating, bedwetting, hyper-vigilance, and sleep problems. Reported behavioral changes featured introversion, separation anxiety or changes in attachment style with parents, regression, and aggression.[81]

If the suffering of children broke the hearts of their caretakers, what was even worse was the fate of those kids without a voice. By July 2024, up to 21,000 children were missing in the chaos of Gaza, many trapped beneath rubble, detained, buried in unmarked graves, or lost from their families. Others had been forcibly disappeared, including an unknown number detained and forcibly transferred out of Gaza, their whereabouts unknown to their families amidst reports of ill-treatment and torture.[82] Furthermore, early on, there were numerous reports of preventable deaths for lack of oxygen and ventilators, and of over 1,000 children that had undergone leg amputations in Gaza, according to UNICEF, some without anesthesia.[83] By June 2024, the UN added Israel to its blacklist of countries that have committed abuses against children in armed conflict. According to a *Children in Armed Conflict* report, more grave violations against children were committed in Gaza, the West Bank and Israel than anywhere else in the world, including Congo DR, Myanmar, Somalia, Nigeria and Sudan.

By late 2024, the testimonies of health professional on location indicated that the deaths of many children in Gaza were not just collateral damage, but outcomes of deliberate, targeted actions. What dozens of doctors, nurses and paramedics in Gaza saw was multiple cases of pre-teen children shot in the head or chest. The testimony of Dr. Feroze Sidhwa, a trauma and general surgeon who had worked at the European Hospital in Khan Younis, was particularly compelling: "I've seen violence and worked in conflict zones. But of the many things that stood out about working in a hospital in Gaza, one got to me: Nearly every day I was there, I saw a new young child who had been shot in the head or the chest, virtually all of whom went on to die."[84]

In March 2025, an independent investigation of the UN Human Rights Council described, on the basis of damning evidence, the "destruction of Palestinians through reproductive violence and harms resulting from the Israeli Security Forces' deliberate attacks on sexual and reproductive health care facilities and the collapsed health care infrastructure in Gaza." It demonstrated a "sharp increase in sexual and gender-based violence perpetrated by members of the Israeli Security Forces and settlers online and in person across the Occupied Palestinian Territory, including rape and other forms of sexual violence.[85]

"Targeting a Collectivity"—Cultural Genocide

"Forcible transfer of children . . ."   Of the four conditions of Article 2 of the Genocide Convention, the last one refers to "forcibly transferring children of the group to another group."[86] In the Convention, this is the only prohibited act that does not lead to physical or biological destruction, but rather to the destruction of the group as a cultural and social unit. It is usually described as occurring when children of the protected group are transferred to the perpetrator group; for instance, boys to be exploited as labor or as soldiers, or girls who are treated as chattel.[87]

In its literal sense, this prohibited act was rare in the Gaza War, just as it has been through decades of Israeli ethnic cleansing of Palestinians within its boundaries and in the occupied Palestinian territories. This, however, did not nullify this characteristic of genocide. It underscored the full extent of the genocide by reflecting Israel's total abhorrence of the targeted group. Palestinians were effectively regarded as sub-human and thus dispensable, reflecting the system of ultra-apartheid and the dehumanization that enables it.

The strategic objective of the Obliteration Doctrine is significantly broader than the four conditions of the Genocide Convention, covering also those conditions that Raphael Lemkin, supported by most countries of the Global South, tried but failed to include in the final Convention, in particular cultural genocide. Lemkin understood that an "attack targeting a collectivity can also take the form of systematic and organized destruction of the art and cultural heritage in which the unique genius and achievement of a collectivity are revealed in fields of science, arts, and literature. The contribution of any particular collectivity to world culture as a whole forms the wealth of all humanity, even while exhibiting unique characteristics."[88]

The framework of the Hague Regulations (1907), the Fourth Geneva Convention (1949), international human rights law, customary international law and relevant treaties has bound Israel since 1967 as an occupying power. Nonetheless, during this period Israel has conducted a series of unlawful acts violating internationally recognized human rights and humanitarian norms, deploying a policy of cultural obliteration, military targeting of cultural property, and the appropriation of cultural heritage. Such actions included removing artefacts of scientific, historical and archaeological interest; carrying out illegal archaeological excavations whose outcomes seek to serve Israel's colonial narrative; and strategically targeting and destroying any cultural sites that do not confirm this narrative.[89]

In other words, Israel adopted actions that are internationally seen as signs of cultural genocide years before October 7. However, at no point in this history has the devastation been as extensive, intensive and irreversible as in Gaza since 2023. During these genocidal atrocities, Israel not only demolished homes and hospitals, but also historic streets, public buildings with important records and archives, including the main public library, as well as all four of Gaza's universities, Gaza's Old City, the ancient port of Gaza, and many museums, even the newly opened Rafah Museum of Palestinian Heritage and the Central Archives of Gaza, with its 150 years of history (Figure 1-5).

Figure 1-5. Cultural Genocide in the Gaza Strip

The al-Amin Muhammad Mosque was destroyed by the Israeli bombing of Khan Yunis on 8 October 2023.

SOURCE: *Wikimedia (Mahmoud Fareed \ WAFA)*

A central characteristic of cultural genocide is *scholasticide*. Used interchangeably with terms like *educide* (Hans-Christof von Sponeck) and *epistemicide* (Boaventura de Sousa Santos), the concept refers to the intended mass destruction of education in a specific place. Typical to past colonialism, epistemicide is used to destroy the existing knowledge systems of the colonized, to replace them with knowledge systems controlled by the colonizer—implying that the targeted population would nonetheless remain. This is not the goal of the Obliteration Doctrine because its final solution relies on the transfer of the target population or, in the absence of ethnic cleansing, on killing them. Scholasticide is a prelude to that end.

In the first six months of the war, two thirds of UNRWA schools in Gaza had been hit; some were bombed out, many severely damaged. In the process, these educational institutions had gone from safe places of education and hope for children to overcrowded shelters and often ending up as places of misery and death.[90] The comprehensive destruction of Palestinian educational institutions and the extermination of educators began in tandem with the obliteration activities after October 7. By January 2024, Euro-Med Human Rights Monitor said that the Israeli army had targeted academic, scientific, and intellectual figures in the Strip in deliberate and specific air raids on their homes without prior notice. Those targeted had been crushed to death beneath the rubble, along with members of their families and other displaced families. Israel had systematically destroyed every university in Gaza. The first stage included the bombing of the Islamic and Al-Azhar universities. The other universities suffered similar assaults; some, like Al-Israa University in southern Gaza, were totally destroyed after initially being used as military barracks.[91]

UN experts raised serious alarm over the systemic destruction of the Palestinian education system in the Gaza Strip. Nearly 90 percent of school buildings had been damaged or destroyed by April 2024, in what seemed to be "an intentional effort to comprehensively destroy the Palestinian education system"; that is, scholasticide.[92]

"Uninhabitable Death War Zone"—Ecocide

The final step of cultural genocide is *ecocide*; that is, the intentional destruction of the environment necessary for the support of human life. It is directly related to the decimation of the reproduction of culture that Lemkin associated with cultural genocide. Over three decades, in parallel with the Madrid and Oslo peace talks, the Gaza Strip had progressively been isolated from the West Bank and the outside world overall, while being subjected to repeated Israeli military incursions. In terms of environmental damage, deterioration had worsened since 2014, when the clearing and bulldozing of agricultural and residential lands by the Israeli military close to the eastern border of Gaza had been coupled with the unannounced aerial spraying of crop-killing herbicides. These illicit practices have not only destroyed entire swaths of formerly arable land along the border fence but also crops and farmlands hundreds of meters deep into Palestinian territory, resulting in the loss of livelihoods for Gazan farmers.[93] In a historical view, such massive bombardment went back to the early days of the Cold War, when the United States dropped bombs on North Korean dams to flood crops and induce starvation among civilians. To compound the same effect, irrigation systems were attacked on the ground.[94] The difference is that in Gaza the scope of destruction was far narrower than in Korea, but the decimation far more effective, intensive and lethal.

From the beginning, "environmental warfare in Gaza" has been marked by colonial violence.[95] It has been an inherent part of the Palestinian expulsions and Israeli occupation since the late 1940s. Furthermore, the destruction is central to the Obliteration Doctrine. In that sense, "the Nakba has also a lesser-known environmental dimension, the complete transformation of the environment, the weather, the soil, the loss of the indigenous climate, the vegetation, the skies. The Nakba is a process of colonially imposed vulnerability to climate change."[96]

At the eve of October 7, World Bank analysts warned that in the West Bank and Gaza, drivers of fragility, development constraints, and vulnerability to climate change were closely interconnected, thanks to decades of the fragmentation of land, restrictions on the movement of people and goods, recurrent episodes of violent conflict, persistent political and policy uncertainty, and the lack of sovereign control over critical natural resources.[97] As the net effect of the Gaza War, widespread damages to built-up areas from the use of explosive weapons resulted in direct impacts on water services and in millions of tons of debris, toxic waste and destroyed agricultural lands. This led to the outbreak of communicable diseases from poor water, health and sanitation conditions, combined with the risk of exposure to a range of additional hazardous materials and the collapse of environmental governance. Hence, the damage to water infrastructure and widescale urban destruction in combination with a severely degraded healthcare system; all of which posed a long-lasting threat to both public health and livelihoods. The future that awaited Palestinians at the end of the hostilities was a Gaza turned into an "uninhabitable death war zone."[98]

By late April 2024, Israel's obliteration of Gaza had created 37m tonnes of debris. That amounts to an average of 300kg of rubble per square meter of land in the Gaza Strip. Worse, much of these piles and heaps of debris and wreckage were laced with unexploded bombs, which could take up to 15 years of extensive work to remove, assuming the availability of 100 trucks on a daily basis.[99] Taking into consideration the fact that on average about 10 percent of weapons failed to detonate when fired, huge demining teams would be warranted for years. The longer the war continued, the longer would the clearance take at its end.

During the first two months of Israel's assault on Gaza, the projected emissions from there exceeded the annual emissions of 20 individual countries and territories. Indeed, the total emissions increased to more than those of over 33 individual countries and territories when the war infrastructure built by both Israel and Hamas is included, such as Hamas's tunnel network and Israel's protective fence or "Iron Wall." In that light, the carbon costs of *reconstructing* Gaza are likely to prove huge. Effectively, rebuilding Gaza will result in a total annual emissions figure higher than that of over 130 countries, putting them on a par with that of New Zealand.[100]

The overwhelming majority of the 281,000 metric tons (MT) of carbon dioxide (CO_2) generated in the first two months of hostilities can be traced to Israel's aerial bombardment and ground invasion of Gaza. Almost half the total carbon emissions were down to U.S. cargo planes flying military supplies to Israel. By contrast, Hamas rockets fired into Israel in the same period generated 713 MT of CO_2, which is equivalent to 300 MT of coal. There was no symmetry in war machinery. The initial brutal offensive by Hamas was overwhelmed by Israel's obliteration of what used to be Gaza. Worse, these estimates are highly conservative because they are based on just two months of the war that had already endured three times longer by June 2024. More importantly, the *actual* carbon footprint could prove five to eight times higher, when emissions from the *entire* war supply chain were included.

Despite all the devastation and the genocidal atrocities, the focus of the U.S. administrations remained on Gaza as the ultimate wrongdoer. In early 2025, Elon Musk, the Trump administration's billionaire partner, recalled that after World War II, when Germany and Japan were defeated, the U.S. helped rebuild Japan and Germany providing financial support to rebuild Japan and Germany, two major U.S. allies today. Similarly, Musk contended, it was very important to make the Palestinian areas prosperous: "You have to bring prosperity and you have to help rebuild."[101] Yet, these practical measures have long been and continue to be undermined by the central role of the military-industrial complex in the U.S. foreign policy.

Accessorial Complicity: The Netanyahu Cabinets[102]

In November 2024, after an investigation of war crimes and crimes against humanity, the International Criminal Court (ICC) issued arrest warrants for the Prime Minister of Israel, Benjamin Netanyahu, and his former Minister of Defense, Yoav Gallant. The two were alleged to be responsible for the war crime of starvation as a method of warfare and for the crimes against humanity of murder, persecution, and other inhumane acts during the Gaza war. Notably, the warrant against Netanyahu was the first against the leader of the a U.S.-led West-backed country for war crimes. But were the two really the only cabinet leaders responsible for the genocidal atrocities?

By supporting Netanyahu and Gallant, there seem to be at least half a dozen cabinet members who contributed to those brutalities, often insisting on effectively more destructive measures and protracted bombardment and obliteration (Figure 1-6).

Figure 1-6. Widening Nets of Accessorial Liability: The Netanyahu Cabinet

SOURCE: *Wikipedia (officials' photos and the group portrait)*

The Minister of National Security, Itamar Ben-Gvir, the leader of the far-right and supremacist Jewish Power party, publicly promoted the expulsion of "non-loyal" Arab citizens, the full blockade of Gaza, the Judaization of all Israel-occupied Palestinian territories and the total elimination of Hamas *and* all who support Palestinian resistance. Ben-Gvir was seconded by Bezazel Smotrich, the far-right leader of the national religious Zionists and Netanyahu's Minister of Finance and Defense, who used the Gaza War to achieve the annexation of the West Bank to Israel proper. A self-proclaimed racist and fascist, Smotrich promoted the blockade of the Gaza Strip, saying fuel will not enter Gaza "under any circumstances." Calling for a "voluntary emigration" of Palestinians from Gaza to other countries, he wanted to have Gaza taken over by the Messianic far-right settlers from the West Bank.[103]

Still another hardliner was Netanyahu's foreign minister Israel Katz. As Netanyahu's Energy Minister in October 2023, Katz had famously declared a complete siege of Gaza: "There will be no electricity, no food, no fuel, everything is closed (to Gaza)." As the Minister of Intelligence, Gila Gamliel was in charge of plans aiming to expunge all residents from Gaza, presumably to the Democratic Republic of Congo. Netanyahu's Heritage Minister Amihai Eliyahu, Ben-Gvir's colleague, suggested that Israel should use nuclear weapons to get rid of the "monsters of Gaza," including women and children. Similarly, Orit Strook, Settlement Minister and Smotrich's far-right peer who opposed ceasefire efforts because Hamas and Palestinians had to be eradicated so that the Messianic settlers could rebuild the Judaized Gaza.[104]

Another set of cabinet members may have been less known internationally but they played a vital role in the protracted genocidal atrocities. Miri Regev, a former brigadier-general in the Israel Defense Forces and IDF spokeswoman, described herself as a "happy fascist," criticizing the efforts to detain Israeli soldiers in the notorious Sde Teiman detention camp, which critics called Israel's Abu Ghraib torture and prisoner center.[105] As Minister of Communications, Shlomo Karhi, who promoted the full removal of all Palestinians from Gaza, had a central role in the censure efforts of international media operating in Israel and the occupied territories, particularly the shutdown of Al Jazeera's Israel bureau. After October 7, then Information Minister, Galit-Distel Atbaryan, posted her infamous tweet: "Erase Gaza from the face of the earth ... Gaza should be wiped off the map, and fire and brimstone on the heads of the Nazis in Judea and Samaria ... We need a cruel, vengeful IDF here. Anything less is immoral."[106] Many of these views were supported by foreign minister Gideon Sa'ar, a longtime promoter of the West Bank's annexation. As Minister of Diaspora Affairs, Amichai Chikli led over 100 civil initiatives to align international sentiments with the cabinet's view that Hamas was comprised of human animals and modern-day antisemitic

Nazis. In turn, May Golan, Netanyahu's openly racist appointee to serve as Israel consul general in New York City, which rejected the appointment, called for the relocation of all Palestinians in Gaza and in retaliation, for "another Nakba" to cleanse Palestinians from Gaza.[107]

Despite their supportive role and accessorial liability, none of these cabinet members got warrants from the ICC.

At one point or another, the Netanyahu cabinet also featured veteran military leaders whose role was crucial in the aftermath of October 7. Their role had been critical in the consolidation of the Obliteration Doctrine, particularly the destruction of urban infrastructure. Benny Gantz, the leader of the conservative centrist party and former IDF chief of general staff, sat in Netanyahu's cabinet through the most devastating phase of Israel's assault against Gaza. Gadi Eisenkot, the former IDF chief of staff, was the architect of the Obliteration Doctrine that Gallant deployed in Gaza. Then there was the controversial Avi Dichter, a former head of Shin bet and veteran politician whose brutal methods in the occupied territories had rendered him vulnerable to war crimes arrest abroad. Just weeks after October 7, Dichter disclosed the not-so-secret goal of the Gaza operation: "We are now rolling out the Gaza Nakba," adding "Gaza Nakba 2023, that's how it will end."[108]

Yet, none of these military strategists was featured among the ICC warrants.

The portrait of Netanyahu's cabinet also features Isaac Herzog, the Israeli president. Right after October 7, Herzog condemned all residents of Gaza for "collective responsibility" for the Hamas attack on Israel, blamed criticism of IDF attacks on Palestinian hospitals as "a 21st-century blood libel," which term he also used for South Africa's case against Israel. Herzog denied any Israeli involvement in the 2024 Lebanon pager explosions, which subsequently turned out to be a blatant lie.[109] The portrait also includes Ron Dermer, Netanyahu's right-hand advisor, who was most intimately linked with the PM's fatal decisions regarding Gaza. These included a covert plan to "thin" the Palestinian population in the Gaza Strip "to a minimum," by the creation of a "humanitarian crisis" to persuade Egypt to allow refugees to flow to other Arab countries, and a second plan to open up sea routes so that Israel "allows a mass escape to European and African countries."[110]

Yet, neither Herzog nor Dermer had to worry about an ICJ warrant.

In light of the track-record of these officials—and it would not be challenging to document the past activities of prior Netanyahu cabinets since the late 1990s and some of its predecessors—the ICC's arrest warrants for PM Netanyahu and his ex-defense minister Gallant would seem to be largely symbolic, albeit consistent with prior warrants by the ICC.

* * *

Tragically, the ineffectiveness of the international intervention in Gaza served to reward Netanyahu's war cabinet, while leaving the last human right defenders in Israel without support, as evidenced by the far-right government's highly controversial effort to destroy B'Tselem, the Israeli Information Center for Human Rights in the Occupied Territories.[111]

What happens in Gaza won't stay in Gaza. The obliteration of the coastal strip casts a long, dark shadow over the future of human rights in Israel. Yet, none of these monstrous feats—blockade and manufactured famine, weaponized starvation, genocidal intent and acts, the consequent human costs, infrastructural decimation, war against women and children, cultural genocide and ecocide—relied on Israel alone. They were made viable by its major ally, the United States, and other partners, such as the UK, Germany and other allies. So, were they complicit in these genocidal atrocities?

CHAPTER 2

WAR PROFITEERING AND U.S. FOREIGN POLICY

When Secretary of State Antony Blinken met Prime Minister Benjamin Netanyahu just five days after October 7, 2023, the latter brought him, in a presumably highly unusual move, straight to his war room in the Kirya, the inner sanctum of Israel's military decision-making. Having introduced Blinken to the core of Israel's political and military leadership who were planning their military response into Gaza, Netanyahu declared:

We need three things: ammo, ammo, ammo.[1]

Having offshored critical elements of its defense ecosystem to the U.S. and its allies, the Netanyahu administration was no longer fully in charge of Israel's protection. It had been a long road. In the 1960s, Israel began to establish defensive military ties with the U.S. In the 1970s, U.S. rearmament was vital to its war effort in the Yom Kippur War. In the 1980s, the Reagan administration made Israel a strategic partner. After the Cold War, these ties have broadened and deepened into a symbiosis.[2]

Knowing fully well how Israel would use the lethal weaponry, the Biden administration nonetheless kept the massive arms flow going. As Israel's defense and military sovereignty has shifted from Tel Aviv to Washington, the degree of U.S. complicity has increased accordingly. This is not to say that the White House was in control of the Israeli undertakings that would soon overwhelm President Biden and his closest confidants. But if that's the case, then who was really in charge?

Relying on a select network of think tanks, many of which it funded, and their corporate proxies, the U.S. military industrial complex itself was in charge. Whatever it wants it gets.

If, since World War I, the U.S. military-industrial complex has been driven by the "merchants of death," then the professional, increasingly Ivy League–schooled and Ph.D.-trained weapons promoters of the early 21st century can be portrayed as the merchants of mass deaths. Ever since the discovery of oil and natural gas in the Middle East, this region has been one of the industry's most favorite playgrounds—presumably, due to the West's great concern for "national security" and "freedom and democracy."[3]

America's Military Dominance in the Middle East

Thanks to its ongoing, indiscriminate military aid to Israel, American credibility in the Middle East has steadily eroded. This outcome wasn't inevitable. It was the net effect of the Cold War and U.S. domestic politics. Initially, U.S. diplomacy was cautious and divided regarding the Middle East, seeking to hedge its bets with the nascent Jewish state and Arab oil. But over time, the deepening of the bilateral military ties and the consequent symbiosis has dragged U.S. administrations into complicity with Israel's miscalculations, while undermining the U.S.'s effective sovereignty.[4]

After the onset of Israel's war with Hamas on October 7, 2023, the United States provided at least $12.5 billion in direct military aid to Israel, including $3.8 billion from a bill in March 2024 and another $8.7 billion in April 2024. The military aid to Israel amounts to $17.9 billion during this period, adding the cost to the U.S. Defense Department of replenishing the stock of weapons provided to Israel. Though the aid goes back to the establishment of the state of Israel in 1948, it has soared since the mid-1970s and skyrocketed with the Gaza War (Figure 2-1).

Figure 2-1. U.S. Military Aid to Israel, 1948–2024

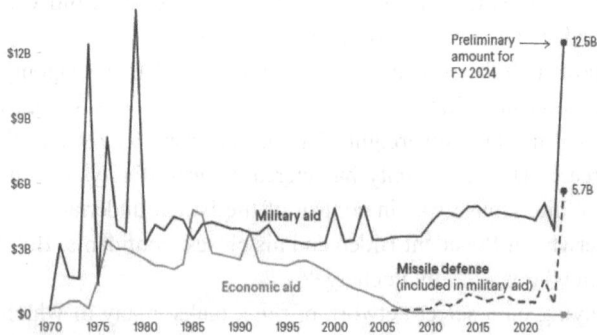

*Data is adjusted to constant 2024 dollars using the price index for the first half of fiscal year 2024.

SOURCES: *USAID; CRS; BEA via Federal Reserve Bank of St. Louis.*

U.S. military and economic ties in the Middle East are not limited to Israel and Saudi Arabia, its two primary allies in the region. They are reflected in U.S. foreign assistance, most of which has been in military aid, designed to support countries that serve to maintain American hegemony in the region. Since 1946, the U.S. has provided $373 billion in foreign assistance to the Middle East, which makes it the largest regional recipient of U.S. economic and security assistance around the world. For years, the bulk of U.S. foreign aid, mainly in the form of State Department-managed military assistance, has been directed to just a few countries: Israel, Egypt, Jordan and more recently, Iraq. However, Israel has been by far the largest cumulative recipient of U.S. foreign aid since its founding, receiving about $310 billion (adjusted for inflation) in total economic and military assistance.[5]

These activities have been exacerbated after the Cold War by huge investments in U.S. military bases during the post-9/11 wars. At the eve of October 7, 2023, before new capacity, there were eight major bases and 11 other military sites to which the Pentagon had access in the Middle East. Interestingly, the figure by the Congressional Research Service does not feature the U.S. bases in Israel, which, though small, played a critical role in the 2023–25 Gaza War (Figure 2-2).

In 2024, over 5,400 active-duty service members were permanently assigned to overseas bases in the Middle East, with the largest number in Bahrain. There were thousands of additional service members on rotational deployments or other temporary assignments, including more than 3,800 in Jordan and 2,300 in Saudi Arabia. They were led by U.S. Central Command (CENTCOM) headquartered in Tampa, Florida, and a forward headquarters at Al Udeid Air Base in Qatar. Their objective comprised efforts in "deterring Iran, countering violent extremist organizations, and competing strategically [i.e., with Russia and China]."[6]

It is this massive delivery of foreign military aid and financing into the region, coupled with the huge aid specifically to Israel, and the elaborate web of U.S. military bases engaging in repeated operations in multiple countries, plus the recurrent efforts at regime change by the U.S. military and intelligence services that define America's structural complicity in the region. These gigantic military and economic activities, in turn, were steered by the U.S. military-industrial-think tank complex and its malleable boundaries among the senior officials of U.S. military, industry and think tank elites.

Figure 2-2. U.S. Overseas Bases in the Middle East

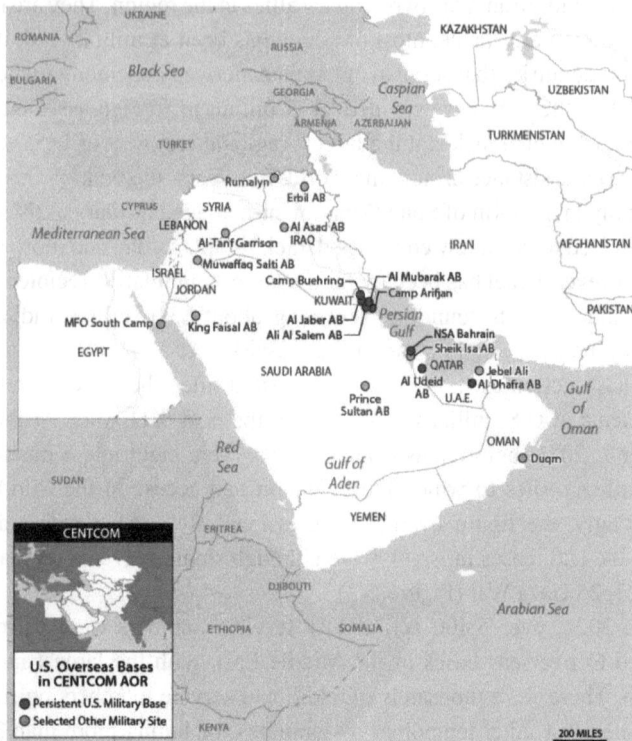

Locations of U.S. bases and sites are based on unclassified sources and do not include all bases and sites in the region.

SOURCE: *CRS; U.S. Naval Institute; Department of Defense; CFR research*

Revolving Doors

In America's foreign policymaking, business leaders and their think tank experts possess a demonstrably outsized influence.[7] Consequently, financial relationships connecting these two raise many questions, especially when the touted policy experts move back and forth from think tanks to public office through the "revolving door," affording the business community significant influence over government policymaking.[8] These revolving doors prevail among the U.S. administrations, America's largest think tanks and the globally-operating U.S. defense contractors that fund them and finance political campaigns paving the way to executive power. The Biden administration was no exception to this rule.

Initially, the rise of the huge U.S. defense complex was not seen as an unalloyed blessing, but as a tradeoff between welfare and security. In his *Farewell Address*, President Dwight D. Eisenhower, who had for years played an inordinate role in building this expansive institutional organism, famously warned against the dangers of the military-industrial complex and the potential "domination of the nation's scholars by Federal employment, project allocations, and the power of money."

> In the councils of government, *we must guard against the acquisition of unwarranted influence, whether sought or unsought, by the military–industrial complex*. The potential for the disastrous rise of misplaced power exists, and will persist.[9]

These huge military contractors function like venture capital giants, hedging their bets like investors among the think tanks that thrive on such seed funding. They multiply the benefits of their investments when the think tanks' luminaries join senior positions in the administration and can then influence huge purchasing decisions to the benefit of the Pentagon, the security and intelligence communities, and the State Department. In the end, American policymaking process is not only about ideas or even influence networks. It is about the money that buys influence and promotes ideas. Despite their great variety, these think tanks share a common denominator. They receive substantial financial support from the U.S. government and private businesses that work for the U.S. government, most prominently defense contractors. Such funding can have a significant, outsized impact on the activities of think tanks. As *The Godfather* demonstrated, there are many ways to kiss the ring. Think tanks may produce reports favorable to a funder. Their scholars work closely with funders' lobbyists. Their experts can offer Congressional testimony in support of funders' interests and so on.

When the Biden administration took office in 2021, at least $1 billion in U.S. government and defense contractor funding went to the top 50 think tanks in America. The top recipients of this funding featured the RAND Corporation, the Center for a New American Security (CNAS), and the New America Foundation (NAF). At least 600 different donations were given to these think tanks, coming from almost 70 different U.S. government and defense contractor sources. The top funders from the U.S. government were the Office of the Secretary of Defense, the Air Force, the Army, the Department of Homeland Security, and the State Department; that is, the critical institutions of national security and foreign policy. In turn, the biggest defense contractors contributing to these think tanks included Northrop Grumman, Raytheon, Boeing, Lockheed Martin, and Airbus; that is, the largest, globally-operating defense contractors—Big Defense.[10]

Along with Big Technology and Big Pharma, Big Defense and the largest think tanks form a complex web, as evidenced by the *top five* such think tanks and the extensive money flows to them from America's largest defense contractors. Among these key actors are the leading Democratic-leaning organizations of the past two decades; namely, the Center for American Progress (which was the preferred think tank of the Obama administration) and the Center for a New American Security (the prime idea machine of the Biden administration). The same applies on the Republican side. In the 2024 election, President Trump's cadres relied particularly on the Heritage Foundation, the think tank par excellence of the Reagan administration, source of the infamous "Project 2025," and on the new America First Policy Institute.

Indirectly, these kingmakers' services feature lobbying, facilitating the transmission of money, the prime contributors and their recipients. In these money flows, the Israel lobby has had a considerable role over time. As its critics have long argued, "well-financed and politically powerful, the pro-Israel lobby is a major force on American foreign affairs that looks to continue America's military and fiscal support of the Jewish nation-state."[11] Particularly cozy with the Netanyahu cabinets, the lobby's successes with the first Trump administration include moving the U.S. embassy in Israel from the internationally recognized capital of Tel Aviv to Jerusalem (a move long advocated by some in the pro-Israel lobby, but opposed by JStreet, one of the larger pro-Israel groups). The lobby has also been undermining Palestinian efforts at a two-state solution and ending all foreign aid to the West Bank and Gaza. In the region, it has pushed for withdrawing from the Iran nuclear deal (JCPOA); and the assassination of General Soleimani which almost brought the U.S. to a brink of war in the Middle East. In 2023–24, half a dozen pro-Israel lobby contributors—most prominently the American Israel Public Affairs Committee (AIPAC), JStreet, Republican Jewish Coalition, Democratic Majority for Israel, and NorPac—accounted for the bulk of the money flows.

Moreover, in the past five years, foreign governments and foreign government-owned entities have donated more than $110 million to the top 50 think tanks in the United States. The most generous donor countries included the United Arab Emirates, the United Kingdom, and Qatar, which contributed $16.7 million, $15.5 million, and $9.1 million to U.S. think tanks, respectively. The Atlantic Council, Brookings Institution, and German Marshall Fund received the most money from foreign governments. In that same period, the top 100 defense companies contributed some $35 million to the top 50 think tanks. The top donors feature Northrop Grumman, Lockheed Martin, and Mitsubishi respectively. The Atlantic Council, Center for a New

American Security (CNAS), and the Center for Strategic and International Studies (CSIS) were the top recipients of Pentagon contractor money. Interestingly, the U.S. government directly has given at least $1.5 billion to American think tanks since 2019. The vast majority of this funding—$1.4 billion—went to the RAND Corporation.[12] Yet, like other U.S. think tanks, RAND, initially a postwar spinoff a project of the Pentagon, U.S. Air Force and Douglas Aircraft (today a part of Boeing), is typically portrayed as an independent entity. The description effectively dilutes RAND's great reliance on the U.S. government monies and foreign donors.

While think tanks exist to produce independent analysis, the prevalence of special interest funding raises questions of intellectual freedom, self-censorship, and perspective filtering. This is compounded by instances in which individual researchers simultaneously hold positions at a think tank and a given foreign government or corporation, a clear potential conflict of interest.

Conflicts of Interest

As one administration replaces another, so do the positions of these think tanks shift and change. In that sense, they are replaceable. But the sources of the money flows aren't. Ultimately, it is Big Defense that maintains, sustains and reproduces these ideas, influence and money flows. The net effect? The proliferation and rise of think tanks able and willing to popularize, support and promote military solutions to a conflict and seemingly at a loss when it comes to proposing peaceful trajectories favoring geopolitical stability and economic development.

Ultimately, Big Defense benefits most from think tanks that are portrayed as centers of security but tend to favor conflict zones that ensure insecurity. For them, conflicts are good business, whereas peace isn't. One might hope that the determination of American foreign policy is the result of judicious consideration of situations with a view to prioritizing the national interest of the United States and the wellbeing of the American people, bearing in mind America's moral values. That, however, is very far from the everyday realities of the actual determination of U.S. foreign policy.

Just like the Reagan administration relied on the Heritage Foundation in the early 1980s, the Biden Democrats in the early 2020s depended on the Center for a New American Security (CNAS), which has functioned not only as a research institution, but as an incubator from which Democratic administrations have selected foreign policy personnel since its founding in 2007. What made CNAS's revolving door syndrome unique is that the Biden administration's key figures targeted by the Gaza genocide cases were, in one way or another, associated with CNAS. Under the Biden administration, at least 16 CNAS alumni were selected for foreign policy positions. The Center exhibited a pattern of conduct in which serious conflicts of interest went unacknowledged and undisclosed. It receives "large contributions directly from defense contractors, foreign governments, and the U.S. government; publishes research and press material that frequently supports the interests of its sponsors without proper disclosure; and even gives its financial sponsors an official oversight role in helping to shape the organization's research."[13]

CNAS is far from alone among Washington think tanks engaging in questionable ethical behavior. Yet, the scale of its conflicts of interest is unique, thanks to its success as the Biden administration's brain incubator. After four years of Trump's devastating trade policies and geopolitics, the Biden administration in 2021 had a historical opportunity to reset both. Instead, it escalated the Trump tariff wars into a broader Cold War with China, while largely building on the previous administration's geopolitics. CNAS, its alumni, their corporate proxies, and the world's largest defense contractors, particularly Northrop Grumman, Raytheon, and Lockheed Martin, played a key institutional role in this economic and geopolitical effort.

Biden's overall policy toward Asia was authored by Kurt Campbell, his Asia czar, who also served as the coordinator for Indo-Pacific affairs on the National Security Council (NSC). In 2019, Campbell and Biden's national security adviser, Jake Sullivan, introduced their China doctrine of intense "competition without catastrophe." It was premised on the pivot to Asia, which Campbell developed during President Obama's first term.[14] And it was manna from heaven for Big Defense, whose profitability is premised on new geopolitical enemies; and it was also manna for the consultancies and advisories in which both Campbell and Sullivan had participated. In 2023–2024 the goals of American grand strategy, largely shared by the Biden administration and its Republican precursor and successor, hovered prominently over the Gaza War (just as it did over Trump's Abraham Accords).

Since 2022, the Biden administration had been in talks with Saudi leaders, urging Riyadh to establish diplomatic ties with Israel. Riyadh had joined the BRICS alliance, remained one of China's largest oil suppliers and was selling oil in multiple currencies. But it was also the world's second-largest arms importer and 75 percent of its weapons came from the U.S. For a long while, Riyadh has been negotiating a security pact with the United States, modeled loosely on the U.S.-Japan mutual defense pact, while seeking cooperation in a civilian nuclear program. Preceded by Israel's peace treaties with Egypt (1979) and Jordan (1994) and the Oslo Accords with the Palestinian Authority (1993–95), Biden's grand bargain was predicated on the Abraham Accords (2020–2021) initiated by Trump between Israel, the UAE and Bahrain, and subsequently with Morocco and Sudan, respectively.

Relying on Washington's revolving-door practices, the primary bene-ficiaries of Campbell's pivot to Asia and the Biden administration's grand strategy in the Middle East were America's gigantic defense contractors (Figure 2-3).

In January 2021, Campbell's appointment unleashed a public debate due to his portfolio of ex-clients, rife with potential conflicts of interests. "Shadow lobbying" outfits like Campbell's firm call themselves consul-tants to avoid restrictions associated with traditional lobbying. Reportedly, Campbell himself received a $25,000 monthly retainer from several defense firms.[15] Yet, his stated stances on the Gaza War reflect as much the Biden administration as those of the CNAS/WestExec interests.

Cashing in on Conflicts

In May 2024, Kurt Campbell stated, in his role as U.S. Deputy Secretary of State, that the Biden administration does not see it likely or possible that Israel will achieve "total victory" in defeating Hamas in Gaza. Likening the situation in Gaza to that of the recurring insurgency that the U.S. faced in Afghanistan and Iraq after its invasions following the Sept. 11 attacks, Campbell said a "political solution" was required.[16] Of course, Campbell was not alone in mixing government business with private-sector money-making. While CNAS was mobilizing American public opinion for a major U.S.-Sino conflict, ex-director of CIA John Brennan too joined WestExec Advisors, headed by Michèle Flournoy, to "advise on strategy and geopolitical risk, and help clients capitalize on key business opportunities."[17]

The WestExec's original co-founders were ex-Obama officials Sergio Aguirre and Nitin Chadda. They needed marquee names; hence, the recruit-ing of Flournoy and Antony Blinken, Biden's secretary of state.[18] Chadda was also WestExec's point man in its "strategic partnership" with Ridgeline, "a venture capital and special situation fund" focusing on military startups.[19] Flournoy was making over $450,000 a year as a head of CNAS, which she had co-founded with Campbell. But that was just a table stake for more. Having served as Obama's undersecretary of defense and a military expert, Flournoy wanted to make money the old-fashioned way; that is, by exploiting the revolving doors between WestExec and the government. When she advised the Boston Consulting Group (BCG) in 2013–16, its defense contracts soared from $1.6 million to $32 million. After Biden's triumph, Flournoy was seen as "a revered member of the defense establishment" who had "practically a lock to run a Biden Pentagon. Her path there ran through ramping up the Afghanistan war."[20]

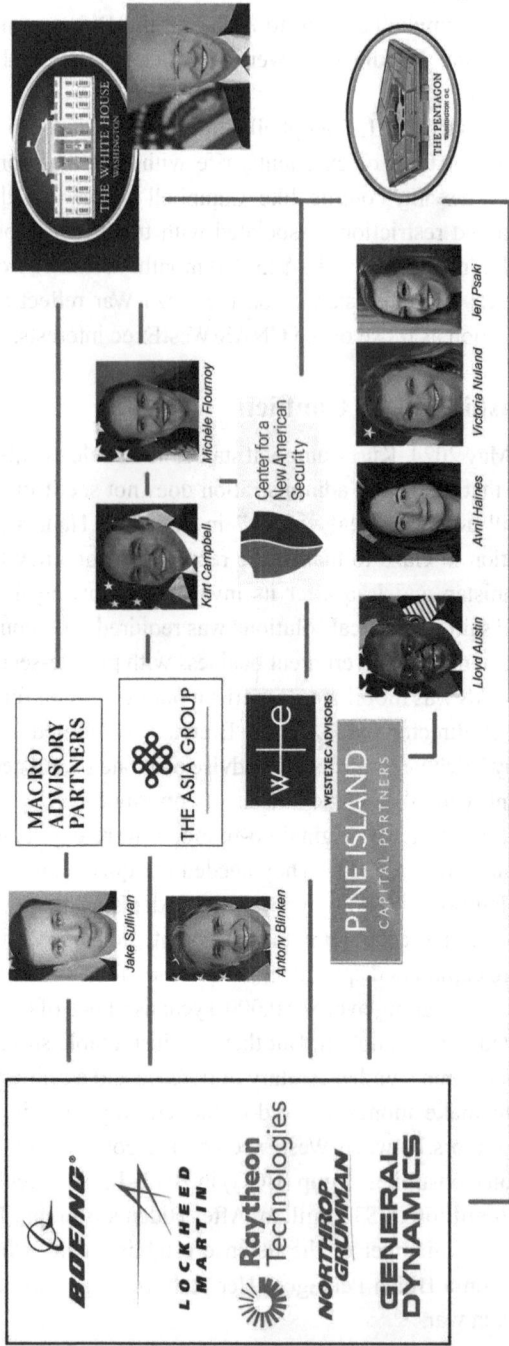

Figure 2-3. Big Defense, Big Think Tanks, Big Advisories and White House

In September 2017, Flournoy co-founded WestExec Advisors. The name of the firm stems from "West Executive Avenue," the closed street that runs between the West Wing of the White House and the Eisenhower Executive Office Building. It is the route to the Situation Room, an intelligence management complex on the ground floor of the West Wing of the White House. As WestExec Advisors boasts on its website, it "brings the Situation Room to the boardroom."[21] The firm purposely sought to employ "people recently coming out of government" with "current knowledge, expertise, contacts, networks."[22] Shrewdly, WestExec and its partners avoided becoming registered lobbyists or foreign agents so that they could enter (or re-enter) government service without delays.[23] Seeking to privatize and thus cash in on executive power, WestExec promised access to big corporate decisionmakers in exchange for big money.

In WestExec, Flournoy quickly learned how to defend the giant contractors. Famously, she made a distinction between "offensive" and "defensive" weapons arguing that Saudi Arabia needed Patriot missiles to protect itself in the Yemeni civil war. By 2019, Raytheon had sold Saudi Arabia over $3 billion worth of bombs that hammered Yemeni targets back into the Middle Ages, "defensively." Raytheon, the contractor, was a major WestExec contributor.[24] Moreover, WestExec's Robert Work, former Deputy Secretary of Defense and ex-CNAS CEO, has been on Raytheon's board since 2017. The top donors of the CNAS included the crème de la crème of Big Defense: Northrop Grumman, Boeing, Lockheed Martin, Raytheon; energy giants Chevron and Exxon, and Soros's Open Society Foundations that often features in the background of regime change operations.[25]

Under a financial disclosure filed by the Biden transition team in December 2020, then-Secretary of State nominee Antony Blinken acknowledged that WestExec clients included "investment giant Blackstone, Bank of America, Facebook, Uber, McKinsey & Company, the Japanese conglomerate SoftBank, the pharmaceutical company Gilead, the investment bank Lazard, Boeing, AT&T, the Royal Bank of Canada, LinkedIn and the venerable Sotheby's." Similarly, Director of National Intelligence-designate Avril Haines disclosed that WestExec had worked with the controversial data-mining company Palantir Technologies.[26]

Non-disclosure agreements conveniently restrict the clients' names from disclosure.[27] Nonetheless, some of these names have been reported. These feature Jigsaw, Google's technology incubator; Windward, an Israeli artificial intelligence firm; Shield AI, a drone surveillance company; and "Fortune 100 types."[28] In the Gaza War, the worst genocidal atrocities occurred in the first few months, when massive bombardments were coupled with AI.[29]

Presidential Privileges

The central actors of the Biden administration, including Secretary of State Blinken and Secretary of Defense Lloyd Austin were connected to CNAS, WestExec or both, and in this capacity and through the administration with the Pentagon and Big Defense. Accordingly, a lawsuit (*Palestine v. Biden*) was filed against President Biden, Blinken, and Austin for the U.S. officials' failure to prevent and complicity in the Israeli government's unfolding genocide against the petitioners, their families, and over 2 million Palestinians in Gaza. It set out how these three defendants not only failed to prevent the genocide of the Palestinian people in Gaza but helped advance this gravest of crimes by continuing to provide Israel with unconditional military and diplomatic support, coordinating closely on military strategy, and undermining efforts by the international community to stop Israel's unrelenting bombing campaign and total siege of Gaza.[30]

President Biden himself was not immune to big money temptations. One of his first acts as president was to issue a new ethics pledge to weaken shadow lobbying. "Special interest groups are not bad people," he'd said as a senator in 2008. "But they are corrosive." When Biden began as Obama's vice president, his net worth was estimated at less than $150,000. Afterwards, he was making $540,000 annually from an academic center with few obligations and a multimillion-dollar book deal. Over the four years he was out of office, he earned $17.3 million.[31] But how did his rise begin?

On October 10, 2023, just three days after the offensive by Hamas and other Palestinian militants against Israeli military and civilians, U.S. President Joe Biden addressed the nation in the White House, pledging unwavering support for Israel, even as Israeli military was pummeling Gaza with aerial bombardment, saying:

When the pure, unadulterated evil is unleashed on this world . . . we must be crystal clear: We stand with Israel . . .[32]

To cope against "unadulterated evil," America would ensure Israel had the military assets it needed to thwart the "sheer evil" that he compared with "painful memories and the scars left by a millennium of antisemitism and genocide of the Jewish people."[33] While sympathy after civilian deaths is always warranted, there was no effort at context, history, or balance, only the certitude of a Manichean world of good and evil, legitimate and illegitimate, Israel and Hamas. It marked the start of the decisions that paved the way to what Senator Bernie Sanders would later call "Biden's Vietnam." But

Biden's views came as no surprise to those who had followed his career since the 1980s. Being an "American Zionist" can pay off, literally.

In the long view, Biden had a special place in the listing of money from the pro-Israel lobby to U.S. senators from 1990 to 2024. During that period, he got a total of $4.2 million, almost twice as much as the next in line.[34] Robert Menendez (I-NC) garnered $2.5 million until his resignation in 2024 following a conviction on 16 counts in a political corruption case. Ranking third, Hillary Clinton (D-NY), another veteran Israeli hawk who had begun her political career as a volunteer for the Republican uber-hawk Barry Goldwater in 1964. Coupling Biden's Senate data from 1990 and his presidential campaigns since 1988, his total amounts to $11.2 million (Figure 2-4).

Figure 2-4. U.S. Presidency, American Zionism

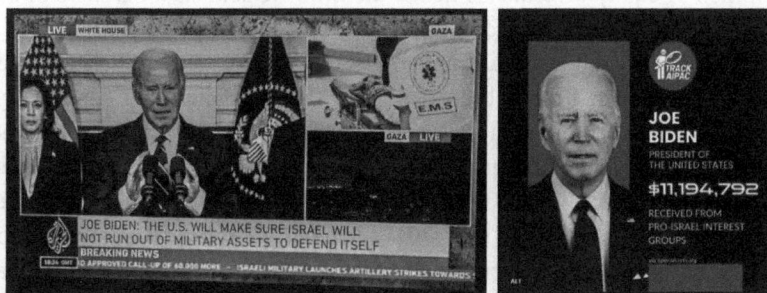

SOURCE: *Screen capture from Al Jazeera; and X/Twitter (AIPACTracker)*

As his key appointees made fortunes in the kind of lobbying that he presumably shunned, Biden marketed himself as "Middle-Class Joe," despite his new status as an aspiring millionaire.[35] The president's critics didn't buy it. Pro-Palestine protesters adopted the term "Genocide Joe" because of Biden's unconditional support of Israel amid its onslaught in Gaza. It was followed by a mass drive by U.S. Campaign for Palestinian Rights: "Tell Genocide Joe: You Are Complicit."[36]

Conflicts of Interest Déjà Vu

Between the Obama and Biden administrations, foreign secretary Antony Blinken co-headed WestExec Advisors with Flournoy. Unsurprisingly, allegations had also been raised about his conflicts of interest.[37] In public, Blinken nurtured an image of a cordial, eloquent international diplomat in the style of Dr. Henry Kissinger, the subject of his undergraduate thesis and his interviewee; even his frequent but futile flights during the Gaza War were depicted as Kissinger-like shuttle diplomacy of the '70s.Through his family background, Blinken has been linked with investment banking (father), diplomats (uncle), a Holocaust survivor, yet controversial international lawyer (uncle Samuel Pisar), who had represented media proprietor and fraudster Robert Maxwell (who maintained links to the British MI6, the Soviet KGB and the Israeli Mossad) and financier and child sex offender, Jeffrey Epstein.[38]

After 25 years in government jobs, Blinken left for the private sector when Hillary Clinton lost to Trump in the 2016 election. With key clientele in the defense industry, private equity, and hedge funds, WestExec, with its colossal military contractors, energy giants, and tech behemoths, had been manna from heaven for him. His financial disclosure report, which lists income from 2019 and 2020, detailed guaranteed payments and distributions of $1.2 million from WestExec. In addition, Blinken noted at least $1.5 million of equity investments tied to the firm. He sold back his share of the business to partners. In addition to WestExec, Blinken began advising a Silicon Valley outfit, Social Capital, where his stake was estimated at over $250,000. It was headed by a master of self-promotion and controversy, Chamath Palihapitiya, whose worth is estimated at $1.3 billion and who subsequently joined Trump's fundraisers. In the U.S., he joined Joe Biden at the Penn Biden Center for Diplomacy & Global Engagement where he presumably worked from May 2017 to June 2019. In just six months of 2019, he earned $80,000 for his efforts, plus $22,000 from CNN as a "global affairs analyst." Biden's campaign trail was another cash machine, generating Blinken another $144,000. In addition to a nice pension from his years in government, the good cash came from the private sector, where he founded his own advisory firm (while his wife worked for Axios Media covering the politics he was contributing to; and got another $96,000 from Biden's transition team). The couple bought a home in Washington suburbia for $4.3 million plus a $1.1 million loan, while accumulating stock in Google parent Alphabet ($195,000), Berkshire Hathaway ($139,000), Apple ($120,000) and Facebook ($80,000), although the Biden administration presumably pledged to "fight the Big Tech."[39]

Only half a decade later, *Forbes* estimated Blinken's worth at about $10 million (Figure 2-5).

Flournoy and Blinken also served as strategic partners in private equity firm Pine Island Capital Partners, led by controversial investment banker John Thain, who played a role in the fall of Merrill Lynch in 2008, while paying himself bonuses along the way. Amid the subprime debacle, Thain spent $1.2 million to remodel his office, including $35,115 for a gold-plated commode on legs. He apologized and reimbursed the company (after he was caught).[40] By 2020, Pine Island Capital was well-positioned to cash in on the U.S. Covid-19 response, investing in government contractors.

Figure 2-5. Blinken's Cash Machine

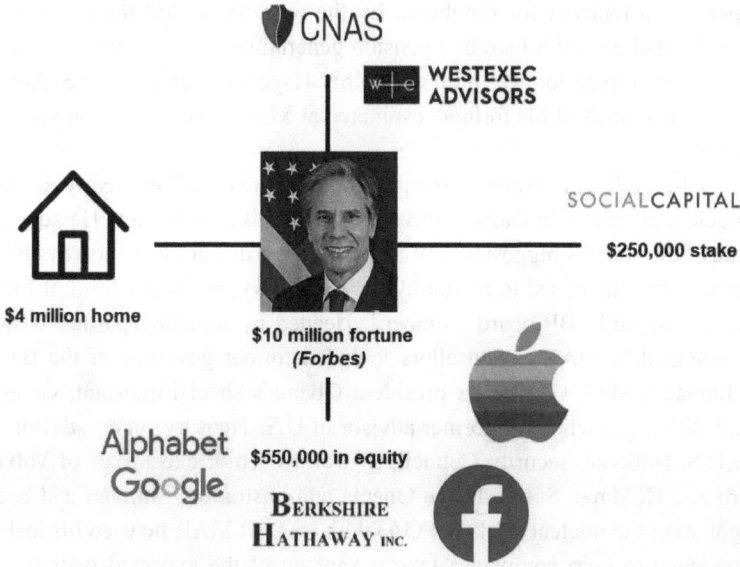

SOURCE: *Data from Forbes; author*

In addition to Blinken, the firm employed Lloyd Austin, the first black secretary of defense and veteran of the U.S. Army (1975–2012). As head of U.S. Forces in Iraq, Austin had befriended President Biden's son, Beau (Hunter, the other son, was later linked with the Trump "Ukrainegate," so named for Trump's effort to coerce Ukraine into investigating corruption by Biden).[41] He was then nominated to become the Army's vice chief of staff. A year later, President Obama tapped Austin to head up U.S. Central Command.[42] After the Trump triumph, Austin left the Army and joined the board of the steel colossus Nucor, a beneficiary of Trump's tariff wars, and the boards of military contractors, including United Technologies Corporation, which in 2020 merged with Raytheon, a Big Defense top lobbying spender. The enterprising Austin earned seven figures from the defense companies until he stepped down from all three board positions following his nomination in 2020. Stock options proved lucrative upon his departure, which earned him as much as $1.7 million. After Austin joined the Biden administration, Raytheon was awarded a new $49 million contract.[43] This defense contractor has played a central role in spreading "freedom and democracy" from Yemen to Ukraine and most recently, to Gaza.

Typically, the three most recent defense secretaries all had served in the military before entering the private sector. James Mattis and Austin were both retired generals serving on the boards of big businesses, whereas Mark Esper was a lobbyist for Raytheon. By the time Austin left the military in 2016, he had earned a lucrative pension generating some $15,000 a month. His military reputation was built during his 41-year career in the U.S. Army, but he made most of his fortune, estimated at $7 million, serving on various boards.[44]

Jake Sullivan, Biden's security adviser, featured indirectly in the genocidal atrocities in Gaza. Sullivan, too, had his money gigs. He advised some of the world's biggest businesses at Macro Advisory Partners (MAP), a secretive firm that used to be run by Sir John Sawyers, former head of MI6, and subsequently BP board member.[45] Headed by founding partner Nader Mousavizadeh, MAP's counsellors included former governor of the Bank of England, Mark Carney, ex-president Obama's special assistant, George W. Bush's legal scholar, a former advisor of U.S. Treasury, an ex-advisor of the U.S. National Security Council, as well as senior executives of Volvo, Ford and Goldman Sachs. In the Obama administration, Sullivan had been negotiating the nuclear deal (JCPOA) with Iran. At MAP, he used his inside knowledge to help companies take advantage of the expected opening of the Iranian economy. Setting aside the ideological contradictions, he also represented the controversial rideshare giant Uber against labor protection legislation.

Like Pine Island, WestExec's other strategic partners are profitable and controversial. In Saudi Arabia, the firm helped Prince Mohammed bin Salman to consolidate power.

The reputations of WestExec and its strategic partners were all overshadowed by lingering allegations of conflict of interest. In the case of WestExec clients, the ties with the Gaza War were more direct. One of these clients was Windward, an Israeli AI venture launched by Israeli naval intelligence officers with the country's former chief of staff, Gabi Ashkenazi, on the board. Ashkenazi had served as director-general of Israel's Defense Ministry when the Obliteration Doctrine was developed and first tested in Beirut. As the IDF Chief of Staff in 2007–2011, he played a vital role in deepening the symbiotic U.S.-Israel ties prior to Gaza's genocidal atrocities. He was in charge of the 2008 Operation Hot Winter in Gaza, which led to the U.S. demand for greater caution to avoid the loss of innocent life and criticism by the UN and the EU on Israel's "disproportionate use of force."

He was responsible for the 2008–2009 war on Gaza that Palestinians termed the "Gaza Massacre," due to Israel's reliance on collective punishment, use of disproportionate force and children as human shields, deployment of white phosphorus and dense inert metal explosives (DIME), which led to charges of misconduct by IDF soldiers, consequent prosecutions and allegations of intent to commit war crimes—military measures that were eventually deployed in the Gaza atrocities.[46]

Responsibility Not To Be Silent

It was a proud moment for Samantha Power, then professor of human rights at Harvard. Following her work as a war correspondent covering the Yugoslav Wars before entering academe, she published her first book, *A Problem from Hell: America and the Age of Genocide* (2002). It built on a paper she wrote while attending law school and contributed to the creation of the doctrine of "responsibility to protect." The bestseller explored America's understanding of, response to, and inaction on 20th century genocides, from the Armenian genocide to the "ethnic cleansings" of the Kosovo War. It popularized Lemkin's name in the United States after half a century of relative silence. It charged American policymakers with having been consistently reluctant to condemn mass atrocities as genocide or to take responsibility for leading an international military intervention. It was the pressure from the American public that forced policymakers to tackle the term "genocide," she argued. Their first preference had long been to prioritize "national interest" or to argue that a U.S. response would simply prove futile and accelerate violence, as a justification for their inaction. Power advocated action against silence. It was America's duty to act.

The book catalyzed her career. In the mid-2000s, she was working in the office of Senator Barack Obama as a foreign policy fellow. In 2009, President Obama appointed her to a position on the National Security Council and in 2013 as U.S. Ambassador to the United Nations, a cabinet-rank position. Following the Trump years, President Biden nominated her to head the United States Agency for International Development (USAID). Just weeks before October 7, 2023, Power's USAID had touted the importance of the *U.S. Strategy to Anticipate, Prevent, and Respond to Atrocities*, presumably a national strategy to pre-neutralize mass atrocities.[47] Based on her lessons, it was depicted as "a core national security commitment and core moral responsibility of the United States, developed pursuant to the bipartisan Elie Wiesel Act."[48]

As Israel began to hammer Gaza, its infrastructure and Palestinians, State Department officials began to debate the U.S. response, criticized their administration and resigned from service. Yet, alternate voices didn't fare well in USAID, despite its famous head. Having built a career as an anti-genocide scholar, Power was now confronted by her own staff, whom she struggled to subdue and silence.

When *A Problem From Hell* won the Pulitzer Prize, it was credited with a bold citation:

> Samantha Power poses a question that haunts our nation's past: Why do American leaders who vow "never again" repeatedly fail to marshal the will and the might to stop genocide?[49]

Instead of stressing the duty to act, as she had in her book, or quitting to protest a flawed policy, as she once pledged she would, Power, like many other senior officials of the Biden administration, chose silence. As the Biden administration got ready to leave the White House, her website still touted her as "a leading voice internationally for principled American engagement in the world."[50]

The failure of genocide prevention is not an unintended side-effect of the Convention that defines it. It is the rule. As we shall see, the Convention was designed to fail: not to prevent, and not to punish, but to condemn belatedly. That represents the best of two possible worlds for those portraying themselves as struggling against actual genocide prevention: a firm moral condemnation, coupled with ineffective action.

A Template for Repression in America

In early 2017, the first Trump administration did not just differ from its precursors. If the prior administrations had failed to restrain Israel, his White House did not even try to do so. Instead, Trump took a far more extreme stance, though one that was in line with the tacit views of PM Netanyahu and explicit statements of Israel's rising Messianic far-right, by approving the Netanyahu cabinets' aggressive settlement expansion, recognizing Jerusalem as the capital of Israel, canceling U.S. aid to the West Bank and Gaza, the aid to the UNRWA, pushing the Abraham Accords sidelining the Palestinians. Trump's second administration began its work by building on this reversal.[51]

From the Secretary of State Marco Rubio, UN Ambassador Elise Stefanik and Defense Secretary Pete Hegseth to Trump's Middle East envoy Steve Witkoff, the key actors of the administration shared ardent pro-Israel stances, intimate ties with pro-Israel groups and in several cases a theologi-cally-bound view of Israel, the willingness to recognize a Jewish unitary state with a minimal Palestinian population and very strong support for continued and expanded arms transfers into the ailing region.

How might these initiatives proceed? Essentially, the Trump administration proposed mobilization to crack down "pro-Palestinian" forces in America, deport Palestinian activists and use these measures as a template to crush democratic dissent at home and increase arms sales to Israel. The blueprint was outlined in Project Esther, the plan to presumably combat antisemitism unveiled by the Heritage Foundation.[52] Purposely, it was published on the 1-year anniversary of October 7 in 2024.

Aiming to dismantle the rising pro-Palestinian movement and the growing sympathy it enjoys in America, it was part of the think tank's *Project 2025*, the ultra-conservative plan to fundamentally alter the U.S. government and consolidate executive power.[53] Project Esther claims that "America's virulently anti-Israel, anti-Zionist, and anti-American 'pro-Palestinian movement' is part of a global Hamas Support Network." Hence, their call to "dismantle the infrastructure . . . dedicated to destroying capitalism and democracy."[54]

This movement capitalizes on the highly controversial "working definition of antisemitism," or the non-legally-binding statement of the International Holocaust Remembrance Alliance (IHRA): "Antisemitism is a certain perception of Jews, which may be expressed as hatred toward Jews. Rhetorical and physical manifestations of antisemitism are directed toward Jewish or non-Jewish individuals and/or their property, toward Jewish community institutions and religious facilities."[55] Accompanying the working definition, but of disputed status, were 11 illustrative examples whose purpose is described as guiding the IHRA in its work, yet seven of which actually relate to criticism of Israel, which is thus tacitly associated with antisemitism.

First published by European Monitoring Centre on Racism and Xenophobia (EUMC) in 2005, the definition was adopted by the International Holocaust Remembrance Alliance (IHRA) in 2016. Three years later, President Trump used an executive order (13899) that rested on this definition. The introduction of the executive order followed the Congressional Anti-Semitism Awareness Acts of 2018 and 2019. The definition, the order and the Acts caused a series of political firestorms among the Palestinians, Jews and civil rights organizations.[56] The problem was that they had the potential to conflate antisemitism and legitimate criticism of Israel while drastically curbing freedom of speech in America. Since 2019, Trump, who himself has been repeatedly charged for the use of antisemitic tropes, had tried to use these orders to crack down on pro-Palestinian groups at home and the international boycott movement against Israel, including the Boycott,

Divestment and Sanctions movement (BDS), a set of academic and cultural boycott campaigns, and disinvestment initiatives.

Project Esther took this objective further. Trump's executive order of January 30, 2025, outlined a broad federal crackdown on "the explosion of antisemitism" in the U.S., especially on college campuses. Trump vowed to cancel visas of foreign students who are "Hamas sympathizers" and deport "pro-jihadist" protesters. The order also laid out how some student protests could be considered a violation of existing federal law that barred individuals from supporting terrorism, directing government officials to encourage schools to monitor and report any such activities by foreign students so they can be investigated and possibly deported. To civil rights activists, it was a gross overreach and unconstitutional effort to exploit student visa policies to punish the expression of free speech protected by the First Amendment. The dark wave of repression was reflected by the notorious and highly controversial detentions of Mahmoud Khalil, a student activist and lead negotiator for the encampment in the 2024 Columbia University pro-Palestinian campus occupations, and Rümeysa Öztürk, a Turkish citizen and a gifted PhD student of Tufts University, and many other students.[57] The White House disagreed. Its fact sheet about the order was unambiguous: "We put you on notice: come 2025, we will find you, and will deport you."[58]

If Project Esther prevails, the Trump crackdown will seek to deport protesters in America on student visas and target universities' tax-exempt status. Though portrayed as an effort to "combat antisemitism," it would serve as a blueprint for other domestic initiatives seeking to repress dissent and political activism. In this self-destructive enterprise, the Palestinians served as a convenient scapegoat and collateral damage.

Collusion of Arms Exporters and Manufacturers

In 2021, a group of half a dozen U.S. foreign policy hawks—including both Flourney and Petraeus—with decades of disastrous policies behind them, were calling on the Biden administration to threaten to attack Iran: "We believe it is vital to restore Iran's fear that its current nuclear path will trigger the use of force against it by the United States." The project of "restoring Iran's fear that it will suffer severe consequences if it refuses"[59] was viewed as essential. In 2008, Hillary Clinton had threatened Iran saying "if I'm the president, we will attack Iran" if it attacks Israel.[60] The point was to crush all resistance in Iran, Lebanon, Iraq, Yemen and Palestine. That was the U.S. national interest as perceived by the CNAS/WestExec and their clients and donors—most importantly Big Defense.

Following the Obama administration's subdued defense spending, U.S. contractors dreamed of a better, more lethal and thereby more profitable future. After a month of the Ukraine War, Raytheon CEO Gregory Hayes disclosed some of his business secrets in a *Harvard Business Review* interview. Hayes noted that "Ukraine has highlighted gaps in U.S. defense technologies," which the contractor colossus offered to fill. He was motivated by Raytheon's "singular mission around defending democracy and connecting the world."[61] Raytheon had suffered from the fall of airline profitability due to the pandemic depression. Like other contractors, it needed wars to sustain profitability. The national interest claim made good business sense. Hayes's salary was "barely" $1 million, but his total compensation had soared to more than $23 million in just a year.[62]

If the proxy war in Ukraine had not occurred, it would have had to be created. From the standpoint of the defense contractors, it was immaterial whether a conflict was precipitated by flag-waving friction or false flag operations. What mattered was that conflicts led to open hostilities in which weapons were necessary.

Internationally, the United States provided the bulk of total aid to Ukraine (62%), while most of the rest came from Europe. The international total of more than $110 billion accounted for over half of Ukraine's pre-war GDP ($200 billion).[63] Ukraine was "a weapons lab," providing ultimate "real-world battle testing."[64] Or as Zelenskyy chimed in, arming Ukraine was a "big business opportunity," as evidenced by his government's new ties with BlackRock, Goldman Sachs and JP Morgan. In December 2022, he revealed that Ukraine had hired BlackRock to "advise" Kyiv on how to use the West's reconstruction funds, which he *then* estimated would have to increase at least to $1 trillion.[65] All of these companies featured as clients or donors or both of CNAS and WestExec.

U.S. Big Defense was the only winner of the proxy war in Ukraine. Not only did these global military contractors arm Ukraine, but they stood to benefit immensely from the re-militarization of Western European countries, Japan, and new NATO members following the depletion of their stocks. Washington had a great economic interest in such geopolitics. Brussels's incentives were harder to fathom, especially as the euro area would pay a hefty post-Ukraine premium on energy and food, which also benefited Washington.

For decades, security cooperation programs have led U.S. forces into unauthorized hostilities alongside foreign partners, particularly in Afghanistan, Iraq, and Libya in the past two decades. But this list is off by at least 17 countries in which the U.S. has engaged in armed conflict through ground forces, proxy forces, or air strikes.[66] The simple reason is money. War may be a racket, but it is a very lucrative racket. In the past two decades alone, the cost of the U.S. global war on terror stands at $8 trillion (plus 900,000 deaths in target countries, where costs are far higher). And this estimate is from fall 2021, more than a year *before* the Ukraine bonanza.[67]

In 2014, Ukrainian military spending was about 3 percent of GDP, increasing to 6 percent in 2022, corresponding to more than $11 billion. Ukrainian military expenditures had doubled since 2014. Meanwhile, its economic growth had tanked. Instead of the expected 3.7 percent real GDP growth in 2022, it plunged dramatically by some 35 percent. Far worse loomed ahead. Reconstruction would require a lot more than $1 trillion. Ukraine as it was then known had ceased to exist. The costs would mortgage Ukrainians to the third generation.

Yet, Big Defense believed that the future was where the money was— Asia. In 2018—following the Obama pivot to Asia and the Trump tariffs against China—General Dynamics CEO Phebe Novakovic said the Asia-Pacific was a growing market for U.S. defense contractors. But she felt Big Defense could do better in the region, just as it had done in the Middle East. So, to win over "unsophisticated buying authorities," Novakovic advocated upgrades "to fight together should the need arise."[68]

Since then, progress has been rapid. Today, Asia is more divided, more vulnerable, and more willing to divert monies from economic development to rearmament. The net effect includes lucrative new markets and new opportunities for Big Defense. At the same time, the Ukraine and Gaza Wars have restored the Middle East as great contributors to their high profit margins. During the past two decades, the stock prices of Big Defense have doubled, quadrupled, even soared sixfold (Figure 2-6). What safer investment was there than in the war machine?

In light of the stock prices, the big change came following September 11, 2001, when the U.S. security state morphed into a global war economy. After the Bush era, there was a brief pause in the Obama first term followed by a return to the normal state of warfare in his second term. Despite the disruption of the Trump era, the floodgates were opened in the Biden era, when two major wars—Ukraine and Gaza—coupled with multiple minor proxy wars around the world. It was a windfall for Big Defense.

Figure 2-6. Soaring Post-9/11 Defense Stocks

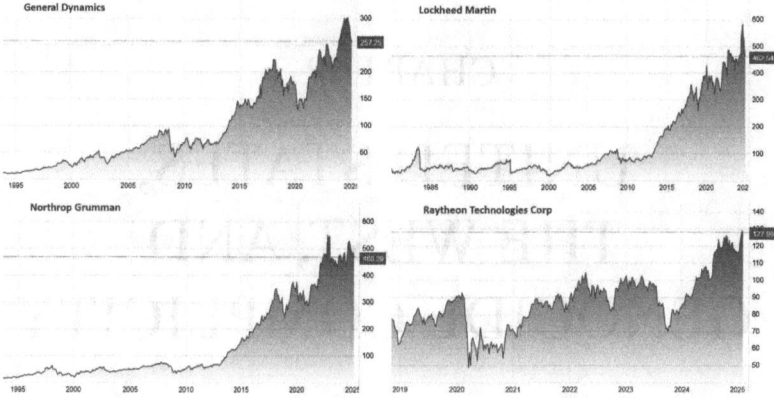

SOURCE: *Tradingeconomics; author, Feb 7, 2025*

CHAPTER 3

UNITED STATES, THE WEST, AND GENOCIDE COMPLICITY

In his book, *War* (2024), journalist Bob Woodward describes the critical moments following the Hamas offensive of October 7, 2023, including the intimate cooperation between the Biden White House and Prime Minister Benjamin Netanyahu's cabinet. President Biden had convened a call with his national security team, including his National Security Advisor Jake Sullivan, Secretary of State Antony Blinken, Defense Secretary Lloyd Austin and CIA Director William Burns. They provided an update on everything they were seeing unfold in Israel. This conversation ensued on the phone later that day:[1]

> "You need to begin messaging Hezbollah to stay out," Netanyahu said to Biden. "Hezbollah needs to get the message from the United States: Don't enter the war. Don't enter the war. Stay out of the war."
>
> Netanyahu, who sounded shaken, was worried that Hezbollah, the powerful Iran-backed militia in Lebanon, would attack Israel from the north.
>
> "These guys think we're weak," Netanyahu said. "And in the Middle East if you're weak, you're roadkill."
>
> "We're with you," Biden said to Netanyahu and reassured him that there would be close coordination ongoing between U.S. and Israeli military and intelligence. [...]
>
> Netanyahu then called Jake Sullivan directly.
>
> "Jake, we need you to basically threaten Hezbollah," Netanyahu implored him. "That's what we need you to do. We need you to tell them that if they mess with us, they mess with you."

In other words, the Israeli Prime Minister told the White House that it needed to tell Hezbollah that an attack against Israel was an attack against America and that it would be treated as such. The tacit assumption was that Hezbollah was Iran's proxy but that Israel was not America's proxy, even if it was fully dependent on U.S weapons and financing.

That afternoon, President Biden took the podium in the State Dining Room of the White House. Flanked by Secretary Blinken, he delivered a warning to Iran and its proxies, including Hezbollah. Israel was under a Hamas-led attack and Biden seized the moment, or as Woodward put it:

> "In this moment of tragedy, I want to say to them and to the world and to terrorists everywhere that the United States stands with Israel. We will not ever fail to have their back." [...]
>
> The day after October 7, Jake Sullivan was looking for deterrence measures or symbols of deterrence in order to cool down the region. No better deterrent than the aircraft carrier.[2]

It was this this military symbiosis that not only triggered the massive escalation in U.S. arms flows to Israel. By "aiding and abetting," it also made possible Israel's genocidal atrocities in and obliteration of the Gaza Strip. But there was more on display than Woodward's intimate access to the White House. Inadvertently, the *Washington Post* author also highlighted the extent of U.S. complicity in Israel's genocidal atrocities.

The United States, Complicity and Genocide

Following October 7, 2023, Israel began to pound northern Gaza with air strikes and ordered the evacuation of more than 1 million Palestinians from the area. Dana Stroul, then the deputy assistant-secretary of defense for the Middle East, warned the White House that the mass evacuation would be a humanitarian disaster. Worse, it could violate international law, leading to charges of war crimes against Israel. Emailing on October 13 to President Biden's senior aides, she was relaying an assessment by the International Committee of the Red Cross that had left her "chilled to the bone." A year later, Reuters reviewed emails between senior U.S. administration officials disclosing that these exchanges revealed alarm early on. Both in the State Department and Pentagon, there was a great concern that a rising death toll in Gaza could violate international law and jeopardize U.S. ties in the Arab world. The messages also showed internal pressure within the Biden administration to shift its messaging from showing solidarity with Israel to including sympathy for Palestinians and the need to allow more humanitarian aid into Gaza.[3]

The Reuters exposé and other similar disclosures highlight U.S. foreknowledge of the impending genocidal atrocities that would violate international law, including the Genocide Convention, and establish the complicity of the U.S. as a key perpetrator, due to its arms exports to Israel and its financing through military aid. Article 3 of the Genocide Convention defines the crimes that can be punished under the convention, and these crimes include complicity. Though occasionally characterized as a secondary participation, the accomplice is often the actual villain who may not dirty its hands but enables the "principal offender" to do so. Think of IBM whose data technologies were deployed in Nazi Germany to develop kill lists of Jews, which paved the way to establishing territories that were seen as *judenrein*, or "clean of Jews." As the Third Reich embarked upon its plan of conquest and genocide, IBM and its subsidiaries helped create enabling technologies, step-by-step, from the identification and cataloging programs in the 1930s to the selections in the 1940s, thus facilitating efficient asset confiscation, ghettoization, deportation, enslaved labor and ultimately annihilation.[4]

In genocide cases, the decisions of the Appeals Chambers suggest that to be complicit, the aider and abettor must have knowledge of the offender's intent, but that he/she need *not* have specific intent to commit genocide.[5] That is, the kind of knowledge that U.S. Secretary of State Blinken discovered right after October 7, following his first talks with the Netanyahu cabinet. At the behest of Western powers, the drafters of the Genocide Convention resisted efforts to criminalize "preparatory acts," such as hate speech and racist organizations. But as the International Court of Justice (ICJ) nonetheless stated in its February 2007 ruling on the Bosnian application against Serbia, responsibility *is* incurred "if the State manifestly failed to take all measures to prevent genocide which were within its power, and which might have contributed to preventing the genocide."[6]

In practice, a State's obligation to prevent "and the corresponding duty to act," arise when the State "learns of, or should normally have learned of, the existence of a serious risk that genocide will be committed. From that moment onwards, if the State has available to it means likely to have a deterrent effect on those suspected of preparing genocide, or reasonably suspected of harboring specific intent (*dolus specialis*), it is under a duty to make such use of these means as the circumstances permit."[7] It is this notion of a *"serious risk"* that casts a long dark shadow over the Biden administration on the very day of October 7 and certainly in its aftermath, particularly for its cooperation with the Netanyahu government, its defense minister and intelligence leaders, and its very vocal far-right members, who have never hidden *their* objectives of ethnically cleansing the Gaza Strip and eventually the West Bank.[8]

In light of the evidence, it would seem that when President Biden, Secretary of State Blinken and Defense Secretary Austin heard about the Netanyahu cabinet's plans, the *obligation to prevent* and the *duty to act* should have been recalled and acted upon, especially as the White House had the means to deter Israel's genocidal atrocities and could reasonably suspect its specific intent to become evident and materialize in genocidal acts.

The Human Costs of U.S. Complicity

The depth of the bilateral complicity is illustrated by the genocidal atrocities in Gaza. Only five days after October 7, 2023, U.S. Secretary of State Antony Blinken arrived in Israel and went straight to see Prime Minister Netanyahu. Israel was preparing for a massive ground assault. But what was Israel's strategic objective regarding the 2.3 million Palestinian residents of Gaza? "We'll take them all into Egypt and let them go there," Netanyahu said. "There won't be a humanitarian crisis in Gaza if no civilians are there," added Ron Dermer, Netanyahu's top aide and right-hand man who, like Netanyahu, had grown of age in the United States.[9]

Even before the Israeli ground assault, the highest echelon of the Biden-Harris administration knew well the final objective of the Netanyahu cabinet: that is, the ethnic cleansing of the Gaza Strip of all Palestinians. And yet, knowing the consequences, the Biden administration, in the next 12 months, increased and almost quintupled the weapons flows to Israel from less than $4 billion to almost $18 billion, which made it possible for Israel to sustain the genocidal atrocities. To make things even worse, with the onset of 2025, the Biden administration notified Congress of an $8 billion weapons package for Israel, including thousands of bombs, missiles and artillery shells, in one of the largest new arms sales since the onset of the Gaza war. The proposed sale featured a set of guidance kits designed to be fitted to large MK-84 2,000-pound bombs, BLU-109 bunker buster bombs, AMRAAM and Hellfire missiles and 155mm artillery rounds.[10] Despite the ICC warrants for PM Netanyahu and former Defense Minister Gallant, and despite efforts to extend legal genocide complicity over President Biden, Secretary of State Blinken and Secretary of Defense Austin, these arms sales delivered an unambiguous message: "We prevent genocides by standing with Israel. We can do whatever we want with impunity and Israel has a right to defend itself. We determine who defines 'genocide' and how. We don't just implement international law. We *are* international law."

Imagine what would have happened if the Biden administration had halted the arms flow after three weeks of Israeli bombardment of Gaza, its infrastructure, and its people, particularly women and children? During that period, over 15,200 Palestinians were killed and some 40,700 were injured. The number of killed alone was more than 10 times the total of Israelis who lost their lives in the period. By late January 2025, a week after the ceasefire became effective, almost 48,000 Palestinians had died and over 111,000 suffered injuries in Gaza. Furthermore, the escalation had cost up to 4,000 deaths and 15,700 injured in Lebanon. So, if a ceasefire had been instituted on October 31, 2023, almost 33,000 Palestinians and 4,000 Lebanese would have survived, while 70,000 Palestinians and nearly 16,000 Lebanese would have avoided injuries. Furthermore, at least 10,000 Palestinians remain buried under ruble and ruins, while tens of thousands, perhaps another 100,000 are likely to lose their lives in coming years, due to indirect health adversities. Finally, more than 2.0 million Palestinians and about 1.3 Palestinians had been displaced (Figure 3-1).

Figure 3-1. Reported Cumulative Palestinian Casualties*

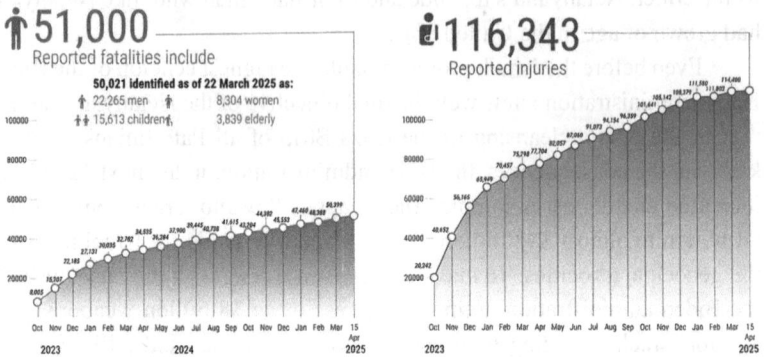

↑51,000
Reported fatalities include

50,021 identified as of 22 March 2025 as:
↑ 22,265 men   ↑   8,304 women
↑↑ 15,613 children↑   3,839 elderly

☝116,343
Reported injuries

2023   2024   2025   2023   2024   2025

*Separately, more than 10,000 people reported missing or under the rubble (source: GMO and PCD).

SOURCE: *Reported Impact Snapshot, Gaza Strip (GMO, PDC), as of Dec. 24, 2024*

That's the nightmare that the U.S. administration—in particular President Biden, Secretary of State Blinken and Defense Secretary Austin—imposed on millions of people, mainly women and children and elderly, of whom only a fraction participated in the Hamas-led offensive on October 7, 2023.

In South Africa's case against Israel the United States remains, as investigative journalist Jeremy Scahill has put it, "the unnamed co-conspirator."[11]

If South Africa laid a meticulous case detailing Israel's genocidal intent, the inconvenient fact is that the U.S. has not only supported but enabled it all. Without U.S. military aid, finance, training, and diplomatic protection, Israel's genocidal atrocities would not have been viable. The world economy may be increasingly multipolar, but American hegemony, based largely on its military might, continues to influence international multilateral organizations such as the International Criminal Court (ICC), even though the United States is not a state party to the Rome Statute, which founded the ICC in 2002. Israel is not a member of the ICC either and rejects its jurisdiction as does the U.S.

Ironically, the Genocide Convention was created in part to avoid future Holocausts, and Israel itself emerged in part as a result of the Holocaust. As the Lemkin Institute for Genocide Prevention argued amid the Israeli ground assault:

> It is the moment when the United States, the 'City on a Hill' that long claimed to be a beacon for humanity, and Israel, the nation state of a stateless people who suffered immeasurable loss at the hands of Nazi Germany, have allied in favor of a very public embrace of a policy of genocide for a marginalized, impoverished, and persecuted people—many of whom are descendants of refugees from the 1948 genocide called the Nakba—who have been humiliated and traumatized by permanent siege and collective imprisonment since 2007.[12]

Palestine et al. v. Biden et al. in U.S. District Court

Following South Africa's launch of genocide proceedings at the International Court of Justice (ICJ), State Department spokesperson Matthew Miller said that the U.S. has not observed acts in Gaza that constitute genocide: "Those are allegations that should not be made lightly ... we are not seeing any acts that constitute genocide." Or as U.S. Secretary of State Antony Blinken put it:

> We believe the submission against Israel to the International Court of Justice distracts the world from all of these important efforts. And moreover, the charge of genocide is meritless.[13]

Those statements ensued after three months of detailed knowledge, starting on the very day of October 7, 2023, of Israeli plans of ethnic cleansing and the application of a military doctrine that would inevitably cause tens of thousands of civilians, most of them women and children, to perish, as well as continuous bombardments and decimation of Gaza's critical infrastructure and civilian institutions. However, this time even the Biden administration was divided, and resignations ensued within the State Department.

Furthermore, 77 groups—representing tens of thousands of lawyers, civil society leaders, and activists from six continents—filed a case in the United States District Court for the Northern District of California against President Biden, Secretary of Defense Lloyd Austin, and Secretary of State Blinken for their alleged "failure to prevent and complicity in the unfolding genocide against Gaza." Along with the human rights organizations, the lawsuit was promoted by Josh Paul who had resigned from the U.S. State Department over arms shipments to Israel; Jewish Voice for Peace; and genocide and Holocaust scholars spearheaded by international lawyer William Schabas. In their *Defense for Children International—Palestine et al v. Biden et al.* case, the plaintiffs proposed, like South Africa, that a genocide, or serious risk of genocide, of Palestinians in Gaza was occurring. But they went further by arguing that the U.S. is violating its duties under international law to prevent and not be complicit in the genocide, and that those U.S. failures contributed to the erosion of "long and widely held norms of international law," including the Genocide Convention and Universal Declaration of Human Rights, both established in 1948 in the wake of World War II.[14]

In its ground assault on Gaza, Israel conducted the bombing attacks, but it did not do so on its own. The Obliteration Doctrine would not have been viable without the steady and incessant flow to Israel of weapons, financial aid and military training by the United States, coupled with support from U.S. bases and installations in Israel and the Middle East at large. Seen in this light, the Gaza War was a proxy war, with Israel an instrument for furthering U.S. policy throughout the region.

As one of the most serious violations of international humanitarian law, "participation by complicity" was considered a crime as early as in the postwar Nuremberg Trials. The requisite *mens rea* for complicity via aiding and abetting meant *"knowledge of* the perpetrator's genocidal intent, rather than *shared genocidal intent"* [my italics]. These allegations include the United States' "significant influence over Israel," in particular through its unparalleled support for Israel's military and provision of political and diplomatic cover to Israel generally, and specifically, since October 7, 2023, "meeting regularly and coordinating with Israeli officials and expressing their unrestrained support" and "unconditional military financial assistance, equipment, and personnel to support and further its assault on Gaza." These allegations established a uniquely strong "capacity to influence effectively the action of persons likely to commit, or already committing, genocide."[15]

As violations of the duty to prevent result from omission, the Complaint further detailed the U.S. refusal to call for a ceasefire and its successful efforts to prevent other states from carrying out *their* duty to prevent genocide through the UN, despite knowledge of, at the very least, a "grave risk of genocide" and facts on the ground establishing an unfolding genocide.[16]

In his declaration, international lawyer William Schabas tackled the issue of U.S. complicity in the Gaza War by scrutinizing it vis-à-vis the Genocide Convention and customary international law, the definition of genocide and of specific intent, and the obligation to prevent genocide. Essentially, Schabas concluded that the U.S. relationship to Israel had many parallels with that between Serbia and the Bosnian Serb forces at the time of the Srebrenica massacre in 1995. "The Bosnian Serb forces were very dependent upon weaponry and other logistical support from Serbia, and there were strong political and economic ties. There has been a close relationship between the United States of America and Israel for many decades." Just as Serbia and its leaders were fully aware of the climate of deep-seated hatred between the Bosnian Serbs and the Muslims in Srebrenica, there was an ominous parallel between it and U.S. cognizance of the antipathy of Israeli Jews towards the Palestinians in Gaza, due to Jewish supremacy doctrines and the rise of the messianic far-right in Israel, and the apartheid rule in the West Bank. In both Srebrenica and Gaza, there was a serious risk of genocide. As Schabas noted, "For the duty to prevent genocide to arise it is sufficient that there be a serious risk the crime will be committed. This is the position of the United States of America, formulated in a Declaration that was submitted to the International Court of Justice in the ongoing proceedings between Ukraine and the Russian Federation based upon the Genocide Convention."[17]

In that Declaration, the U.S. referred to its "long history of supporting efforts to prevent and punish genocide," citing the *Bosnia v. Serbia* judgement of the ICJ. It went on to refer to the vital paragraphs italicizing the words "serious risk":

> A State's obligation to prevent, and the corresponding duty to act, arise at the instant that the State learns of, or should normally have learned of, the existence of a *serious risk* that genocide will be committed.[18]

Hence, Schabas' conclusion was that, regardless of the outcome of the *Ukraine v. Russia* case, by the U.S.'s own Declaration in that case, it demonstrated its awareness of its legal duties to intervene in such instances:

...the Declaration of the United States is a unilateral act that has legal effects, and that the United States is bound by the interpretation of the duty to intervene that it set out, including its endorsement of the reasoning of the International Court of Justice.[19]

In brief, the Defense for Palestine's case argued that the United States was in breach of its obligation under the 1948 Genocide Convention and international law.

The Controversial "Political Question Doctrine"

Nonetheless, the *Palestine et al. v. Biden et al.* case was dismissed by the U.S. Court with a ruling that while "it is plausible that Israel's conduct amounts to genocide," U.S. foreign policy was a political question over which courts lacked jurisdiction. But the devil was in the details. In a written decision, U.S. District Judge Jeffrey White quoted approvingly from the preliminary ruling issued the week before by the ICJ in the case brought against Israel by South Africa, which found Israel's current conduct in Gaza may plausibly amount to genocide and ordered it to stop killing and wounding Palestinians:

> The undisputed evidence before this Court comports with the finding of the ICJ and indicates that the current treatment of the Palestinians in the Gaza Strip by the Israeli military may plausibly constitute a genocide in violation of international law.[20]

While Judge White conceded that there was strong evidence that Israel's "military siege in Gaza is intended to eradicate a whole people and therefore plausibly falls within the international prohibition against genocide," he noted that under well-established legal standards, the so-called political question doctrine applied:

> Foreign policy is constitutionally committed to the political branches of government, and disputes over foreign policy are considered non-justiciable political questions.

Hence, White's ruling held that the court had neither the competence nor the authority to decide on the matter. And so, the case was dismissed.

Just a few days later, U.S. District Judge Matthew Kacsmaryk in Amarillo, Texas rejected the Biden administration's bid to dismiss a lawsuit brought by Republican Representative Ronny Jackson and three others that alleged President Biden and Secretary Blinken violated the 2018 Taylor Force Act (TFA) and put U.S. visitors to Israel under increased risk of harm by providing economic aid to the West Bank and Gaza. The case was filed in 2022, well before the October 7 attack. The U.S. Department of Justice had urged Kacsmaryk to conclude that Jackson and the others who regularly visited Israel could not sue to challenge the foreign aid. The Justice Department argued that the plaintiffs, represented by America Legal First, a legal group founded by former Trump White House adviser Stephen Miller, lacked legal standing to sue because their claims of an increased risk of harm were "wholly conjectural." It also argued that any risk of future harm was due to actions by others besides the U.S. government, such as overseas militants, and contended that dismissal was warranted to avoid entangling the courts in a high-level foreign policy matter. Nonetheless, Kacsmaryk, an appointee of former President Trump, ruled that the individuals had demonstrated a "legitimate and warranted" fear of harm if the funding continues, which "recent world events further substantiate." And so the federal judge in Texas rejected the Biden administration's bid to dismiss a lawsuit seeking to block U.S. aid to the West Bank and Gaza.[21]

Central to U.S. constitutional law, the political question doctrine is premised on the idea that a constitutional dispute, which requires knowledge of a non-legal character—or the use of techniques not suitable for a court, or explicitly assigned by the Constitution to the U.S. Congress, or the President of the United States—lies within the *political* rather than the *legal* realm to resolve. The assumption is that these two realms are independent. As a result, judges customarily, though not always, refuse to address such matters.

The idea of a political question is intimately associated with the concept of justiciability, since it comes down to a question of whether or not the court system is an appropriate venue in which to hear the case. This system is seen to have the authority to hear and decide a legal question, but not a political one. Legal questions are perceived as justiciable, whereas political questions are non-justiciable. The historical origin of the political question doctrine goes back to the Supreme Court case of *Marbury v. Madison* (1803) in which Chief Justice John Marshall drew a distinction between two different functions of the U.S. Secretary of State, thus rendering legitimacy to the analytical if not theoretical divide between a legal and a political realm. Unsurprisingly, this doctrine remains debated among jurists.[22]

Nonetheless, irrespective of the wide-ranging debate, "it is impossible to deny that the doctrine plays an important role in shaping the relationship between U.S. courts and foreign affairs."[23]

Not every case or controversy that touches on foreign relations lies beyond judicial cognizance. So, the court analyses each question on a case-by-case basis. Nonetheless, the contrasting application of the doctrine in the two politically charged cases—one seeking to prevent harm to Palestinians, and the other relating to halting aid from reaching them—reflects the inability or unwillingness of U.S. courts, like many other U.S. institutions, to maintain their independence and objectivity in issues relating to the Israel-Palestine conflict. The tacit corollary, whether intended or not, is that Palestinian lives have lesser significance than those of their adversaries.

Accessorial Complicity:
DAWN v. Biden et al. in the ICC

In February 2025, Democracy for the Arab World Now (DAWN) requested the International Criminal Court (ICC) to investigate former U.S. officials—President Joe Biden, Secretary of State Antony Blinken and Secretary of Defense Lloyd Austin—for their accessorial roles in aiding and abetting, and for intentionally contributing to, Israeli war crimes and crimes against humanity in Gaza. Founded in 2020 by Saudi journalist Jamal Khashoggi before his assassination, the U.S.-based non-profit submitted a 172-page communication detailing a pattern of deliberate and purposeful decisions by these officials to provide military, political, and public support to facilitate Israeli crimes in Gaza, despite knowledge of how such support had and would substantially enable grave abuses.[24]

DAWN wanted the ICC to investigate Biden, Blinken, and Austin for violating Articles 25(3)(c) and (d) of the Rome Statute. These crimes featured those identified in the ICC arrest warrants against Israeli Prime Minister Benjamin Netanyahu and his former Defense Minister Yoav Gallant.[25]

DAWN's "Article 15 submission" to the ICC refers to the Rome Statute's mechanism for sending communications to the Office of the ICC Prosecutor, providing information about alleged crimes that fall under the court's jurisdiction, such as war crimes, crimes against humanity, or genocide, which could potentially trigger an investigation by the Prosecutor. Article 15 communications are the primary way that civil society organizations, individuals, and even victims, can provide information and evidence to the court. Although U.S. officials were aware of exactly what Israel was doing, their support never stopped." As DAWN's executive director Sarah Leah Whitson put it: "They provided Israel with not only essential military support but equally essential political support by vetoing multiple ceasefire resolutions at the UN Security Council to ensure Israel could continue its crimes."[26]

Intriguingly, the DAWN submission widened the net of "accessorial liability" to include several other U.S. officials. In terms of military support, a central role in Israel's genocidal atrocities in Gaza belonged not just to President Biden but to Jake Sullivan, his National Security Advisor, who advised the President on the strategic implications of arms transfers and ensured the coordination between defense, diplomatic, and intelligence agencies; and Gina Raimondo, Secretary of Commerce, who oversaw dual-use technology exports. In terms of political support, Ambassador Linda Thomas-Greenfield had a critical role in the UN Security Council where she vetoed seven resolutions calling for immediate ceasefire, humanitarian assistance and limits to Israeli attacks against civilians.

In addition to Secretary of State Blinken, U.S. military support relied on his subordinates who failed to raise the alarm on the use of arms transfers to Israel in disregard of U.S. foreign policy, domestic legal standards, and international obligations, including Bonnie Jenkins, the Under Secretary of Arms Control and International Security, and Stanley L. Brown, acting as Assistant Secretary Political-Military Affairs, which coordinates between the State and Defense Departments on arms transfers and oversees the Directorate of Defense Trade Controls. In addition to Defense Secretary Austin, Israel's military support also relied on the Pentagon's senior officials, such as Amanda Dory, Under Secretary of Defense for Policy, who provided strategic direction for international arms sales, and Mike Miller, as Director of the Defense Security Cooperation Agency.

During her failed presidential campaign, Vice President Kamala Harris touted her readiness for executive responsibility by supporting continued military aid to Israel, even as she acknowledged that Gaza was a "humanitarian catastrophe" and denied she would shift policy from Biden and said she would not end arms sales to Israel.[27] As Secretary of Treasury, Janet Yellen pledged the U.S. could afford to offer massive amounts of military aid to both Ukraine and Israel at the same time, thus enabling the ceaseless flow of arms in both wars. She also warned Iran that nothing was "off the table" for sanctions if Tehran were to be linked to the Hamas-led attack on Israel.[28] Similarly, the idea that the CIA Director William J. Burner and the Director of National Intelligence Avril Haines were not intimately linked with the Biden cabinet's actions regarding the Gaza atrocities would be extraordinarily naïve (Figure 3-2).

**Figure 3-2. Widening Nets of Accessorial Liability:
President Biden's Cabinet**

SOURCE: *Wikipedia (officials' photos and the group portrait)*

So, in addition to the big three and the supportive six members of the Biden cabinet, the widening net of accessorial liability seemed to include half a dozen other heads of executive departments and some ten cabinet-level officials. Moreover, a case could be made that, by building on and in certain cases radicalizing further these controversial policies which rest on war crimes, crimes against humanity and genocide, the subsequent Trump administration and its senior officials have knowingly also played an accessorial role in aiding, abetting, and intentionally contributing to Israeli war crimes and crimes against humanity in Gaza. If anything, the administration seemed to be perfectly willing to play a direct role in ethnic cleansing by supporting a U.S. takeover of the Gaza Strip, forcibly relocating the Palestinian population to other Arab states, establishing Gaza as a special economic zone, rejoining the bombing of Houthis in Yemen and threatening Iran with devastation.

Domestically such measures were mirrored by efforts to crush civil society opposition to genocidal atrocities in Gaza, efforts to deport particularly Palestinian demonstrators, undermine free speech in the nation's leading institutions of higher education and so on.

In these actions, the key roles belonged to President Trump, his Vice President JD Vance, Secretary of State Marco Rubio, Secretary of Defense Pete Hegseth, and Secretary of Homeland Security Kristi Noem. Reflecting the president's maximalist interpretation of executive power and the objectives of the controversial far-right Project 2025, the Trump administration not only built on but radicalized Biden's policies regarding Gaza.[29] These efforts included the controversial ploy to "privatize" humanitarian assistance, one that the UN and most of its member states opposed. The scheme envisioned U.S. companies operating in southern Gaza, under the supervision of the Israeli military, in a "humanitarian compound" with over 2 million Palestinians surrounded by barbed wire. Since the Cold War, the U.S. had relied increasingly on private contractors, which made wars an even more lucrative business. Now the idea was to diversify such revenue flows with not-so-humanitarian aid by military mercenaries, at the expense of civilian populations.[30]

In other words, by 2025 U.S. complicity and accessorial liability in Gaza was no longer confined to one administration, but increasingly institutionalized by a bipartisan consensus. In this regard, it also reflected the symbiosis between the U.S. and Israel, which itself has experienced a comparable institutionalization. In the process, the peace process of the 1990s has been replaced with "forever wars" aiming at a unitary Jewish state within the pre-1967 Israeli borders *and* Gaza and the West Bank—thanks to incessant U.S. arms transfers and financing.

Accessorial Complicity: *GIPRI v. European Commission President Ursula von der Leyen*

After the first mass atrocities of the Israeli ground assault in late 2023, the charges for complicity were no longer limited to the U.S. administration. Following in the footprints of South Africa's case against the Israeli leaders, the Geneva International Peace Research Institute (GIPRI), an NGO with UN consultative status, requested the opening of an investigation against the European Commission president, Ursula von der Leyen, for complicity in war crimes and genocide against Palestinian civilians. The complicity was attributed to "violations of Articles 6, 7 and 8 of the Rome Statute by her positive actions (military, political, diplomatic support to Israel) and by her failure to take timely action on behalf of the European Commission to help prevent genocide as required by the 1948 Genocide Convention."[31] Having been repeatedly informed of violations of international humanitarian law committed in Gaza, von der Leyen was now charged with aiding and abetting these mass atrocities.

The GIPRI charge reflected three important developments and tensions between Brussels and the European member states. First, there was the gross double standard. Although European leaders portrayed themselves as proponents of the liberal international order that President Trump was repudiating, they were lining up with Trump to support the resumption of Israel's genocidal atrocities against Palestinians. The net effect translated to a tacit endorsement of mass slaughter. Second, there were the deepening divides within Europe regarding the atrocities in Gaza. While the EU's former foreign policy chief Josep Borrell had warned of such double standards and condemned the atrocities, von der Leyen, a former German defense minister herself, made unconditional statements of support for Israel, even as over 800 EU staff and diplomats pled for a ceasefire and protection of civilian life. Finally, GIPRI's actions reflected a broader development the devastation of Gaza had escalated. The case raised the stakes on genocide complicity. As Richard Falk, a renowned international scholar and former Special Rapporteur on Palestine, saw it, the GIPRI initiative illustrated "the breadth of the ICC's potential, and exhibits an effort of civil society to invoke international law, given the failure of the UN or the inter-governmental system to prevent and punish such a transparent genocide."[32]

Clearly, there was a case to prosecute a senior EU figure, even if it represented a break with precedent. Yet, in light of the ICC's scarce actions, it seemed unreasonable to expect the ICC prosecutor to take the case up.[33] In the absence of appropriate policy stances against ethnic cleansing and genocidal atrocities in Gaza, it was the whistleblowers who held the promise of promoting alternative, more peaceful and humane futures, particularly in the United States.

Testimonies of the Whistleblowers

Unlike constitutional legal scholars, many Americans in public service did not find the over-two-centuries-old doctrine very convincing in the case of Gaza. They believed the United States *was* in breach of its obligation under the 1948 Genocide Convention and international law. It was a matter that caused a great amount of anxiety to many longstanding, often highly qualified members of U.S. diplomatic, intelligence and military bureaucracies, prompting their private protests, resignations and whistleblower accounts.

By May 2024, more than half a dozen senior officials of the Biden administration had resigned, including Andrew Miller, the deputy assistant secretary for Israeli-Palestinian affairs, and Alexander Smith, a contractor for the U.S. Agency for International Development (USAID). A group of officials who publicly resigned over the Biden administration's Gaza policy—Josh Paul, Harrison Mann, Tariq Habash, Annelle Sheline, Hala Rharrit, Lily Greenberg Call, Alex Smith, and Stacy Gilbert—banded together to support ongoing dissent and pressure the government to change course. They believed their perspectives, expertise and concerns were not being heeded, and that the Biden administration was willfully ignoring the humanitarian toll caused by Israel's military campaign. They were particularly vocal about the damage they felt U.S. policy on the war was having on America's credibility and their sense that the administration did not fully grasp that impact.[34]

Many of these protests were triggered by an extraordinary debacle. In a highly anticipated report to Congress in May 2024, the U.S. State Department said the assurances given by Israel and a handful of other countries under scrutiny that they had been using U.S.-supplied weapons in accordance with international humanitarian law (IHL) were "credible and reliable." Mandated under National Security Memorandum 20 (NSM-20), the report itself expressed deep misgivings about Israeli compliance:

> Given Israel's significant reliance on U.S.-made defense articles, it is reasonable to assess that defense articles covered under NSM-20 have been used by Israeli security forces since October 7 in instances inconsistent with its IHL obligations or with established best practices for mitigating civilian harm ...
>
> [W]e do not currently assess that the Israeli government is prohibiting or otherwise restricting the transport or delivery of U.S. humanitarian assistance within the meaning of section 620I of the Foreign Assistance Act.[35]

That noted, the report nonetheless concluded that the U.S. did not have sufficient evidence about individual cases to recommend that U.S. arms supplies be suspended. In the light of cumulative evidence of such violations by international media in the prior months, it was both a stunning and critical judgment. Under a clause in the Foreign Assistance Act, the U.S. would be obliged to cut arms sales and security assistance to any country found to have blocked delivery of U.S. aid.

Soon thereafter, Stacy Gilbert, a 20-year veteran of the State Department who had worked in several war zones, resigned. Gilbert was one of the

Department's experts on these matters who had drafted the controversial report. She said the report went *against* the consensus of the experts, as the U.S. State Department deliberately falsified the report in an effort to absolve Israel on Gaza aid. Gilbert argued that Israel played a role in limiting the amount of food and medical supplies crossing the border into Gaza. The report had been taken out of the experts' hands as it approached completion in April, when they were told it would be edited at a higher level. When it was released, Gilbert saw a huge gap between the experts' consensus views and the edited conclusions. Setting aside the breach, the report was the first official admission that the U.S. government believed Israel *was* using U.S. weapons inconsistent with IHL. Yet, according to Gilbert, the State Department made the "patently, demonstrably false" conclusion to avoid triggering section 620I of the Foreign Assistance Act, which requires the U.S. to halt weapons transfers to a country if that country is found to be obstructing humanitarian assistance (Figure 3-3). In her resignation letter she said, "As death, disease, displacement, and destruction escalates in Gaza, that report will haunt us."[36]

**Figure 3-3. U.S. Report Falsified Israel's
Violations of International Law**

SOURCE: *Screen capture of Gilbert's interview by Democracy Now.*

    Alexander Smith became another U.S. official to resign over the Biden administration's Gaza policy. A contractor for the U.S. Agency for International Development (USAID), he said he was given a choice between resignation and dismissal after preparing a presentation on maternal and child mortality among Palestinians, which was cancelled by USAID before it was due to be delivered. Smith was asked to make redactions, including removing a slide outlining applicable international humanitarian law. He was also to edit out any language implying recognition of a Palestinian state, including references to agencies which have Palestine in their title, like the UN Family Planning Association (UNFPA) Palestine.[37] The requests suggested USAID was uncomfortable with any possible references to ongoing violations of international law in Gaza *and* with any allusion to the Palestinian people or sovereignty, despite the U.S. stated support for the two-state solution.

Such resignations did not come out of the blue. In November 2023, more than 1,000 officials at USAID signed an open letter asking Biden to call for a ceasefire.[38] In a joint statement entitled "Service in Dissent," over a dozen resigned officials wrote that "America's diplomatic cover for, and continuous flow of arms to, Israel has ensured our undeniable complicity in the killings and forced starvation of a besieged Palestinian population in Gaza. This is not only morally reprehensible and in clear violation of international humanitarian law and U.S. laws, but it has also put a target on America's back." In addition to Gilbert, Smith and Paul, still other senior officials resigned in private. Most referred to the importance of the Leahy Act, which prohibits aid to foreign military units involved in crimes, and Section 620(I) of the Foreign Assistance Act stating that no aid shall be provided to any government that "prohibits or otherwise restricts, directly or indirectly, the transport or delivery of United States humanitarian assistance."

As far as they were concerned, Israeli authorities had both prohibited and restricted such assistance, as verified by evidence. In addition to the issue of U.S. complicity, legal contradictions, stemming from violations of various policies, compounded this apprehension.

Nicaragua v. Germany: The Quest to Address State Complicity

The charge against American complicity was not limited to the case in the U.S. court. In January 2024, South African Attorney Wikus Van Rensburg stated that the proceedings against Israel in the International Court of Justice (ICJ) were just a "precursor." If these proceedings were to be successful, Van Rensburg pledged to pursue civil action against the U.S. and Britain "for their complicit conduct in this Israeli process and the bombardment within Gaza, as well as the West Bank."[39] Leading a group of 50 lawyers in a class-action lawsuit against the U.S. and the UK for their complicity in Israel's actions in Gaza, Van Rensburg said the two countries "must be held accountable for the conduct and what is happening within Gaza."[40]

Unlike most nations in the world, the United States has been reluctant to join several international agreements seeking to regulate arms transfers worldwide. That is very much in the interest of the nation that accounts for almost two-fifth of global military expenditures and remains, by far, the world's largest arms exporter. So, it should not come as a surprise that the U.S. domestic statutes governing arms transfers ensure the executive branch with broad discretion in making such transfer decisions and do not explicitly require consideration of whether recipient countries are or may be in violation of IHL or genocide prohibitions.[41]

Comprising the body of treaties and customary international law, international humanitarian law (IHL) governs states' conduct during armed conflicts. The Geneva Conventions, which are among the major components of IHL, provide various protections for civilians and others not actively participating in hostilities. The United States is a party to all four Geneva Conventions (Figure 3-4).

Figure 3-4. Geneva Conventions

1. The First Geneva Convention "for the Amelioration of the Condition of the Wounded and Sick in Armed Forces in the Field," (adopted in 1864, revised in 1906, 1929, and finally 1949);

2. The Second Geneva Convention "for the Amelioration of the Condition of Wounded, Sick and Shipwrecked Members of Armed Forces at Sea" (adopted in 1949, successor of the Hague Convention [X] 1907);

3. The Third Geneva Convention "relative to the Treatment of Prisoners of War" (adopted in 1929, last revision in 1949);

4. The Fourth Geneva Convention "relative to the Protection of Civilian Persons in Time of War" (adopted in 1949, based on parts of the Hague Convention [II] of 1899 and Hague Convention [IV] 1907).

With two Geneva Conventions revised and adopted and two added in 1949, the treaties had been ratified, in whole or with reservations, by 196 countries.

These Conventions direct parties to criminalize violations listed as "grave breaches." In the U.S., Congress implemented this obligation through the War Crimes Act of 1996. The Act also criminalizes additional IHL violations that may be applicable both to conflicts between states and conflicts involving state and non-state actors. While the Geneva Conventions apply only in the context of armed conflict, the Genocide Convention's obligations apply in time of war and peace; that is, at all times. In addition to prohibiting the commission of genocide, the Genocide Convention prohibits complicity in genocide and requires states *to prevent* genocide. Hence, the international interest in the *Nicaragua v. Germany* case brought before the ICJ.

In April 2024, Nicaragua filed a case against Germany alleging that Germany's provision of arms to Israel for use in its military campaign in Gaza violated the Genocide Convention and IHL as codified in the Geneva Conventions. In its case, Nicaragua argued that Germany was aware of "violations being committed by Israel from the moment of their first occurrence," including Israel's alleged intent to "target the civilian population, a clear act of collective punishment." It cited the remarks of the Chancellor of Germany, Olaf Scholz, who went so far as to say that "Israel's security is a German raison d'état," as it concerned sending supplies of weapons to Israel; ignoring concerns expressed about harm to Palestinian civilians and a risk of genocide. The Nicaraguan case argued that German policy on aid towards Palestinians "increased the vulnerability of the Palestinian population, particularly Gazans, and contributed to the very present risk of irreparable prejudice." It further argued that Germany suspended funds to UNRWA on the basis of allegedly unreliable Israeli allegations that members of the UNRWA were involved in Hamas's attack of October 7. submitted that funding for UNRWA was "relied upon" for the continuation of its work, on which "over two million people [depend]" including for health services, environmental health, pest control, water quality, education, and microfinance. Nicaragua cited UNRWA's warning that suspension of funding could lead to the cessation of its operations "by the end of February," despite the presence of widespread hunger in the Gazan population according to UN reports.[42]

Intriguingly, Nicaragua's case was "the first to allege *contribution to the act* of genocide rather than the *commission of the act* itself"[43] [my italics]. Nonetheless, the ICJ denied Nicaragua's request for a preliminary order requiring Germany to stop transferring weapons. Yet, the case remains pending on the ICJ's docket. This is unsettling from the standpoint of those U.S. interests that would like to have minimal constraints to U.S. arms shipments and deny all allegations by South Africa about genocide in Gaza. The *Nicaragua v. Germany* case could eventually lead the tribunal to issue an opinion addressing states' obligations under the Genocide and Geneva Conventions when providing arms to other states. However, the ICJ's decisions are binding only on the parties to a given case. In that sense, *Nicaragua v. Germany* does not have direct implications for the United States. However, as U.S. Congressional research has acknowledged,

> the ICJ's decisions are considered to be highly authoritative and thus can contribute to the interpretation and development of international law. The ICJ's decisions in *Nicaragua v. Germany* thus may impact the United States in the sense that they may provide the ICJ's interpretation of international legal obligations that are binding on the United States as a party to the Genocide and Geneva Conventions and as a matter of customary international law.[44]

U.S. Complicity in Light of the Genocide Convention

In its 2007 ruling on the Bosnian genocide, the International Court of Justice (ICJ), clarified that "conspiracy to commit genocide" and "complicity in genocide" involve not only *individual* criminal responsibility but also the international responsibility of *states*. Furthermore, Nicaragua's lawsuit against Germany at the ICJ, due to Germany's involvement in Israel's genocide in Gaza and other Palestinian territories, enables the responsibility of states that contribute to, participate in, or act contrary to their obligation to prevent genocide to be brought before international courts. The most important of these agreements is the Genocide Convention. In particular, Article 3 defines the crimes that can be punished under the Convention:

(a) Genocide;
(b) Conspiracy to commit genocide;
(c) Direct and public incitement to commit genocide;
(d) Attempt to commit genocide;
(e) Complicity in genocide.[45]

(a) Genocide: Since Israel's actions in Gaza can be found to violate the Genocide Convention, the United States and other states can be held accountable for complicity in Israel's genocidal atrocities. The ruling of the International Court of Justice (ICJ) of January 2024 suggested that the evidence presented in the case brought by South Africa against Israel was "reasonable."

(b) Conspiracy to commit genocide: As we have seen, the U.S. was aware of the genocide, thus making it possible to hold it responsible for complicity. The Biden administration was keenly aware of the maneuverings and Israel's military response and its stated purpose, due to the symbiotic

bilateral cooperation. Moreover, the cessation of arms sales to Israel in the course of hostilities by many countries, including Western states, the ICJ's rulings, and even Washington's restrictions on arms sales to Israeli settlers, demonstrates U.S. cognizance of the atrocities committed in Gaza. Yet, the U.S. administration continued to provide arms to Israel, which would seem to meet the conditions for the crimes of "conspiracy to commit genocide" and "complicity in genocide."

(c) *Direct and public incitement to commit genocide*: Since U.S. military aid to Israel comprised materials that were essential and directly facilitated the commission of the genocidal atrocities that resulted from the Israeli ground assault, the U.S. can be held responsible for complicity in genocide. Moreover, U.S. military aid to Israel at the time when its highest echelon engaged in public incitement to commit genocide suggests the U.S. administration was indirectly supporting such views and sentiments.

(d) *Attempt to commit genocide:* Cognizant of the mass atrocities committed by Israel in Gaza, the U.S. had an obligation to prevent genocide and to refrain from supporting Israel. Yet, by summer 2024, the provision of over 100 military sales, including thousands of precision-guided munitions, bombs, missiles targeting underground shelters, light weapons, and other lethal materials, along with the preparation to provide $18 billion worth of equipment related to 50 F-15 fighter jets, coupled with the latest $8 billion deal, evidenced how the U.S. provision of arms supplies were directly used by Israel to commit atrocities. Since adopting the Genocide Convention Implementation Act on Nov. 25, 1988, the U.S. has been a party to the Genocide Convention, which imposes a duty to prevent genocide on the U.S. and its officials. Despite having the ability to stop Israel's actions in Gaza, the U.S. failure to deploy this power demonstrated a violation of its duty to prevent genocide.

(e) *Complicity in genocide:* The U.S. reservation to Article 9 of the Genocide Convention, which allows the ICJ to adjudicate on violations of the Convention, would seem to pose an obstacle to bringing a genocide case against the U.S. before the ICJ. There is no obstacle, however, to prosecuting senior American officials for being complicit in the genocide in Gaza as part of the ongoing investigation into Palestine at the International Criminal Court (ICC). In the U.S., such efforts were seen as synonymous with a declaration of war, however.

"Target Israel and We Will Target You"

The tone was set by Elliott Abrams, a pro-Israel neoconservative uber-hawk. After the prosecutor called for the arrest warrants for top Israeli officials against Israel's Prime Minister Benjamin Netanyahu and Defense Minister Yoav Gallant, Abrams blasted ICC Director Khan's statements, which alluded to complicity: "Those who seek to defend Israel and stop the malicious, deeply antisemitic action against its leaders and against the Jewish state are now being told that their words and actions may also be a crime."[46]

Abrams had a personal stake in any complicity issue relating to genocidal atrocities. He was a key player in the Reagan administration's atrocities in Central America (Nicaragua, Guatemala, El Salvador) who had been convicted in 1991 in the Reagan administration's Iran-Contra scandal for unlawfully withholding information from Congress (he was subsequently pardoned by President George H.W. Bush).[47] He was a signatory of the 1998 *Project for the New American Century* (PNAC) letter demanding the removal of Saddam Hussein and a key architect of the misguided Iraq War. In the subsequent George W. Bush era, Abrams led the "democracy promotion" efforts worldwide, while serving in key positions in both the Trump and Biden administrations.

In Washington, Abrams was no anomaly. Following the ICC arrest warrant, a dozen U.S. Senators wrote to the ICC playing hardball:

> If you issue a warrant for the arrest of the Israeli leadership, we will interpret this not only as a threat to Israel's sovereignty but to the sovereignty of the United States. Our country demonstrated in the American Service-Members' Protection Act the lengths to which we will go to protect that sovereignty.
>
> The United States will not tolerate politicized attacks by the ICC on our allies. Target Israel and we will target you. If you move forward with the measures indicated in the report, we will move to end all American support for the ICC, sanction your employees and associates, and bar you and your families from the United States. You have been warned.[48]

The reference to the American Service-Members' Protection Act was a deliberate legal tactic to suppress charges of U.S. complicity. This act, also known as The Hague Invasion Act, is a U.S. federal law described as "a bill to protect U.S. personnel and other elected and appointed officials of the U.S. government against criminal prosecution by an international criminal court to which the U.S. is not party."[49] Legally, the Act gives the president power to use "all means necessary and appropriate to bring about the release of any U.S. or allied personnel being detained or imprisoned by, on behalf of, or at the request of the International Criminal Court." Furthermore, the subsection (b) of the Act specifies that this authority does not extend only to "covered U.S. persons," but also to broadly defined "covered allied persons" worldwide.[50]

While it is challenging to envision such an invasion in practice, the ease by which the U.S. senators seized upon it to bolster their case against charges of complicity does suggest the sensitivity and apprehension of vulnerability on the topic in the U.S. Congress. When the Act was launched in the early 2000s by two ultra-conservative Republicans, Jesse Helms and Tom DeLay, it was quickly condemned by the European Parliament, the Netherlands, and the Coalition for the International Criminal Court, which called the act a "dangerous symbolic opposition to international criminal justice."[51] Nonetheless, when U.S. Representative Ilhan Omar tried to repeal the bill in 2022, it was quickly buried in Congress and no vote was ever taken.[52]

The Hague Invasion Act

In summer 2024, when Israel was still busy bombarding Gaza, the U.S. State Department delivered to Congress its annual report on U.S. efforts to prevent mass atrocities, based on the Elie Wiesel Genocide and Atrocities Prevention Act of 2018 (P.L. 115-441). That report charged Hamas for an effort to "annihilate Israel" but dismissed Israel's genocidal atrocities in the name of its "inherent right to defend itself."[53] Reflecting the kind of diplomatic coercion that the U.S. administrations have favored in the past decade or so, the senators were led by Senator Tom Cotton. The tough-talking former army officer who once hoped to incarcerate U.S. journalists writing on Iraq for violating "espionage laws," denied that waterboarding was torture and wanted to house "more prisoners at Guantanamo."[54] In foreign policy, the war hawk advocated tougher measures against Iran, Russia, North Korea, as well as China—effectively any country that opposed or seemed to oppose American supremacy.

In 2017, Cotton co-sponsored the bipartisan Israel Anti-Boycott Act (S.270) that criminalized foreign-led boycotts of U.S. allies. In October 2023, Cotton condemned Hamas's actions, denying that Israel was committing war crimes in the Gaza Strip, and saying, "Israel can bounce the rubble in Gaza. Anything that happens in Gaza is the responsibility of Hamas."[55]

Hence, the opposition of Cotton and his fellow Republicans against Khan, the ICC and any international law that seemed to limit U.S. strategic maneuverability. After the ICC issued arrest warrants for Netanyahu and Yoav

Gallant in late November 2024, Cotton described it as a "kangaroo court" and the prosecutor, Karim Khan, as a "deranged fanatic." On X/Twitter, he went further, calling for The Hague to be invaded should Netanyahu be arrested: "Woe to [Khan] and anyone who tries to enforce these outlaw warrants. Let me give them all a friendly reminder: the American law on the ICC is known as The Hague Invasion Act for a reason. Think about it."[56]

Outside the United States, the threats of Cotton and his fellow senators weren't persuasive. By then, more than a dozen countries had announced their intention to intervene in the context of South Africa's ICJ genocide case against Israel. Nicaragua, Colombia, Mexico and Spain filed an official request. Others took a political stance by announcing their intention to participate in the trial to support South Africa, such as Belgium, Egypt, Ireland, and Cuba. Still others were following in their footprints, including Türkiye, Chile, Maldives and Bolivia.

Subsequently, the president of the ICC, Tomoko Akane, said the court faced "coercive measures, threats, pressure and acts of sabotage" without naming the United States and Russia. These attacks, she warned, "jeopardize its very existence." Worse, the court was being "threatened with draconian economic sanctions by another permanent member of the Security Council, as if it was a terrorist organization."[57]

Expectedly, these threats translated to action in January 2025, when the House passed a bill to sanction ICC officials in the last session of Congress by a vote of 247 to 155, with 42 Democrats joining Republicans in support. The bill was heading to the Senate, where a Republican majority was sworn in earlier in the month. The legislation seeks sanctions for any foreigner who helps the ICC in its attempts to investigate, detain or prosecute a U.S. citizen or citizen of an allied country that does not recognize the authority of the court. The sanctions include the freezing of property assets, and denial of visas to any foreigners who materially or financially contribute to the court's efforts.

"America is passing this law because a kangaroo court is seeking to arrest the prime minister of our great ally, Israel," Representative Brian Mast, the Republican chairman of the House Foreign Affairs Committee, said in a speech before the House vote. Mast was a Trumpian politician and U.S. military veteran who had lost both his legs while serving as a U.S. Army explosive ordnance disposal technician in Afghanistan in 2010. In 2015, he volunteered with the Israel Defense Force through Sar-El, working at a base outside Tel Aviv. Following the 2023 Hamas-led attack on Israel, he wore his IDF uniform in Congress. Like the Israeli far-right, he regarded the Palestinians as Nazis and advocated collective punishment:

I would encourage the other side to not so lightly throw around the idea of innocent Palestinian civilians, as is frequently said, I don't think we would so lightly throw around the term 'innocent Nazi civilians' during World War II. It is not a far stretch to say there are very few innocent Palestinian civilians.[58]

Mast rejected any criticism against Israel by international groups and the UN. He called for disbanding the UN agency for Palestinian refugees, UNRWA. Like President Biden, he is a favorite of the Israel lobby. In 2015, his campaign received funds from Duty Free Americas of the Falic family, owners of the chain of 180 stores. The Falics are known for their financial contributions to Jewish settlements in the occupied territories, including the far-right anti-Arab extremists. In 2023–24, he also got almost $200,000 in political donations from the American Israel Public Affairs Committee (AIPAC), the largest and most controversial member of the Israel lobby. He benefited even more from individual contributions.[59]

Israel's Foreign Military Accomplices

In January 2024, the International Court of Justice (ICJ) ordered Israel to prevent and not commit genocidal acts against Palestinians, prevent and punish public incitement to commit genocide, ensure the provision of humanitarian aid, preserve evidence related to allegations of genocide and submit a compliance report within one month. These orders had (or at least should have had) a significant impact on the provision of weapons to Israel since governments arming genocide can be held accountable for genocide themselves.

In the past half a decade, only three countries—the United States, Germany and Italy—have supplied most of Israel's arms. Yet, many others supplied vital military components, ammunition or services.[60] Moreover, countries that had boldly declared they would suspend their exports of military items to Israel, most prominently the United Kingdom, continued their arms flows nonetheless, while allegedly deliberately misleading the British parliament. In effect, the UK had sent more than 8,600 separate munitions since the suspensions took effect.[61] So, even as the Starmer government was depicting itself as having an ethical conscience, it was busy transferring bombs, grenades, torpedoes, mines, missiles and arms components to Gaza, thereby advancing ethnic cleansing and genocidal atrocities in the Strip.

During the prior decade, Israel had significantly increased its imports of arms. In 2019–23, it was the world's 15th largest importer of major arms, accounting for 2.1 percent of global arms imports in the period. In the prior period (2009–13), it ranked only 47th. What contributed to the change was the collapsed peace process, the recurring Gaza wars and the increasingly lethal occupation of the West Bank, coupled with the multi-billion-dollar annual U.S. military aid that continued to flood in, despite growing concerns about its uses in the occupied territories.

In effect, America is the court supplier of all major military powers in the Middle East. In the case of its closest allies, the U.S. provides 60 to 80 percent of their lethal imports (Israel, Kuwait, Saudi Arabia). In the rest, it accounts for 50 to 60 percent of the total (UAE, Iraq, Qatar), followed by Egypt (34%) whose primary suppliers are mainly America's NATO allies (Germany, Italy), as well as Russia (Figure 3-5).

Figure 3-5. How America Is Arming Forever Wars in the Middle East*

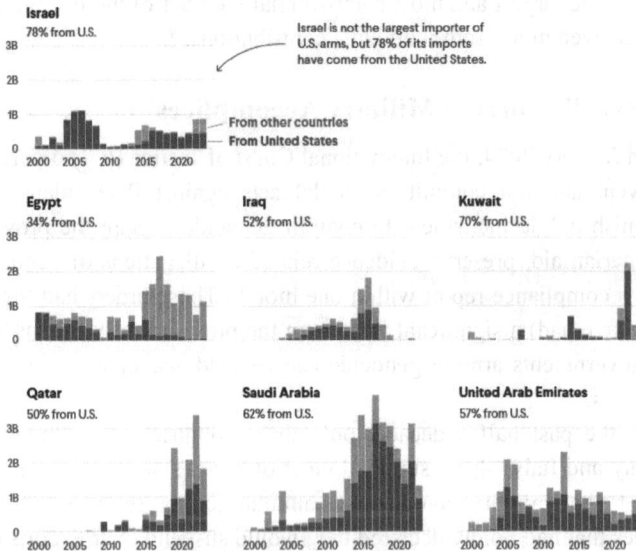

*Estimated military value of arms import: military value is expressed as "trend-indicator-value," a unit developed by the SIPRI that represents the military capability of arms sales.

Note: These countries include the largest recipients of U.S. arms sales in the Middle East. SOURCE: *SIPRI*

This steady, progressive flow of arms into the troubled region has been the primary contributor to its geopolitical volatility and economic uncertainty, particularly since America's strategic partnership with Israel in the 1980s. The flow of arms has never been non-preferential, however. It has been orchestrated by the United States to maintain Israel's military supremacy in the region. Israel's military supremacy has not been the simple result of its technological innovation. It reflects the net effect of American technology exports inscribed in U.S. legislation; that is, the U.S. is legally bound to preserve Israel's "qualitative military edge" (QME). QME serves as Israel's military insurance by ensuring that the country will always be the first in the region to get access to the most sophisticated U.S. military weapons and platforms, such as the F-35 stealth fighter.[62]

America's complicity in most weapons flows into the Middle East was coupled with its diplomatic coercion of Israel's perceived adversaries. The Biden administration denounced the arrest warrant for Prime Minister Benjamin Netanyahu over alleged Israeli war crimes as "outrageous." Prior to the issuing of the ICC's arrest warrant for Netanyahu, a group of U.S. Republican senators went further, engaging in effective strong-arm tactics by threatening ICC prosecutor Karim Ahmad Khan. Similarly, Secretary of State Blinken said the administration would work with the U.S. Congress on potential sanctions against the ICC. The House passed a bill to sanction ICC officials on June 4, 2024.[63]

Just weeks later, Netanyahu addressed a joint session of the U.S. Congress in a blatant violation of the ICC arrest warrant and the mass protests against Netanyahu in Israel. This reflected not just an effort to support a major non-NATO ally but also a tacit attempt to deny the validity of such charges, and thereby of U.S. responsibility and complicity in Israel's ongoing genocidal atrocities in Gaza, including of the role of the U.S. President, Secretary of State and Secretary of Defense, and the full Congressional collusion with such activities and their fatal objectives. To the victims of the genocidal atrocities in Gaza, it all looked like a monsters' ball (Figure 3-6).

Such arms transfers to Israel in the context of its facing ICJ and ICC charges related to genocide would seem to also violate customary international law, including the International Law Commission's Draft Articles on Responsibility of States for Internationally Wrongful Acts, and International Humanitarian Law, including Common Article 1 to the four Geneva Conventions of 1949. Originating from the end of the Cold War in the late 1980s and civil society concerns about the unregulated global arms trade and its detrimental impact on human security, the Arms Trade Treaty (ATT) entered into force in December 2014. It is a multilateral treaty that regulates the international trade in conventional weapons. Some 116 states have ratified the treaty, and a further 24 states have signed but not ratified it.[64]

Figure 3-6. Cooperation, Collusion, Complicity

Israeli Prime Minister Benjamin Netanyahu addresses a joint session of Congress in Washington, D.C. with House Speaker Mike Johnson and Senator Ben Cardin (July 24, 2024).
SOURCE: *Wikimedia (Johnson's X account)*

The ATT prohibits states parties from fueling genocide and other international crimes with weapons. All countries supplying weapons to Israel are party to this treaty, except for the United States. Under the ATT's legal framework, a state party is prohibited from transferring weapons "if it has knowledge at the time of authorization that arms or items would be used in the commission of genocide, crimes against humanity, grave breaches of the Geneva Conventions of 1949, attacks directed against civilian objects or civilians protected as such, or other war crimes as defined by international agreements to which they are a Party."[65] For states that are members, arms transfers to Israel violate the Arms Trade Treaty and—taking into consideration the European allies' military exports to Israel—the EU's Common Position on Arms Exports, and the Principles Governing Conventional Arms Transfers of the Organization for Security and Cooperation in Europe (OSCE).[66]

Altogether, these agreements have the potential to bind states to a system of collective responsibility. Similarly, the Genocide Convention prohibits both the commission of genocide and complicity in it. Although South Africa has charged Israel at the ICJ, there are ongoing efforts to charge governments complicit to genocide at the Court later. The continued, incessant flow of weapons to Israel could also render states complicit in internationally wrongful acts through the aiding or abetting of war crimes and crimes against humanity. This, in turn, could give rise to individual criminal responsibility of senior officials of these states under the Rome Statute of the International Criminal Court.

Until recently, it has been challenging to hold the weapon companies—the CEOs of Lockheed Martin and Raytheon and all the corporations making billions from genocides, wars, and armed violence worldwide—to account as responsible parties. The UN Working Group on Business and Human Rights has acknowledged that accountability for the arms industry is challenging, particularly because it is the government officials that make the decisions about whether or not to sell weapons or grant licenses to a particular recipient. However, the Group has made note of the lack of separation between the entity producing the weapon and the entity approving its sale (read: Big Defense and the Pentagon), which is a recipe for corruption and for the continued export of violence in the name of profits or "national interest."[67]

During his 2024 campaign, President Trump promised to serve as a peacemaker. Yet, his early actions suggested that he was not only embracing complicity but eager to take it to its logical end by ending American aid to Palestinians and the completion of ethnic cleansing in Gaza.

Undermining UNRWA, Completing Ethnic Cleansing

In May 2024, Israeli settlers launched several attacks on the headquarters of the UN Relief and Works Agency for Palestine Refugees in the Near East (UNRWA), setting fire to the perimeter of the building in East Jerusalem. The attacks against UNRWA came after months of far-right settler protests outside of the building. More than 5.9 million Palestinians, including three of four Palestinians in Gaza, were registered with UNRWA as refugees. It is the longstanding lifeline of U.S. humanitarian aid to Palestinians, particularly after the devastation of Gaza. Hence, the Israeli and U.S. efforts to dismantle the Agency.[68]

After achieving an initial truce in the 1948 Arab-Israeli War, Count Folke Bernadotte, a Swedish diplomat, used it to lay the groundwork for the UN Relief and Works Agency (UNRWA) for Palestine Refugees in the Near East. Just hours after his proposal, Bernadotte was assassinated in Jerusalem by the Jewish paramilitary Stern group, while pursuing his official duties. One of those who planned the killing was Yitzhak Shamir, the future prime minister of Israel, and the predecessor and onetime mentor of Benjamin Netanyahu, Israel's current PM.[69]

Ever since then, UNRWA has been a lifeline to generations of Palestinians in the West Bank, the Gaza Strip and the adjacent Arab countries. Created as a temporary measure, UNRWA's mandate has been subject to renewal every three years. Historically, the United States has been UNRWA's largest financial contributor, with more than $7.3 billion since 1950. From the start, these contributions have been subject to a variety of legislative conditions and oversight measures. Decades of U.S. policy toward Israel and the occupied territories, however ambiguous, was reversed almost overnight, when the Trump administration executed a set of dramatic policy changes in 2018 and canceled nearly all U.S. aid to the West Bank and Gaza, plus $360 million in annual aid previously given to the UNRWA. Subsequently, the Biden administration restored much of the funding, yet continued to provide Israel weapons and financing for the mass atrocities against those the UNRWA funding was supposed to help.[70]

After allegations surfaced connecting a few of the 30,000 UNRWA employees with the October 7 Hamas-led attacks against Israel, UNRWA fired nine staff members following a UN investigation, but denied allegations that the agency has widespread links to Hamas. Yet, Congress enacted a March 2024 prohibition on U.S. funding to UNRWA (P.L. 118-47), which is set to last until late March 2025.[71] To put it all into context: The Empire State Building is said to have 21,000 employees. Imagine what would happen if six of them were suspected of terrorism and *therefore* the entire building would have to be dismantled and all employees fired? It would seem to represent collective punishment of many for the alleged crimes of a few.

Additionally, certain provisions of Israeli laws scheduled to take effect in early 2025 could have far-reaching consequences for UNRWA's ability to operate in Gaza, the West Bank, and Jerusalem, endangering the lives of hundreds of thousands of Palestinians. The new U.S. and Israeli legal measures emboldened Jewish settlers, particularly the Messianic far-right, prompting several attacks on the UNRWA headquarters in East Jerusalem in May 2024. These assaults came after months of far-right settler protests outside of the building, following Israeli claims of UNRWA-Hamas links that lacked verification, according to U.S. intelligence. Among the protesters was Aryeh King, a deputy mayor of Jerusalem and a prominent advocate for settlements, who described Palestinian Gazans as "Muslim Nazis" and "sub-human," calling for captured Palestinians to be "buried alive" in December 2023.[72]

By April 2025, some 290 UNRWA staff had been killed in hostilities since October 7, 2023.

During Trump's first term, his administration gradually cut all U.S. assistance to UNRWA. It was only the fragile ceasefire that delayed the catastrophe. The stakes were extraordinarily high in the UNRWA debacle. In Gaza, nearly two million Palestinians were displaced and dependent on aid for food, water and medical services. U.S. officials acknowledged there was no serious backup plan for providing humanitarian supplies and services to Palestinians.

The hope of some that President Trump would offer a more peaceful alternative fell finally apart in early February 2025, when he said in a joint press conference with PM Netanyahu that "the U.S. will take over the Gaza Strip." Asked to elaborate whether he was willing to send U.S. troops to fill a security vacuum in Gaza, Trump did not rule it out. "We're going to take over [Gaza] we're going to develop it." He added: "I do see a long-term ownership position, and I see it bringing great stability to that part of the Middle East, and maybe the entire Middle East." The former real estate tycoon suggested, Gaza could become a "Riviera of the Middle East."[73]

Around the world, observers were shocked. But the statement did not come out of the blue. Barely a week after October 7, Israel's intelligence ministry, which oversees policies related to the intelligence organizations Mossad and Shin Bet, prepared a secret memorandum. It recommended the forcible transfer of Gaza's 2.3 million residents to Egypt's Sinai as the preferred course of action. It encouraged Israel's government to lead a public campaign in the West to promote the transfer plan, which was depicted as a "humanitarian necessity." As the plan was leaked, an international debacle ensued with all Arab countries and European leaders rejecting the idea. Yet, that's the idea Trump was touting and one that his son-in-law and former Middle East advisor Jared Kushner had promoted a year before.[74]

By early 2025, the Trump administration, by supporting the Netanyahu cabinet's ideas of the not-so-voluntary transfer of the Palestinian population, was effectively promoting ethnic cleansing in Gaza. As a result, the administration seemed to make itself complicit in the kind of violations of international law that had undermined the credibility of the Biden administration not just in the Middle East but worldwide. The failure of genocide prevention went far further back in history, however.

PART II

THE FAILURE
OF GENOCIDE
PREVENTION

CHAPTER 4

RAPHAEL LEMKIN AND GENOCIDE POLITICS

The history of the legal definition of genocide is intertwined with the life of Raphael Lemkin, a Polish-Jewish lawyer who played a critical role in the establishment of the Genocide Convention. What is less understood is that his understanding of genocide emerged from a critique of colonialism that originates from the 16th century. In his published work, Lemkin built on the history of natural law, European philosophers and lawyers. He approached the issue historically and, like most Europeans of his time, listed genocide cases dating from those perpetrated against the early Christians, the Jews in the Middle Ages and the indigenous peoples in Latin America to the Nazi Holocaust. In his unpublished manuscripts, he depicted the role of settler-colonialism in relation to genocide as an extended process that often-involved destructive episodes and events.[1]

Lemkin's critique of imperialism and warfare targeting civilians dates from the Spanish conquest of the Americas. He set the Genocide Convention into larger historical context believing that "the history of genocide provides examples of the awakening of humanitarian feelings, which gradually have been crystallized in formulas of international law." Tracing the rise of a world consciousness abhorring genocide, he went back to the historical moment, "when the world community took an affirmative stand to protect human groups from extinction." He believed that Francisco de Vitoria's and Bartolomé de las Casas's denunciations of Spanish atrocities in the Americas were the first "links in one chain leading to the proclamation of genocide as an international crime."[2]

Genocide in the Americas: "The Natives Don't Have a Soul"

After the first voyages of Christopher Columbus to the Americas, Catholic conversion had served as the colonial pretext for enslaving the indigenous peoples, mining their silver and gold, and developing their land for agricultural production. The colonists saw the natives as devoid of soul and thus devoid of rights. After all, if they weren't human, they didn't have to be treated as such. But not everybody accepted the compulsory Christianization, plunder and brutal enslavement of the indigenous people. As the first officially appointed "Protector of the Indians," Bartolomé de las Casas (1484–1566), a Dominican friar from the School of Salamanca, oversaw the administrative office of the Spanish colonies responsible for the well-being of the indigenous people. He believed that since all humans shared the same nature, they had the same rights to life and liberty.

Las Casas saw a great breach between the material interests of the colonizers and the values they presumably professed. For decades, he had preached against the ruthless colonial conquests, but by 1542 his tone grew alarmed. With the natives being worked to death, he began to promote New Laws to end the colonial *encomienda* system. Although it was supposed to offer benefits to native laborers, the system was effectively functioning as communal slavery. Even as las Casas was being accused of treason and his life was being threatened by the colonists, the bold friar wrote *A Short Account of the Destruction of the Indies* (1542–52), in which he accused the Spanish Empire of responsibility for the "fire and sword" that had devastated several kingdoms in Americas.[3] Over just three decades, he said, the "despotic and diabolical behavior of the Christians," had caused the "unjust and totally unwarranted deaths" of millions of natives:

> There are two main ways in which those who have travelled to this part of the world pretending to be Christians have uprooted these pitiful peoples and wiped them from the face of the earth. First, they have waged war on them: unjust, cruel, bloody and tyrannical war. Second, they have murdered anyone and everyone who has shown the slightest sign of resistance...
> The reason the Christians have murdered on such a vast scale and killed anyone and everyone in their way is purely and simply greed. They have set out to line their pockets with gold and to amass private fortunes...[4]

The natives' deaths were being attributed mainly to diseases for which they had no immunity, whereas las Casas stressed the role of war, slavery and overwork. New research tends to concur. Between 1492 and 1550, "a nexus of slavery, overwork, and famine killed more Indians in the Caribbean than smallpox, influenza, and malaria. And among these human factors, slavery has emerged as a major killer."[5]

There is a lethal line of continuity from these early colonial atrocities to contemporary genocides. In light of the population size, the extermination of the indigenous peoples in the early 16th century resulted in two to four times more deaths than the Holocaust of six million Jews in the 20th century. Nonetheless, the two genocides share common threads, including slave work in extermination camps; dehumanization of the victims; preemption of reproduction between men and women; and labor until extinction, among others. It was such parallels that likely led Lemkin to link settler-colonial mass atrocities with genocide as an extended chain of devastatingly destructive events (Figure 4-1).[6]

Figure 4-1. Five Centuries of Extermination Camps

Pre-Industrial Spanish Atrocities | Industrial Genocide in Bergen-Belsen

SOURCES: *Spanish atrocities in Cuba: Illustration of Las Casas' Destruction of the Indies: Bergen-Belsen concentration camp, April 1, 194: No 5 Army Film & Photographic Unit. Wikimedia*

The two genocides are also marked by parallels in the quest for historical legitimacy. In the case of the Holocaust, it took decades to overcome historical denialism; that is, the distortion or rejection of the historical record. Distressingly, such efforts at de-legitimation have intensified in the past decade or two, with the spread of secular stagnation in Western economies. In the case of colonial exterminations and their legacies, denialism was the rule until not so long ago. Nonetheless, Lemkin saw early modernity as both the architect of the ultimate decimation—cultural genocide—and as "the awakening of humanitarian feelings" that gradually gave rise to principles of international law.

In these developments, the Valladolid debate marked the symbolic beginning. The disclosures of las Casas gave rise to the first moral and theological debate about the Spanish conquest of the Americas. Certainly, the debate disguised the cold material facts. The colonial settlers had not risked their lives in the New World in pursuit of divine glory in the afterlife. Their earthly quest was about lucrative fortunes. When the natives were seen to resist that quest, they were exterminated.

Held in the city of Valladolid (1550–51), more than half a century after the first colonial massacres, the Spanish debate was the first to question the fatal treatment of the indigenous people by the European colonial settlers. Did the natives have a human soul like the colonizers or were they just sub-human beasts? To settle the matter, the King of Spain Carlos V (Charles V), the grandson of Fernando and Isabel, ordered las Casas to argue his case against Juan Ginés de Sepúlveda, a doctor of theology and law. Though he had never been to the Americas, de Sepúlveda was supported by the colonists, and the landowners. According to his *Just Causes of War against the Indians,* the natives were unable to rule themselves and thus had to be pacified and governed forcefully.[7]

In one form or another, this argument hasn't disappeared. It looms behind Kipling's "White Man's Burden" and the British Empire, the "civilizing mission" of the colonial French, and the imperial version of the American "Manifest Destiny." There is a long line of continuity from the liberal apologies of John Stuart Mill to U.S. postwar presidents from the Cold War to the post-9/11 wars and the canon of the "responsibility to protect." This doctrine or pretext portrays the consequent military devastation under the rubric of the Global War on Terror (GWOT) and later Overseas Contingency Operations (OCO), as necessary and just.

To validate his stance, de Sepúlveda obviously did not refer outright to the value of the resources to be acquired, unlike some contemporary American legislators seeking to affirm the pretexts for plunder. Instead, he resorted to Aristotle and the philosopher's blessing for slavery in the nonetheless widely touted Greek democracy:

Those who are as different [from other men] as the soul from the body or man from beast—and they are in this state if their work is the use of the body, and if this is the best that can come from them—are slaves by nature.[8]

Since the natives were but "slaves by nature," de Sepúlveda argued that it was to their advantage that they should be ruled thus. After all, neither small children nor animals knew what was best for them. It was the same argument John Stuart Mill seized in the 19th century to legitimize British colonial repression as a force of civilization against the barbarian insurgents. However, las Casas disagreed. He held that Aristotle's views on barbarians and natural slaves were not applicable to the natives who were capable of reason and could be converted to Christianity without force. Both las Casas and de Sepúlveda saw conversion vital to the civilizing mission of the Spanish colonists. They only disagreed about the means.

Dehumanizing arguments of the colonized as "slaves by nature" still prevail in the early 21st century. When Israel's defense minister Yoav Gallant ordered a "complete siege" of Gaza after October 7, denying Palestinians electricity, food, water and fuel as Israel continues its bombardment of Gaza, his justification was: "We are fighting human animals and we are acting accordingly."[9] Subsequently, several members of the Netanyahu cabinet repeated the metaphor. After all, there was nothing new in such statements. Already a decade before, a member of the Israeli parliament, Eli Ben-Dahan, Netanyahu's then-defense minister, stated that Palestinians are "like animals, they are not human."[10] In the Israeli scene, such rhetoric reiterated rabbi Meir Kahane's Jewish supremacy doctrines in the 1970s, even the prior Eurocentric orientalist metaphors that some Jewish colonial settlers, including certain labor Zionist leaders, embraced a century ago.[11]

In other words, these genocidal actions and their supporting rhetoric follow a predictable trajectory initially catalyzed by self-interest, none of which comes out of the blue.

Unsurprisingly, the Valladolid debate produced no ultimate winners. Las Casas was supported by the monarchy, which sought to control the colonists' might, whereas de Sepúlveda was promoted by the colonists and landowners who sought to deny the monarch's right to interfere with their plunder. The ultimate winner of the Valladolid debate may have been the Spanish Crown. It benefited from the continuing extraction of natural resources while portraying the monarchy as a passionate supporter of the natives and Christianity. Las Casas failed to end Spanish conquests in the New World, while de Sepúlveda failed to overturn the New Laws that ostensibly restricted the colonists' power but effectively did not.[12]

The rise of other European colonial powers set the stage for the legitimization of occupation and seizure of native lands by waves of white settlers and subsequent legal justifications of effective genocides predicated on the colonists' property rights. This turn of events inspired Lemkin's bold project to preempt future genocides, to try to nip the entire horrendous process in the bud.

Raphael Lemkin's Quest for a *Preventive* Genocide Convention

Born in a large farm near Wolkowysk, Raphael Lemkin (1900–1959), understood very early in life that the suffering of the Jews in eastern Poland was part of a broader and more systemic pattern of violence manifested throughout history and around the world. Every genocide had its unique characteristics, but they also shared uniformities. The challenge they posed was comparative and international.[13] In *The Axis Rule in Occupied Europe* (1944), his early master treatise, Lemkin coined the term genocide from the Greek *genos* (family, clan, tribute, race, stock, kin) and -*cide* (Latin for -cidium, killing). He also understood the close link between the ideas of ethnic supremacy doctrines and massacres, noting that genocide could equally be termed "ethnocide," with the Greek *ethno* meaning "nation."[14]

Historical evidence showed Lemkin "the real purpose behind the Nazi war policy" which was that "this war was being waged by the Nazis not only for frontiers, but mainly for the alteration of the human element within these frontiers." In turn, this alteration meant that "certain people were to be annihilated and supplanted by Germans. Their destruction would be irrevocable and their cultures erased forever."[15]

In the early 20th century, genocidal atrocities, due in part to their comprehensive nature, unfolded gradually over time. In the early 21st century, these atrocities, though still sequenced, can proceed faster, more efficiently and destructively, thanks to post-industrialization, greater lethality, and the obfuscatory transnational troll farms that can elevate disinformation into mainstream conventional wisdom worldwide, in just a matter of hours.

Nonetheless, the basic phases that genocide pioneer Raphael Lemkin identified in the 1930s still remain: "one, the destruction of the national pattern of the oppressed group, the other, the imposition of the national pattern of the oppressor."[16] Hence Lemkin's initial broad definition of genocide in *The Axis Rule*:

> Generally speaking, genocide does not necessarily mean the immediate destruction of a nation, except when accomplished by mass killings of all members of a nation. It is intended rather to signify a coordinated plan of different actions aiming at the destruction of essential foundations of the life of national groups, with the aim of annihilating the groups themselves. The objectives of such a plan would be disintegration of the political and social institutions, of culture, language, national feelings, religion, and the economic existence of national groups, and the destruction of

the personal security, liberty, health, dignity, and even the lives of the individuals belonging to such groups. Genocide is directed against the national group as an entity, and the actions involved are directed against individuals, not in their individual capacity, but as members of the national group.[17]

After World War II, Lemkin worked on the legal team of the U.S. prosecutor at the International Military Tribunal (IMT) in Nuremberg (1945–46). The Nuremberg indictment did make reference to war crimes, crimes against humanity, conspiracy, and crimes against peace. However, the trials did not prosecute Nazi atrocities targeting ethnic and religious groups. Though controversial in its time for the *retroactive* criminalization of aggression, the IMT is often seen as "the true beginning of international criminal law."[18]

Lemkin had a different take. He saw the IMT as a failure. How could the Nuremberg tribunal bring legal justice for the horrors of the Jewish Holocaust, when it rejected the very principle of trying Nazi leaders for their crimes against the Jews? True, the tribunals dispensed retributive justice and "created a feeling that . . . crime should not be allowed to pay." Yet, the judgment "only partly relieved the world's moral tensions," Lemkin wrote, while "the purely juridical consequences of the trials were wholly insufficient."[19] (Figure 4-2)

Figure 4-2. "Allies Refused to Envisage Future Hitlers"

Raphael Lemkin (1900 –1959) | Nuremberg Trials (1945–46): A Failure?

SOURCE: *Center for Jewish History, NYC (Wikimedia); Judges' bench during the tribunal in Nuremberg, Allied-occupied Germany (Wikimedia)*

As Lemkin saw it, "the Allies decided their case against a past Hitler but refused to envisage future Hitlers." To Lemkin, the IMT had proven that the world's states cared only to protect states against aggression by other states and had no interest in protecting populations. To him, people came first, while the mainly Western powers did not want to, or could not, "establish a rule of international law that would prevent and punish future crimes of the same type."[20] The quest for an international convention to prevent the rise of "future Hitlers" became Lemkin's obsession and life mission. This preemptory objective marked his life project from the very start. The point was not merely to develop international legal instruments to punish but to *prevent* future genocides.

Ostensibly, Lemkin's quest was realized in December 1948, when the just-created United Nations approved the Genocide Convention, based largely on his proposals. The full name—the Convention on the Prevention and Punishment of the Crime of Genocide (CPPCG)—reflects the three central tenets of the project (in this order): *prevention* and *punishment* of the *crime* of genocide obligating state parties to pursue the enforcement of its prohibition.

The Genocide Convention was unanimously adopted by the UN General Assembly on December 9, 1948, during its third session.[21] The Convention entered into force on January 12, 1951, and has today 153 state parties.[22] Maps of the parties to the Convention suggest near-universal support and acceptance (Figure 4-3). Nothing would be further from the realities.

Figure 4-3. Parties to the Genocide Convention

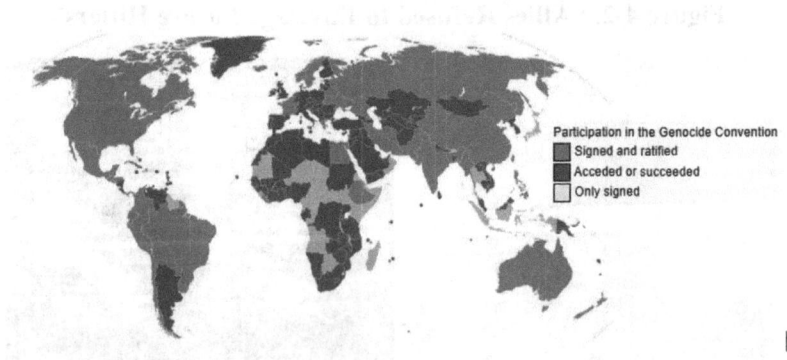

Participation in the Genocide Convention
☐ Signed and ratified
☐ Acceded or succeeded
☐ Only signed

SOURCE: *Wikimedia, Jan. 2025*

Lemkin's life work became more widely known only in the 1990s, when international prosecutions of genocide began in response to atrocities in the former Yugoslavia and Rwanda.[23] It took almost half a century before the Security Council would refer to "acts of genocide." That happened only in June 1994 with respect to Rwanda (Resolution 925), which was the first time that the word "genocide" was used in a resolution.[24] The timing matters.

The Genocide Convention was developed prior to but only became effective in the early, escalatory phase of the Cold War. These four decades cast a long dark shadow over the realization, interpretation and implementation—or more precisely, non-implementation—of the Convention.

The Genocide Convention is often portrayed as a pillar of the West's rules-based international order. Yet, the realities are more nuanced. For all practical purposes, the West's prosperous industrialized states, particularly the former colonial powers, sought to dilute not just the key clauses of the Convention, but to suppress and suspend what Lemkin saw as the core of the original drafts, including cultural genocide, political killings, ethnic cleansing and preparatory attacks. As a net consequence, the final Convention itself was the result of an exclusionary process, which purposely omitted the elements that Lemkin himself saw critical to genocide.

There is a beautiful fragmentary marble statue, called the Belvedere Torso, in the Vatican Museum. A copy originating from the 1430s, the 1.6-meter-tall statue represents a colossal nude male torso, bereft of the head, arms and lower legs. If the full original is comparable to the Genocide Convention, then the existing torso represents what's left of the original Convention draft. It is mutilated.

The Removal of Cultural Genocide

Ever since 1947, Lemkin had sought financial assistance for his planned book on genocide. In that ambitious project, he hoped to examine "every genocide of importance" from ancient times to the present. In this enterprise, las Casas and the Americas held a privileged role. Las Casas estimated that the total of Indians killed in Spanish America exceeded 20 million. Lemkin added that this figure did not include those who died from overwork, the slaves killed in the mines, or the Indians killed during active combat, or the prisoners who were executed.[25]

As Lemkin began to push hard for the Genocide Convention and its international codification, he drew from his book on global genocide, relying on a historical and comparative approach that built on and extended his definition of genocide in *Axis Rule*. This objective was significantly broader than the restricted and narrow torso that is today known as the Convention.[26]

Similarly, the original drafts of the Convention still classified this crime relying on three headings: physical, biological and cultural. In this view, physical genocide featured massacre and mutilation, deprivation of livelihood, including starvation and exposure often by deportation), slavery and ultimately exposure to death. In turn, biological genocide translated to separation of families, sterilization, and destruction of fetus. Finally, cultural genocide included desecration and destruction of cultural symbols (books, objects of art, religious relics, etc.), loot, destruction of cultural leadership, destruction of cultural centers (cities, churches, monasteries, schools, libraries), prohibition of cultural activities or codes of behavior, forceful conversion and demoralization. In contrast to Lemkin and his champions particularly in the Global South who favored a broad view of genocide, the final draft, after long debates, multiple exclusions and wheeling and dealing, featured mainly physical genocide and aspects of its biological dimension. It no longer featured the classification, nor any agreement that cultural genocide was an inherent part of the Convention. Perhaps one reason that cultural genocide was booted from the Convention was that it was too reminiscent of "ethnic cleansing."[27]

Cultural genocide could take place in many ways. Cultural centers were destroyed. Religion served as an important instrument in the "subtle kind of cultural genocide" committed by the Spanish missions. Once the Indians yielded to the admonitions of the fathers, they could no longer escape the snare of the church or the mission. Typically, the missionaries gave mass in Latin and Spanish, making no effort to learn the native tongue. Corporal punishment was inflicted on Indians of both sexes who failed in their religious duties. If an Indian escaped from the mission village, he was brought back by soldiers and lashed. There was looting and pillaging of Indian wealth. There was destruction of Indian leadership through the murder of one chief or king after another. With few exceptions the colonists of New Spain were guilty of genocide: "the colonists were guilty on all counts." Hence, Lemkin's criticism of Columbus and his historical example for future colonization in the Americas:

> After his discovery of the West Indies and the first flush of excitement at finding such peaceful and friendly natives in a charming country, hardened to become a model to the later colonists. He may have been disappointed at not discovering the riches he had hoped for. At any rate he mismanaged his colony and tolerated all kinds of genocidal crimes. To atone for the growing stories of poor discoveries and of his mismanagement, he sent Indian slaves to Spain. Natives to him constituted the principal wealth of the island and he wanted to impress the crown with them and derive a profit in turn. Thus, he set the infamous example for what was to become the shame and scandal of Spanish conquest in the New World.[28]

Predicating his struggle against mass atrocities on the idea of cultural genocide, Lemkin felt his most painful sacrifice was the original Article 3 of the ad hoc committee draft on *cultural genocide*. It deemed that "genocide also means any deliberate act committed with intent to destroy the language, religion, or culture of a national, racial, or religious group" through acts such as "prohibiting the use of the language of the group in daily intercourse or in schools, or the printing and circulation of publications in the language of the group" or "destroying or preventing the use of libraries, museums, schools, historical monuments, places of worship, or other cultural institutions and objects of the group."[29] As he saw it, the article on cultural genocide represented the full breadth of national cultural autonomy.[30]

When Lemkin began to push the Convention draft in the just-established United Nations in 1946, he considered genocide inherent in colonization. Consequently, the original Convention drafts still referred to acts of cultural genocide. The final version no longer did. In retrospect, it is hardly surprising that it was the delegates from African countries, "on whom genocide was practiced" during the period of European colonization, who were the most receptive to a proposal to outlaw genocide. Instinctively, Lemkin turned to those countries that would first show their international clout in the 1955 Bandung Summit of the Non-Alignment Movement; that is, countries that today are collectively known as the Global South (Figure 4-4).

Figure 4-4. Global South

The developed Global North is highlighted in blue and the Global South in red. The latter comprises emerging and developing Africa, Latin America and the Caribbean, Asia, and Oceania. Actually, since the income levels in Russia and most of Eastern Europe are similar to those in emerging economies, they could be included among the Global South.

SOURCE: *UNCTAD (Wikipedia)*

Lemkin saw as his task to assemble the African nations, along with a number of Latin American and Asian states, to form a coalition that "the European delegations could not refuse to follow, especially after the Holocaust." If smaller states could bring a law against genocide to the agenda, then "the Allies of the recent war would have to say yes, because they could not afford to be led but must themselves lead." Importantly, it was the support of the Muslim nations of Lebanon, Egypt, Saudi Arabia, Pakistan, and Iran that provided the core of the Genocide Convention's political support at the UN, forcing the major powers to the bargaining table. Moreover, the contribution of individual women and of women's organizations to the issue proved considerable. The role of the Global South and gendered support was critical to the genesis of the Genocide Convention.[31]

Furthermore, China rendered its support to the Convention because the *Axis Rule* had demonstrated how the commission of genocide could be facilitated through forced drug and alcohol use. The Chinese delegates noted that the Japanese occupation authorities in northeastern China had forcibly imposed narcotic drugs upon Chinese citizens to "[undermine] the resistance and [impair] the physical and mental wellbeing of the Chinese people."[32] Indeed, ever since the late 18th century, the British East India Company had expanded the cultivation of opium in the Bengal Presidency, selling it to private merchants who transported it to China and covertly sold it on to Chinese smugglers. The opium was thus purposely weaponized to weaken China prior to two Opium Wars (1839–42, 1856–60), which contributed to the disintegration of the Chinese Empire, its colonization, Japanese invasion, and Civil War—that is, the "century of [colonial] humiliation" (Figure 4-5).

Figure 4-5. Weaponizing Drugs for Genocide

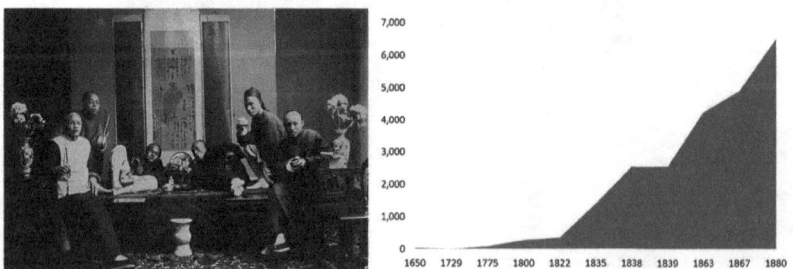

[Left] Opium smokers ca. 1880. *[Right]* Opium imports into China 1650–1880.

SOURCE: *Wikimedia (Lai Afong); [Right] Wikimedia (TilmannR)*

Nonetheless, Lemkin faced consistent opposition on the part of the United States and the United Kingdom; the mightiest old empire and its still-more powerful new successor. What he did not know at the time was that these two governments, despite their public rhetoric, had also issued private orders to their delegates to either bury the Convention in subcommittees or confirm genocide in a vaguely worded resolution that could satisfy the humanitarian activists until the issue faded.[33]

London had little interest in genocide investigations in different part of the British Empire. Washington was concerned about international attention being directed to its racial segregation and the many lynchings of African Americans, and the genocidal massacres of Native Americans. Hence, the Senate's refusal to ratify the Convention throughout most of the Cold War on the grounds that the treaty gave international courts jurisdiction over domestic U.S. affairs, potentially allowing the U.S. and American citizens to be charged with genocide against African Americans and Native Americans.[34] In turn, the French hoped to keep genocide strictly an international crime, which would have undermined efforts to accuse France of committing genocide in French colonies that the government in Paris claimed were part of the French republic and thus not under the jurisdiction of international law.[35]

Such concerns were also typical to other former colonial states, including the Netherlands, Canada and Sweden, and the defeated Germany, Italy and Japan. Ultimately, the UN delegates wanted a Convention that could be used against their geopolitical opponents, but not against themselves. So, Lemkin knew that the issue of cultural genocide would have to be conceded to Washington, but only in exchange for keeping international tribunals and having the Convention also apply to times of peace.[36]

Since the drafts on cultural genocide were vehemently opposed by the Anglo-Saxon settler countries (UK, the U.S., Canada, Australia and New Zealand) and European colonial powers (France, Netherlands, Belgium, Denmark), the concept was shelved.[37] And so it was that judicial recourse for some five centuries of calamitous colonial atrocities was suppressed and redacted from the final Convention. These genocides ranged from Spanish conquistadors and the British East India Company to the American Indian Wars, the transatlantic slave trade that led to the deaths of 20 million Africans, and the Herero and Nama genocide in Africa that paved the way to the industrially organized assembly-plants of extermination during the Holocaust. The UN General Assembly in 2007 estimated that for a period of over 400 years, more than 15 million men, women and children were the victims of the tragic transatlantic slave trade in one of the darkest chapters in human history (Figure 4-6). However, the total slave trade out of Africa likely amounts to 25 million and some estimates are over two times higher.[38]

Figure 4-6. Slave Trade out of Africa, 1500–1900

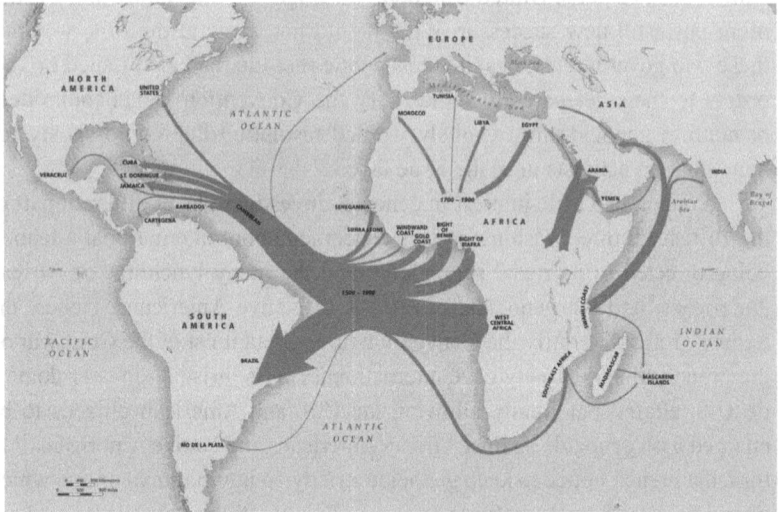

Overview of the slave trade out of Africa, 1500–1900. Eltis, David and Richardson, David. 2019. Atlas of the Transatlantic Slave Trade. New Haven.

SOURCE: *United Nations*

Similarly, the genocidal atrocities in Gaza can be seen as "part of a century-long project of eliminatory settler-colonialism in Palestine, stain on the international system and humanity" that the UN Special Rapporteur Francesca Albanese calls "genocide as colonial erasure."[39]

Ironically, the price of the creation of the Genocide Convention that the West exacted was the exclusion of their colonial genocides that had set the stage for the establishment of that Convention.

The Removal of Political Killings

Lemkin's early drafts also included the notion of *political killing*. According to conventional wisdom in the West, political groups were excised from the Convention at the behest of the Soviet Union. The assumption is that Soviets plotted to exclude political groups out of unease that the Kulak massacres, purges of regime adversaries, and wartime executions like the Katyn´ massacre could fall within the scope of genocide. In reality, the drafting history offers a far more nuanced debate on this subject, and a fairly large consensus for exclusion of political groups. Presumably, the United States switched its position in a spirit of compromise. In effect, Washington had long planned to exclude political groups from the Convention. In turn, the

Soviets and their allies in Eastern and Central Europe had not voted for the removal of political groups from the Convention; they abstained. At the end, the resolution to drop the political groups was adopted by a large majority.[40]

By October 1948, Lemkin had to abandon his theory of genocide and lobby the delegates to excise political groups from the draft. Now he argued that "the destruction of political opponents should be treated as the crime of political homicide, not as genocide." Second, he conceded, perhaps in the context of Latin American politics, that "every revolutionary regime comes to power by destroying some of its opponents. Later this regime is recognized by other nations, sometimes the whole world. Should political groups be included in the definition of genocide, recognition of a revolutionary regime would imply acceptance of genocide as legal. This would kill the Genocide Convention before it took root in world society."[41] Nonetheless, Lemkin was not averse to using anti-Communist sentiments when trying to promote his Convention. Hence, his turn to the Lithuanian, Polish and Ukrainian diasporas to lobby elected officials.

The simple reality is that the Genocide Convention treaty was drafted, contested, and diluted amid the early Cold War tensions and ideological struggles between the United States and the Soviet Union. Unsurprisingly, the political objectives of the superpowers rendered the convention a weak instrument for addressing abuses against human rights. Accordingly, the Soviets saw the genocide treaty as a political document that the West would exploit in its ideological warfare, fearing repercussions directed against it. All things considered, the Kremlin wanted to keep the subjugation of Eastern Europe and the vast system of forced labor camps out of the genocide discourse. In turn, the American Bar Association and Senate Committee on Foreign Relations worried that the Convention could be used against America, particularly in relation to the plight of African Americans.[42] In these heated discussions, humanitarian concerns for human rights to prevent future genocides were first sidelined, then suppressed.

Lemkin's misguided battle to exploit the Cold War division to facilitate the inclusion of political killings in the Genocide Convention backfired. Eventually, these points, too, were removed from the Convention. In effect, the idea was challenging to the United States in the sense that the stated objective of the Cold War—containment to "prevent the spread of Communism"—would rely on ideologically-motivated genocidal atrocities and "dirty wars" to achieve these objectives, as subsequently evidenced by the abject obliteration of North Korea, followed by Operation Gladio in Europe, Operation Condor in Latin America, Operation Phoenix in Vietnam and so on.[43]

Lemkin's political effort to promote the Convention did not change his own view of genocide as basically a settler colonial project that left its lethal impact on both Nazi antisemitism and the segregationist America's racism. Yet, his attempt to ride on the McCarthy-era anti-Communist paranoia in order to codify the Convention led him into an unwarranted battle with prominent civil rights leaders who had begun to use the word genocide to describe the treatment of black Americans in the early 1950s.[44]

These civil rights activists based their case precisely on Lemkin's own notions.

America's Black Genocide

In *The Souls of Black Folk* (1903), the black civil rights pioneer W.E.B. Du Bois famously said that: "The problem of the 20th century is the problem of the color line."[45] It was a view that would become the foundation of American civil rights movement in the postwar era. Paralleling Lemkin's quest for the Genocide Convention, one might have expected these two powerful drives for social justice to converge. But that's not what happened.

The battle between Lemkin and the prominent early civil rights leaders climaxed in 1951, when the Civil Rights Congress (CRC) published its petition charging the United States with committing genocide against its black population. The full title tells the story: "The Historic Petition to the United Nations for Relief from a Crime of the United States Government Against the Negro People."[46] The basic argument was simple and persuasive:

> Out of the inhuman black ghettos of American cities, out of the cotton plantations of the South, comes this record of mass slayings on the basis of race, of lives deliberately warped and distorted by the willful creation of conditions making for premature death, poverty and disease. It is a record that calls aloud for condemnation, for an end to these terrible injustices that constitute a daily and ever-increasing violation of the United Nations Convention on the Prevention and Punishment of the Crime of Genocide...
>
> We maintain, therefore, that the oppressed Negro citizens of the United States, segregated, discriminated against and long the target violence, suffer from genocide as the result of the consistent, consciously unified policies of every branch of government.[47]

The CRC had used a two-pronged strategy of litigation and demonstrations to call attention to racial injustice in America. Relying on extensive public communications, its major tactic was publicizing cases, especially in the segregated South. The CRC was successful particularly in raising inter-national awareness about such cases, which occasionally sparked protests to the president and Congress. During the dark years of the McCarthyistic Red Scare, the CRC was classified as subversive, due to the Communist Party affiliations of some of its members. Under President Harry S. Truman, U.S. Attorney General Thomas Clark labelled the CRC a "Communist front" and it was branded as "subversive" by the House Committee on Un-American Activities, which managed to undermine its future.

Yet, *We Charge Genocide* was methodically researched, and promoted by leading black intellectuals, including W. E. B. Du Bois, documenting the killing of "10,000 Negroes" between 1945 and 1951. Rightly, the petition highlighted parallels between the U.S. treatment of blacks and the German and Austrian pogroms at the beginning of the Nazi genocide.[48] Yet, when the CRC founder William Patterson presented the document to the UN in Paris, his passport was revoked by the State Department. Blocked from traveling, Paul Robeson and W.E.B. Du Bois went to the UN offices in New York. Though well received in Europe, the document was ignored in the UN, which did not acknowledge receiving the petition (Figure 4-7).[49] Robeson in particular seems to have paid a high price for his initiative and ideolog-ical commitment, which led to a string of health problems his son believed stemmed from the CIA's and MI5's attempts to "neutralize" his father and from being "subjected to mind de-patterning under MK Ultra," a covert CIA human experimentation program. What is certain is that he would be under systematic government harassment for years.[50]

Figure 4-7. "We Charge Genocide"

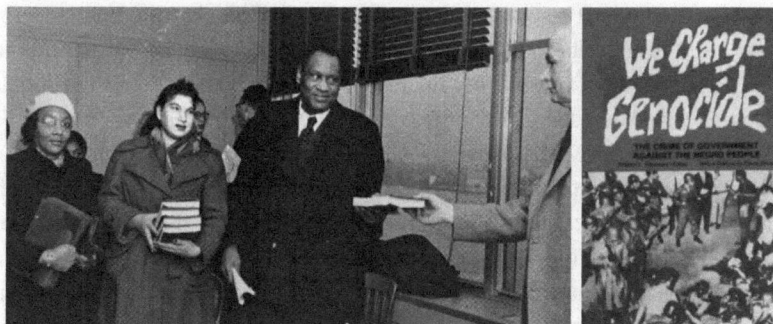

Paul Robeson presents We Charge Genocide to UN Secretariat in New York on December 17, 1951

SOURCE: *Zinn Education Project (Civil Rights Movement Archive)*

At the height of the Red Scare in America, Lemkin dismissed as part of a Communist-orchestrated "maneuver to divert attention" from the Soviet crimes of genocide and belittled the historical impact of slavery and segregation in America. And yet, even as Lemkin was battling with the black civil rights leaders, he was writing chapters for his planned *Introduction to the Study of Genocide* in which his central argument was that modern racism evolved in the era of European colonial expansion to legitimize the exploitation of human beings.[51]

Lemkin's obsession to have the Convention drafted, even at the cost of its critical tenets, did not compromise his understanding and theory of colonial history as the breeding-ground of contemporary racism and genocides. But it did undermine the rise of a broader progressive front for the original draft in America.

Obfuscation of "Ethnic Cleansing"

In historical view, the term "ethnic cleansing" could be derived from the Nazis' "racial hygiene" programs, which were concerned for racial purity and thus "cleansing" (*Säuberung*), which presumably accounted for their objective to make Germany *judenrein*; literally, "clean of Jews."[52] In this sense, the term served German expansionism and its strive for greater *Lebensraum*, or living space, by the Aryan master race through colonization and enslavement. Following World War II, Poles and Czechs used this sense of (reversed) ethnic cleansing in efforts to purify their countries of Germans and Ukrainians.

The conventional wisdom is that the term next resurfaced in 1981 in Yugoslav media accounts of the establishment of "ethnically clean territories" in Kosovo. It re-entered the international vocabulary in 1992 when it was used to describe policies being pursued by a variety of participants in the Yugoslav wars, presumably to create ethnically homogeneous territories. But the term had been tacitly implied after the 1967 Six-Day War by Israel's Defense Minister Moshe Dayan. Right after the war, Dayan reneged on the idea of returning territory in exchange for peace. The terms of his address left an aspiring young author Amos Oz breathless. In his polemic against the minister, he deliberately used the German translation of Dayan's Hebrew term "living space"—that is, "Lebensraum," Nazi Germany's pretext for expansion and atrocities in occupied Eastern Europe. It was a term that should have raised harrowing memories, particularly in Israel. Yet Dayan relied on it as a pretext for colonization. As Oz saw it:

Living space means one thing: disenfranchising the foreigner, the inferior "savage" and making place for the superior and the civilized—the powerful....
Not for that did we fight.... The expression "living space" defiles our war.[53]

When the idea of living space was coupled with that of national security and the dream of Greater Israel and subsequently linked with Jewish supremacy doctrines and the Messianic far-right, demands for Palestinian expulsions grew more popular.

During the drafting of the Genocide Convention, there were also efforts by the U.S., Canada and Sweden to move the entire Article 3 from the Convention, putting it beyond the purview of international law. After all, its key clauses supported punishment for genocidal activities that were a part of the history of the colonial settler states, including genocide; conspiracy to commit genocide; direct and public incitement to commit genocide; attempt to commit genocide; and complicity in genocide. The attempts to eject such activities from the Convention were deflected by the vocal opposition of Pakistan, which saw Article 3 as vital to the millions of Muslims who faced massacres and cultural extinction in India. These lethal massacres ensued after the British Partition, as did ethnic cleansing and massacres in the British Mandatory Palestine. Hence, the strong opposition by Pakistan, Egypt and Syria after Israel's unilateral declaration of independence in May 1948.

Although "ethnic cleansing" has been characterized as a euphemism for genocide by scholars, it was eventually excluded from the Convention—but not without a debate. In the Sixth Committee of the General Assembly, Syria proposed an amendment to the definition of genocide corresponding closely to the contemporary notion of ethnic cleansing. The proposed amendment read: "imposing measures intended to oblige members of a group to abandon their homes in order to escape the threat of subsequent ill-treatment." The Syrian representative said "[t]he problem of refugees and displaced persons to which his delegation's proposal referred had arisen at the end of the Second World War and remained extremely acute." Yugoslavia supported the amendment, citing the Nazi displacement of Slav populations from a part of Yugoslavia in an effort to consolidate a German majority. "That action was tantamount to the deliberate destruction of a group," said the Yugoslav delegate. "Genocide could be committed by forcing members of a group to abandon their homes." Yet, these efforts were quickly buried by the U.S. and the UK. The former argued the Syrian proposal "deviated too much from the original concept of genocide," whereas the UK acknowledged seriousness of the problem but claimed the amendment "did not fall within the definition of genocide." Ultimately, the Syrian amendment was resoundingly defeated.[54]

But why this exclusion? Ostensibly, the U.S. and UK interventions were about definitional issues. But if they are viewed from the standpoint of perceived interests, the ensuing picture looks quite different. In addition to the ethnic expulsions of Palestinians, the induced flight and expulsion of Germans toward the end of World War II and the postwar period (1944–50) compelled millions of people, both ethnic Germans and German citizens, to be moved from Central and Eastern Europe. By 1950, about 12 million Germans—14.6 million, according to the West German government—had fled or been expelled from east-central Europe into Allied-occupied Germany and Austria. The largest numbers came from former eastern territories of Germany ceded to Poland and the Soviet Union (7 million) and from Czechoslovakia (3 million).[55] As Alfred de Zayas has argued in *A Terrible Revenge*, unlike the Nazi atrocities, the fate of the displaced Germans remains less known. All over Eastern Europe, the inhabitants of these communities were either expelled or killed. More than two million Germans did not survive.[56] Officially, of course, these expulsions were supposed to be "orderly and humane." Yet, it was the largest recorded episode of what is today known as "ethnic cleansing."[57]

The UK had somewhat similar reasons to suppress the idea of ethnic cleansing as a prelude to genocide and mass atrocities. As the British Empire began to crumble in the postwar era, London engineered several partition plans, most prominently in both Mandatory Palestine (Israel/Arabs) and colonial India (India/Pakistan). In the former case, these plans sparked waves of ethnic cleansing and mass atrocities, multiple wars and extraordinary regional escalation. In the latter case, an estimated 12 to 20 million people were displaced along religious lines sparking massive refugee crises and large-scale violence causing the deaths of up to 2 million people.[58] In both cases, inter-state and inter-communal tensions prevail even today, as do mass atrocities. Like Washington, London had ample reasons to decouple "ethnic cleansing" from "genocide." In addition to their documented quest to suppress, dilute and undermine legal pursuits to fully execute the original, broader goals of the Genocide Convention, the U.S. and the UK sought to maintain the disconnect between the two terms. In brief, the definitional debate was the public façade of the proverbial iceberg.

Furthermore, even as the drafting process was taking place, Palestinians were being subjected to expulsions and thus to "ethnic cleansing" in areas that became the new state of Israel.[59] Indeed, the Egyptian delegate noted that there were genocides "being committed in the Holy Land," and "certain metropolitan powers in non-self-governing territories . . . were attempting to substitute their own culture for the ancient one respected by the local population." The Egyptian delegation argued that the Convention should be able to hold more than states and state leaders responsible for committing genocide, offering as proof accounts of Zionist massacres in Palestinian villages before May 1948, prior to the establishment of the state of Israel.[60] Toward the end of that year, the *New York Times* published an open letter condemning the Israeli terrorist groups—Irgun and Stern (whose leaders, Menachem Begin and Yitzhak Shamir respectively would serve as prime ministers from the late 1970s to the early 1990s) as being behind the massacre in Deir Yassin—and associating their methods, organization, politics and appeal with that of "the Nazi and Fascist parties." The letter's signatories included physicist Albert Einstein and philosopher Hannah Arendt.[61]

Ethnic Cleansing as a Path to Genocide

The drafters of the Convention did not believe that mass displacements of population from one region to another constituted genocide. However, they did seem to think that such displacements could "become genocide if the occupation were attended by such circumstances as to lead to the death of the whole or part of the displaced population (if, for example, people were driven from their homes and forced to travel long distances in a country where they were exposed to starvation, thirst, heat, cold and epidemics)."[62] The implication was that ethnic cleansing could be codified as genocide only after it had first happened—that is, *ex post facto*—which undermined the very objective of the Convention to prevent such tragedies in the first place.

In the 1970s, South African apartheid was declared a crime against humanity, defined by the Apartheid Convention as "inhuman acts committed for the purpose of establishing and maintaining domination by one racial group of persons over any other racial group of persons and systematically oppressing them."[63] Yet, as human rights experts have noted, certain practices of apartheid should be characterized as genocide, including (a) the institution of crowded and impoverished group areas ("Bantustan policies"); (b) restrictions of mobility; (c) population policies favoring lower birth rates among the underprivileged, but favoring immigration of ruling population; (d) imprisonment and ill-treatment of the political leaders of the underprivileged group; (e) killing the underprivileged through tied labor.[64] Except for the last one, many of these apartheid characteristics have long described the role of Palestinians in the West Bank as well.[65]

What complicates *legal* accounts of ethnic expulsions are the elusive terms used to understand them. *Crimes against humanity* feature systematic attacks against civilians involving inhumane means, such as extermination, forcible population transfer, torture, rape, and disappearances. *War crimes* are grave breaches of the Geneva Convention including willful killing, willfully causing great suffering or serious injury, extensive destruction and appropriation of property, and torture. *Ethnic cleansing* is the removal of a particular group of people from a state or region using such means as forced migration and/or mass killing.[66] Nonetheless, ethnic cleansing is not defined as an atrocity crime under the Rome Statute of the International Criminal Court. However, Article 7 of the Statute, which outlines crimes against humanity, includes as one of its listed acts "deportation or forcible transfer of population." And that is understood to mean "forced displacement of the persons concerned by expulsion or other coercive acts from the area in which they are lawfully present."[67]

The brutal realities of ethnic cleansing were re-evoked with gusto during the Yugoslav wars when many commentators were inclined to equate them with genocide and when a UN General Assembly resolution in 1992 also evoked "the abhorrent policy of 'ethnic cleansing,' which is a form of genocide."[68] This contrasted with the 1948 Genocide Convention that had explicitly rejected the equation. Understandably, the delegates sought words for the horror they sensed, but as they failed to confront the legacy of the 1948 rejection, their resolution proved hollow and ineffectual.

In October 1992, the report of the Commission of Experts, appointed by the Security Council to examine violations of international humanitarian law in the former Yugoslavia, stated that the practices of ethnic cleansing "constitute crimes against humanity and can be assimilated to specific war crimes. Furthermore, such acts could also fall within the meaning of the Genocide Convention."[69] Nonetheless, a year after the Rome Statute, reflecting the ambivalence of the Prosecutor on genocide charges, Slobodan Milosevic and four of his colleagues were indicted for crimes against humanity with respect to the ethnic cleansing of Kosovo, but not for genocide.[70] Initially, even the judges appeared distressed by the Prosecutor's prudence, criticizing the reluctance to describe "ethnic cleansing" for what it was; that is, the crime of genocide. The Tribunal even proposed the indictment could be reconsidered. But oddly enough, in the first genocide cases to go to trial, "the judges of the trial chambers were unsatisfied with the evidence of a campaign to physically exterminate Bosnian Muslims as a group, and dismissed the charges of genocide," as William Schabas subsequently noted. "Such activities might have been 'ethnic cleansing' but they were not, apparently, genocide."[71]

Typically, ethnic expulsions are included as a distinct category of mass atrocity, despite the absence of a formal legal definition. Collectively, legal scholars refer to these crimes, including ethnic cleansing, as atrocity crimes; that is, *mass atrocities*.

So, is "ethnic cleansing" genocide or one of its forms, as some have long argued? In his analysis, William Schabas took a pragmatic stance:

> The crime of genocide is aimed at the intentional destruction of an ethnic group. "Ethnic cleansing" would seem to be targeted at something different, the expulsion of a group with a view to encouraging or at least tolerating its survival elsewhere. Yet ethnic cleansing may well have the effect of rendering the continued existence of a group impossible, thereby effecting its destruction. In other words, forcible deportation may achieve the same result as extermination camps. But there is strong evidence that at least in the early years of the development of the concept of a crime of genocide, the forced expulsion, transfer or deportation that we now describe as "ethnic cleansing" was not meant to be included within the definition.[72]

On the other hand, in light of Lemkin's broader definition of colonial genocide—the one that Western powers suppressed and diluted—ethnic cleansing seems to be typical of an early phase of genocide, which is characterized by "destruction of the national pattern of the oppressed group," followed by "the imposition of the national pattern of the oppressor. This imposition, in turn, may be made upon the oppressed population which is allowed to remain, or upon the territory alone, after removal of the population and the colonization of the area by the oppressor's own nationals."[73]

In this view, ethnic cleansing and genocide are neither identical nor is one a form of the other. Rather, they are two manifestations of different phases in the historical process of genocide. While this broad definition was diluted in the drafters' final definition of the Genocide Convention, it was central to the way Lemkin defined genocide as a historical, essentially colonial process of displacement, dispossession and devastation.

Genocidal Acts and Punishable Crimes

In his *Axis Rule in Occupied Europe*, Raphael Lemkin outlined several "techniques of genocide in various fields": physical and biological, political, social, cultural, religious, economic and moral. Building on a broad definition, he stressed acts of genocide directed at these various aspects of the life of a group.[74] This broad view of genocide was still reflected in the original draft convention by Saudi Arabia, an eager proponent of the draft in late 1946.

But for all practical purposes—following the adoption of General Assembly Resolution 96(I) in late 1946—it became obvious that international consensus on the scope of genocide would be significantly narrower.

In the process, Lemkin's reference to culture and cultural genocide fell victim to an association between genocide and homicide stressing the physical dimension. In criminal law, analysis of an offense builds on a basic distinction between the physical element (the *actus reus*) and the mental element (the *mens rea*). The prosecution must prove specific material facts and establish the accused's criminal intent or "guilty mind." Similarly, the definition of genocide in the 1948 Convention separates the two elements. The Article 2 addresses the mental side of the crime of genocide, that is, the "intent to destroy, in whole or in part, a national, ethnical, racial or religious group, as such." The five subparagraphs, in turn, list the criminal acts (Figure 4-8).[75]

Effective since 1951, Article 2 of the Genocide Convention (Resolution 260, III) defined genocide by certain *acts with intent*:

... any of the following acts committed with intent to destroy, in whole or in part, a national, ethnical, racial or religious group, as such:

(a) Killing members of the group; Causing serious bodily or mental harm to members of the group;

(b) Deliberately inflicting on the group conditions of life calculated to bring about its physical destruction in whole or in part;

(c) Imposing measures intended to prevent births within the group;

(d) Forcibly transferring children of the group to another group.[76]

Article 3 of the Genocide Convention focuses on criminal participation, such as accomplices, and incomplete or inchoate offences, such as attempts and conspiracy. It defined the *punishable crimes* under the convention:

(a) Genocide;

(b) Conspiracy to commit genocide;

(c) Direct and public incitement to commit genocide;

(d) Attempt to commit genocide;

(e) Complicity in genocide.[77]

Figure 4-8. The Genocide Convention (1951)

278	*United Nations — Treaty Series*	1951

No. 1021. CONVENTION[1] ON THE PREVENTION AND
PUNISHMENT OF THE CRIME OF GENOCIDE.
ADOPTED BY THE GENERAL ASSEMBLY OF THE
UNITED NATIONS ON 9 DECEMBER 1948

THE CONTRACTING PARTIES,

HAVING CONSIDERED the declaration made by the General Assembly of the
United Nations in its resolution 96 (I) dated 11 December 1946[2] that genocide
is a crime under international law, contrary to the spirit and aims of the United
Nations and condemned by the civilized world;

RECOGNIZING that at all periods of history genocide has inflicted great
losses on humanity; and

BEING CONVINCED that, in order to liberate mankind from such an odious
scourge, international co-operation is required,

HEREBY AGREE AS HEREINAFTER PROVIDED:

---

[1] Came into force on 12 January 1951, the ninetieth day following the date of deposit of the
twentieth instrument of ratification or accession, in accordance with article XIII.

The following States deposited with the Secretary-General of the United Nations their instruments
of ratification or accession on the dates indicated:

Ratifications	*Accessions*
AUSTRALIA . . . . 8 July 1949	*BULGARIA . . . . 21 July 1950
By a notification received on 8 July 1949 the	CAMBODIA . . . . 14 October 1950
Government of Australia extended the ap-	CEYLON . . . . 12 October 1950
plication of the Convention to all terri-	COSTA RICA . . . . . . 14 October 1950
tories for the conduct of whose foreign	JORDAN . . . . 3 April 1950
relations Australia is responsible.	KOREA . . . . 14 October 1950
*Czechoslovakia . . . . . 21 December 1950	LAOS . . . . 8 December 1950
ECUADOR. . . . . 21 December 1950	*MONACO . . . . 30 March 1950
EL SALVADOR . . . . . . 28 September 1950	*POLAND . . . . 14 November 1950
ETHIOPIA . . . . 1 July 1949	*ROMANIA . . . . 2 November 1950
FRANCE . . . . 14 October 1950	SAUDI ARABIA. . . . . . 13 July 1950
GUATEMALA . . . . . . 13 January 1950	TURKEY . . . . 31 July 1950
HAITI . . . . 14 October 1950	VIET-NAM . . . . 11 August 1950
ICELAND . . . . 29 August 1949	
ISRAEL . . . . 9 March 1950	
LIBERIA . . . . 9 June 1950	
NORWAY . . . . 22 July 1949	
PANAMA . . . . 11 January 1950	
*PHILIPPINES . . . . . . 7 July 1950	
YUGOSLAVIA . . . . . 29 August 1950	

* With reservations. For text of reservations, see pp. 314-322 of this volume.

[2] United Nations, document A/64/Add. 1. 31 January 1947.

SOURCE: *UN*

A central aspect of the Convention is the "intent to destroy." It is the
mens rea. For an act to be classified as genocide according to the Convention,
it must be demonstrated that the perpetrators have a deliberate and specific
intent to physically destroy the group, based on its real or perceived national-
ity, ethnicity, race, or religion. If that intent is not established, the act remains

punishable, but not as genocide, but likely as a crime against humanity or a crime under ordinary criminal law. Intent is challenging for prosecutors to prove because offenders avoid leaving recorded statements about their intent, although courts sometimes seek to ascribe intent based on other factors.[78] Offenders also portray their acts as efforts to remove a group from a given territory rather than as an act of destruction, or argue that genocidal acts were collateral damage of military activity (the "war is war" argument).[79]

There has been a longstanding debate on whether Lemkin meant special intent constituted prior intent evident in the psychological state of the perpetrator (*dolus specialis*); or as conditional intent, where intent is constituted by the act (*dolus eventualis*). For all practical purposes, Lemkin seems to have implied conditional intent; that is, the net effect. As a lawyer, he knew that the emphasis on intention would be more challenging to prosecute. So, to him genocidal intent was mainly a juridical issue rather than a philosophical question.[80] In *Axis Rule*, Lemkin stressed intent less than effect. The spotlight was on the fact that groups of people were being destroyed; not on the level of intention behind the act.

As the drafters of the Convention argued, war may fall outside the scope of genocide because it is—or should be—directed at the total destruction of the enemy *combatants*. However, when non-combatants become targets, the situation changes:

War may, however, be accompanied by the crime of genocide. This happens when one of the belligerents aims at exterminating the population of enemy territory and systematically destroys what are not genuine military objectives. Examples of this are the execution of prisoners of war, the massacre of the populations of occupied territory and their gradual extermination. These are clearly cases of genocide.[81]

Such a characterization could serve as a shorthand—but not as a full definition of what will here be called the Obliteration Doctrine. But it is largely Article 2 that has been used in the scrutiny of Israel's atrocities in the Gaza Strip, whereas Article 3 and the complicity issues it raises has been widely suppressed.

Nonetheless, during the four long decades of the Cold War, the genocide cases were purposely ignored. This is particularly distressing in light of the fact that, as the ICJ has commented, there is no explicit temporal limitation in the Genocide Convention to prevent it from having a retroactive effect.[82] In theory at least, the Convention made it possible to prosecute cases that were contemporary and cases that weren't.

What compounds the complexities associated with genocidal acts and punishable crimes is the deep wedge that the Gaza War has driven between the two groups of genocide scholars. One sees Jewish genocide during World War II—the Holocaust—as unique and exceptional. This narrative has been promoted by Jewish Holocaust scholars (Yehuda Bauer, Emil Fackenheim, Saul Friedländer) and their more recent offspring (Deborah Lipstadt, Danie Goldhagen, Lucy Dawidowicz). Another group of scholars depicts Jewish genocide as distinctive yet typical to a history of genocides, marked by colonial beginnings. In the postwar era, it was typified by political philosopher Hannah Arendt who associated Israel with colonial settler domination.[83] This group of scholars underscores the affinities of Jewish genocide with historical and colonial mass atrocities (Dirk Moses, Omer Bartov, William Schabas, John Docker).[84]

Nonetheless, Raphael Lemkin's inclusive view of genocide convention can only be aligned with a narrative that, like Lemkin himself, sees Jewish genocide as a unique yet typical component of genocides in history, overshadowed by settler colonialism.

Toward a More Inclusive Genocide Convention

Times did not favor Lemkin's original draft for Genocide Convention in the late 1940s, when its main supporters were countries of the Global South and large international women's organizations. The Dutch were still struggling to undermine the independence of Indonesia. The French resorted to extraordinary brutality to retain their supremacy in Indochina (Vietnam, Cambodia, Laos). The United Kingdom would not agree to decolonization until the "winds of change" took over after 1960. And Belgium, in cooperation with other colonial powers and the United States, fought the Congolese independence struggle even then. In parallel, the United States was effectively filling the vacuum left by the former European colonial powers, from Indonesia and the Korean Peninsula to Southeast Asia and across Africa. Since the U.S.-led Western powers could not bury the Convention, they did what they could to weaken and dilute it.

Following the end of the Cold War, there have been some ad hoc tribunals and the International Criminal Court (ICC) does exist. Although even a torso of the original Convention is better than nothing, Lemkin's original broader definition merits a new scrutiny. But how could his goals be fully realized today?

Restoration of Lemkin's Broader Convention Definition. This venue could restart the arduous though necessary project to restore the broad approach to genocide, as defined by Lemkin's original draft. The objective would be to include the key aspects of genocide as these are known in history, particularly, the notions of cultural genocide and political killings, and ethnic cleansing. It is an initiative that would cause much noble posturing, bitter divides and leverage ploys. Yet, making the process public could spark a new interest in historical wrongs that have never been corrected—and that climaxed in the atrocities of Gaza.

Adding an Optional Protocol. Typically, human rights treaties are followed by "Optional Protocols" which provide for procedures with regard to the treaty or address a substantive area related to the treaty. Optional Protocols to human rights treaties are seen as treaties in their own right, and are open to signature, accession or ratification by countries who are party to the main treaty. In the case of the Elimination of All Forms of Discrimination Against Women (CEDAW), the Optional Protocols did evolve between the mid-1970s and the 1990s.[85] In the process, such optional protocols were said to be needed particularly for "serious international crimes" such as apartheid and racial discrimination. If that was the case already half a century ago, why should these protocols not be adopted today in the case of Genocide Convention itself?

There is a caveat, however. These protocols are called "optional" because they are not automatically binding on the states which have ratified the original treaty. It is up to each state to decide whether or not it wants to be bound by an Optional Protocol. If it wants to be bound then it must ratify the Optional Protocol. Those countries that wanted to dilute the original convention may speak eloquently for the protocols, but are unlikely to ratify them.

Joint Intervention. In late 2023, half a dozen Western states filed a joint application before the International Court of Justice (ICJ)—not the ICC—arguing for a full and expansive understanding of genocide.[86] Legal scholars have regarded this intervention as important because of "how it interprets past genocide cases, and in terms of what this could mean for the ICJ's future determinations regarding states' commission of genocide."[87] Canada, Denmark, France, Germany, the Netherlands and the UK made their intervention, as it is legally called, regarding the genocide case The Gambia filed against Myanmar in 2019. The case revolves around the violent expulsion of the Rohingya people from Myanmar into Bangladesh. The intervention argues that genocide concerns "destruction," which need not be death. According to the current Genocide Convention, killing is not a necessary aspect of genocide and other forms of violence may also be genocidal. Indeed, Lemkin's original notion of cultural genocide makes this point most explicitly. Moreover, the intervention focuses on how sexual and gender-based crime can contribute to a finding of genocide. It seeks to link these crimes to the intent standard in the crime of genocide, and to standard of the group destruction. Furthermore, the intervention argues that the threshold for how genocide is constituted should be lowered when considering crimes against children because they are more vulnerable and such crimes can define generations. These arguments would seem to highlight atrocities in Gaza because up to 70 percent of the tens of thousands who perished and almost 120,000 of those who were injured and maimed were women and children.

What makes the joint intervention typical to past cases is that, once again, the Western countries target some of the poorest developing countries. All six are former colonial powers. The Gambia itself is a former British and French colony.[88] Myanmar, along with India and Pakistan, resulted from the British partition of the Indian Empire and the secession from Pakistan, somewhat as Israel and Palestine ensued from the partition of British Mandatory Palestine. In the early 2020s, all of these six Western countries were struggling with anti-immigration sentiments and various degrees of Islamophobia, yet each was presumably eager to support the Rohingya in their fight for survival. Had they experienced an overnight change of heart? Hardly.

Military crackdowns of the Rohingya have taken place since 1978, 1991–1992, 2012, 2015, and particularly in 2016–2018, when most of Myanmar's Rohingya were expelled into neighboring Bangladesh, as a result of what has been called ethnic cleansing that could amount to crimes against humanity, and an unfolding genocide.[89] Yet, the Western countries filed their case only half a decade later. Most of them supported Myanmar's National Unity Government (NUG) seeking to overthrow the junta, which made the joint intervention one instrument to reinforce NUG amid its armed struggle. Perhaps some of these countries were positioning for post-junta Myanmar which remains rich in minerals, including metal ores, petroleum, and natural gas, and has significant deposits of precious and semiprecious stones. Furthermore, these Western states did not express interest in applying the implications of their intervention in the case of Gaza, which was burning when they expressed their moral disgust over Myanmar's persecution of the Rohingya. Perhaps one motivation for this reluctance was the fact that they were also among Israel's arms suppliers and thereby complicit in the mass atrocities in Gaza.

Nonetheless, the importance of the joint intervention goes beyond the motives of its initiators. What makes it significant is that it realized the *erga omnes* jurisdictional mandate of the Genocide Convention. This mandate makes all state parties to the Convention responsible for genocide prevention everywhere around the world. The Gambian case against Myanmar is the first time that the Convention was raised between two unrelated states rather than states in conflict with each other. In this way, it opened still another possible venue to expand Genocide Convention in a manner that would bring it closer to Lemkin's original broader definition.

* * *

Nonetheless, if genocide politics has narrowed the definition of Genocide Convention, the question remains, why has its enforcement also proved sparse and selective since the Cold War?

CHAPTER 5

INADEQUATE ENFORCEMENT OF THE GENOCIDE CONVENTION

L emkin's quest to bring into being the Genocide Convention was motivated in large part by the inadequacies of the Nuremberg Trials. Until then, the prosecution of war crimes had been restricted to cases where the victims were residents in occupied territories. Horrified by the Nazi concentration camps, the Nuremberg Trials prosecutors seemed to go beyond such limitations but not without strings attached. Effectively, "they were holding the Germans accountable for atrocities committed against Germans but resisting a more general principle that might hold them responsible for atrocities perpetrated within their own borders or in their colonies." The failure to appropriately criminalize crimes against humanity mirrored, as genocide scholar William Schabas has argued, the foundational ambiguities of the Charter of the United Nations, adopted in June 1945. The latter pledged to promote respect for human rights, even as it pledged that "the UN would not intervene in matters which were 'essentially within the domestic jurisdiction of any state.'"[1]

Origins of the International Criminal Tribunals

In the long view, the origins of international criminal prosecutions can be dated, as some scholars do, from the medieval precedents of the Holy Roman Empire. However, *modern* international tribunals evolved with the onset of the modern international system. Effectively, genocide tribunals should have ensued with 1904–1908 and the Herero and Nama genocide; that is, a campaign of ethnic extermination and collective punishment conducted in German South West Africa (now Namibia). It is often recognized as the first genocide in the 20th century, which featured genocidal atrocities, massacres, starvation, extermination through forced labor, but also starvation and human experimentation.[2] With up to 100,000 Herero deaths and 10,000

Nama killed, it set a rough template for the subsequent path from colonialism to Auschwitz and Gaza. The horrific extermination was well known at the time, including the medical experimentation (Figure 5-1)

Figure 5-1. Herero and Nama:
The First Genocide in the 20th Century

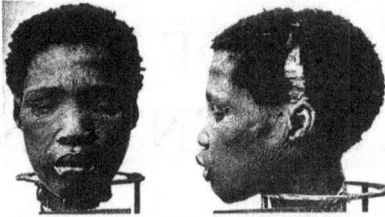

[Above] Head of Shark Island prisoner used for medical experimentation.

[Right] Political cartoon from the German socialist magazine Der Wahre Jakob (1906): "Even if it hasn't brought in much profit and there are no better-quality goods on offer, at least we can use it to set up a bone-grinding plant."

SOURCE: *Wikimedia*

The effort to set up an international criminal ad hoc tribunal arose during World War I and its aftermath. In May 1915, diplomatic sources reported on the Armenian population being massacred in the Ottoman Empire, issuing a warning to the crumbling power.[3] Unsurprisingly, this first reference in international relations to crimes against humanity was motivated by both concern and geopolitics. Following the hostilities, the Germans, also defeated in the war, were similarly supposed to be prosecuted in a "special tribunal" of five judges, representing the victors; that is, the United States, Britain, France, Italy and Japan. Yet, neither the prosecution nor the tribunal ever materialized. Instead, Kaiser Wilhelm rushed to the Netherlands where he obtained asylum. The Dutch refused to extradite the accused arguing that this would mean "retroactive punishment"; a concept that the victors of World War II eventually revised.[4]

Nonetheless, the Great War, as World War I was initially known, was a massive shock to European sensibility. This, the deadliest conflict in history, resulted in an estimated 10 million military dead, more than 20 million wounded, coupled with the deaths of 10 million civilians. During the interwar period several international bodies, most of them unofficial, reviewed proposals for a permanent international criminal court. The League of Nations eventually adopted an agreement aiming at the creation of such a court. But in history, as in all dramatic arts, timing matters. And by 1937, time had run out.

The United States never joined the League and its credibility had been fragile from the start. With the rise of the far-right in Europe and Asia, Germany and Japan (1933), Italy (1937) and Spain (1939) left the League while the Soviet Union, which had joined in 1934, was expelled half a decade later. In the Atlantic Charter (1941), Churchill threatened to hold the Nazi leadership responsible for what he called "the crime without a name." By October 1943, Roosevelt, Stalin, and Churchill spoke in the Moscow Declarations of "evidence of atrocities, massacres and cold-blooded mass executions which are being perpetrated by Hitlerite forces in many of the countries they have overrun and from which they are now being steadily expelled."[5] The Statement on Atrocities, the fourth Moscow Declaration, was largely drafted by Winston Churchill, and led to the setting up of the European Advisory Commission which drafted the London Charter. Though these three powerful leaders had flirted with the idea of summary executions of Nazi leaders, they ultimately opted for tribunals to deliver justice. These had been promised at Versailles in 1919. It was time to set them up.

The Nuremberg Tribunals

It was with the Nuremberg trials following World War II that ad hoc tribunals focusing on criminal cases against individuals were established to deal with major international crimes. Encompassing a series of parallel and follow-up trials, coupled with denazification procedures, these consolidated the criminal justice model as the main instrument in the Allies' dealing with postwar Germany. Nonetheless, the Tribunal's jurisdiction was restricted to three primary categories: crimes against peace, war crimes, and crimes against humanity. A fourth category, the conspiracy charge, made leaders, organizers, instigators, and accomplices who participated in development or implementation of a common plan or conspiracy to commit any of the other crimes individually responsible, but it was always linked to one of the three indicated crimes. It was only subsequently that the Genocide Convention—particularly its Article 2 that defined the genocidal acts and Article 3 that defined the role of complicity and conspiracy in those acts—incorporated both genocide and conspiracy as the fourth category of these "unimaginable atrocities."

As U.S. Chief Prosecutor at Nuremberg, judge Robert H. Jackson stated in his aspirational opening statement that all state leaders were subject to the rule of law:

We are able to do away with domestic tyranny and violence and aggression by those in power against the rights of their own people only when we make all men answerable to the law.[6]

Between November 1945 and October 1946—at the eve of the inception of the U.S. security state and the Cold War—the International Military Tribunal (IMT) in Nuremberg tried 22 of important surviving Nazi leaders in German politics, military, and its economy, and six German organizations. The IMT verdict proclaimed the crime of plotting and waging aggressive war "the supreme international crime."[7] At the time, the retroactive criminalization of aggression was considered controversial. So, holding these individuals responsible for violations of international law is considered "the true beginning of international criminal law." The genocide played a central role in the creation of the IMT, but the Tribunal did not sentence a single Nazi leader for "intent to destroy, in whole or in part, a national, ethnical, racial or religious group, as such." This was the great deficit of justice that Lemkin hoped to overcome.

In the United States, 12 further trials were conducted against mainly lower-level perpetrators, which focused more on the Holocaust.[8] Nonetheless, at the same time, both the Pentagon and the just-created Central Intelligence Agency (CIA), the successor of the OSS, engaged in large-scale naturalization of major Nazi scientists, military officials, politicians and industrialists, to exploit their presumed skills, use them as spies and rally them against the Soviet Union in the Cold War. The most prominent of these activities was Operation Paperclip, the secret U.S. intelligence program from 1945 to 1959, which brought to America more than 1,600 German scientists and engineers.[9] The group included Wernher von Braun, a member of the Nazi Party and *Allgemeine* SS, the leading figure in the development of rocket technology, and later a pioneer of rocket and space technology in America whose team was assimilated into NASA. The genocidist rose to the top of the U.S. military-industrial complex (Figure 5-2).

As America became a safe haven for Nazis, they were used to consolidate the new national security state and to make the world safe for American capitalism. It had a "destructive impact on [U.S.] domestic and foreign policy," ultimately reflecting "American ambivalence about the military-industrial complex and the viability of an 'ends justifies the means' solution to external threats."[10]

Figure 5-2. Genocidists in Cold War America

Wearing his Nazi badge, Von Braun with Fritz Todt, the founder of a military-engineering organisation that supplied German industry with forced labor across occupied Europe.

Von Braun with President Dwight D. Eisenhower, 1960. The happy times followed the 1957 Sputnik crisis, when von Braun was given key role in the design of space rockets.

SOURCE: *Wikipedia (Bundesarchiv and NASA/Marshall Space Flight Center)*

As the onset of the Cold War ensured generous denazification, which amounted to a sort of covert amnesty, the establishment of the Federal Republic of Germany in 1949 meant putting the past to rest.[11] Chancellor Konrad Adenauer initiated a policy of reconciliation with the West, aligning Germany with the U.S. Cold War against the Soviet Union and reparations for Israel and the Jews, fostering Israel's fragile economy at a challenging moment of its early history.[12] These moves set the stage for a *de facto* blanket amnesty, while war criminals sentenced prior to 1949 were released. The amnesties were completed by the mid-1950s, both in Germany and in the European countries that had been occupied by the Nazi regime. What followed was a mood of "collective amnesia."[13] In the mid-1950s the takeaway from the Nuremberg Trial attributed solely to Hitler and his inner circle all responsibilities for the crimes of the Nazi regime. The painful effort to regain collective memories was re-ignited only in the 1960s, fueled as it was by three important trials: the 1961 Eichmann trial in Jerusalem and the 1963–65 Auschwitz and 1975–81 Majdanek trials in Germany. The importance of the trials was mainly due to the fact that for the first time they made the victims visible and heard in Germany. If justice in Jerusalem could still be ignored, that was no longer the case with the Auschwitz trial, the "key event"[14] that hit the message home for German society, particularly for the younger generation—as illustrated by the critically-acclaimed, *The Interpreter of Silence* (2023), the German historical TV miniseries.

Germany was not alone with its lingering collective amnesia. In the aftermath of World War II, Washington's reverse course also led the Western partners of its wartime anti-Nazi alliance to recruit of many of Hitler's mass killers into the anti-communist cause after 1945. In the early Cold War, Britain, France and the United States put numerous war criminals on the payroll of their intelligence services, presumably to contain communism. In effect, years before the Nuremberg Trial got under way, whole detachments of Nazi collaborators from the occupied territories of Central Europe (Yugoslavia, Hungary, Czechoslovakia, Romania) and Eastern Europe (Ukraine, Byelorussia, the Baltic states, Russia) had been rounded up and recruited by the West. These initiatives included *Operation Shrapnel* by the British secret intelligence service and the U.S. spy agency's *Pica* network (officially Project Huntington). They were mainly used as anti-communist guerrillas in their former homelands and as intelligence agents to assist Western operations to topple Soviet supremacy in the region. In parallel, Western intelligence hid accused war criminals from the Allied teams, who were hunting them to bring them to justice, while collaborating with the Vatican to smuggle many of them to Argentina and other South American nations where they would foster the subsequent Operation Condor networks. Toward the end of World War II, the Nazis used the "ratline" to escape the advancing Red Army to Genoa, with the support of some in the Vatican. Subsequently, U.S. Intelligence relied on ratlines to remove certain Nazi strategists and scientists via Spain to Argentina and elsewhere in South America.[15] While Western nations initiated important humanitarian immigration programs to millions of refugees in postwar Western Europe, they also lent a helping hand to large numbers of Nazi mass killers, making them citizens. "Many were then promptly put on the payroll of the domestic counter-intelligence services in their adopted homelands," Mark Aarons concludes. "For the next 35 years, the Governments of the United States, Canada, Britain, Australia and New Zealand lied about the Nazis they had knowingly allowed to settle in their cities and towns."[16]

It was only when declassified intelligence and diplomatic files surfaced in the mid-to-late 1970s and 1980s that the truth emerged on this particular dark side of Western history with far-belated efforts to bring a few of the genocidists to justice. The failure to deal with known perpetrators has been repeated again and with other atrocity perpetrators. Nonetheless, though the "civilizing influence" of the Nuremberg trial took several decades to materialize, some observers hope today's international landscape may facilitate faster justice:

> The Nuremberg Trial was conducted in a perpetrators' environment, and allowed the perpetrators to feel as victims. Today,

victims are present and have a voice. This contributes to more unambiguous moral messages and clarification.[17]

But as the genocidal atrocities in Gaza after October 7 attest, even if victims are present and have a voice, that is no assurance that they will be seen and heard.

The Tokyo Tribunal

Between 1946 and 1948, the Nuremberg Trials were followed by the International Military Tribunal for the Far East, or the Tokyo Trial, legislatively a slightly modified version of the Nuremberg statute. It lasted twice as long as its German precursor. Building on the Nuremberg Charter, 28 high-ranking Japanese military and political leaders were tried by the court. They were charged with 55 separate counts, including waging wars of aggression, murder, and various war crimes and crimes against humanity. Thousands of other "lesser" war criminals were tried by domestic tribunals in Asia and the Pacific by Allied nations, with most concluding by 1949. Like in Nuremberg, none of the leaders of Imperial Japan were charged for genocidal atrocities, despite the racial Yamato doctrine; the ideological foundation of Japanese war crimes in East and Southeast Asia that remained hidden until the 1980s.[18]

Evidence that would incriminate Emperor Hirohito and his family was simply excluded from the Tribunal. In this insulation, MacArthur's point man was Brigadier General Bonner Frank Fellers, an ex-OSS operative who had also served as director of psychological warfare. As liaison between the HQ and the Imperial Household, Fellers authored influential memoranda arguing that keeping Emperor Hirohito in place would benefit the occupation, Japan's reconstruction and U.S. long-term interests. Meeting with the major defendants of the Tokyo tribunal, Fellers was assigned to coordinate their stories basically to exonerate Hirohito and all members of his family of war crimes. Codenamed "Operation Blacklist," Fellers worked for MacArthur, who rejected the idea of the prosecution of the Emperor or his family.[19] The Supreme Commander for the Allied Powers, U.S. General Douglas MacArthur, believed the U.S. needed Emperor Hirohito to maintain stability in Japan and to achieve the postwar *reverse course;* that is. the shift of the occupation policy from the demilitarization and democratization of Japan to its economic reconstruction and remilitarization to support U.S. Cold War goals in Asia.

Even before the war crimes trials convened, the prosecution representatives and court officials worked behind the scenes to prevent the imperial family from being indicted and to skew the testimony of the defendants, to ensure the exoneration of the emperor.[20] Three justices wrote a legal opinion about the criminal responsibility of Hirohito. "No ruler can commit the crime of launching aggressive war and then validly claim to be excused for doing so because his life would otherwise have been in danger," as Judge-in-Chief William Webb concluded.[21]

In Japanese human experiments, the Chinese victims had been routinely dehumanized and internally referred to as "logs," just as their facilities were called "log cabins." Serving the Yamato supremacy doctrine, dehumanization was central to the brutality. In Imperial Japan, Nobusuke Kishi, who later became Prime Minister, had similarly used emergency laws to enslave 1.5 million Chinese in the Japanese puppet state Manchuko, the wartime Manchuria. Legal procedures were viewed as unwarranted because the Chinese were more like dogs than human beings and would only understand force. Instead of being sentenced as a Class A war criminal, U.S. occupation authorities did not charge, try, or convict Kishi, the maternal grandfather of the subsequent PM, Shinzo Abe. The 42 suspects, including Kishi, were imprisoned to be prosecuted at a second Tokyo Tribunal. Yet, instead of being charged, they were released in 1947 and 1948. These measures skewed the sense of history in postwar Japan, but they were very much in line with the objectives of the U.S.-led West's reverse course and the Cold War. And so it was that Kishi was released in 1948 and de-purged in 1952, which made possible his election to the National *Diet* in 1953. With overt and covert U.S. support, the subsequent PM consolidated Japanese conservatives against perceived threats from the Japan Socialist Party, and in 1955 was instrumental in forming the Liberal Democratic Party (LDP), which remains Japan's dominant party.[22]

And like in Nuremberg, those war criminals whose skills could be exploited, or who could be used as spies and rally Japan against China found new jobs as U.S. partners, assets and allies in the Cold War. Thanks to U.S. interventions, the Tokyo Trials did not charge the military leaders behind Unit 731, the notorious covert biological and chemical warfare research and development unit of the Imperial Japanese Army. Between 1937 and 1945, this unit and its clones engaged in lethal human experimentation and biological weapons manufacturing. Cooperating with the Nazis, the crimes of these units were at par or exceeded the human experiments in the Nazi camps by the infamous SS officer Josef Mengele, Auschwitz's "Angel of Death."[23]

What united these experiments in Auschwitz and Unit 731 was the scientific interest in what was racially desirable and utter disregard of those seen as racially undesirable. But in the death factories of General Shirō Ishii, the science of evil went further, was more diversified and of different magnitude.

These experiments included disease injections, controlled dehydration, biological weapons testing, hypobaric pressure chamber testing, vivisection, organ harvesting, and amputation, and standard weapons testing. In Harbin, China, Unit 731 single-handedly murdered an estimated 14,000 victims featuring kidnapped Chinese males, women, children and babies born from the staff's rapes. Moreover, at least 300,000 individuals died due to infectious illnesses caused by the unit and its affiliated research facilities. It was led by General Ishii, who got an immunity deal, thanks to an intervention by the U.S. Occupation leader, General Douglas MacArthur, and was never prosecuted for any war crimes or crimes against humanity.[24]

Responsibility for the germ-warfare program extended to top Japan's government leaders and many respected scientists, all of whom escaped indictment. Instead, U.S. military intelligence in Tokyo insinuated itself into the Tokyo Trial by blocking prosecution access to key witnesses and then classifying incriminating documents. Washington decisionmakers, supported by General MacArthur, hoped to acquire Japan's biological-warfare expertise to gain an advantage over the Soviet Union. Ultimately, U.S. national-security goals left the victims of Unit 731 without vindication and historical wounds that still cry for closure.[25] (Figure 5-3) After World War II, Mengele, Auschwitz's Angel of Death, escaped justice, which was systematically obstructed by U.S. military and the CIA. Ishii, the Monster of Unit 731, could have been sentenced along with his superiors, but instead was given immunity by General MacArthur. It was all for the greater good of freedom and democracy, presumably.

Both the U.S. and Soviet Union garnered data from these units after the fall of Japan. After their collaboration, the Soviets sentenced the Japanese to Siberian labor camps for 2–25 years, whereas those captured by the U.S. were secretly given immunity. Instead of death sentences, the U.S. covered up the human experimentations, granted stipends to the perpetrators and co-opted their bioweapons knowledge for use in America's warfare program; and the knowledge was used by the Pentagon in biological and chemical weapons during the Korean War.[26] In particular, Ishii was hired by the U.S. government to lecture American officers at Fort Detrick on bioweapons and the Unit 731's "findings."[27] During the Korean War, Ishii was among the Japanese war criminals sent to Korea to participate in the U.S. Army's alleged biological warfare activities.[28]

Just as Operation Paperclip had corroded American domestic and foreign policies, so too did the cooptation of Japanese war criminals linked with the subsequent history of human experimentation in America, including the exposure of humans to chemical and biological weapons, human

Figure 5-3. How Genocidists Escape Justice

Josef Mengele, "the Angel of Death" of Auschwitz, lived happily ever after until his death hiding in São Paulo until 1986. (*Auschwitz Album*)

Shirō Ishii, the monster of the Unit 731, lived happily ever after until his death in Tokyo in 1959. (*Pacific Atrocities*)

SOURCE: *Wikimedia*

radiation experiments, injections of toxic and radioactive chemicals, surgical experiments, interrogation and torture experiments, and tests which involve mind-altering substances. Reflecting America's long interest in eugenics and segregation, many tests were performed not just on children, but on the sick, and mentally disabled, while a disproportionate share of the subjects were poor, racial minorities, and prisoners. Human experimentation has a dark history in America, but following World War II it was used systematically by the military-industrial complex.[29] The experiments included Project MK Ultra, a CIA human experimentation program by the CIA to develop drugs for interrogation and forced confessions through brainwashing and psychological torture.[30]

On the back of Nuremberg and Tokyo, there were efforts to codify norms of international criminal law and to create a permanent international tribunal. The UN International Law Commission drafted a Code of Offences Against the Peace and Security of Mankind, while scrutinizing procedural questions on the operation of an international court. But the faster the Cold War polarized the international community, the more the original enthusiasm waned. As the U.S. Congress steered the spotlight toward the Soviet massacre of Polish military and political leaders at Katyn in 1952, the remaining British and French empires were crumbling and credible reports surfaced on atrocities by colonial police and soldiers from Kenya to Algeria. In parallel, the United States was taking the mantle of the old European colonial powers in the Third World, particularly in the former French Indochina and soon committing similar genocidal atrocities that the Soviet Union eagerly spotlighted in international fora.

Victor's Justice

The *legal* argument of "victor's justice" goes back to the aftermath of the postwar International Military Tribunals (IMT). After World War II, most Germans initially thought that the IMT at Nuremberg was fair, but a few years later, following the massive ethnic cleansing of Germans from Eastern Europe, many saw it as unfair; and with the passage of time, as illegitimate victor's justice.[31] This reassessment was in part fueled by the U.S. reverse course, which turned old enemies into new allies against the Soviet Union in the Cold War, and the consequent refusal of the U.S. Army to release the Nuremberg IMT record in German for concern that it would undermine the battle against Communism.[32]

Withholding the truth and misrepresenting the realities was legitimized in the name of national security. That seems to be the common denominator of these mass atrocities from Auschwitz and Hiroshima to Vietnam and Gaza.

Subsequently, the term "victor's justice" was also used in a reassessment of the IMT in Tokyo.[33] The indiscriminate bombing of the Chinese cities, a precursor of the Obliteration Doctrine, was never raised. Due to the U.S. exoneration of the imperial family and protection of Prince Asaka as member of the imperial family, coupled with the suppression of evidence, the 1937 Nanjing Massacre, which caused the deaths of up to 200,000–300,000 civilians and prisoners of war, was not prosecuted as a genocidal atrocity but as a war crime. Only general Iwane Matsui was indicted by the IMT for "deliberately and recklessly" ignoring his legal duty to "secure the observance and prevent breaches" of the Hague Convention. Other Japanese military leaders responsible for the Nanjing Massacre were not tried. The same goes for many other mass atrocities in China, Korea and Southeast Asia. Instead of prosecution, Shirō Ishii, the Japanese commander of Unit 731 responsible for inhumane medical experimentation, and his colleagues were spared and given immunity in exchange for cooperation with their U.S. counterparts in biological and chemical warfare. Later, the IMT judges bitterly complained that "centrally ordered Japanese war criminality of the most disgusting kind was kept secret from the Court by the U.S. government."[34] By then, the story was no longer in the headlines.

Similarly, more than 40 high-level war criminals, including Nobusuke Kishi, were never charged but released in the late 1940s. In addition to these

Japanese "Class A" war criminals, "Class B" war criminals were found guilty of war crimes *per se*, while "Class C" war criminals were guilty of crimes against humanity. Yet, most perpetrators of Japanese colonial atrocities in East and Southeast Asia were not sentenced. The matter was too sensitive to colonial Britain, France, Netherlands, and the U.S. These four-nation members of the Tokyo trials feared that *their* colonial atrocities might be targeted as crimes against humanity. And so, the masses of victimized in Asia who had survived the horrific brutalities in the hands of Imperial Japan, were left without any recourse in the international legal system.[35]

In his dissenting opinion, Indian jurist Radhabinod Pal believed the refusal to try Allied crimes, especially the use of atomic bombs, significantly weakened the tribunal's authority. He dismissed the legitimacy of the Tokyo Tribunal as victor's justice. Similarly, in a subsequent reassessment, Richard Minear quoted Japanese general and statesman Tojo Hideki: "In the last analysis, this trial was a political trial. It was only victor's justice."[36] But should one throw the baby out with the bathwater? Serving as PM of Japan in the fatal years of 1941–1944, Tojo's rule was overshadowed by extraordinary state violence and imperialism. He was directly complicit in the 1937 invasion of China, Pearl Harbor in 1941 and many mass atrocities. After a failed suicide in 1945, Tojo was tried by the IMT for war crimes, sentenced to death and hanged.[37]

To discard the very idea of justice because it has failed in the past is no pretext for greenlighting mass atrocities and releasing their perpetrators in the future. Nonetheless, it is vital to recognize the historical verity that the West has never been that eager to subvert victor's justice. The idea that history is written by the victors is ancient, as is its corollary, that the advantage of the stronger is just. The proposition that "might makes right" goes back to Plato's *Republic* (340a).[38] And power is portrayed as its own justification. Victor's justice is not the side-effect of the postwar era, or even the rise of Western modernity in the 15th century. It can be traced to the origins of the West itself—particularly its colonialism.

It was the discontent with the limitations on crimes against humanity in Nuremberg that contributed to the recognition of genocide as an international crime by the UN General Assembly in December 1946 and the adoption in 1948 of the Genocide Convention, which became effective in 1951. In parallel, the UN General Assembly adopted the Universal Declaration of Human Rights with its corollary, the individual accountability for violations of human rights, reflected by the embrace of the Genocide Convention as a promising historical first step. But then, the horrors of Auschwitz and Dachau gave way to the concerns of the Cold War and the kind of actions that violated the very foundations of the Genocide Convention.

Although the Nuremberg and Tokyo trials are often portrayed as the genesis of international criminal law, this is only a part of the actual narrative. Only a few perpetrators were charged for war crimes and crimes against humanity, but none for genocide—until the end of the Cold War.

The Cold War: Suppressed Genocide Prevention

With the onset of the Cold War, the "free world" was redefined to exclude the Soviet Union and China, formerly U.S. allies in World War II, without which the triumph against Nazism and Fascism would have been inconceivable. Instead, it included America's wartime enemies—Germany, Italy, and Japan—that the Grand Alliance had fought and defeated. Ironically, many of the new members of the free world were military dictatorships or would become such.[39] Known at the time as the *reverse course*, it was a dramatic reversal of wartime policies. Instead of the initial plans of political and economic reforms and demilitarization, the reverse course led the U.S. to reward and strengthen its wartime enemies as its new Cold War allies.[40]

If the reverse course served to suspend the Convention externally, the establishment of the *security state* in the United States drove that purpose internally. A top-secret policy paper by the National Security Council (NSC 68), drafted by the Departments of State and Defense and presented to President Truman in April 1950, played a key role in the militarization of the Cold War that ensued in 1950. Widely considered one of the critical U.S. policy statements in the Cold War, it "provided the blueprint for the militarization of the Cold War from 1950 to the collapse of the Soviet Union at the beginning of the 1990s."[41] NSC 68 and its subsequent amplifications resulted in a massive U.S. rearmament, the development of a hydrogen bomb, and increased military aid to allies. Rejecting all alternative policies of friendly détente and containment of the Soviet Union, NSC 68 made the rollback of "global communism" the official U.S. geopolitical priority.[42]

Before NSC 68, U.S. military expenditure was falling. With the Korean War, NSC 68 dramatically reversed the trend as foreign military and economic aid soared fourfold. The creation of the U.S. military-industrial complex that ensued made it possible to station large numbers of troops abroad with bases and naval stations to support them, to intervene in foreign countries' internal affairs, engage in proxy wars against Soviet client states, conduct overt and covert operations against foreign governments, as well as extend an expansive military assistance program and continuing economic aid beyond 1952 when such aid was supposed to cease with the winding down of the Marshall Plan in Western Europe and its variant in Japan.[43]

Neither the reverse course nor the security state was in alignment with the use of the Genocide Convention not only to prosecute genocidal atrocities but to preempt their occurrences. Instead, these trajectories effectively nullified efforts to deploy the Convention between the early 1950s and early 1990s. As a result, the Convention was not applied to prosecute and certainly not to preempt the genocidal atrocities of the period. Reflecting conventional wisdom, Wikipedia offers one list of genocides in the Cold War period:

- Massacre of Maya civilians during the Guatemalan Civil War (1960–1996);
- Massacre of blacks following the Zanzibar Revolution (1964);
- Ethnic cleansing of Bengalis amid the 1971 Civil War (1971);
- Massacre of Acholi and Lango people in Uganda (1972–78);
- Ikiza series of mass killings committed in Burundi (1972);
- "Pacification campaigns" in East Timor (1975–99);
- Killing of Cambodians by the Khmer Rouge (1975–79);
- Sabra and Shatila massacre of mostly Palestinians and Lebanese Shias in Beirut (1982);
- Massacre of the Ndebele people in Zimbabwe (1983–87);
- Anfal campaign against Kurds in Iraq (1986–89);
- Massacre of Isaaq civilians in Somaliland/Somalia (1988–91).

Most of the Wikipedia genocides took place against the backdrop of the tumultuous decolonization and independence struggles of the countries of the Third World, today better known as the Global South, and the rule-and-divide legacies left behind by the former British, French, Dutch and Italian colonial powers and by those governments they supported in South Africa, Rhodesia and Israel. Curiously enough, most of these struggles—many of which would seem to fulfill many or most conditions of the Genocide Convention—are not even included in conventional lists of genocides that took place during the decades of the Cold War. The same goes for the U.S./NATO-led Operation Gladio in Europe, the U.S. role in the Indonesian genocide and the Guatemalan "disappearances" in the 1960s, the U.S.-led "dirty wars" associated with Operation Condor in Latin America, the apartheid-regime in South Africa, the subsequent Operation Phoenix and the use of napalm in Vietnam, support for the Khmer Rouge in Cambodia and many similar campaigns in other countries, mainly in the Global South.[44] What about the post-Cold War era?

Toward Ad Hoc Tribunals

Following more than four decades of silence and inactivity, the UN General Assembly eventually greenlighted the efforts of the International Law Commission to draft a statute for a permanent court. In 1990, the West tried to establish an international court with jurisdiction over Iraq's invasion of Kuwait. Since the crisis ended in a military stalemate, the West's focus shifted to the Balkans, the break-up of Yugoslavia and the concomitant ethnic cleansing, war crimes and gender violence. In early 1993 the UN Security Council voted to establish the International Criminal Tribunal (ICT) for what once was Yugoslavia (ICTY) and its sister court for Rwanda (ICTR). Elements of the Convention and its definition of the crime of genocide were incorporated into the statutes of the two ad hoc tribunals created by the Security Council to judge those accused of genocide and other crimes in the former Yugoslavia and Rwanda.

Since then, special courts have also been set up to prosecute domestic and international crimes. Examples of such hybrid tribunals can be found in Kosovo, Bosnia Herzegovina, East Timor, Sierra Leone, Cambodia, and most recently Lebanon. At the same time, talks intensified on the creation of a permanent international court, which led to the Statute of the International Criminal Court (ICC), with the Statute entering into force in July 2002. In the Rome Statute, the body of substantive law features four components: genocide, crimes against humanity, war crimes and the crime of aggression. Furthermore, there have been frequent references to genocide in the resolutions, declarations and statements of the UN organs, particularly in the works of expert bodies and special rapporteurs. Nonetheless, major efforts by the international community to preempt genocides have been effectively absent until recently.

After World War II, the nascent Cold War politicized and chipped away the efforts at establishing international tribunals. In the 1990s, it was déjà vu all over again, but this time the process was more subtle and discrete. After all, the historical moment differed from its precedent in 1945, when the U.S. dominated half of the world economy, international politics and global military. In the 1990s, America's monopolistic role in global governance was premised particularly on its military prowess that would come back to haunt it during the post-9/11 wars. Moreover, there was the issue of soaring costs. While the Yugoslavia and Rwanda tribunals still operated out of the general budget of the UN, their successors were financed by "voluntary contributions" from states and, in the case of Lebanon, a contribution from the government. That risked moral hazards and potential conflicts of interest, as those controlling the purse like to link financial support with the "right outcome."

The ultimate problem is in the implementation dimension, however. Originating from 1948–51, the Genocide Convention contains a narrow but enduring definition of the crime of genocide but deals inadequately with enforcement and related matters. Here's the bottom line: Prosecution is reserved to the courts of the territorial state, but dispute settlement is assigned to the International Court of Justice. In contrast with human rights treaties, there was "no dedicated organ for implementation."[45]

These insufficient mechanisms of the Convention have often been criticized, with a range of initiatives advanced over the years. There have also been efforts to enlarge the mandate, for instance by adding the term "mass atrocities," so as "to make it broader in scope without the need to determine first whether a specific situation has a 'genocidal' character."[46] But over time, such attempts have been frustrated. Moreover, new genocidal atrocities were ignored, including the massacres of Hutus during the First Congo War (1996–97), the extermination of the Bambutis in the Democratic Republic of the Congo (2002–2003), and the killing of ethnic Darfuri people (2003). Coupled with the misguided U.S. war against Afghanistan and Iraq, these neglected mass killings fostered new interest and attention to genocidal atrocities. The international community grew increasingly concerned about the abuses of disproportionate military power against non-armed civilians.

There was also a Special Tribunal on Lebanon. But it was not about the devastation of Dahiya, Beirut. It was about the interests of Western powers in Lebanon and, well, a single billionaire.

Special Tribunal for Lebanon: Billionaire versus Obliteration

In mid-February 2005, the motorcade of former Prime Minister of Lebanon Rafic Hariri drove near St George Hotel in Beirut's central district. Then a truck bomb, with explosives equivalent to 1,800 kilograms was detonated. In a flash, two dozen people, including Hariri, were killed, and 220 more were injured. It was a murder mystery even by the ailing Beirut's standards.

The assassination triggered a dramatic international response as Hariri's friends, U.S. President George W. Bush and French President Jacques Chirac, sprang into action. Meanwhile, as tensions were escalating between Israel and Hezbollah in Southern Lebanon, the UN Security Council in March 2006 requested the Secretary-General to consult the Lebanese government on the establishment of the Special Tribunal of Lebanon (STL), or the Hariri

Tribunal. While Kofi Annan gave way to Ban Ki-Moon as the head of the UN, no effort was wasted to create the STL, even amid the 2006 Lebanon War, as tens of thousands of Israelis returned to Southern Lebanon and the IDF launched airstrikes and artillery fire on both Hezbollah military targets and Lebanese infrastructure, including Beirut's newly-named Rafic Hariri International Airport, imposing an air-and-naval blockade on the country.[47] While entire Lebanese towns were covered in cluster bombs, 23 tons of high explosives in a single raid were dropped on Dahia in southern Beirut, according to U.S. officials.[48]

All political violence is terrifying. Yet, there is something deeply unsettling about the fact that through this 2006 horrific test run of the Obliteration Doctrine when UN and Lebanese authorities worked intensely to establish the STL, the causal triggers of the military mass devastation were largely shunned. In early 2007, the UN and Lebanon signed an STL agreement, but the Lebanese parliamentarians refused to ratify it. So, the UN Security Council hammered out Resolution 1757. Two years later, the tribunal convened in the Netherlands. It was the first UN-based international criminal court to try "a terrorist crime" committed against a specific person. Subsequently, the assassination was attributed to a young male suicide bomber, while a UN investigation linked Syria to the assassination. A decade later, several Hezbollah supporters were indicted and tried in *absentia*. The full investigation took 15 years.[49]

From the start, Hezbollah leader Hassan Nasrallah, later assassinated by Israel during its Lebanon assault in 2024, condemned the investigation as an Israeli project intended to escalate tensions in Lebanon, due to an audio recording of an alleged Israeli agent and intercepted Israeli aerial drone footage of Hariri's route. Nasrallah believed Israel wanted to assassinate Hariri to create political chaos and force Syria to withdraw from Lebanon.[50] The turmoil set the stage to a political reaction, which brought to power Hariri's successors (until it was their turn to flee).

The Hariri assassination sparked the 2005 Cedar Revolution, a set of peaceful demonstrations demanding the withdrawal of the Syrian troops from Lebanon. With the resignation of the incumbent government, the general election, and the establishment of the STL, the main goals of that revolution were presumably achieved. It was a variant of the not-so-spontaneous "color revolutions" that were supported by the West, particularly in the subsequent "Arab Spring" of the early 2010s. Even the term "Cedar Revolution" was not coined by the Lebanese, but by U.S. Under Secretary of State for Global Affairs Paula J. Dobriansky, an appointee of President George W. Bush, whose Ukrainian-American father, Dr. Lev Dobriansky, was a prominent anti-communist through the Cold War and who herself played a central role in the hawkish U.S. policies regarding the Middle East, Russia and China.[51] In the case of the Lebanese tribunal, such "revolutions" seem to have aimed at a new concept of an international crime; that is, "international terrorism," that constitutes an "attack on universal values," as the STL Appeals Chamber in February 2011 concluded. In this view, insurgencies can be framed as such attacks, whereas the historical context of those uprisings is discretely shuffled under the carpet.

During his tenure, Rafic Hariri had led five Lebanese cabinets (1992–98, 2000–2004). Once regarded as one of the world's 100 wealthiest,[52] he was close to the West, even though his governments were haunted by allegations of corruption and human rights violations. His assassination paved the way for the rise of his son, Saad Hariri, as the prime minister (2009–2011, 2016–2020), and the son's resignation following the 2019 popular protest movement demanding accountability and transparency. Hariri Jr. waited patiently for a new opportunity until two flight attendants sued him for alleged sexual assault in 2023. Life was rough. His net worth of $2 billion had shrunk to $1.4 billion.[53]

Officially, the Special Tribune for Lebanon ceased operations at the year-end of 2023, after a protracted struggle with financial difficulties. The mission had not fully achieved its goals.[54] Born amid the 2006 Lebanon War and the test run of the Obliteration Doctrine, it closed shop amid the mass atrocities in Gaza and ahead of the new Israeli assault on Southern Lebanon.

Of course, new tribunals are possible, theoretically. As the International Court of Justice has suggested, there is no explicit temporal limitation in the Genocide Convention to prevent it from having a retroactive effect.[55] Nonetheless, "any one of the five [permanent members of the UN Security Council] can always veto the establishment of an international justice mechanism that comes too close to home. For this reason, criminal tribunals for Israel, Myanmar, or Sri Lanka have never been seriously entertained."[56] That is why the two great philosophers, Bertrand Russell and Jean-Paul Sartre, set up the 1966 International War Crimes Tribunal in Stockholm to tackle American atrocities in Vietnam. Any official effort would have been torpedoed by the U.S. veto in the Security Council. An unofficial tribunal can make a determination in accord with international justice—but it cannot achieve effective and internationally-binding outcomes.

If consensus does not prevail among the permanent members of the UN Security Council, it cannot intervene. The STL is a textbook case. Despite their disagreements on the Iraq War, Presidents Bush and Chirac agreed on the case of Hariri, their friend, so the STL had been established through fire and rain. But when the brutal conflict between Israel and Hezbollah devastated much of the country, the Council did nothing.[57]

In addition to the tribunals, the international bodies that are tasked to implement the Convention, including the ICC, have been subjected to pressure for years.

Undermining the ICC

In late May 2024, the prosecutor of the International Criminal Court (ICC) in The Hague, Karim Khan, said he would file applications for arrest warrants against Prime Minister Benjamin Netanyahu and Defense Minister Yoav Gallant. Soon thereafter, the *Guardian* in Britain revealed that Mossad director Yossi Cohen had been personally involved in a secret plot to pressure Khan's predecessor, Fatou Bensouda, to drop the investigation into Israel's alleged war crimes and crimes against humanity in the occupied territories. Reportedly, Israeli intelligence had some 60 people under surveillance—half of them Palestinians and half from other countries, including UN officials and ICC personnel. Presumably, Shin Bet installed NSO's Pegasus spyware, previously used in the infamous Khashoggi murder, on the phones of multiple Palestinian NGO employees, and two senior Palestinian Authority officials.[58]

The prior Trump campaign against the ICC had been a joint operation in which sanctions were adopted against Bensouda and her top officials because Trump feared U.S. armed forces could be prosecuted. To Netanyahu cabinets, the ICC was a source of great unease since the ICC is a criminal court that prosecutes individuals, targeting those deemed most responsible for atrocities. Effectively, Israel had run "a decade-long secret 'war' against the ICC, deploying its intelligence agencies to surveil, hack, pressure, smear and allegedly threaten senior ICC staff in an effort to derail the court's inquiries."[59] As the Israeli cabinet officials vehemently denied the disclosures and the Bensouda debacle, Israeli newspaper *Haaretz* reported how these same authorities had not only confirmed the newspaper's findings already back in 2022, but also how Israeli government officials had used emergency powers to prevent the story from being published at the time.[60] When Cohen's predecessor at the head of Mossad, Tamir Prado, was asked to comment on the debacle, the ex-Mossad chief said: "It sounds like Cosa Nostra–style blackmail."[61]

After Bensouda had been contained, Khan and the ICC were targeted by direct public pressure by both Israel and the United States. But there were still other odd affiliations suggesting tacit influencing. When the ICC began to scrutinize South Africa's genocide case against Israel, one of the 17 judges was Julia Sebutinde, the Ugandan jurist who had served in the court since

2012 and was the first African woman to sit on the ICC. As fate would have it, Sebutinde became acting president in January 2025 upon the resignation of president Nawaf Salam, the first Lebanese judge to hold the office, after the parliament of Lebanon nominated him as prime minister. The departure of Salam after Israel's ground invasion paved the way to the rise of Sebutinde. Unlike Salam who was critical of Israel's action, she voted against *all* the provisional measures in South Africa's case against Israel. In effect, she was the *only* permanent judge to vote against any measures.[62]

In a dissenting opinion, Sebutinde concluded that the dispute in question was basically political rather than legal. Setting aside abundant evidence by South Africa on the genocidal atrocities, she stated that "South Africa has not demonstrated, even on a prima facie basis, that the acts allegedly committed by Israel ... were committed with the necessary genocidal intent and that, as a result, they are capable of falling within the scope of the Genocide Convention."[63] Shunning empirical evidence, it was a stunning argument, sort of an ICC version of the controversial "political question doctrine."[64] The judge rejected the court's call for the Israeli military to halt deliberate assaults on civilians, end its forced population displacement, and cancel its planned invasion of Rafah. Subsequently, even the Ugandan Ministry of Foreign Affairs stated it supported South Africa's position and Sebutinde's vote did not in any way reflect the position of Uganda.[65]

What made Sebutinde's dissenting opinion even more stunning was the fact that it was copied. Several critical sentences in her opinion were plagiarized, without any reference to the original sources. She drew from a controversial commentary, "The Forgotten History of the Term 'Palestine'," by Douglas J. Feith, a national security senior fellow of the Hudson Institute, a far-right U.S. think tank, known as an architect of the 2003 Iraq War and a prime supporter of the Big Defense contractors which are among Hudson's key funders. Feith was also a member of a neoconservative report for then newly elected Israeli PM, Benjamin Netanyahu, setting the stage for his harsh rule, the demise of the peace process and record-high arms sales.[66] Where Feith's commentary blurred the history of Palestine, Sebutinde used it as a historical document underscoring her point that "the controversy between Israel and Palestine is historically a political one." She supported accounts of the Jewish presence in the biblical land of Israel, omitting any mention of UN resolutions or international law she was mandated to represent.

There was a common denominator between Feith and Sebutinde, however. The former is a revisionist Zionist; the latter, a Christian Zionist whose sympathy to Israel is linked with her faith. Christian Zionists espouse the return of the Jewish people to the Holy Land because the eschatological "Gathering of Israel" is seen as a prerequisite for the Second Coming of Jesus

Christ.[67] It was all in line with the Christian Zionism she had professed as a member of Watoto, a Pentecostal megachurch in Kampala, Uganda's capital, under the tutelage of a Canadian "end of times" pastor Gary Skinner. As Skinner saw it, the future was Manichean: "If you bless the Jews, you will be blessed. If you curse the Jews, you will be cursed."[68]

Sanctioning the ICC

Ever since the establishment of the International Criminal Court (ICC), the U.S. stance toward the court has shifted with administrations and political fluctuations. In 2002, President George W. Bush had formally declared that the U.S. did not intend to become a party or recognize any legal obligations arising from the U.S. signature of the Rome Statute. During the Obama administration, the U.S. began participating in the Statute parties' meetings as a non-state party observer. By contrast, its successor, the Trump administration, expressed strong disapproval of the ICC's investigation of whether U.S. military and intelligence personnel committed war crimes in Afghanistan, issuing an executive order in 2020 that declared a national emergency and authorized sanctions against certain ICC officials involved in the investigation. That executive order was rescinded by the Biden administration in 2021 and again began participating as a non-party observer in the ICC meetings.[69]

Taking into consideration the prior shifts, it is hardly surprising that when Trump returned to the White House, he signed an executive order that sanctioned the ICC once again. But now the tone was tougher, the scope of sanctions broader, and the concern focused not just on the Israelis but on the U.S. system of global military alliances and American soldiers:

> The ICC, as established by the Rome Statute, has engaged in illegitimate and baseless actions targeting America and our close ally Israel. The ICC has, without a legitimate basis, asserted jurisdiction over and opened preliminary investigations concerning personnel of the United States and certain of its allies, including Israel, and has further abused its power by issuing baseless arrest warrants targeting Israeli Prime Minister Benjamin Netanyahu and Former Minister of Defense Yoav Gallant. The ICC has no jurisdiction over the United States or Israel, as neither country is party to the Rome Statute or a member of the ICC. Neither country has ever recognized the ICC's jurisdiction, and both nations are thriving democracies with militaries that strictly adhere to the laws of war. The ICC's recent actions against Israel and the United States set a dangerous precedent, directly endangering current and

former United States personnel, including active service members of the Armed Forces, by exposing them to harassment, abuse, and possible arrest. This malign conduct in turn threatens to infringe upon the sovereignty of the United States and undermines the critical national security and foreign policy work of the United States Government and our allies, including Israel.[70]

The ICC condemned Trump's decision and said it stands firmly behind its "personnel and pledges to continue providing justice and hope to millions of innocent victims of atrocities across the world.[71] Through his ICC sanctions and intimate cooperation with PM Netanyahu and his far-right government, Trump seemed to make himself and his administration complicit to genocidal atrocities.

Unlike many international human rights treaties, the Convention has not been endowed with a formal monitoring mechanism, or a treaty body, to monitor the implementation of the treaty provisions and to provide states with advice on preventive and corrective action. The earliest Convention draft envisioned such a mechanism, but this idea was diluted from the final text. As Louise Arbour, the UN High Commissioner for Human Rights and a former Chief Prosecutor of the tribunals for the former Yugoslavia and Rwanda, argued over 15 years ago:

Properly designed, a monitoring mechanism could provide an authoritative early warning of situations at risk of degenerating into genocide. Such situations are almost invariably preceded and characterized by a discernable escalation of systematic or gross violations of human rights.

If the necessary political will is mustered, the gestation of this mechanism needs not be long and complex.[72]

The key term, of course, is the "necessary political will." It takes the discourse back to the failure of prevention. Do the ICC's arrest warrants indicate that the necessary political will had now been garnered? No, but the recent ICC actions do suggest that times are changing and that the old anomalies are pushing the world courts toward an existential impasse edge or an inclusive transformation.

The Gaza War is a case in point. The first Trump administration sanctioned several senior ICC prosecution officials preventing them from traveling to U.S. territory and creating other challenges (e.g., using personal credit cards). But by targeting *anyone* aiding the court, the new sanctions could prove far more threatening. And so, the ICC Prosecutor Karim Khan became the first person to be hit with U.S. economic and travel sanctions. Ironically, Khan began his ICC activities by "deprioritizing" (read: sidelining) allegations against the U.S. in Afghanistan. Following a year of the proxy war in Ukraine, Khan issued arrest warrants against President Vladimir Putin and other senior Russian officials; and in January 2025, against Taliban leadership.

What the ICC actions and the consequent debacles did suggest was the return of the repressed: the all-too-familiar situation in which the prosecutor seems to be faced with two seemingly irreconcilable demands (universal jurisdiction, state sovereignty) that keep coming back to disrupt the court's activities.

What the Biden and Trump administrations were coping with is the compromise the states agreed to at the 1998 Rome Conference. At the time, the scope of the court's jurisdiction was among the most heated topics. Many championed universal jurisdiction, but the U.S. proposal pushed for UN Security Council authorization. The talks resulted in a compromise, which is reflected in the ICC's *jurisdiction* and the principles of *complementarity* and *cooperation*.[73] The Court may exercise jurisdiction in a situation where genocide, crimes against humanity or war crimes were committed on or after July 1, 2002 and:

- the crimes were committed by a state party national, or in the territory of a state party, or in a state that has accepted the jurisdiction of the Court; or
- the crimes were referred to the ICC Prosecutor by the UN Security Council (UNSC) pursuant to a resolution adopted under Chapter VII of the UN charter.[74]
- As of July 17, 2018, a situation in which an act of aggression would appear to have occurred could be referred to the Court by the UNSC, acting under Chapter VII of the UN Charter, irrespective as to whether it involves states parties or non-states parties.

In the absence of a UNSC referral of an act of aggression, the prosecutor may also initiate an investigation on his/her own initiative or upon request from a state party.

By design, the ICC is intended to complement, not to replace, national criminal systems. It prosecutes cases only when States are unwilling or unable to do so. Finally, as a judicial institution, the ICC does not have its own police force or enforcement body. It relies on cooperation with countries worldwide for support, particularly for making arrests, transferring arrested persons to the ICC detention center in The Hague, freezing suspects' assets, and enforcing sentences.

Importantly, this structure allows the court to investigate and prosecute the nationals of *non-member states* when their alleged crimes take place on the territory of a member state. This compromise enabled the ICC Prosecutor Karim Khan to go after PM Netanyahu and his former Defense Minister Gallant. Like the U.S., Israel is not a member of the ICC, but the alleged crimes took place in occupied Palestine, which is a member-state.

From Hollow Universalism to Effective Multipolarity

After two decades of trial and error, the ICC's track record suggests a dual challenge. On the one hand, the broad mandate coupled with limited economic resources and state support has constrained ICC ambitions. On the other hand, the ICC has wide jurisdiction but with weaker political support. It can aim high, but to shoot effectively it would need the resources it lacks. So, when the ICC launched its activities in 2003, it initially moved cautiously by either requesting court intervention (Congo DR, Central American Republic, Uganda) or with the UN Security Council's authorization. But as several new crises surfaced, the pattern changed and the double-bind inherent in the ICC's mandate escalated.

In 2010, the ICC launched its first investigation without state support, when prosecutor Luis Moreno Ocampo charged then-Deputy Prime Minister Uhuru Kenyatta, along with five other government leaders, as an indirect co-perpetrator in the violence that followed Kenya's 2007–2008 post-election violence.[75] A popular politician and the son of the legendary anti-colonial leader Jomo Kenyatta, Uhuru readied to fight back, however. Meanwhile, the ambitious Ocampo found himself in intense public scrutiny, due to close ties with organizations funded by the billionaire speculator George Soros since the 1990s. These originated from the early 1990s, when Soros infused funds into a real estate conglomerate (IRSA) serving as a prominent backer of Ocampo's NGO in Argentina. In the mid-'90s, Ocampo began to oversee work on Latin America by Transparency International, a corruption watchdog that has been criticized for bias against developing countries. A decade later, while serving as the ICC prosecutor he participated in a roundtable by the Open Society, funded by Soros: "Restoring American Leadership—the International Criminal Court."[76] Such coincidences still went without major controversies. However, when the UN Security Council assigned Ocampo the task of investigating war crimes in Libya, he reportedly shared confidential information about ongoing investigations with a party to the conflict, the French foreign minister's cabinet chief. Ocampo indicted Gaddafi and his son Saif al-Islam for war crimes in 2011 before leaving his job at the ICC for a lucrative career in private practice. Though a champion for transparency, Ocampo made millions of dollars in questionable deals routing monies to his offshore companies in several tax havens, as evidenced by the Panama Papers. "Offshore companies are not illegal," he said. He just wanted to "try to make some more millions."[77]

Despite the ICC process, Uhuru was elected Kenya's president in April 2013. In Kenya, the effort to prosecute him led to the parliament's call for withdrawal from the ICC and the African Union summit in which Uhuru accused the ICC of being "a toy of declining imperial powers."[78] After a three-year juridical chaos, the ICC charges were dropped in March 2015 for lack of evidence.

From the standpoint of the Union, for a decade or two the ICC had gone after the poorest countries mainly in Africa, which has suffered the most from colonial plunder. And this status quo remained even in early 2025, when there were 12 ongoing and five concluded investigations—most of them in Africa (Figure 5-4).

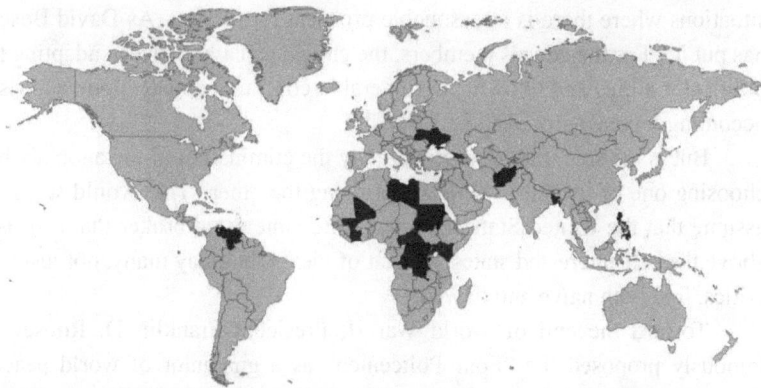

Figure 5-4. ICC Situations Under Investigation
SOURCE: *ICC Office of the Prosecutor, Feb. 2025*

Nonetheless, in the course of those years, the ICC initiated several investigations that dragged it into friction with multiple non-member states, including Russia (Georgia, Ukraine), Libya (civil war), Myanmar (Rohingya), United States (Afghanistan) and Israel (Gaza). And yet, as high-profile cases amounted, actual results seemed few and the hoped-for demonstration and deterrent effects, coupled with the threat of court prosecution, failed to mate-rialize. Furthermore, an increasing number of ICC countries began to defy court arrest warrants or suggested they would not respect them in the future. In the case of the Gaza War, France suggested PM Netanyahu had head-of-state immunity. Although Article 89 of the Rome Statute maintained that its 125 states parties "shall, in accordance with the provisions of this Part and the procedure under their national law, comply with requests for arrest and sur-render," French foreign ministry said Netanyahu "and the other ministers con-cerned" were immune from arrest. The argument was that "a State cannot be required to act inconsistently with its obligations under international law with respect to the immunities of States not party to the ICC."[79] While Germany seemed to follow in the footprints, Poland said it would allow Netanyahu to visit the country, irrespective of the arrest warrant. Unsurprisingly, the ICC's convictions were against citizens of member countries, whereas cases against non-member state nationals seemed to go nowhere.

In the U.S. debate, some legal scholars argued that with or without a Security Council–mandated pause, the United States should work with sym-pathetic countries that have not joined the court to urge reform of the ICC's reach. Armed with the threat of broad sanctions, the White House could pressure ICC member states to adopt an implementing agreement or another code of conduct prioritizing some investigations over others and stressing situations where there is a reasonable prospect for success. As David Bosco has put it: "For the court's members, the choice is really between adapting to political realities and allowing a vulnerable court to navigate alone and risk becoming increasingly dysfunctional."[80]

But is the sole viable solution really the elimination of the anomaly by choosing one of its sides, while suppressing the other? That would seem to assume that the United States is a neutral, disinterested broker that can rise above the self-interested states; a point of view that today many, not just the critics, find both naïve and flawed.

Toward the end of World War II, President Franklin D. Roosevelt famously proposed the "Four Policemen" as a guarantor of world peace. These four featured the victorious Allies of World War II: the United States and the United Kingdom, the Soviet Union and China. The Four Policemen would keep order within their spheres of influence: the U.S. in the Western Hemisphere, Britain in its empire and Western Europe, the Soviet Union in Eastern Europe and the central Eurasia, and China in East Asia and the Western Pacific. To Roosevelt, this idea was the key to the United Nations that he saw as the single most important outcome of the world war. Unlike the old League of Nations, the UN would not be just a "debating society," but an effective international force supported by the great powers.[81] Following Roosevelt's death, the idea endured, but as a torso, somewhat like the subsequent Genocide Convention. The Big Four nations became the permanent members of the UN Security Council, but with much less power than had been envisioned in Roosevelt's original proposal, even though France was later added as the fifth permanent member of the Council.

Of course, the proposal had its contradictions and liabilities even initially. Yet, it captured something very essential about the emerging new world order that would not be dominated by any single nation, not even the United States. Roosevelt's proposal sought to ensure a peaceful and stable balance of power in the new spheres of influence. Today, these Four Policemen have undergone great changes. While the U.S. remains the economic leader in the Americas, the eclipse of continental powers has resulted in the rise of a united Europe. After the Brexit, the UK is an even paler shadow of its former imperial glory. In East Asia, the postwar rise of Japan and South Korea has been augmented by the more recent emergence of China and Southeast Asia, particularly Indonesia. Similarly, South Asia has witnessed the expansion of India, Pakistan and Bangladesh. In the Middle East, the rise of the Gulf States, led by Saudi Arabia, has had a great impact on the world's energy and financial markets. Despite its post-colonial frictions and wars, sub-Saharan Africa, too, has some of the fastest-growing states. In brief, Roosevelt's Four Policemen proposal has been replaced by multipolarity, as evidenced by the BRICS bloc led by the largest economies of the Global South.

In this new international status quo, the role of the Global South can no longer be shunned in any international configuration claiming to represent the wide majority of humankind, including the world courts and the Genocide Convention—whether it is a question of enforcement or, even more importantly, prevention.

CHAPTER 6

THE FAILURE OF GENOCIDE PREVENTION

In the Genocide Convention, the issue of preparatory attacks, which was addressed by Article 3(d) by including an "other act," was seen to cover attempted genocide. In its convention draft, the Secretariat initially included a more far-reaching provision to tackle preparatory acts, which may morph into conduct that becomes punishable. This was considered vital because the gravity and criminality of genocide necessitates a determined effort to prevent its commission beyond simple reliance on post hoc punishment as a deterrent.

Indeed, the Secretariat deemed the crimes of genocide to feature "the following preparatory acts: (a) studies and research for the purpose of developing the technique of genocide; (b) setting up of installations, manufacturing, obtaining, possessing or supplying of articles or substances."[1] This provision was strongly promoted by the Soviet Union, but it was torpedoed by the United States and the United Kingdom. Eventually, it was excluded and ultimately forgotten.[2]

Certainly, nothing should be as offensive to human sensibility than indifference to incessant violence. Nonetheless, past efforts to reinforce the Genocide Convention and its stress on prevention are predicated on the idea that "if only we knew about the horrific mass atrocities that were going on, we would have stopped the bloodshed." What makes indifference such a formidable challenge is the simple fact that when it serves the interests of powers to be, it is not only allowed but fostered.

Today, we know that Britain and later its American ally were fully aware of even the minute details of the Nazis' mass killings from the beginning of the German invasion of the Soviet Union in June 1941; even earlier, after the invasion of Poland on September 1, 1939.[3] The British decrypts of German police radio traffic recorded almost every detail of the *Judenaktionen* (a code for the mass killings of Jews) carried out by the *Einsatzgruppen* (the mobile killing units) which accompanied the German Army into Russia, the

Ukraine, Byelorussia and the Baltic states. Yet, these mass crimes on the Eastern front were purposely permitted to prevail, which set the stage to the "Final Solution" in the January 1942 Wannsee Conference.

Even thereafter, there were still opportunities to disrupt the genocidal atrocities in Auschwitz, Treblinka and so many others, thanks to the flow of reports on the concentration camps and gas chambers. Technically, there were no obstacles to bombing the railway bridges *en masse* or destroying the chambers and crematoria. But that did not happen. Even though the synthetic rubber factory at Auschwitz was bombed several times by the Allies, the apparatus of mass murder in the adjoining facilities at Birkenau was never targeted. Decisionmakers like John J. McCloy, Assistant Secretary of War and former banker, argued that no bombs should be wasted on the death factories at Auschwitz. American planes were directed elsewhere to destroy industrial targets rather than to preempt industrial mass atrocities. Later, as the Commissioner of the U.S. Zone of Occupied Germany, McCloy ordered the release of senior Nazis imprisoned in war crimes trials, including the most notorious commanding officers of mass-killing units. Instead of controversy, these decisions earned him exceptional credibility, prestige and clout in the postwar American establishment. During the Cold War, McCloy was an architect of the CIA, a member of the famous foreign policy group "the Wise Men," president of the World Bank, chair of Chase Manhattan Bank and the Council on Foreign Relations, and a prominent adviser to all U.S. presidents from Roosevelt to Reagan.[4]

With this caveat in mind, it is easy to understand why, from the beginning, the prevention of genocide was Raphael Lemkin's primary objective, even if it often contradicted the logic of the Cold War and the U.S. grand strategy.

Identifying Preparatory Attacks

As we have seen, the Genocide Convention is a torso relative to the original draft. Though legally termed the Prevention and Punishment of the Crime of Genocide (CPPCG), the critical preemptory mandate has been suppressed. There is no reason why it should remain so, however. Alternative preventive measures do exist. The real question is not just why weren't they applied in the original drafting, but what (or who) is preventing their further legal clarification and entrenchment?

In the aftermath of the Cold War, the concern for genocide prevention intensified at the UN following the brutal ethnic cleansing and genocidal atrocities in former Yugoslavia and Rwanda. In 2004—that is, two to three years *before* the first application of the Obliteration Doctrine in Beirut—the

UN Secretary-General established a Special Adviser on the Prevention of Genocide, a senior position within the Secretariat with responsibility for warning the institution of threatened catastrophes.[5]

The institution of the Special Adviser's office was an effort to fill the implementation deficit in the Convention. That year, UN Secretary-General Kofi Annan established the position of Special Rapporteur on the prevention of genocide.[6] The mandate derived from Security Council Resolution 1366 (2001) in which the Security Council noted "the lessons to be learned for all concerned from the failure of preventive efforts that preceded such tragedies as the genocide in Rwanda [...] and the massacre in Srebrenica." The idea was to take appropriate action, coupled with the efforts of member states, "to prevent the recurrence of such tragedies."[7]

In the view of the UN, genocide often occurs in societies in which different national, racial, ethnic or religious groups become locked in identity-related conflicts. It is not the differences in identity per se that generate conflict, but the gross inequalities associated with those differences. Accordingly, the Special Adviser's task became to "act as a catalyst to raise awareness of the causes and dynamics of genocide, to alert relevant actors where there is a risk of genocide and to advocate and mobilize for appropriate action."[8] The UN mandate is clear about the obligation of the international community:

> If a State is manifestly failing to protect its populations, the international community must be prepared to take collective action to protect populations, in accordance with the UN Charter.[9]

In 2007, still another effort was undertaken to establish a complementary position within the Secretariat of "Special Adviser on the Responsibility to Protect."[10] By then, the efforts at international justice were clearly on the rise (Figure 6-1). These efforts intensified in parallel with the Palestinians' democratic elections, the triumph of Hamas, the pioneering test of the Obliteration Doctrine in Beirut, and the consequent sanctions and blockade of the Gaza Strip by Israel and the West, which paved the way to October 7, 2023.

What happened to Special Advisers on genocide prevention and the responsibility to protect, to the idea of preempting the recurrence of genocides? Were they not qualified for the task? Hardly.

Since 2005, the Special Adviser's job has been held by figures with impressive records as activists and advocates for human rights. The first to hold the mandate, Juan Méndez, was Special Adviser from 2004 to 2007. Representing political prisoners, Méndez had been arrested in the late 1970s amid Argentina's "dirty war" by the military dictatorship and subjected to torture and administrative detention. He was followed by Francis Deng,

Figure 6-1. Rise of International Justice

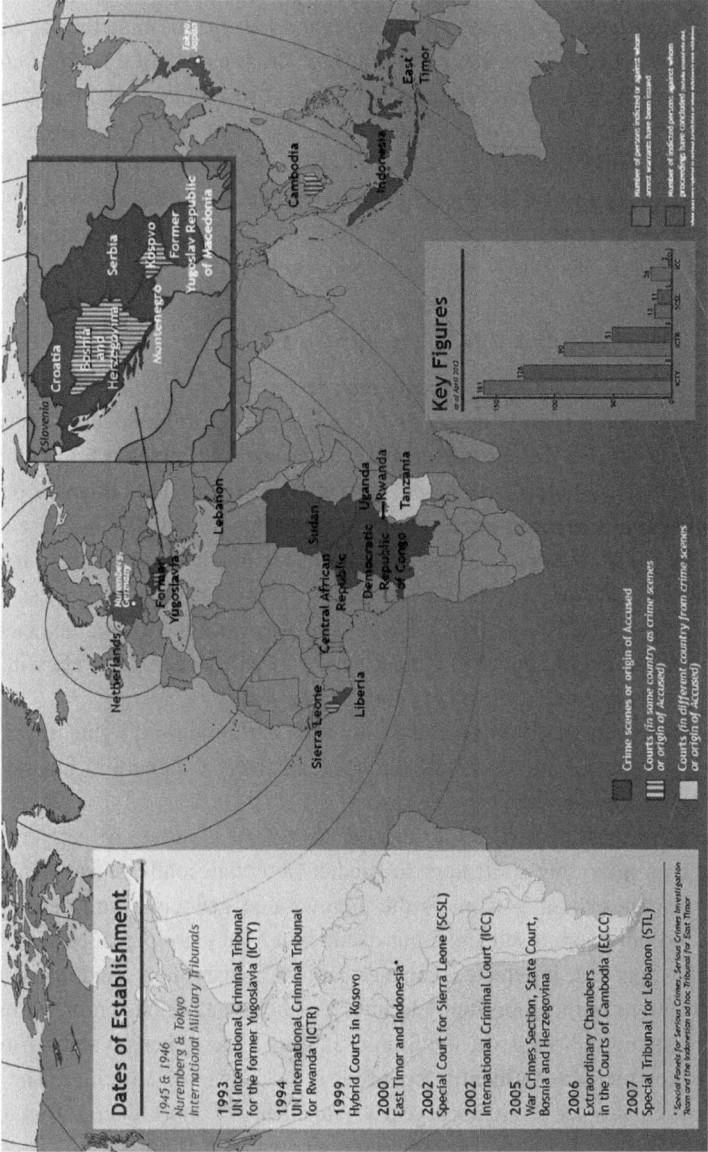

Dates of Establishment

1945 & 1946
Nuremberg & Tokyo
International Military Tribunals

1993
UN International Criminal Tribunal
for the former Yugoslavia (ICTY)

1994
UN International Criminal Tribunal
for Rwanda (ICTR)

1999
Hybrid Courts in Kosovo

2000
East Timor and Indonesia*

2002
Special Court for Sierra Leone (SCSL)

2002
International Criminal Court (ICC)

2005
War Crimes Section, State Court,
Bosnia and Herzegovina

2006
Extraordinary Chambers
in the Courts of Cambodia (ECCC)

2007
Special Tribunal for Lebanon (STL)

*Special Panels for Serious Crimes, Serious Crimes Investigation
Team and the Indonesian ad hoc Tribunal for East Timor*

SOURCE: *UN, International Criminal Tribunal for the former Yugoslavia*

who served until 2012. The Sudanese politician and diplomat had served as the UN's first Special Representative on the Human Rights of Internally Displaced Persons. Deng was succeeded by Adama Dieng, the Registrar of the International Criminal Tribunal for Rwanda and consultant for international organizations. Then came Alice Wairimu Nderitu, the first female Special Adviser. The peace researcher was one of the founders of a Kenyan conflict prevention agency encouraging citizens to use mobile communications to report indicators of violence, linking early warning to early response.

The qualifications of these advisers have never been in dispute. Yet, as Special Advisers on the Prevention of Genocide, their track record has been relatively impotent. They are not the issue. Given earlier warnings, some critics argue, responses would not follow belatedly.

Early Warnings, Late Responses

Early warning of genocide requires an ability to identify and recognize the initial symptoms. In 2010, the UN Office of the Special Adviser on the Prevention of Genocide developed an analysis framework to determine whether there is a risk of genocide in a given situation. The Office encourages other institutions and organizations to adopt this framework in their analysis of the risk of genocide. It spotlights eight factors that cumulatively increase that risk. Let's apply these categories to our findings. As the figure suggests, at the eve of 2006 the risk of genocide was prominent in every category of the framework, both individually and particularly cumulatively with each category reinforcing the other (Figure 6-2).

Despite these multiple and cumulative blinking red lights, there were strong condemnations, moral outrage and mass indignation, but no truly effective intervention.

The past decade has witnessed the rise of a variety of early warning systems providing indicators to predict potential conflicts and genocides. What unites these systems is the premise that genocides and mass atrocities do not happen suddenly, out of the blue. They are preceded by a set of early signs that, if detected, can alert national governments and international institutions to the opportunity to intervene before atrocities erupt. Partnering with Dartmouth College, the Simon-Skjodt Center relies on state-of-the-art research methods to identify countries at risk for mass atrocities. The Early Warning Project produces a yearly ranked list of more than 160 countries based on their likelihood to experience a new mass killing. It also uses crowd forecasting tools to provide real-time updates and produces in-depth reports on selected high-risk countries. The Center hoped to assist policy makers who in early 2024 faced the challenge of "simultaneously responding to ongoing

Figure 6-2. Obliteration Doctrine and Cumulative Genocide Risk

Cumulative Risk of Genocide	Obliteration Doctrine in the Gaza Strip, 2023–24
1. Tense inter-group relations, including a record of discrimination and/or other human rights violations committed against a group;	1. Tense inter-group relations since the 1920s, incl. a record of discrimination of Israeli Arabs since 1948, apartheid rule in occupied territories and/or other human rights violations against Palestinians;
2. Weak institutional capacity to prevent genocide, such as the lack of an independent judiciary, ineffective national human rights institutions, the absence of international actors capable of protecting vulnerable groups, a lack of impartial security forces and media;	2. Eroded institutional capacity to prevent genocide, incl. undermined independent judiciary (e.g., 2018 nation-state law, quest for judicial reforms since 2023, ineffective national human rights institutions, the unwillingness of international U.S.-led actors, capable of protecting vulnerable groups, a lack of impartial security forces, media under military censor; colonial Emergency laws;
3. The presence of illegal arms and armed elements;	3. Expansion of illegal arms and armed elements among Jewish settlers; underground extremists, Messianic far-right paramilitaries supported by the 'dual state'
4. Underlying political, economic, military or other motivation to target a group;	4. Underlying political ('Greater Israel'), economic (cheap labor, captive consumers), military and security (test labs of new weapons, surveillance exports);
5. Circumstances that facilitate perpetration of genocide, such as a sudden or gradual strengthening of the military or security apparatus;	5. Circumstances that facilitate perpetration of genocide, incl. disproportionate investments into military and security apparatus since 1940s; U.S. military cooperation and multi-billion-dollar military aid since the '80s;
6. Acts that could be elements of genocide, such as such as killings, abduction and disappearances, torture, rape and sexual violence, 'ethnic cleansing' or pogroms or the deliberate deprivation of food;	6. Acts that could be elements of genocide, such as such as killings, incl. abduction and disappearances of Palestinians in WB/G; torture of Palestinians; rape and sexual violence by extremist groups; systematic 'ethnic cleansing' since the 1940s, elevated anti-Arab pogroms and deliberate deprivation of food, esp. in Gaza;
7. Evidence of the 'intent to destroy in whole or in part';	7. Longstanding and abundant evidence of the "intent to destroy in whole or in part" the Palestinian people;
8. Triggering factors, such as elections.	8. Triggering factors, incl. Palestinian 2006 election of Hamas, which triggered Israel's blockade, supported by the U.S. and EU paving the way to October 7, 2023.

mass atrocities, such as those in Burma, China, Ethiopia, South Sudan, and Syria, and trying to prevent entirely new mass atrocity situations."[11] At the surface, they are impressive and persuasive. In practice, things are a bit different.

Intriguingly, the Center's top 30 countries by estimated risk of new mass killing *excluded* not only the United States, the absolute leader of mass shootings which accounted for nearly one-third of the entire world's mass shootings in the past half a century,[12] but also Gaza and the West Bank; that is, Palestine. Yet, the report was released following two months of the Gaza War and the worst genocidal atrocities since World War II. This silence went far. All terms referring to the Palestinian people are excluded from the Center's "heat map," which does not recognize either "Gaza" and the "West Bank" or "Palestine" and "Palestinians." The Center's Early Warning Project, by its own testimony, "excludes situations in which an armed group (state or nonstate) residing in one country attacks civilians in another country's territory ... This means our definition of mass killing does not include Russian forces' deliberate targeting of civilians in Ukraine, civilian killings in Yemen perpetrated by the Saudi-led coalition, or civilian killings in the war between Israel and Hamas." According to the Center, the decision to exclude these mass killings does not involve a value judgment, but "only a pragmatic judgment about what we are able to forecast more reliably."[13] As a result, the Center only makes reference to Hamas, but simply to explain its exclusion as an effect of statistical modeling.

If quantitative modeling in such early warning initiatives washes away the baby with the bath water, it suggests a defective model or the politicization of its application, or both. Launched in 2013, the Center is affiliated with the United States Holocaust Memorial Museum and grew out of the work of the Committee on Conscience. In turn, the Museum is the creation of President Jimmy Carter and Holocaust author Elie Wiesel and it was launched with private funding in which Richard Krieger, the Jewish liaison with the Republican National Committee, played a major role. The Center's modeling built on the work of Jay Ulferder, a political scientist known for his work on anticipating various forms of political instability and interest in democratization around the world. From 2001 to 2010, Ulferder had served as research director of the Political Instability Task Force (PITF), which was funded by the Central Intelligence Agency (CIA).

The Simon-Skjodt Center is not the only one of its kind. Its story highlights not only the potential importance of early warning indicators but also the subtle and not-so-subtle ways in which such indicators can be used and exploited in world politics to either promote genocide suppression agendas or to ensure silence about others. Belated response is not the only challenge.

So are flawed and misguided early warnings. Besides, early warnings, even when they are viable and valid, are no assurance of adequate prevention.

In addition to various early warning indicators, citizen activism, often operating through social media, has also contributed to new and innovative methods in global citizen activism.

Global Citizen Activism

On January 29, 2024, the Rajab family hoped to flee the inferno of Gaza. Determined to find a safe place somewhere else, their black Kia was rushing away from Tel al-Hawa, a neighborhood of Gaza City when an Israeli army tank shot their car, killing Hind Rajab's aunt and uncle, and four cousins. The only other survivor, Hind Rajab's 15-year-old cousin Layan Hamadeh, called the Palestinian Red Crescent for emergency aid. But when the dispatchers called back, Hind answered the call, saying everyone else in the car was dead. Injured in the back, hand and foot, the six-year-old girl was told to hide in the vehicle. After hours of waiting, the Red Crescent was given the green light to send the ambulance.[14]

Then Rajab was killed by the Israeli army in a "planned execution." Using a U.S.-made missile, the IDF also killed the Red Crescent paramedics sent to rescue the young girls. Shell fragments of an American-made M830A1 projectile were found at the site of the bombed Red Crescent ambulance that was looking for Rajab and her family. The sales of these particular projectiles to the Israeli military were approved by Secretary of State Blinken in mid-December 2023; just weeks before the Israeli Merkava tank killed Rajab, six of her family members and the paramedics coming to rescue.[15] Most likely, they were killed by Israeli fire (Figure 6-3).[16]

Figure 6-3. The Death of Hind Rajab

Hind graduating from senior kindergarten | A mural in her remembrance.
SOURCE: *The Hind Rajab Foundation*

In mid-2024, independent experts appointed by the UN Human Rights Council stated Rajab's killing might amount to a war crime.[17] Later, the legal foundation of the activist March 30 Movement was named the Hind Rajab Foundation (HRF). The Movement itself had been created in memory of the Land Day of 1976, when Israeli security forces shot dead six Arab Israelis who were protesting the expropriation of Arab-owned lands. The Belgian political activist group has filed multiple lawsuits against people who served in the Israeli military during the Israel-Gaza War, sending the names of more than 1,000 Israeli soldiers to the International Criminal Court (ICC).[18]

During their lethal service in Gaza, as well as Lebanon and Syria, these soldiers left behind not just physical footprints but digital fingerprints. Just as they might have in peacetime conditions, many soldiers posted thousands of selfie videos and photos on Instagram, Facebook, TikTok and YouTube. These posts by the soldiers themselves provide evidence of their commission of war crimes in Gaza.

In October 2024, a year after fighting in Gaza, Al Jazeera exposed Israeli war crimes in the Strip through the medium of photos and videos posted online by the soldiers themselves. Building up a database of more than 2,500 social media accounts, including thousands of videos, photos and social media posts, the network's investigative arm (I-Unit) released damning materials revealing a range of illegal activities. The conduct displayed in the photos and videos ranges from crass jokes and soldiers rifling through women's underwear drawers to what seems to be the murder of unarmed civilians. Some of the videos show large numbers of detainees stripped to their underwear, being held in stress positions and mocked for having soiled themselves. One shows naked and near-naked detainees, bound and blind-folded, being kicked and dragged around on the floor. In one video, a French Israeli soldier films a detainee being pulled from the back of a truck and says: "Look, I'm going to show you his back. You're going to laugh at this. He was tortured." Most of the photos and videos fell into one of three categories: wanton destruction, the mistreatment of detainees and/or the use of human shields. All three may be violations of international humanitarian law (IHL) and war crimes under the Rome Statute of the International Criminal Court. According to Rodney Dixon, an international law expert, the database is "a treasure trove which you very seldom come across . . . something which I think prosecutors will be licking their lips at."[19]

Where the HRF has demonstrated the complicity of Israelis with dual citizenship in likely war crimes and genocidal atrocities, the I-Unit exposed the complicity of Western governments, particularly the use of RAF Akrotiri in Cyprus as a base for surveillance flights over Gaza. Historically, such complicity goes back to the 1956 Suez Crisis when the military airbase was used to serve British objectives in the Sinai Campaign, seeking to overthrow President Nasser's government in Egypt in cooperation with French and Israeli troops. In the 1960s, the airbase was used to suppress the EOKA revolt to end British rule in Cyprus, to provide conventional support in the Arabian Peninsula and a nuclear striking capability as part of the Baghdad Pact. In the 1970s, the base cooperated with CIA and American reconnaissance aircraft to monitor the region. In the 1980s, it had a role in the U.S. retaliatory attacks against Libya. In 2006, when Israel pioneered the use of the Obliteration Doctrine in Lebanon, the base served as a transit point for mass evacuations. From the NATO-led military intervention in Libya in the early 2010s to assisting Israel in its battle against Hamas after October 7, NATO, too, has been complicit to genocidal atrocities in Gaza and its strikes against Israel.[20]

Just as law enforcement organizations use social media posts as leads and evidence of crimes in peacetime conditions, many NGOs scrutinize them hoping to bring Israeli soldiers to trial. The Hind Rajab Foundation hopes to have Israeli soldiers tried for war crimes or charges of genocide. In January 2025, the group filed a case in Brazil—500 pages of judicial records—against IDF soldier and Nova festival massacre survivor Yuval Vagdani. Israel's Foreign Ministry had to rush Vagdani out of Brazil where he was vacationing. By then, such complaints have been filed not only in Brazil, but Sri Lanka, Thailand, Belgium, the Netherlands, Serbia, Ireland and Cyprus over alleged war crimes in Gaza.[21]

Global citizen activism can respond to atrocities after they have occurred; at best, in parallel. Gaza is the first "livestreamed genocide." In this task, global citizen activism can contribute to and greatly enhance the work of media and courts. Nonetheless, it is still recording rather than preventing genocide.

Preventing or Merely Recording Genocides?

The wider international debate on Israel's genocidal atrocities began soon after the IDF ground assault in Gaza following the Hamas-led offensive of October 7, 2023. Yet, the military doctrine that set the stage for these massacres had been developed and first tested *two decades* before, when Israel Defense Forces (IDF) deployed what is here termed the Obliteration Doctrine in Dahiya, Beirut. Ruthlessly exterminating civilian lives and infrastructure, the execution turned the vibrant, largely Shia neighborhood into ruins and rubble. It was no longer a reflection of simple collateral damage but of the wholesale decimation of civilian infrastructure and civilians themselves, particularly women, children and the elderly. And yet, when Israel applied this doctrine to Gaza after October 7, 2023, the international community acted as if it came out of the blue.

As we have seen, the narrow legal definition of the Genocide Convention excludes aspects of genocide that its prime pioneer, Raphael Lemkin, saw as inherent to the term, such as colonial conquest, cultural genocide, political killings, and ethnic cleansing. This broader definition could have made the Convention more effective in the future, assuming political consensus on its use. After all, the task for the Convention was to serve as deterrent by punishing crimes of genocide. Yet, in its current form, the Convention can identify a genocide only *ex post facto*. No meteorological report is perfect, but many anticipate probable realities. Such reports are critical before the occurrences of tornados, not after they have occurred. Yet, that is the effective status of the current Convention. It is like a weather report that's released only after the tornado has obliterated communities and their people. If genocide is to be regarded as the ultimate violation of human rights, it would seem to deserve the harshest possible punishment—not a free license to enable murders that might have been prevented.

The responsibility for the silence in the face of genocide does not lie with the UN Office or the UN Special adviser. Nor does it lie with the final torso form of the Genocide Convention. At the end of his *Genocide in International Law*, William Schabas returned to the central yet elusive question of the "crime of crimes":

Perhaps the greatest unresolved question in the [Genocide] Convention is the meaning of the enigmatic word "prevent." The title of the Convention indicates that its scope involves prevention of the crime, and, in article I, States parties undertake to prevent genocide. Aside from article VIII, which entitles States parties to apply to the relevant organs of the United Nations for the prevention of genocide, the Convention has little specific to say on the question. The obligation to prevent genocide is a blank sheet awaiting the inscriptions of State practice and case law.[22]

How might these state practices proceed? While "the debate on this is unresolved, and is likely to remain so, at least until the next episode of genocide," Schabas envisioned two alternatives. A "conservative interpretation" of the provision requires states only to enact appropriate legislation and to take other measures to ensure that genocide does not occur. Whereas a more "progressive view" requires states to take action not just within their own borders but outside them, activity that may go as far as the use of force in order to prevent the crime being committed.[23]

This comment by Schabas highlights the status quo of the Genocide Convention at the turn of the 2010s. Nonetheless, even these two interpretations pose problems of their own. As an outcome of genocidal atrocities and as an occupying power, Israel has legislation to preempt genocide, deemed necessary by the progressive interpretation, yet it has engaged in mass atrocities in the name of national security. Furthermore, the Israeli war cabinet relied on similar arguments to take action outside its own borders to invade Lebanon and to threaten such action in Iran. And to make things still more challenging, in both cases Israel was aided and abetted by the United States, relying on similar interpretations. By aiding, the U.S. was providing support and assistance to Israel's atrocities; and by abetting, it was effectively encouraging Israel to commit what many saw as a heinous crime.

Indeed, it would seem that both conservative and progressive interpretation have a dark track record, at least when genocidists—as Lemkin used to call the perpetrators—claim to fight genocide.

Furthermore, even when the UN representatives highlighted genocidal threats, their voices quickly faded away into the background muzak of resigned neglect. A week after October 7, UN Special Adviser Alice Wairimu Nderitu condemned the situation in and around the Gaza Strip.[24] Over a year later, she called for prioritizing "all possible diplomatic efforts to bring an end to the ongoing hostilities in the Middle East and to redouble all efforts to strengthen the protection of innocent civilian populations, as well as to ensure the delivery of the necessary humanitarian assistance to those in dire need of receiving it."[25] Meanwhile hostilities had spread to Lebanon with spillovers in Jordan, Syria, Iraq, Yemen and Iran.

The Problem with *Ex Post Facto* Arguments

The devil is in the enforcement. Furthermore, the thresholds of genocide are habitually defined in a way that virtually ensures they will not, and even worse, *cannot* be prevented. Here's the problem in a nutshell: the Genocide Convention articulates conditions that are specific, empirically validated but necessarily *ex post facto*. For a genocide to be confirmed as such, it must first have taken place. Even though this procedure effectively violates the very purpose of the Convention—genocide *prevention*—it prevailed in the UN drafting process. As suggested by the original Latin term "from a thing done afterward," *ex post facto* law refers to law that retroactively makes criminal conduct that was not criminal when performed. It is thus limited to punishment for crimes already committed.

The articles of the Genocide Convention specify the conditions that serve as a checklist for a cumulative process. As those conditions cross the specified legal threshold, they define the formal occurrence of genocide. But it is an elusive procedure because the definition of genocide (Article 2 of the Convention) is smuggled into the analysis as a normative framework and genocide cannot be identified as such until it has taken place. In the process, the most central aspect of the Convention and its first term—*prevention*—is shuffled aside. The result is a procedure that, though seemingly specific and factual, suppresses action on meaningful prior facts on the ground, and is deemed only *ex post facto*. The premise is that a crime can be prevented only by first letting it happen.

These ideas of *ex post facto* genocide can be illustrated with an asymptote. In analytic geometry, an asymptote is a straight line that constantly approaches a given curve without ever touching it. Building on this metaphor, the *ex post facto* argument envisions genocide at some undefined threshold point. When the atrocities are seen to cross that threshold, they have become an (*ex post facto*) genocide. The procedure dramatically narrows the scope of the Convention in that only a genocide that has happened can qualify as *de jure*. To exaggerate the point: the goal is no longer to prevent the rise of future Hitlers but to first enable the final solution.

Furthermore, the *ex post facto* procedure serves to suppress responsive measures by the international community, as efforts concentrate on debating whether the operational conditions of the threshold point have been crossed rather than preventing the atrocities in the first place. Like Cervantes's *Don Quixote*, genocide analysts are forced to engage in a quest for the impossible, in the sense that they are in an eternal but, by definition, a frustrated pursuit of the end of the asymptote. The Convention, which was created to preempt future genocides, has been turned upside down to codify past genocides.

Obviously, the self-identification by the states where genocide has occurred cannot be relied upon as the criterion for finding that genocide has occurred or for its legal pursuit. Indeed, countries have an embedded interest in denying the horror they have caused. To overcome this conundrum, it is useful to re-frame the issue from the perspective of institutionalism.[26] As we shall see, it can restore *ex post ante* genocide as an organizing framework by stressing the original purpose of the Genocide Convention to prevent the crime of genocide. Such an alternative and more preventive approach would have to focus on the prior, preparatory conditions presaging the onset of genocide. That, however, is easier said than done.

Nonetheless, genocide scholars and international lawyers have proposed alternative measures to tackle preventive challenges. Instead of an amendment to the Convention to elaborate on genocide prevention, realistically a highly unlikely prospect, these mechanisms could include a commitment by states to use force to prevent genocide, but such commitments could be cumulative or escalatory while *avoiding* the use of force, by means of General Assembly resolutions, or collective decisions to the same effect by regional bodies, such as the Organization for Security and Cooperation in Europe (OSCE), the Organization of American States (OAS) and the Organization of African Unity (OAU). However, the suggested utility of such mechanisms downplays the role of hegemonic pressure and coercion that often narrow the adjudication process for determining which cases are framed as genocides and which are not.[27] Typically, while created to promote cooperation among its member states within the Americas, the OAS is located in Washington, D.C., conveniently close to the White House and the United States accounts for half of its budget.[28] Similarly, the EU is the biggest donor of the OAU and, together with a few European member states, the prime funder and backer of the peace support operations and of the program's budget.[29]

What about extending the scope of punishable acts, whether by additional protocols or by amendments to the Convention, as it was initially intended? Realistically, there are political reasons for the relatively narrow definition of the Convention; for instance, the efforts of the former colonial states to avoid charges of genocide in their colonies, or the U.S. effort to avoid legal condemnations of its mass atrocities, including the American Indian Wars, thousands of lynchings and so on. Lemkin and his colleagues had to fight long and hard to keep some of the core elements in the Convention, even as they were forced to compromise on others.

Another possibly useful mechanism to help resolve the stalemated status quo with the Convention would be to create a reporting system, somewhat like those developed by the International Labour Organization (ILO) and the major human rights treaties, or possibly build on the Universal Periodic Review (UPR), a mechanism of the UN Human Rights Council (HRC), paying particular attention to early warning indicators.[30] Yet, the cycles of such reviews are too slow and rigid to respond in a timely manner to genocidal atrocities. Such aspirations have steadily increased in the past two decades or so, as evidenced by ongoing efforts of UN human rights bodies to preempt, for instance, the role of mercenaries, mercenary-related actors and private military and/or security companies in the exploitation of natural resources.[31]

As the genocidal atrocities in Gaza suggest, preventive reporting is critical. Then again, as these atrocities also attest, the massacres have prevailed, despite one report after another—by the UN bodies, Human Rights Watch and other rights organizations, Amnesty International and a wide variety of

NGOs—condemning such violence and violations. Clearly, reporting, documenting, publicizing is not the same as having options that could bring to bear more conducive measures of prevention.

Incitement as a Separate Inchoate Crime

In December 2024, after the International Criminal Court's (ICJ) arrest warrants for Israel's Prime Minister Benjamin Netanyahu and his former Defense Minister Yoav Gallant, law professor Omer Shatz of Sciences Po (Paris Institute of Political Studies) filed a 170-page report with the ICC prosecutor's office. Submitted on behalf of French-Palestinian victims, it alleged that eight prominent Israeli officials and public figures were responsible for incitement to genocide. These were identified as Netanyahu, Gallant, President Isaac Herzog, current Defense Minister Israel Katz, retired army general Giora Eiland, Finance Minister Bezalel Smotrich, National Security Minister Itamar Ben-Gvir and journalist Zvi Yehezkeli. Instead of directly charging Israeli officials for committing genocide in Gaza, Shatz hoped to establish a pattern of incitement to genocide.

It was not the first time Shatz sought justice to victims of genocidal atrocities. Following October 7 in 2023 Gallant simply replicated measures he had deployed already 15 years ago, as we have seen. At the time, Shatz had co-filed a petition in Israel's High Court of Justice against the then-IDF general Gallant for alleged war crimes in Gaza. "We know you will reject this case, but if you don't intervene, one day, in 10 years or so, this will reach the Hague," he and his colleagues cautioned the justices. After October 7 "told you so" realization, he decided to use a different tactic to go after the genocidists: "Israeli officials' statements meet the legal criteria for direct and public incitement to genocide. For example, Gallant's [October 2023] statement referring to Palestinians as 'human animals' and declaring that 'all restraints have been removed' points to the labeling of civil facilities as military ones and removal of proportionality in military actions. Similarly, [President] Herzog's claim that 'there are no innocents in Gaza' reinforces a blanket justification for targeting civilians," he continues. "These statements, combined with cutting off electricity, water and fuel to Gaza [at the start of the war], create living conditions calculated to bring about the destruction of part of the targeted group—a genocidal act under Article 6 of the Rome Statute. This is what the ICC determined in its decision to issue arrest warrants against Netanyahu and Gallant."[32]

As we have seen, Article 3(c) of the Genocide Convention, which defines the punishable crimes under this convention, features "direct and public incitement to commit genocide." If genocide were to be committed, then incitement could also be prosecuted as complicity in genocide, prohibited in Article 3(e), without the incitement necessarily being direct or public.[33] Regarded as an extreme form of hate speech, incitement to genocide is an inchoate offense and is theoretically subject to prosecution even if genocide does not occur, although charges are typically brought in an international court following mass violence.[34] Incitement to genocide is often cloaked in metaphor and euphemism. Hence, too, the coded references to "Amalek" by Israeli soldiers and Prime Minister Netanyahu during the Gaza War. A historical enemy of the Israelites, the term Amalek is often used metaphorically to represent those who presumably seek to destroy the Jewish people and who thus justify the mandate to destroy Amalek. After all, to the faithful, social turmoil can serve as a divine sign because they expect the redemptive process to climax in the restoration of Jewish sovereignty over Amalek, the enemy nation of the Israelites.[35]

From the legal perspective, incitement to genocide is an inchoate crime since it is technically prosecutable even if genocide is *not* committed.[36] Some 15 years ago, legal scholars did consider similar measures against Iran's president and his threats of Israel's destruction. But as they lamented at the time, "no international court has ever brought an incitement prosecution in the absence of a subsequent genocide or other directly-related large-scale atrocity."[37] In the case of Gaza, such threats had been followed by what seemed a subsequent "genocide and other directly-related large-scale atrocity."

For all practical purposes, the separate inchoate approach seemed to offer several benefits to prosecute incitement rather than prosecuting incitement as part of the crime of genocide. Since real life offered the causality between incitements and subsequent violence, it obviated the challenging task of proving a causal connection between the two. Moreover, it permitted people to be charged with aiding and abetting incitement. Furthermore, and in contrast to say war crimes or crimes against humanity, it permitted incitement to genocide be prosecuted even when the subsequent violence cannot be proven to have been genocidal. Finally, it seemed to make possible the prevention of genocide since prosecuting incitement could now serve as a deterrent to genocide.[38]

Obviously, Shatz's effort was fueled by the fourth possible benefit, the urgency to prevent future genocide: "The ICC prosecutor has a duty not only to prosecute past crimes, but also to prevent future or terminate ongoing ones."[39]

The evidence on incitement was "coupled with the Israeli Attorney General Gali Baharav-Miara's notification to the Israeli Supreme Court that she decided not to open any investigation against the inciters, citing "no public interest."[40] To many observers, it was a stunning move not only because it went so blatantly against the realities in Gaza, but because the failure to address war crimes locally would lead to them being tried internationally in line with the ICC complementarity principle: If domestic courts do not act, international courts gain jurisdiction. In this view, the AG's notification effectively set the stage for the ICC's intervention and involvement. Some of Netanyahu's insiders had warned the PM of the potential of such a trajectory, while others had urged him to set up a state commission of inquiry into the government's handling of October 7 and the war, to placate possible ICC proceedings. The fact that Netanyahu rejected both efforts was seen as his failure. Yet, the PM may have shrewdly calculated that neither process was needed because the U.S. Congress would cover his war cabinet's activities, just as it would protect U.S. sovereignty from any potential interference by the world court, while a Trump election triumph in late 2024 would further solidify his position and keep ICC at bay.

Another liability was structural rather than legal. Theoretically, a separate and inchoate incitement prosecution could disrupt and prevent genocide. Yet, it remained vulnerable to demands that causality between incitement and violence is credible, if not provable. If, on the other hand, such incitement prosecution takes place after the genocide has already occurred, it falls into the *ex post facto* category that records rather than prevent genocides. The legal effectiveness of the criminalization of incitement is also haunted by the Rome Statute of the ICC, which seems to reduce the status of incitement from a separate crime to a form of criminal participation.[41]

The Proxmire Act: Genocide Incitement in America

The reckless voices of Israel's Messianic far-right for ultimate obliteration of the Palestinians in Gaza were augmented by similar calls in the United States, Israel's powerful military and financial ally. Amid the first peak of famine in Gaza, congressman Tim Walberg (R-MI), a former pastor, speaking to group of constituents in spring 2024, warned against U.S. humanitarian aid in Gaza. America "shouldn't be spending a dime on humanitarian aid." Instead, Gaza "should be like Nagasaki and Hiroshima. Get it over quick."[42]

The Republican congressman was seconded by Senator Lindsey Graham (R-SC), an influential Trump ally, on *Meet the Press*: "When we were faced with destruction as a nation after Pearl Harbor, fighting the Germans and the Japanese, we decided to end the war by the bombing [of] Hiroshima [and] Nagasaki with nuclear weapons. That was the right decision." Graham urged Americans to "give Israel the bombs they need to end the war. They can't afford to lose."[43] (Figure 6-4)

Figure 6-4. Treating Gaza "Like Hiroshima and Nagasaki"

SOURCE: *Screen captures from YouTube and X*

The Genocide Convention obligates countries to prosecute genocide within their own borders. In the United States, the Genocide Convention Implementation Act of 1987 (Proxmire Act) amended the Federal criminal code to establish the criminal offense of genocide as specified acts committed with the intent to destroy a national, ethnic, racial, or religious group.[44] To President Reagan, it was a proud moment as it allowed America to "formally join 97 nations of the world in condemning genocide and treating it as a crime." Giving his speech in remembrance of the Kristallnacht, the infamous "night of broken glass," when the Nazi pogroms paved the way to the Holocaust, Reagan added:

> Under this legislation, any U.S. national or any person in the United States who kills members of a national, ethnic, racial, or religious group with the specific intent of destroying that group in whole or in substantial part may spend his or her life in prison. Lesser acts of violence are punishable by as much as 20 years in prison and a fine of up to $1 million.[45]

Under the Act, federal prosecutors conceivably could initiate legal action against Senator Graham. However, Graham and U.S. courts would likely take advantage of domestic case law on free speech to present *their* interpretation of direct and public incitement. In turn, the U.S. court would be expected to rule that Graham's statements are protected under the First Amendment. This interpretation would be reinforced by the Senate's ratification of the Genocide Convention only in 1986—35 years after the Genocide Convention became effective—and on the reservation that nothing in the Convention requires or authorizes legislation or other action by the U.S. prohibited by the U.S. Constitution, as interpreted by the U.S.[46]

Furthermore, were Graham and Walberg advocating nuclear war or inciting? The Genocide Convention criminalizes only the latter, which is challenging to prove in a court. Legal scholars stress that the choice of the word "incitement" by the Genocide Convention's delegates reflects their intention to criminalize speech that calls for the commission of *acts* of genocide, not *speech* that encourages others to act.[47] The distinction is present in the Convention, but as we have seen, it reflects a political compromise that allowed the enactment of the Convention following the exclusion and dilution of its key elements.[48] However, like the Genocide Convention, the First Amendment does not protect incitement to commit a crime. Similar to the preparatory works of the Convention, it prohibited incitement from the beginning. But the outcomes have been debated.

In *Brandenburg v. Ohio*, the U.S. Supreme Court overturned a state statute that punished a Ku Klux Klan leader for advocating or teaching about the use of violence to achieve political change, since the statute did not distinguish between advocacy and incitement. The Proxmire Act defines "incites" as "to urge another to engage imminently in conduct in circumstances under which there is a substantial likelihood of imminently causing such conduct."[49] In *Brandenburg*, however, the court decided that what had taken place was "advocacy," though the term itself and the difference between the two is not exactly defined. It would seem that overlapping and unclear definitions, coupled with a wide variety of different interpretations make the task of prosecution highly challenging, whether inadvertently, by design, or both. The net effect is strong and bold official condemnation of genocide, accompanied by weak and timid reluctance to effectively prosecute the crime of crimes.

Interpreting an individual's stated objectives and intent matters. Holding the keys to the weapons arsenals and purse strings, an American senator or a member of the Congress has far more influence on Israel than a marginal podcaster or even a mainstream pundit. The Senate and House can actually influence how Israel conducts its war, should they really want to do so.

Of course, neither Graham nor Walberg were the first to resort to nuclear threats. In April 2007, Republican presidential contender Sen. John McCain (R-AZ) joked about bombing Iran during a campaign appearance in South Carolina. McCain was asked by an audience member about possible U.S. military action in Iran. In response, McCain said, "That old, eh, that old Beach Boys song, Bomb Iran"—which elicited laughter from the crowd. McCain then chuckled before briefly singing—to the tune of the chorus of the Beach Boys' classic "Barbara Ann"—"Bomb, bomb, bomb, bomb, anyway, ah ...." The audience responded with more laughter.[50]

The bomb lyrics go back to the Iran hostage crisis in 1979–81, when several publicly-known parodies were actually written, recorded and copyrighted, including "Bomb Iran." The lyrics were repurposed in 1990, when the Rush Limbaugh Show featured a parody of "Barbara Ann" called "Bomb Iraq" following the start of the Gulf War.[51] In the United States, these lyrical threats are explained away as humorous jests. While Americans have been treated to images of popular Iranian anger in response to attacks on Islam or their country, one wonders how the White House, the Congress and American audiences at large would react to Iran's president, Supreme leader and parliamentarians courting their audiences with lyrics like "Bomb, bomb, bomb the USA" with audiences' reckless laughter at the idea of American civilians being fried alive.

Engaged with their constituencies and audiences, both Graham and Walberg seemed to be publicly encouraging the use of nuclear weapons in Gaza and inciting genocide. Legal scholars have argued that "at minimum, this question should be discussed at the highest levels of international law before 'incitement' results in action."[52] Distressingly, such discussions have been largely absent at both domestic and international levels.

Still another possibility could be to direct international attention to preemptive *institutional* analysis. But to be effective, even an institutionalist scrutiny would have to be premised on international cooperation enabling such preemption.

Institutional Changes as Early Warnings

From organizations to states, the analysis of institutions has proved a promising approach focusing on both the constraining and enabling effects of formal and informal rules on the behavior of individuals and groups.[53] Historically, it has intensified since the rise of social sciences and economics in the late 19th century, when it was closely intertwined with the rise of classic political economy such as the pioneering works of Karl Marx, Max Weber and Emile Durkheim. In the United States, this tradition inspired "economic interpretation" in the early 20th century. This paradigm did not propose that "economic relations exert an exclusive influence," as Erwin R.A. Seligman argued, "but that they exert a preponderant influence in shaping the progress of society."[54] Shunning conventional wisdom, his protégé Charles A. Beard, America's most popular historian at the time, ignited a huge debate by documenting how the U.S. constitution was informed by the class interests of its founding fathers, thereby reflecting the emergence of a counterrevolution of sorts.[55] In sociology, Beard was succeeded by John R. Commons, who developed an analysis of collective action by the state and other institutions, which he saw as essential to understanding economics.[56]

Contemporary institutionalists stress the difference between "old" institutionalism, focused on analyzing the formal institutions of government and the state in comparative perspective, and behavioral revolution which has brought new perspectives to the social sciences.[57] In practice, this distinction is a line drawn in water. Both variants of institutionalism have inspired new strands of analysis via sociological institutionalism,[58] new institutional economics (Robert Coase, Douglass North, Daron Acemoglu)[59] and historical institutionalism.[60] Relevant to any analysis of military strategy and organization, in particular, are the works of Alfred D. Chandler Jr. on business history. Chandler's *Strategy and Structure* (1962) one of the most influential management books in history, sees strategy as determination of the long-term goals, adoption of necessary courses of action and allocation of resources. As the underlying economic environment changes, new strategies are developed to shape new organizational structures, which, in turn, affect performance.[61]

In the institutional theory of genocide, changes in the organizational capacities and structures serve as evidence of institutional shifts and thereby of policymaking intents. The consequent insights are useful in classifying a situation as preparatory to genocide when no formal declaration occurs. After all, it is very much in the interest of the offending state (in this case, Israel) and those that are complicit in its actions (United States, Germany and Israel's other arms suppliers) that terms like "genocide" are suppressed from public discourse. Following October 7, 2023, for example, when Israel began to bombard civilians in Gaza in preparation for the massive and lethal ground assault, the U.S. State Department was already discouraging diplomats working on Middle East issues from making public statements, suggesting the U.S. wants to see less violence, according to internal emails. In messages circulated, State Department staff wrote that high-level officials do not want press materials to include three specific phrases: "de-escalation/ ceasefire," "end to violence/bloodshed" and "restoring calm." The net effect was an institutionalized *carte blanche* to Israel to dramatically escalate genocidal atrocities with seeming impunity, initiating efforts at ethnic cleansing in and pushing for "voluntary population transfers" from the Gaza Strip.[62]

Due to the horrific moral and political implications of genocide, states have a vested interest in denying and covering up information disclosing that they have committed genocidal atrocities. To solve this obfuscation, the most important indicator suggesting the occurrence of genocide or its impending reality is a change in a state's organizing normative framework. If there is a change in the strategy (here, military doctrine), it means a change in the organizational structure (military organization), which translates to change in the performance (consequent activities).

It was this change in Israel's military strategy and the consequent transformation of its military organization in the late 20th century to serve the new doctrine that articulated the changes in the performance in the first two decades of the 21st century. Evolving amid the Palestinian uprising in the occupied territories, tested in the Shia neighborhood of Beirut in 2006, the Obliteration Doctrine was executed in full force in the Gaza Strip after October 7, 2023. It didn't come out of the blue. In just a matter of weeks, its destructive power exceeded the darkest devastation of World War II and anything subsequent to it. It was shock and awe, 21st century style. And it set a horrific precedent and blueprint for monsters' balls to come.

CHAPTER 7

THE PATH TO THE OBLITERATION DOCTRINE

The ultimate objective of obliteration can be defined as the total destruction of something so that nothing of it remains. This erasure ranges from physical devastation of critical infrastructure, urban hubs and settlements, public buildings and hospitals, to both combatants and non-combatants and the entire ecology of the environment. Another aspect of the term suggests a more figurative eradication: removing something from memory. Hence, the obliteration of museums, libraries, institutions of learning, arts and culture; or what Raphael Lemkin used to call "cultural genocide." Out of sight, out of mind, gone forever. A third sense of the term that is central here refers to the concerted effort to curtail, reverse or undo future development, and thus entirely undermine all economic progress. In this sense, obliteration has affinities with de-development and un-development.

In the long view, the doctrine and practice of obliteration has precursors that were already known in antiquity, including scorched-earth policies, collective punishment and civilian victimization. In turn, these historical precedents were re-deployed against the decolonization and independence struggles of the Third World. During the period that roughly coincides with the Cold War, they were repurposed to serve the former colonial powers' maintenance of their economic, political and military advantages in the new era, particularly through emergency dictates that instigated insurgencies, which were then repressed via counterinsurgency operations.

Origins of the Obliteration Doctrine

In historical view, the kind of obliteration seen in Gaza in 2023–2024 is reminiscent of the *scorched-earth policy*, a longstanding military strategy of destroying everything that allows an enemy military force to fight a war, including the critical infrastructure, military and state institutions, buildings, crops, livestock, security and so on. Even in antiquity, Egyptian and Mesopotamian leaders destroyed the fields and orchards of their enemies, forcing the besieged to choose between capitulation and starvation.[1] Typically, it has been deployed by a retreating army to leave no critical assets or by an advancing military to defeat unconventional warfare. Relatively recent historical examples feature the American Civil War and American Indian Wars[2], and Nazi Germany's war against the Soviet Union. However, the Obliteration Doctrine goes further insofar as it aims at either devastating the entire infrastructure of the target population or destroying it, in order to achieve "voluntary" mass displacement, dispossession and ultimately extermination. The deployment of scorched-earth policy against non-combatants is nonetheless banned under the 1977 Geneva Conventions.[3]

Another historical component of the Obliteration Doctrine is *collective punishment,* typically imposed on a group or entire community of people for acts presumably perpetrated by a member, or some members of that group, in a given area, city or community. The punished group often has no direct association with the perpetrators other than residing in the same area, city or community. Collective punishment violates the principle of individual responsibility since it targets individuals who are not responsible for the perpetrated acts. By the same token, it undermines modern legal systems, which habitually restrict criminal liability to individuals. Yet, it has been widely deployed throughout history, from late medieval Florence to American Civil War and Nazi occupation of Poland and Yugoslavia to postwar anti-colonial liberation struggles. Like scorched-earth policy, collective punishment is prohibited in both international and non-international armed conflicts.[4]

The third historical element of the Obliteration Doctrine is *civilian victimization,* or the purposeful use of violence against noncombatants in a conflict. This kind of victimization can feature both lethal, including killings, and non-lethal forms of violence, such as forced expulsion, torture, and rape. Occasionally, the distinction between collateral and intended damage can be blurry, or clouded by intentional obfuscation.[5] Nonetheless, in civilian victimization, violence is often deployed strategically in different ways, including to foster civilian cooperation and isolate the military adversary from its civilian proponents by removing civilians from an area,[6] as applied in the U.S. Strategic Hamlet program during the Vietnam War.

During the Cold War, both the United States and the Soviet Union provided military and financial backing to governments and groups engaging in irregular civil wars that often involved the deployment of violence to control civilians and territory.[7] After the Cold War, the involvement of major actors has been less direct but still substantial. Like scorched-earth policy and collective punishment, civilian victimization is prohibited by the Geneva Conventions.[8]

Since the postwar era, these old sources of obliteration have been coupled with largely indiscriminate area bombardment. In Gaza, it set a historical precedent.

The World-Historical Scale of Gaza's Bombardment

Aerial warfare should comply with laws of war, which regulates the conditions for initiating war (*jus ad bellum*) and the conduct of hostilities (*jus in bello*). In particular, aerial operations should comply with the principles of humanitarian law: that is, of military *necessity, objective, and proportionality*.[9] Among other things, compliance is critical to protection of the victims of the conflict and refraining from attacks on protected persons, such as medical personnel. These laws were often violated by area bombing during World War II when bombs were dropped over a fairly general area of a target. In "carpet bombing," a large area bombardment proceeded progressively to damage every part of the selected zone.

In historical view, the first aerial carpet bombing was the bombardment of Barcelona in March 1938, when 1,300 people perished and some 2,000 were wounded. It was preceded by the bombing of Guernica by the same belligerents in April 1937.[10] If area bombing refers to the indiscriminate bombing of an area, obliteration bombing or terror bombing describes intensified bombing aiming to totally devastate a city or a large part of it. Based on Article 51 of Protocol I of the Geneva Conventions, carpet bombing has been considered a war crime since 1977, conveniently *after* the Vietnam War. Nonetheless, bombardment should abide by the laws of war, as previously defined by the Hague Convention of 1907 (Hague IV):

> Article 25: The attack or bombardment, by whatever means, of towns, villages, dwellings, or buildings which are undefended is prohibited.

> Article 26: The officer in command of an attacking force must, before commencing a bombardment, except in cases of assault, do all in his power to warn the authorities.

> Article 27: In sieges and bombardments all necessary steps must be taken to spare, as far as possible, buildings dedicated to religion, art, science, or charitable purposes, historic monuments, hospitals, and places where the sick and wounded are collected, provided they are not being used at the time for military purposes.

Note that Article 27 is central to preempt the kind of cultural genocide that Lemkin considered inherent to genocide, but that some drafters, particularly the U.S. and UK delegates, managed to exclude from the Genocide Convention.

During the first year of the Gaza War, the U.S. spent at least $22.8 billion on military aid to Israel and related U.S. operations in the region.[11] What did these lethal American weapons and their generous U.S. financing enable in the Gaza Strip, one of the most densely inhabited areas in the world? By late April 2024, after barely half a year of hostilities, Israel had dropped over 70,000 tons of bombs over Gaza, surpassing the World War II bombing of Dresden, Hamburg, and London *combined.*

Taking place in mid-February 1945, the Dresden bombing was a joint British and American aerial attack in which up to 3,900 tons of high-explosive bombs and incendiary devices were dropped on the city, resulting in a firestorm and up to 25,000 killed.[12] In Hamburg, the Allied bombing between 1939 and 1945 caused 9,000 tons of bombs to be dropped and an estimated 37,000 people to perish.[13] In London, the German bombing campaign or the Blitz endured from September 1940 to May 1941. More than 30,000 tons of bombs were dropped, and some 43,000 people lost their lives.[14] During the first half a year of the Gaza War, Israeli airstrikes damaged or destroyed Palestinian refugee camps, schools, hospitals, mosques, churches, and other civilian infrastructure (Figure 7-1).[15]

The targets in Gaza are typical of the kind of mass atrocities and infrastructural devastation that would seem to be covered by the Genocide Convention. Moreover, by most accounts, more than two-thirds of the perished in Gaza are women, children and elderly. In brief, the bombing of Gaza was not only world-historical in terms of the scale of bombs and the number of perished, injured and maimed. It appears to have been a deliberately targeted campaign with intent to destroy, in whole or in part, the Palestinians and the Palestinian people as a national, ethnical, and religious group. Furthermore, the scale of destruction in Gaza became viable only with the incessant flow of U.S. weapons, guaranteed by U.S. military aid and funding to finance it. The aid is a result of half a century of bilateral military cooperation, starting with Israel's military ties with apartheid South Africa and participation in the U.S. "Dirty Wars" in Latin America, sub-Saharan Africa, and even Asia since the 1970s and '80s.[16]

The destruction of Gaza and the effort to eradicate and cleanse its Palestinian residents reflects the West's willingness to undertake mass civilian destruction, reflecting its track record from the horrific firebombing of Tokyo and the atom bombs of Hiroshima and Nagasaki to the non-military targets

Figure 7-1. Scale of Gaza's Devastation = Hamburg + London + Dresden

[Top left] Bombing of Hamburg, 1943 (Dowd J., Royal Air Force official photographer). [Top right] German bombing of London, 1940–41 (National Archives). [Left] Dresden after U.K./U.S. bombing, Feb. 13–15, 1945 (Bundesarchiv). [Right] Damage following an Israeli airstrike on the Rimal area in Gaza City on Oct. 9, 2023.

Source: *Wikimedia*

of the early 21st century. There is a critical caveat, though. Since 1945, such campaigns have targeted primarily the states and people of the Global South rather than those of the West. Hence, the tacit supremacy doctrines—that is, belief systems that a certain group of people are superior to and should have supreme authority over another group or others—in the perpetrator states to legitimize the unlegitimizable. Indeed, the more intense the obliteration has proved, the greater have been the efforts to justify and thereby legitimize it, as evidenced by the alleged Israeli effort to use the 10,000 kg, the GBU-43/B Massive Ordnance Air Blast (MOAB) bomb, to destroy the deep underground bunkers of Iran's nuclear facilities.[17]

Supremacism and Obliteration

Such indifference to human life would seem to be marked by what Lemkin termed cultural genocide, or the wholesale erasure of a group of people in a given territory. Typically, genocidal atrocities have been preceded and legitimized by doctrines of exceptionalism, including racialized supremacy dogmas, typical to white settler societies. Hitler had praised America as the one state that had made progress toward the creation of a healthy racist order, which is what the 1933 Nuremberg Race Laws were intended to establish in Germany. Jim Crow laws were only a part of Hitler's interest in U.S. segregation. American citizenship and anti-miscegenation laws were even more relevant to the Nuremberg Laws resting on presumed white Aryan supremacy. The German Aryan master race (*Herrenvolk*) proposed to displace indigenous people, who were seen as racially inferior (*Untermenschen*, a German translation of "under-man" by Lothrop Stoddard, the American political scientist and white supremacist). The Law for the Protection of German Blood and German Honor forbade marriages and extramarital intercourse between Jews and Germans and the employment of German females under 45 in Jewish households, and the Reich Citizenship Law, which declared that only those of German or related blood were eligible to be Reich citizens.[18]

In Italy, Mussolini's Fascists saw imperial expansion as necessary for the economy and national prestige. The *spazio vitale* (literally "living space") rested on a vision of a reborn Imperial Italy that would dominate the Mediterranean countries and Northern Africa. As Mussolini's ideologist Giuseppe Bottai saw it, this living space was a historic mission to restore the realm of Ancient Rome. Mussolini's Italian Empire—the New Rome—would "illuminate the world" with advanced administration, structure, knowledge and arts. As in the Old Rome, the subjugated peoples could retain their native languages and cultures. Yet, after Italy's war against Ethiopia and the rise of Hitler, Bottai supported Aryan supremacy and war. Italy's mission no longer precluded genocides.[19]

In Japan, the Meiji Restoration had been initiated with the Imperial Oath, followed by the industrial takeoff, rapid urbanization and demographic expansion. Like Bismarck in late 19th century Germany, the Meiji government initially responded to labor unrest and socialism with harsh suppression but was then compelled to introduce social legislation. However, military elites regarded modernization and Westernization as misguided without national purpose. After the economic damage of the Shōwa financial crisis in the late 1920s and followed by the Great Depression, Japan, like Germany and Italy, witnessed a resurgence of the radical right and eventually Prime Minister Fumimaro Konoe's proclamation of a new order in East Asia: the "Greater East Asia Co-Prosperity Sphere." Like Bottai's *spazio vitale*, it initially stressed inclusion and cooperation. But like its parallels in Germany and Italy, it soon waned into a vicious colonialism and supremacism. The Yamato race theory, based on a secret government report, justified racial population policy in the Asia-Pacific under Japanese rule.[20]

Far from disappearing after World War II, these ideas of racial supremacy have recently resurged as thinly veiled undercurrents in major economies, particularly amid the secular economic stagnation, aging population
and the consequent cost-of-living crises in the West. Unsurprisingly, there
have been efforts to revive the old supremacist doctrines—from the members
of the Liberal Democratic Party in Japan to restore Hakko Ichiu and those
of the German far-right to promote Lebensraum against immigration and
Italian neo-Fascist movements, to the nativism and xenophobia of the Trump
administrations.

Just as America had pursued its westward expansion to conquer the
Frontier, German colonial expansion into the east was *its* "historical destiny."
Germany needed *Lebensraum* in the East.[21] In the 19th century, Americans
justified weaponized mass starvation by the need to displace the native
"savages," whereas Nazis simply saw the Jews and the Poles as sub-human
Untermensch. Similarly, after October 7, 2023, Israelis saw their perceived
enemy, the Palestinians, as "human animals."

In *Les Damnés de la Terre* (*The Wretched of the Earth*, 1961), Frantz
Fanon, the French Afro-Caribbean anti-colonial philosopher and psychoan-
alyst, showed the dehumanizing effect of the colonial settler class on their
victims but also their own brutalization. Fanon witnessed it intimately in the
Algerian War of Independence in which he fought the French as a member of
the Algerian National Liberation Front (FLN). In Algeria, as in other colonies,
the settlers saw themselves in a Manichean world in which the natives were
not members of the same species. In their eyes, the settlers represented the
forces of good, while the natives were incapable of ethics and thereby were
the embodiment of absolute evil and deserving of collective punishment.
Taken to its logical conclusion, this Manicheism dehumanizes the colonized,
turning them into animals:

> In fact, the terms the settler uses when he mentions the native
> are zoological terms. He speaks of the yellow man's reptilian
> motions, of the stink of the native quarter, of breeding swarms,
> of foulness, of spawn, of gesticulations. When the settler seeks
> to describe the native fully in exact terms, he constantly refers to
> the bestiary.[22]

By legitimizing what cannot be legitimized, the process of dehumanization paves the way to displacement, dispossession and devastation.

States of Emergency: From Korea to Israel

In the postwar era, the boundaries between the scorched-earth tactics, collective punishment and civilian victimization blended in the emergency rule many former colonial states applied when fighting decolonization and in justification of their counterinsurgency operations. During a state of emergency, a government can impose policies that it would not or could not normally do, presumably for the safety and protection of its citizens. These repressive policies have served as convenient pretexts to justify the suspension of rights and freedoms amid a state of emergency. Depending on the perceived threat, states have used different legal definitions for specific states of emergency. In order of severity, these feature civil emergency, states of siege and martial law.

During the Cold War, declarations of a state of emergency were deployed in several theaters, starting with the Korean War (1950–1953) when present-day North Korea became one of the most heavily bombed countries in history. As virtually all major cities in the Korean Peninsula were destroyed, the U.S.-led war caused the death of an estimated 12–15 percent of the North Korean population or about 10 million people.[23] The Korean obliteration was paralleled by the Malayan Emergency (1948–60) where, in order to subjugate the indigenous independence fighters, the British resorted to the extrajudicial killings of unarmed villagers, massacres, and forced relocations of hundreds of thousands into concentration camps. Hoping to starve the Malaysians, the British exploited scorched-earth policies with food rationing, killing livestock, and aerial herbicide spraying (Agent Orange). These operations relied on precedents in other British colonies and mandates, including Palestine, Kenya, South Yemen and Dhofar (Oman), Cyprus, and Northern Ireland.[24] Similarly, the Algerian War (1954–62), which eventually resulted in Algeria winning its independence from France in the extraordinarily brutal decolonization struggle, was riddled with French war crimes. Historians estimate the death toll of almost eight years of revolution at some 1.5 million Algerian deaths.[25]

Following the French Indochina War, the U.S.-led Vietnam War (1955–75), including the wars in Laos and Cambodia, exacted horrific human costs, with up to 3 million Vietnamese killed. The economic costs include 20 percent of South Vietnam's jungle and 20 to 50 percent of the mangrove forests destroyed, with U.S. military spraying over 20 million gallons (75 million liters) of toxic herbicides.[26] Like the British in the course of the Malayan Emergency, the U.S. committed similar war crimes in Vietnam but in much larger scale, unleashing a major ecocide, and in several post-9/11 wars, particularly the misguided Iraq War (Figure 7-2).[27]

Figure 7-2. The Obliteration Doctrine in Postwar History

[Left] Pyongyang after U.S. bombing in May 1951, during the Korean War. ("We Accuse," 1951, East Berlin/Twitter). [Right] British allied headhunters in a Royal Marine base posing with the decapitated head of a suspected pro-independence guerrilla in May 1952. (*Daily Worker/Morning Star,* April 30, 1952)

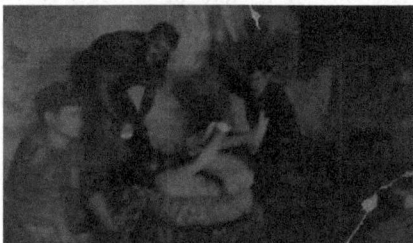

[Left] An Algerian insurgent is submerged in water and tortured by the French army using electricity, while two tires serve as containers, June 1961. [Right] Kenyan Mau Mau rebels in British concentration camps (*TalkAfricana*)

[Left] Kim Phúc in the center, running down a road naked near Trảng Bàng after a South Vietnam Air Force napalm attack in June 1972 (Nick Ut, Associated Press). [Right] Sabrina Harman poses for a fun photo behind naked Iraqi detainees forced to form a human pyramid, while Charles Graner watches. (U.S. Army/Criminal Investigation Command).

Source: *Wikimedia*

These are seen as wars of extermination—a term that some UN ambassadors used during the drafting of the Genocide Convention in the late 1940s—in which the war powers, representing colonial settler societies and their proxies, whether client states or proxy non-state actors, set out to obliterate the perceived enemy in its entirety, typically in the name of "freedom and democracy."

In Israel, the legal pathway to the Obliteration Doctrine was enacted in May 1948, when Israel's Provisional Council of State passed an ordinance that gave the Council power to declare a state of emergency, which it did immediately.[28] Since its establishment, Israel has seen itself as facing "threats of war, armed attacks and campaigns of terrorism" justifying a state of emergency, although the rationale was formally acknowledged only in 1991.[29]

These emergency regulations have a long colonial history. In the 19th century, the British had used a variety of legal and institutional approaches in Ireland, which refused to submit to British authority. Subsequently, the repressive measures were exported to other parts of the empire, including India, South Africa, and Nigeria. In each case, they served to reduce and displace the potential for more direct violence by the indigenous populations, but at the cost of legitimizing repressive practices.[30] In Palestine, the British Army had already deployed them with devastating effect in the suppression of the Arab Revolt of 1936–1939, following its "long tradition of pacification."[31] After World War II, the British used such emergency laws to suppress independence fighters in their colonies, portraying this as a "struggle against communism" during the early Cold War.[32]

In Mandatory Palestine, the emergency laws permitted detention without trial along with deportation, curfew, and suppression of publications. First propagated in 1945, the British repealed the regulations before withdrawing from Palestine in 1948. Nonetheless, most were incorporated into Israel's domestic legislation. The state of emergency was originally authorized under Section 9 of the 1948 Law and Administration Ordinance and has been in continuous effect ever since. As amended, these regulations form a central part of the legal system in the West Bank, permitting military tribunals, prohibitions on books and newspapers, house demolitions, indefinite administrative detention, extensive powers of search and seizure, the sealing off of territories and the imposition of curfews.[33] It is a seemingly legal way to maintain illegal realities.

In the postwar decades, a comparable "strategy of tension" was exploited in several countries considered vital to the U.S.-led West. In Italy, it resulted in two decades of extraordinary social turmoil, political violence and economic volatility. It was also marked by a wave of false flag terror, originally attributed to the far-left but later linked with the far-right, as well as Italian and U.S. intelligence agencies.[34] The strategic objective was to use a general sense of insecurity related to targeted groups to facilitate the buttressing an increasingly repressive government. Even though economic welfare suffers as geopolitics replaces development, the perceived common enemy is expected to "unite the nation."[35] Historically, the strategy of tension has paved the way to neoliberal economic policies, such as the 1973 Pinochet regime's reliance on U.S.-trained Chicago economists in Chile.[36]

In the aftermath of the 1973 Yom Kippur War and the rise of U.S.-Israel military ties, the long emergency in Israel contributed to extra-parliamentary efforts at violent ethnic expulsions in the West Bank, thanks to the Messianic far-right militants and their American-Jewish idol, Meir Kahane, whose role has been central ever since to Jewish supremacy doctrines, anti-Arab settler violence, efforts at the expulsion of Palestinians, and particularly the rise of the Messianic far-right.

Yet, the Gaza War was not a kind of proxy "civil war" like the Korean and Vietnam wars. Nor was it a direct confrontation between an imperial power and its colony, such as the Malayan Emergency. While sustaining the incessant flow of weapons and financing to Israel throughout most of the conflict, the United States has struggled to limit the perception of its complicity in the consequent devastation. Yet, the genocidal atrocities in Gaza would have been inconceivable without U.S. arms, financing, logistics and intelligence.

Far from complying with the laws of war, the Obliteration Doctrine violates the basic principles of humanitarian law. Even attacks against "protected persons," such as medical personnel, have been common. And this is because the doctrine rests on the idea that the civilians and civilian infrastructure are the backbone of the enemy; that attacking both must be the military objective; and that this attack against civilians and civilian property must be disproportionate so that it can foster effective deterrence. In this sense, Israel's bombardment operations in Gaza were reminiscent of area bombing during World War II, when bombs were first dropped over a fairly general area of a non-military target. Despite the regular use of the qualifier "targeted," Israeli operations mimicked carpet bombing. The horror of Guernica prompted Picasso's painting because of the massacre of 1,700 civilians; a figure that pales in comparison with the daily terror in the Gaza Strip since October 7, 2023.

Due to the continuous, long emergency—that is, the longstanding and still-continuing state of emergency—Israel has been able to apply a set of extraordinary provisions, which were initially adopted for Mandatory Palestine by Great Britain, and which have served its militarized quest for national security.

Israel's (Militarized) National Security

In 1953, Israel's first prime minister, David Ben-Gurion, crafted a strategy to respond to its national security challenges. It laid down the pillars of Israel's national security doctrine until the 1967 War. Subsequent formulations have matched neither the scope nor the influence of the original document. In Ben-Gurion's view, Israel's Arab neighbors hadn't and wouldn't accept Israel's presence in the region. Unlike some other members of his cabinet, he believed Arab countries were determined to destroy Israel and that over time their demographic size and resources would allow them to acquire advanced weapon systems and military capacity.[37]

However, Israel also had its advantages. While its small size did not allow "strategic depth," it could move troops fast from one location to another. Thanks to immigrants, it benefited from more qualified human capital. Unlike the large but disunited Arab world at the time, Ben-Gurion saw Israel as a united singular actor. Hence, the need for an advanced air force and intelligence to keep its neighbors in check; expansive immigration to build a larger qualified population with requisite educational and science systems; mandatory military service with huge reserves that could be mobilized rapidly; and an overwhelming ethos of unity that would ensure that the small "nation in uniform" would be more effective than a simple sum of its parts.[38]

The consequent security state would serve as an "iron wall," which assertive revisionist Zionism thought necessary, so that the Arabs would eventually be resigned to the enduring presence of a predominantly Jewish state in the Middle East. Despite his ideological differences with revisionist Zionism, Ben-Gurion's grand strategy was predicated on the "Iron Wall" concept of his arch-enemy Ze'ev Jabotinsky, the prophet of revisionist Zionism.[39]

Since Israel would not be able to halt Arab wars, an effective deterrence was seen as vital to keep the enemy at bay and the wars less frequent. If that failed, Israel then needed an early warning system to respond to the challenge in time. In case of conflict, a decisive and fast victory was critical. The more stunning the triumph, the more it would buy time to prepare for the next attack.[40] Hence, too, Israel's early preoccupation with cross-border friction in the 1950s and the misguided 1956 Sinai War, mainly to create new security "buffer zones" and to expand the state borders and increase strategic depth, coupled with the displacement, dispossession and devastation of Palestinian lands and people.

Following the 1967 Six-Day War and the subsequent 1973 Yom Kippur War, the occupied territories became the primary threat. Until then, the PLO with its reluctance to recognize Israel had been seen as the main obstacle to peace. Now, with the aggressive expansion of the settlements, the right-wing

Likud governments refused to recognize the Palestinian case, even after Arafat had recognized the right of Israel to exist in 1988 (and Hamas leaders made statements to similar effect in the late 1990s).[41] In the absence of viable alternatives, Palestinians had few alternatives but to fight back, which Israel sought to crush with disproportionate force, hoping to project an effective deterrence. Hence, the First Intifada (1987–93), the rise and fall of the peace process, the Second Intifada (2000–2005) and a series of Gaza wars paving the way to October 7, 2023.

From the very beginning of its existence, Israel has been a warring state. But over time, there have been dramatic shifts in the nature of these wars. Since the late 1940s, Israel has waged essentially three kinds of wars: (1) ostensibly *wars of survival* in which it has faced the joint forces of its neighboring Arab states; (2) *wars of expansion,* which have effectively served as counterinsurgency campaigns against Palestinian uprisings; and (3) *wars of obliteration* dominated by a doctrine first tested in Dahiya, a mainly Shia neighborhood in Beirut. The latter were limited to compounds, blocks of settlements or neighborhoods until the Gaza War, in which the civilian populations were subjected to far broader mass atrocities. In this long view, the peace process of the 1990s was a temporary blip in the longer trend of expansion paving the way to the wars of obliteration.[42]

None of these catastrophes could have happened without the complicity of the United States, and to a lesser degree Germany and certain other states.[43] These allies provided Israel a defensive cushion. On the other hand, their very presence and decisive contributions disguised a new reality. For the first time in its history, Israel is no longer able to fully protect itself. Nothing illustrated this better than Iran's Operation True Promise on April 13, 2024. As President Biden followed the events in the Situation Room at the White House, he watched the events very silently until the integrated defenses kicked in, as told by journalist Bob Woodward:

> U.S. military coordinators in Israel were leading the ballistic missile defense: You take down those, we'll take down these, the Brits have those, the Saudis have these. It was an extraordinary integrated defense operation.
>
> A lot of history was made as they watched. This was the first time Iran had ever directly attacked Israel and the first time the U.S. military had ever directly defended Israel. Saudi Arabia and Jordan had come to Israel's defense. It was unprecedented. A major power move against Iran ...

When Iran announced the end of its military operation, the U.S. and its partners had intercepted and shot down almost all of Iran's missiles and drones, nearly 300 in total, proving for the moment the enormous power in collective defensive capability.[44]

Biden told Netanyahu that Israel had "won" and no other move was warranted. Netanyahu wouldn't hear any of it. Israel would strike back, again. And so, new U.S. weapons, American surveillance systems and cooperation with U.S. allies, all of these states became complicit to Israel's new escalation and atrocities.

But Israel had not contained Iran's attack. It was the U.S. and its partners that had intercepted and shot down most of Iran's missiles and drones, albeit some did get through. The Netanyahu cabinet had effectively offshored its military sovereignty. Accordingly, it had become subject to the U.S.-led collective defensive capability.

From Targeted Killings to Institutionalized Obliteration

The tacit doctrine of what is here conceptualized as a "war of obliteration" emerged more fully in the course of the 2006 Lebanon War in which up to 1,300 Lebanese were killed. It severely damaged Lebanese civil infrastructure and displaced 1 million Lebanese and 300,000–500,000 Israelis, primarily in northern Israel.[45] Structurally, the conflict stemmed from the 1967 Six-Day War, which triggered the first cross-border attacks from southern Lebanon into Israel by the Palestine Liberation Organization (PLO). These offensives intensified after 1971 when the PLO and its leadership arrived in the area after the Jordanian civil war, itself an outcome of the 1967 War that caused several hundred thousand Palestinians to be expunged from the Israeli-occupied Palestinian territories into Jordan. Demographic tensions contributed to the Lebanese Civil War (1975–2000).[46] The rise of the Hezbollah was the outcome of Israel's 1982 invasion of Lebanon and the group's consequent cross-border raids, which subsequently led to the tacit U.S.-Israel collaboration to eliminate Hezbollah from southern Lebanon.[47]

The strategic objective seems to have been the effort to alter the fragile equilibrium of Lebanon, even at the cost of the ailing country's economy. In the course of the war, the Israeli Air Force (IAF) flew 11,900 combat missions; more than the number of sorties in the 1973 October War and almost double the number during the 1982 Lebanon War. The Israeli performance had been poor, but nonetheless large parts of the Lebanese civilian infrastructure were destroyed.[48] It was then that Chief of Staff Dan Halutz deepened the cooperation of the IAF with the IDF ground forces and Israel's internal security service, developing a "targeted killings policy" that enabled the IAF to implement targeted killings of Palestinian militants within minutes following intelligence. On July 23, 2002, an IAF warplane dropped a 1-ton bomb on a Gaza apartment building in a densely populated residential neighborhood. The bomb killed not just senior Hamas commander Salah Shehade, his wife and daughter, but over a dozen other civilians. Israel's then-prime minister Ariel Sharon characterized the operation as a success. Yet, it was conducted just hours *after* Hamas leader Ahmed Yassin had offered to end suicide bombing and the Palestinian Authority (PA) was working out a deal with Hamas to end the terror attacks. The bombing sparked a resumed terror wave and a number of new civilian deaths in Israel.[49]

These basic elements—devastating tactics of targeted killings with unwarranted civilian collateral damage, the absence of a coherent political strategy and efforts to neutralize pragmatic negotiations to make way for extremist leaders who could then be blamed for Israeli reluctance to engage in talks, along with concerted efforts at rule-and-divide measures between the PA and Hamas—all these are an integral part of the targeted killings not just of Shehade, but of Hamas leader Ahmed Yassin (2004), and Shehade's successors, Ahmed al-Jabari (2012) and Mohammed Deif (2024).[50] In the absence of U.S. and international sanctions and interventions, the perception among Israel's conservative cabinets was that they enjoyed impunity, which was then exploited by broadening the scope of targeted killings. Consequently, domestic dissent in Israel was increasingly suppressed, including the protests of Brig. Gen (res.) Iftach Spector who charged Halutz's targeting killings with compromising the ethical principles of the IDF culture. He was one of 27 reserve and former pilots refusing to fly missions against targets in the West Bank and Gaza, opposing "illegal and immoral" attack orders that continued to "harm innocent civilians."[51] In response, Chief of Staff Dan Halutz had the pilots grounded.[52]

The rise of the Obliteration Doctrine in Israel reflects the institutional preconditions of the military, particularly the shift of political balance among the chiefs of staff from moderate left to hard right from 1948 up to the present. In its early period (1948–73), their military doctrines were aligned with the dominant labor coalition. Moreover, many grew of age in collective *kibbutzim* and cooperative *moshavim* (Figure 7-3).

Figure 7-3. Israel's Wars and Chiefs of Staff

Wars of Survival (1948-1973) Labor-led "Land-for-peace"	Wars of Expansion (1973-1991) Likud-led "Iron Wall" security	"Peace Process" (1991-2005) Labor-led Two-State	Wars of Obliteration (2005-Present) Harsh-right Greater Israel
Yaakov Dori (1947-49)	David Elazar (1972-74)	Ehud Barak (1991-95)	Moshe Ya'alon
Yigael Yadin (1949-52)	Mordechai Gur	Amnon Lipkin-Shahak	(2002-2005)
Mordechai Maklef	(1974-78)	(1995-98)	Dan Halutz (2005-2007)
(1952-53)	Rafael Eitan (1978-83)	Shaul Mofaz	Gabi Ashkenazi
Moshe Dayan (1953-58)	Moshe Levi (1983-87)	(1998-2002)	(2007-11)
Haim Laskov (1958-61)	Dan Shomron (1987-91)		Benny Gantz (2011-15)
Tzvi Tzur (1961-64)			Gadi Eisenkot (2015-19)
Yitzhak Rabin (1964-68)			Aviv Kohavi (2019-23)
Haim Bar-Lev (1968-72)			Herzi Halevi
			(2023-Present)

SOURCE: *Steinbock 2025, op. cit., Chapters 4 and 11, respectively.*

During the wars of expansion (1973–91), these doctrines were replaced by very different views, starting with those of Rafael Eitan who actively armed and formed an alliance with the Lebanese Phalangist militia, paved the way to the Lebanon War and allowed the Sabra and Shatila Palestinian massacre to occur. As a gung-ho supporter of the Israeli alliance with apartheid-era South Africa, Eitan saw Israeli Arabs and Palestinians in occupied territories as similar to blacks in South Africa who "want to gain control over the white minority just like the Arabs here want to gain control over us. And we, like the white minority in South Africa, must act to prevent them from taking over."[53] As Netanyahu's political career took off, Eitan gave his support to the harsh-right Likud.

During the peace process in the 1990s, the chiefs of staff supported the more peaceful objectives of Prime Minister Rabin and, after his assassination, those of Shimon Peres. Hence, the terms of Ehud Barak, the future Labor PM; Amnon Lipkin-Shahak, a dovish veteran soldier who severely criticized Netanyahu's policies while calling for a labor-center coalition; and Shaul Mofaz, a transitional figure who supported Ariel Sharon in politics while resorting to harsh measures during the Second Intifada in 2000–2005. But as the peace process crumbled, IDF's chiefs of staff, whether they believed in a two-state solution or a Likud-style unitary Jewish state, began to favor increasingly hawkish measures; not just as tactics toward a strategic goal, but as a strategy that dictated tactical measures. In 1996, the Israeli military fired artillery shells at a UN compound sheltering around 800 Lebanese civilians, causing the Qana massacre. It triggered a lawsuit against chief of staff Moshe Ya'alon who had greenlighted the killing of Hamas commander Shehade. The bombing in Gaza City caused 14 civilian deaths and in 2006 a warrant for Ya'alon's arrest for alleged war crimes during his fund-raising tour in New Zealand. In 2014, Ya'alon served as defense minister when the IDF conducted Operation Protective Edge, which led to another series of allegations of war crimes against Israel. By then, as his relationship with Prime Minister Netanyahu fell apart, he warned that "extreme and dangerous elements have taken over Israel and the Likud Party."[54] Subsequently, he called the government a "dictatorship of criminals."[55] But it was a cabinet for whom his past stances had paved the way.

Ya'alon was succeeded at the head of the IDF by Dan Halutz in 2005. Halutz had played a key role in the "targeted killings" by cementing cooperation between the Israeli air force, ground forces and internal security, coupled with the massive employment of UAV drones. Halutz saw no moral issues with such killings. After increasing criticism and international controversy, he resigned, claiming that his decision was based on "strong ethics, loyalty to the organization and integrity." Yet it turned out that, while still the chief of staff, Halutz sold off his investment portfolio in August 2006, just hours after two Israeli soldiers were captured by Hezbollah, leading to the outbreak of war. Though technically legal,[56] his action and the ensuing scandal demonstrated that the legal definition of "insider information" in the military elite was too narrow. It also highlighted the conflicts of interests and economic perks associated with the military-industrial complex and the nascent genocide business.[57]

Subsequent Israeli chiefs of staff have continued to follow in the footprints of Gadi Eisenkot, who refined and perfected the Obliteration Doctrine in 2005, as we shall see, and his successors.

Eventually, Yoav Gallant, who served as Netanyahu's defense minister for a year, was targeted by the ICC prosecutor. But it was not the first time Gallant was accused of violations of international law. He used to serve as the head of Southern Command and was widely criticized for the execution of the Obliteration Doctrine in the 2008–2009 Gaza War and condemned by the famed Goldstone Report. His command role in Operation Cast Lead and his lobbying against an investigation of an IDF commander who approved an air strike resulting in multiple civilian deaths led critics to charge him as a suspect in "grave violations of international law."[58] Two months before October 7, 2023, Gallant paved the way to charges of genocide by threatening to attack Hezbollah and "return Lebanon to the Stone Age," if Israel was attacked. Two days after the Hamas offensive, Gallant ordered a complete siege on the Gaza Strip: "We are fighting human animals and we are acting accordingly."[59] Just days later, when he met U.S. Secretary of Defense Lloyd Austin, Gallant called on Palestinians to evacuate northern Gaza, including Gaza City, stating that "we are going to destroy Hamas infrastructure, Hamas headquarters, Hamas military establishment, and take these phenomena out of Gaza and out of the Earth." To leave no doubt about his intentions, he added:

> Gaza won't return to what it was before. Hamas won't be there.
> We will eliminate everything.[60]

So, Austin, Biden and Blinken were fully familiar with the Israeli objectives from the very beginning. Not only did they hear those goals in person, as we have seen. They supported these objectives. By November 2023, Gallant warned that Beirut could meet the same fate as Gaza.[61] It was a threat that he would execute in fall 2024.

The Test Laboratory of Dahiya, Beirut

So it was that just a few years later, the military strategy compounding civilian collateral damage was succeeded by a further elaboration which targeted the civilian infrastructure itself for destruction. In the process, the devastation doctrine that had targeted individuals in the past was expanded to include buildings and compounds, even the urban neighborhood that would initially name the nascent doctrine.

Indeed, Dahiya had been an Israeli target for decades. The predominantly Shia Muslim suburb, located in southern Beirut, is one of its most densely populated. Today, it is a largely residential and commercial area encompassing malls, retail stores and busy *souks*. Before the Lebanese Civil War in 1975, it was a rural settlement under rapid urbanization with a mixed community of Christians and Shia Muslims. Many of the latter had come from Southern Lebanon and the Beqaa valley where they had fought the French mandate in the interwar period. Another wave of Shi'ites moved into the area in the early 1960s in part to flee rural hardship in the south and in part to access the perceived benefits of urbanization. After Jordan's civil war in 1971, still another wave of refugees followed. So, when the Lebanese civil war took off, some 45 percent of the country's Shi'ites were living in Greater Beirut.[62]

After just a year into the civil war, some 100,000 Shi'ites were displaced from eastern Beirut following several massacres. When Israel initiated its 1978 and particularly 1982 invasions into Lebanon, another 250,000 Lebanese were displaced, many of them Shia, and an estimated 80 percent of Lebanese villages were devastated.[63] And in 1986 the South Lebanon security belt was established with Israeli logistics and military support, leading more Shi'ites to move to Beirut. By then, an estimated 800,000 Shias, that is, the overwhelming majority of Shia in Lebanon, had experienced displacement.[64]

So, when the Gaza War spread from the Strip to Lebanon, the IDF bombed Southern Lebanon in general and Dahiya in particular and demanded a security zone in the region, it was a déjà vu all over again for the Shi'ites. What made the Israeli operation of 2006 different from earlier devastations was their new military doctrine. Asymmetric warfare combined two heretofore forbidden characteristics of modern warfare: the deliberate destruction of the civilian infrastructure and the deployment of disproportionate force. The net effect was a dual war crime par excellence. Under international humanitarian law, warring parties are required to distinguish between combatants and civilians, to ensure that attacks on legitimate military targets are proportional, and that the military advantage of such attacks outweighs the potential harm done to civilians.[65] Since violations of such laws are considered war crimes, the 2006 Lebanon War sparked widespread condemnation by Amnesty International, Human Rights Watch and the United Nations, which all charged both Hezbollah and Israel of violating international humanitarian law (though the equation of the two sides made little sense in terms of their respective firepower and capabilities).[66]

The pioneering Obliteration Doctrine was first outlined in 2005 by Gadi Eizenkot. Interestingly, he was no extremist. Subsequently an influential Israeli military leader and politician, Eisenkot supported Israeli democracy and a two-state solution. But as a military strategist, he opened the Pandora's Box that both Israel's right-wing Likud and Messianic far-right would embrace. Eisenkot was appointed head of the Northern Command following Maj. Gen. Udi Adam's resignation amid criticism over his conduct in the 2006 Lebanon War. Adam had led Israeli forces against Hezbollah until he was effectively sidelined when another general was appointed above him.[67] At the time, it was seen as still another fallout of the Lebanese crisis. Many Israelis were frustrated that the military had failed to secure a comprehensive victory over the Hezbollah militia or retrieve the two soldiers whose capture had triggered the conflict. It was this popular frustration that set the stage for "tougher measures."

Eisenkot's strategy was based on the idea that the IDF would have to severely damage Dahiya to create effective deterrence against Hezbollah.[68] After all, his predecessor had been compelled to quit for having been "too cautious." The assumption was that the deployment of disproportionate power would end Hezbollah for good, or at least for a sustained period. Hence, Eisenkot's new strategy of disproportion:

With an outbreak of hostilities [with Hezbollah], the IDF will need to act immediately, decisively, and with force that is disproportionate to the enemy's actions and the threat it poses. Such a response aims at inflicting damage and meting out punishment to an extent that will demand long and expensive reconstruction processes. The strike must be carried out as quickly as possible, and must prioritize damaging assets over seeking out each and every launcher. Punishment must be aimed at decision makers and the power elite...

Israel's test will be the intensity and quality of its response to incidents on the Lebanese border or terrorist attacks involving Hezbollah in the north or Hamas in the south. In such cases, Israel again will not be able to limit its response to actions whose severity is seemingly proportionate to an isolated incident. Rather, it will have to respond disproportionately in order to make it abundantly clear that the State of Israel will accept no attempt to disrupt the calm currently prevailing along its borders. Israel must be prepared for deterioration and escalation, as well as for a full-scale confrontation. Such preparedness is obligatory in order to prevent long term attrition.[69]

In 2006, Dahiya served as Hezbollah's stronghold. In the war of that year, following the group's rockets on Israeli border towns, Israel's military focused on major civilian targets in Lebanon, including infrastructure and public works, ports and factories, power systems, civilian homes and industrial plants, even ambulances. UN Emergency Relief authorities called Israel's offensive "disproportionate" referring to the "horrific" leveling of "block after block" of buildings in Beirut. They regarded it as a violation of international humanitarian law. A third of the killed were children, while 900,000 Lebanese were displaced (Figure 7-4).[70]

Figure 7-4. The Obliteration Doctrine: July–August 2006

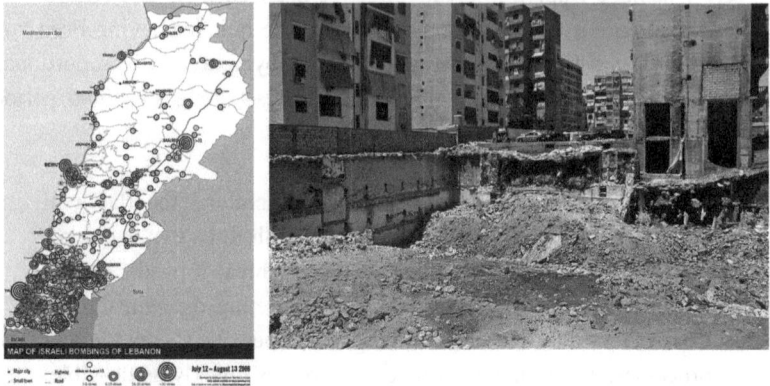

[Left] Lebanese areas targeted by Israeli bombs, July 12 to Aug. 13, 2006. (*Lestat de Lioncourt*) [Right] Crater from destroyed buildings in Beirut suburb of Dahiya two years after the Second Lebanon War of 2006. (*Magne Hagesæter*)

Source: *Wikimedia*

When the IDF embraced the nascent Obliteration Doctrine, the Cold War was history, ad hoc tribunals had been set up, the Genocide Convention was in the ICC's Rome Statute, UN organs had many references to it and the UN even had its special adviser with a mandate for warning the UN on the *Prevention* of Genocide. Ostensibly, things were in place to deal with this kind of military doctrine that explicitly targeted civilians and civilian infrastructure.

Yet, when Eisenkot stated in public that Israel would embrace a new military doctrine—that of extreme disproportion which virtually ensured genocidal atrocities—there was no consequential international outcry, not to speak of intervention, despite the IDF's track-record since the 1980s, the demise of the peace process, the rise of Jewish supremacy doctrines and Messianic far-right in Israel, and the Israel-U.S.-EU blockade of Gaza after Hamas rose to power following a democratic election—which made a new war a matter of time rather than a matter of principle.

The Doctrine of Obliteration

In the Obliteration Doctrine, the army deliberately targets civilian infrastructure to wreak massive suffering on the civilian population, thereby seeking to establish an effective deterrence. Following the 2006 Lebanese War, the same doctrine was deployed in the 2008–2009 Gaza War, or Operation Cast Lead, as Israel called it. This was a three-week armed conflict between the Gazan Palestinian groups and the IDF. It caused 1,200–1,400 Palestinian and a dozen Israeli deaths. Over 46,000 homes were destroyed, making more than 100,000 people homeless.[71] As Eisenkot saw it,

> What happened in the Dahiya quarter of Beirut in 2006 will happen in every village from which shots will be fired in the direction of Israel. We will wield disproportionate power and cause immense damage and destruction. From our perspective, these are military bases.... This isn't a suggestion. It's a plan that has already been authorized.... Every one of the Shi'ite villages is a military site, with headquarters, an intelligence center, and a communications center. Dozens of rockets are buried in houses, basements, attics, and the village is run by Hezbollah men. In each village, according to its size, there are dozens of active members, the local residents, and alongside them fighters from outside, and everything is prepared and planned both for a defensive battle and for firing missiles at Israel.[72]

After pilot efforts, the Obliteration Doctrine was effectively in place. It had been developed by Israel's military leaders in close cooperation with the country's cabinet and political leaders. It targeted the civilian infrastructure for devastation, deliberately and purposefully. Civilian devastation was no longer unfortunate collateral damage, but the very focus of a new military doctrine, supported by Israel's political and military elites that understood well the inevitable consequence of civilian decimation.[73] As Col. (Ret.) Gabriel Siboni, Eisenkot's frequent co-author, noted 15 years before the post-October 7 Gaza atrocities:

> This approach is applicable to the Gaza Strip as well. There, the IDF will be required to strike hard at Hamas and to refrain from the cat and mouse games of searching for Qassam rocket launchers. The IDF should not be expected to stop the rocket and missile fire against the Israeli home front through attacks on the launchers themselves, but by means of imposing a ceasefire on the enemy.[74]

A central element in the Obliteration Doctrine relates to the (hoped for) purpose of ending the conflict in the shortest possible time. Furthermore, Eisenkot pledged that "in the next clash with Hezbollah, we won't bother to hunt for tens of thousands of rocket launchers and we won't spill our soldiers' blood in attempts to overtake fortified Hezbollah positions. Rather, we shall destroy Lebanon and won't be deterred by the protests of the 'world.'"[75]

Replace the terms "Hezbollah" with "Hamas" and "Lebanon" with "Gaza," and the implications are unambiguous.

By 2008, some 15 years *before* October 7, 2023, there was a broad public consensus among both the Israeli military elites and their observers that "in the next war the IDF would deploy disproportionate force" and that this force would feature heavy firepower, "immense destruction"; even if the targets chosen would be different than those in prior conflicts. Oddly enough, the very public launch of and debate on what was then described as the "Dahiya Doctrine" attracted little attention from those international bodies and authorities presumably dedicated to genocide prevention. Hence, the subsequent note by the former UN Special Rapporteur. Professor Richard Falk, sparked by Eisenkot's claim that the Shi'ite villages of south Lebanon had been transformed "into platforms for terror," an inflammatory shorthand for armed resistance to Israel's occupation of southern Lebanon.

> It is notable that this claim is put forward without the slightest effort on Eisenkot's part to reconcile the Dahiya Doctrine with international humanitarian law, which imposes a limit of proportionality on any use of force in situations of international combat. It also neglects to take note of the fact that before encounters with Hezbollah, Israel routinely struck back disproportionately at its enemies.[76]

As far as Falk was concerned, there was a broad agreement at the UN and by legal experts that an occupying power like Israel cannot invoke "self-defense" arguments in support of using force and collective punishment against an occupied people, such as the Palestinians, particularly taking into consideration the historical context. In 1967, the UN Security Council Resolution 242 had unanimously looked toward the withdrawal of Israel's armed forces from the occupied territories following the Six-Day War. Furthermore, Israel is subject to specific legal duties in the 4th Geneva Convention to protect civilians subject to its administration, and to refrain from efforts to displace the occupied people by interfering with their underlying rights of self-determination.[77]

The Israeli take was very different, however.

"Exterminate All the Brutes!"

There was nothing inevitable about the genocidal atrocities of Gaza. There was no divine fate that pre-determined one future over another. It is thus a future that was chosen among several alternatives. In effect, another future was conceivable even in 2016, when Yair Golan, as the deputy chief of staff of the IDF, prepared for his speech on Holocaust Day. At the time, he was widely seen as the next Chief of Staff. In contrast to most of his contemporaries and more like the first generation of Israeli military leaders, Golan grew of age in the leftist Labor movement and still shares its values and ideas. So, it was hardly surprising that he drew a parallel with the Nazi era and the conditions in modern Israel, saying:

It's scary to see horrifying developments that took place in Europe begin to unfold here. The Holocaust should bring us to ponder our public lives and, furthermore, it must lead anyone who is capable of taking public responsibility to do so. Because if there is one thing that is scary in remembering the Holocaust, it is noticing horrific processes which developed in Europe—particularly in Germany—70, 80, and 90 years ago, and finding remnants of that here among us in the year 2016.

The Holocaust, in my view, must lead us to deep soul-searching about the nature of man. It must bring us to conduct some soul-searching as to the responsibility of leadership and the quality of our society. It must lead us to fundamentally rethink how we, here and now, behave towards the other.

There is nothing easier and simpler than in changing the other. There is nothing easier and simpler than fear-mongering and threatening. There is nothing easier and simpler than in behaving like beasts, becoming morally corrupt, and sanctimoniousness.

On Holocaust Remembrance Day, it is worthwhile to ponder our capacity to uproot the first signs of intolerance, violence, and self-destruction that arise on the path to moral degradation.[78]

Calling for national soul-searching, Golan's speech was widely reported as a bombshell in Israel. Prime Minister Netanyahu called the comments "outrageous" saying they "do injustice to Israeli society and create contempt for the Holocaust." Meanwhile, Culture Minister Miri Regev called for his resignation and right-wing Twitter users charged him of "forgetting the lessons of the Holocaust."[79] Golan never became IDF's Chief of Staff. Nor did he ever retreat from his message. In 2021, following a killing of a Jewish settler in West Bank by a Palestinian, other settlers attacked a man from the Palestinian village of Burqa, damaging houses and desecrating graves. The violence enraged Golan: "Those people who come to settle there, riot in Burqa, destroy gravestones, committed a pogrom. Do we abuse gravestones? These are not people, these are sub-humans, despicable people, the corruption of the Jewish people."[80] It triggered an even broader firestorm in Israel, just months before Netanyahu embraced the Messianic far-right in his cabinet—that is, the very same people representing those who destroyed gravestones and committed pogroms against Palestinians.

Almost two decades ago, the senior proponents of the Obliteration Doctrine included General Eisenkot, his co-author Colonel (Res.) Gabriel Siboni and Major General (Res.) Giora Eiland, ex-head of the National Security Council. At the time, the three thought mainly in terms of the Shi'ite strongholds in Lebanon. Eiland spelled out the implications. In the next war, whenever it would take place, the enemy combatants would have to be destroyed, along with the civilian infrastructure (Figure 7-5).

Figure 7-5. Major Champions of the Obliteration Doctrine

General (Res.) Gadi Eisenkot   Colonel (Res.) Gabriel Siboni   Major General (Res.) Giora Eiland

SOURCE: *Wikimedia, screen capture from X/Twitter*

Subsequently Eisenkot, in cooperation with Siboni, outlined the *Guidelines for Israel's National Security Strategy* (2019) urging Israel's security establishment to ensure effective deterrence because "once deterrence collapses, it is imperative to stop the threat as rapidly and clearly as possible to renew deterrence, return to routine life, and allow an extended period of calm based on security strength."[81]

That was the objective of the Netanyahu war cabinet in 2023; one in which it thoroughly failed. After just one month of the Gaza War, Eisenkot charged the Netanyahu cabinet for "near-criminal behavior" as the PM tried to hide protocols, leak lies to media and sway war goals to appease the Messianic far-right.[82] With advancing obliteration, Eisenkot lost his own son and two nephews in a war he now opposed. Yet, the doctrine that was foundational for the obliteration was to a great extent his own handiwork. Colonel Siboni stuck to the obliteration script. Any expectations of an imminent end to combat in Gaza were unrealistic, he said in an interview to an Israeli think tank which had advocated ethnic cleansing and Palestinian population transfers from Gaza. Just as Israel had been fighting in the West Bank "since 2002, and we are still fighting, and probably in Gaza, we will fight for decades ahead."[83]

In November 2023, Major General (Res.) Giora Eiland took the doctrine even further, arguing as the Messianic far-right had done since the days of rabbi Meir Kahane and the prophecies of ultra-nationalist rabbis in the 1970s, that since most Gazans support Hamas, effectively all Gaza women are the mothers, sisters, and spouses of Hamas murderers. So, Israel was not only entitled but morally obligated to ignore their pain. Collective punishment was not a violation of international law or a perverse moral code. Somewhat like Joseph Conrad's Mr. Kurtz in *The Heart of Darkness* (1899), his solution was: *"Exterminate all the brutes!"*

Behind every terrorist stand dozens of men and women, without whom he could not engage in terrorism. Now this also includes the mothers of the martyrs, who send them to hell with flowers and kisses. They should follow their sons, nothing would be more just. They should go, as should the physical homes in which they raised the snakes. Otherwise, more little snakes will be raised there ...

The international community warns us of a humanitarian disaster in Gaza and of severe epidemics. We must not shy away from this, as difficult as that may be. After all, severe epidemics in the south of the Gaza Strip will bring victory closer and reduce casualties among IDF soldiers ...

And no, this is not about cruelty for cruelty's sake, since we don't support the suffering of the other side as an end but as a means.[84]

It was the ultimate ethical dictum of inhumanity. Just as the Nazis evoked collective punishment against Jews, Poles, Communists and gypsies in the 1940s, Eiland seized on it to suggest that what the military might not achieve, biowarfare might: "Epidemics in the South [of Gaza] will bring victory closer and will decrease casualties among IDF soldiers."[85] These arguments unleashed a broad Israeli and international condemnation, but they were aligned with the strategic objectives of the Obliteration Doctrine.[86]

Following a year of abject obliteration in the Gaza Strip, Eiland's name surfaced again in international debate. He was the lead author of the highly controversial "General's Plan," which proposed that the Israeli military gives all civilians in northern Gaza one week in which to evacuate the area, after which they would be considered combatants and targeted for death by the military. Hamas would "either have to surrender or to starve."[87] What got lost in the translation was the fact that even though the international debate escalated in October 2024, Eiland had already talked about the outlined plan in April. In other words, half a year before the intended implementation of the plan, it was well known. Had the ceasefire been imposed *then*, tens of thousands of Palestinians, quite likely 100,000 to 200,000—most of them children, women and elderly—would have survived.

But that would have undermined the Obliteration Doctrine.

EPILOGUE

Right following October 7, 2023, the Israeli army expanded its authorization for bombing non-military targets, thereby loosening the constraints regarding expected civilian casualties. For the first time, it used artificial intelligence (AI) to generate potential targets, which proved terrifyingly efficient. The decision to allow algorithms to dictate not just who will die, but also to take out others in their proximity, typically family members and other families; all of them civilians; that was something new.[1] It violated the basic tenets of international law. But it was strategic in the sense that it was well-aligned with the Obliteration Doctrine. It transformed the ethics of warfare into a dark real-life survival game in which life and survival had little to do with one's conduct, but everything with probability degrees of destruction.

As IDF spokesperson Daniel Hagari acknowledged only two days after the Hamas offensive, "the emphasis is on damage and not on accuracy."[2] Yet, two long months of massive Israeli bombing took place before the U.S. intelligence community would acknowledge in public that nearly half of the air-to-ground munitions used in Gaza had been *unguided*, while the rest were precision-guided munitions.

The use of these less precise "dumb bombs" poses a greater threat to civilians, especially in densely populated areas.[3] It suggests that the intent had been to expunge all Palestinian presence from the territory altogether; not just the individuals and infrastructure, but all traces of Palestinian culture and history. It exemplified the kind of physical, mental, intellectual and spiritual "cultural genocide" that Lemkin had hoped but failed to see included in the Genocide Convention.

Necrotizing the Living Dead

Deploying AI for maximum devastation, Israel's mass assassination factories were premised on programs like *Lavender, Where's Daddy?* and *The Gospel,* particularly in the early days of the Gaza War. These notorious programs enabled the identification of the most desired targets and their location, usually when at home with their families. In the past, comparable targeting was subjected to protocol constraints to minimize collateral damage. After October 7, the Israeli military gave officers sweeping approval to embrace the Lavender kill lists, fully knowing that the system made "errors" in about 10 percent of cases and occasionally targeted individuals who had little or no connection to militants. As the attacks usually took place at night when entire families were present, civilian collateral damage was maximized. For every Hamas operative marked by Lavender, it was permissible to kill up to 15–20 civilians. It was the implicit indicator of the difference between the net worth of human beings, as tacitly inscribed in international law, and the Palestinians, as evidenced by the killing fields of Gaza. Backed with AI, the Israeli military purposely used "dumb bombs" hitting these homes.[4]

"The smell of death is everywhere as bodies are left lying on the roads or under the rubble," warned the head of the UN agency for Palestinian refugees (UNRWA) Philippe Lazzarini. "In northern Gaza, people are just waiting to die. They feel deserted, hopeless and alone. They live from one hour to the next, fearing death at every second."[5]

In the early 2000s, Cameroonian historian Achille Mbembe used the cases of Palestine, Africa, and Kosovo to illuminate "necropolitics," which created zones of death, or new forms of social existence in which "vast populations are subjected to living conditions that confer upon them the status of the living dead."[6] These zones have long been the daily life of subjugation in the occupied territories. But today the scope of such death worlds goes well beyond politics. It is far more extensive. It could be called *necrotization*. Necrotization seeks to transform a world of life into a world of death because that is what displacement, dispossession, devastation and particularly the Obliteration Doctrine ultimately require. It is not personal. A killer wants to kill his victim. A necrotizer seeks to decimate his victims and everything about them, as if they never existed. Necrotization means the collective elimination of those who have nothing more to lose and still refuse to submit; who fight amid the wreckage of their homes and risk a further descent into nothingness. Like Lemkin's original concept of cultural genocide, it is physical, social and cultural; and so are the efforts to eradicate, "with intent to destroy, in whole or in part, a national, ethnical, racial or religious group."[7]

In addition to physical devastation, Israel's necrotization—or necro-violence—seemed to target all reminders of cultural heritage, including historical buildings, libraries, museums, heritage sites, universities and other repositories of knowledge, even mosques, churches and cemeteries. In the Gaza Strip, Israeli forces damaged and destroyed at least 16 Palestinian cemeteries, according to verified evidence. The necro-violence targeted corpses as well. In addition to the desecration or destruction of cemeteries, it featured withholding of bodies from families, thus preventing the mourning of loved ones. What it did offer were the "cemeteries of numbers," where graves are marked only with numbers and not names, thus dehumanizing the dead. Israeli forces also conducted a number of activities in cemeteries, including establishing military bases and exhuming bodies for the purposes of (failed) attempts to locate the bodies of hostages. In other cases, a corpse was violently scooped up with a bulldozer, a hundred bodies were reburied in a mass grave in Rafah, with some bodies missing organs.[8]

Necrotization is not synonymous with weaponization, which is more instrumental, seeking to exploit trade, technology, currency and other things, typically for economic benefit, geopolitical advance, or both. Instead, necrotization turns homes full of life into craters of lethal quiet as it transforms buildings, schools and universities into rubble and ruin, poisons the water, the air, the very earth upon which the victims reside. Necrotization can target a nation's politics, its polity. It can zoom in on an entire society and its culture. An economy can be necrotized, and so can an entire population and the land it inhabits, even its entire ecology. Nothing as destructive has existed in the past. In that sense, necrotization, despite its precursors, represents something thoroughly new. In an algorithmic genocide or *algocide*, the combination of ultra-modern information and communication technology facilitates a necrotization process that is capital-intensive, stunningly rapid and lethally effective.[9]

In the Gazan mass bombardments, targeting was subject to artificial intelligence, which necrotized the intended targets by accepting certain probabilities of error, allowing algorithms to dictate not just who will die, but also to take out others in their proximity. The genocidist quants who developed these systems essentially coupled cutting-edge technology with the most horrific killing machines, while anchoring their performance with pre-calculated probabilities on how many would die, how fast. When innocent observers saw children playing amid the surreal ruins that once was Gaza, these genocidists perceived living dead in potential death worlds, framed by various probability degrees of death, injury and survival. As human beings, they may be the kindest of men and women to their families and relatives, neighbors and acquaintances, even pets. But as genocidists, their job is to ensure that every target will be decimated within a certain probability, time and place.

From drones to cyberweapons and artificial intelligence, the doctrines and technologies of devastation have played a central role in warfare and in genocidal atrocities. But in the final analysis, they are instruments deployed to certain ends. While the path leading to the 2023–2025 Gaza War is littered with massacres ever since Mandatory Palestine, these trajectories moved to a new stage some two decades ago with the Dahiya doctrine. This isn't a new phenomenon unique to Israel, either. It has a long history in "scorched earth" wars—in the postwar era particularly from Nazi Germany to British and French counterinsurgency doctrines and America's calculated destruction in North Korea and Vietnam. What made it different was Israel's frankness about the ultimate ends of the Obliteration Doctrine, its effort to systematize devastation and its inclusion of methods that are usually considered war crimes. And the global social media that exposed it for an aghast world public to see.

The Dream to "Nuke Gaza"

If for Lenin imperialism represented the highest stage of capitalism, necrotizing the living dead is the ultimate phase of the Obliteration Doctrine. Theoretically, the surest, deadliest way to achieve that objective is to use nuclear weapons. And that idea, too, is something that both members of the Israeli cabinet and of the U.S. Congress have recently flirted with.

Just days after October 7, Revital Gotliv, a conservative Israeli lawyer with a penchant for superlatives, released multiple posts on X/Twitter calling for the use of nuclear weapons in Gaza: "Doomsday weapons fearlessly against our enemies," for "crushing and flattening Gaza . . . without mercy! without mercy!" Gotliv ignored the possible damage to Israel proper from fallout, to say nothing of rendering the land useless for future habitation.[10]

A month later, Prime Minister Netanyahu's heritage minister Amichai Eliyahu suggested Israel could drop a nuclear bomb on the Gaza Strip. As the story spread internationally, it was disavowed by Netanyahu, but he did not fire his minister. The far-right Eliyahu objected to allowing any humanitarian aid into Gaza, saying "we wouldn't hand the Nazis [ironically the reference is to Palestinians] humanitarian aid because there is no such thing as uninvolved civilians in Gaza."[11]

Gotliv belonged to Netanyahu's conservative Likud party. Eliyahu represented the far-right Otzma Yehudit in the war cabinet. Both had built their career on extremism, which sparked controversies internationally but rewarded them domestically.

By late April 2024, Israel had dropped over 70,000 tons of bombs over Gaza, surpassing the bombing of Dresden, Hamburg, and London combined during World War II. That amounts to more than 30 kilograms of explosives per individual. The weight of the U.S. nuclear bombs dropped on Hiroshima and Nagasaki in Japan was estimated at about 15,000 tons of explosives. Even before the Rafah offensive, Gaza had been bombed almost five times more than that.[12]

In January 2024, the International Court of Justice (ICJ) delivered its order on the provisional measures in South Africa's genocide case against

Israel. A key piece of this decision focused on those who could be prosecuted for inciting genocide. It was supported by abundant evidence. By then, the Law for Palestine project, a British human rights organization, had documented over 500 statements made by Israeli officials which amounted to incitement of genocide.[13]

But what about the threat or use of nuclear weapons themselves? Is this permissible under international law and Genocide Convention?

Nuclear Warfare as Genocide

When Daniel Ellsberg passed away in 2023, he was remembered as the famous whistleblower behind the release of the *Pentagon Papers* that cast new light on the Vietnam War. Yet, from 1958 to 1971, his primary job had been as a nuclear war planner for the Eisenhower, Kennedy, Johnson, and Nixon administrations.[14] In addition to the Vietnam files, Ellsberg also secretly copied files on the Pentagon's nuclear plans to "decapitate" Russia and China. Additionally, these plans focused on Asia (North Vietnam, North Korea), the Middle East (Iraq, Iran, and Libya) and India. In the case of China, Beijing's role in the Korean War and the Taiwan Strait crises triggered successive U.S. nuclear plans (1950, 1954–55, 1958).

In 1961, Ellsberg was handed a top-secret memo in a White House office.[15] It was the answer to his question that President John F. Kennedy had addressed to the Joint Chiefs of Staff: "If your plans for general [nuclear] war are carried out as planned, how many people will be killed in the Soviet Union and China?" The lowest number was 275 million; the highest, 325 million. Ellsberg also drafted another question, asking for a total breakdown of global deaths from U.S. attacks. In that answer, another 100 million deaths were predicted in Eastern Europe from direct attacks on Warsaw Pact bases and air defenses, and from the fallout. There might be 100 million more from fallout in Western Europe, depending on which way the wind blew. Still another 100 million deaths were predicted from fallout in the mostly neutral countries adjacent to the Soviet bloc and China, including Afghanistan, India, Japan, Austria, Sweden and Finland, which would be wiped out by fallout from U.S. ground-burst explosions on the Soviet submarine pens in Leningrad (Figure E-1).[16]

Figure E-1. 1,100 U.S. Nuclear Targets in 1956

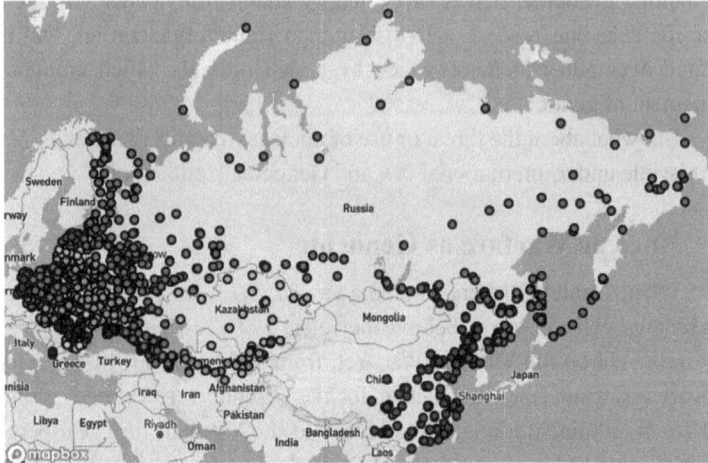

In 2016, The National Security Archives published a declassified list of U.S. nuclear targets from 1956, which spanned 1,100 locations across Eastern Europe, Russia, China, and North Korea.

SOURCE: *Screen capture close-up of "Nukemap" by Future of Life Institute*

The total deaths from a U.S. first strike amounted to "roughly 600 million dead; that is, a hundred Holocausts."[17] Effectively, the U.S. nuclear war plan sought the "destruction of China and Soviet Union as 'viable' societies." Oddly, the nuclear strategy linked a "general war" to legitimizing a first strike against the Soviet Union *and China,* even if Beijing had had nothing to do with such a conflict. Nonetheless, the Pentagon stipulated that the "military objective in general war . . . [was] to defeat the Soviet Bloc alone or in combination with the Asian communist Bloc." To destroy China, the Joint Staff would aim at destroying 30 cities so that "China would no longer be a viable nation."[18]

In Ellsberg's view, nearly every U.S. president from Truman to Trump had "considered or directed serious preparations for possible imminent U.S. initiation of tactical or strategic nuclear warfare."[19] *Deterring* a surprise Soviet nuclear attack or responding to such an attack had never been the only or primary purpose of America's nuclear preparations. The real purpose has been to limit the damage to the U.S. from Soviet or Russian retaliation to a *U.S. first strike* against the USSR or Russia. The devastating impact of "nuclear winter" and "nuclear famine," both of which have been known since the early 1980s, are systematically ignored by these nuclear planners. If American plans were to be carried out, it would mean "smoke and soot *lofted* by fierce firestorms in hundreds of burning cities into the stratosphere, where it would not rain out and would remain for a decade or more." It would envelop the globe and block most sunlight. It would lower annual global temperatures to the level of the last Ice Age and kill all harvests worldwide, thereby "causing near-universal starvation within a year or two."[20]

Nonetheless, the basic Doomsday Machine plan, officially known as the Single Integrated Operational Plan (SIOP) is thought to still be directed against the perceived U.S. adversaries, including "Russia, China, North Korea, and Iran."[21] And in October 2022, the Biden administration unveiled a Cold War strategy for "nuclear threats from Russia and China."[22] Nuclear preparedness—and the ensuing self-destruction—doesn't come cheap. The projected costs of the U.S. nuclear forces are likely to total $756 billion over the 2023–2032 period, or an average of over $75 billion a year.[23] Already half a decade ago, the price tag for operating the existing weapons and building new ones had soared to a staggering *$2 trillion.*[24]

The key beneficiaries of these expenditures are the major contractors for new nuclear delivery vehicles and the operators of the national nuclear weapons complex. In the United States, a small oligopoly of global contractors and operators—Big Defense—reaps the profits. Northrop Grumman has identified major suppliers for its new ICBM in 32 states. Its 12 largest subcontractors include the nation's most prominent defense companies, including Lockheed Martin, General Dynamics, L3Harris, Aerojet Rocketdyne, Honeywell, Bechtel, and the aerospace division of Raytheon. This is pretty much the same lethal oligopoly that drives the military-industrial complex.[25]

Like the Israeli Obliteration Doctrine, the de facto U.S. nuclear doctrine has been known to be operational for years, even decades. Each has genocidal implications. In both cases, institutional ramifications, which are known internationally, correlate with massive death tolls and unimaginable pain. But is the threat or use of nuclear weapons permissible under international law or the Genocide Convention?

The issue of the use of nuclear weapons in an armed conflict was actually already raised in 1950 by the International Law Commission (ILC).[26] But it was suspended throughout the Cold War. After some tentative efforts by the World Health Organization (WHO) and the Non-Aligned Movement (NAM) in 1993, a year later the UN General Assembly did request an opinion of the International Court of Justice (ICJ) on the question: "Is the threat or use of nuclear weapons in any circumstances permitted under international law?"[27] Altogether, 42 states participated in the written phase of the pleadings. It was the largest number ever to join in proceedings before the Court. As was the case with the enactment of the Genocide Convention at the turn of the 1950s, many of the participants were developing countries of the Global South, which had previously not contributed to proceedings before the ICJ. In the landmark case, *Legality of the Threat or Use of Nuclear Weapons* (1996), the Court's unanimous opinions were that

> There is in neither customary nor conventional international law any specific authorization of the threat or use of nuclear weapons;
> A threat or use of force by means of nuclear weapons that is contrary to Article 2, paragraph 4, of the United Nations Charter and that fails to meet all the requirements of Article 51, is unlawful;
> A threat or use of nuclear weapons should also be compatible with the requirements of the international law applicable in armed conflict, particularly those of the principles and rules of international humanitarian law, as well as with specific obligations under treaties and other undertakings which expressly deal with nuclear weapons;
> There exists an obligation to pursue in good faith and bring to a conclusion negotiations leading to nuclear disarmament in all its aspects under strict and effective international control.[28]

Legal scholars argue that the resulting compromise provision gutted the proposed text embodying the customary international humanitarian law (IHL) prohibition against indiscriminate weapons due to unnecessary suffering. Given that the Rome Statute does not grant the ICC jurisdiction over the violation of customary international humanitarian law regarding prohibited weapons, the avenues that remain for enforcing these prohibitions include "domestic prosecution under national law, dispute resolution mechanisms developed under the various weapons conventions (often, negotiations or referral to the UN Security Council) and the specific IHL enforcement mechanisms enshrined in the Geneva Conventions and their Protocols, such as Protecting Powers and international fact-finding missions."[29]

Sticking to the current interpretation and implementation of the Genocide Convention would allow observers to record the path to a nuclear genocide, but only after it has taken place—assuming there are still observers left to record the nightmares.

The Rise of the Global South

Certainly, there is today more clarity about the importance of the duty to prevent, and the scope of this obligation. It is particularly reflected in the February 2007 judgment of the International Court of Justice in the *Bosnia v. Serbia* case and its development on the subject of the duty to prevent genocide. Similarly, genocide is increasingly acknowledged as a subset of crimes against humanity. However, neither clarity about the duty to prevent nor the recognition of genocide as a crime against humanity has been the primary constraint against the deployment of the Convention. Geopolitics *has*.

Ever since the aftermath of World War II, the Convention and some of its key instruments have been in place, others have been diluted and still others eroded. Nonetheless, some critical elements remain in place. The problem is that they have not been deployed, mainly because of geopolitics. The development of the Genocide Convention ensued in the aftermath of World War II, but its drafting took place between the late 1940s and early 1950s, in parallel with the reverse course; that is, the establishment of the security state paving the way to the Cold War. Hence, the near-suspension of the Convention throughout the Cold War, mainly due to the superpower rivalry between the United States and the Soviet Union.

It was the aftermath of World War II—the discovery of the Nazi concentration camps, gas chambers and the realities of industrial-scale mass atrocities—that set the stage for the Nuremberg Trials and eventually for the enactment of the Genocide Convention by the victors of World War II. Except for the Soviet Union and China, most of these nations were industrialized and former colonial powers, which resisted and suppressed the pioneering applications of the Convention through the Cold War.

In the immediate post-Cold War era, early applications were still initiated mainly by the Western Powers. Yet, the rise of China and the Global South since the early 2000s has gone hand in hand with an increasing number of litigation efforts seeking to use the Convention against the genocidist states and non-state actors.

At the turn of 1980, advanced countries still dominated 64 percent of the world economy, as opposed to 35 percent by the emerging and developing economies. By the turn of the 1990s, the share of the advanced countries began a steady decline. A reversal of roles ensued right before the West's financial crisis in 2008. By 2030, emerging and developing economies could dominate the world economy, as advanced countries did in 1980 (Figure E-2).

Figure E-2. Global North and South:
Share of World Economy, Per Capita Income

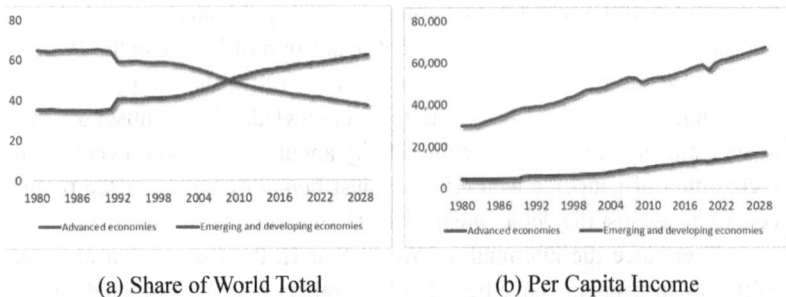

(a) Share of World Total   (b) Per Capita Income

(a) GDP based on purchasing-power-parity (PPP). (b) GDP per capita, constant prices (2017 international dollars).

SOURCE: *Data from IMF; author*

Yet, peaceful long-term economic trends are no longer assured, due to the West's increasing protectionism via trade and tariff wars. Another caveat is that the rise of the Global South largely reflects China's economic expansion and, to a lesser degree, that of India, Indonesia and other large emerging economies. This is one reason why China has been targeted in the West's trade and technology wars. The third caveat is methodological. While it is appropriate to use purchasing power parity to compare living standards in different countries, comparisons of entire economies overstate the strengths of the Global South and the weaknesses of the West. In 1980, per capita income in the Global South was less than 15 percent of that in the prosperous West. Today, that ratio is 24 percent. But it remains 76 percent behind the West.

These economic facts have significant implications even in issues relating to genocide and particularly its prevention. The growing economic weight of the Global South is a reality in both international relations and international law, but its political leverage hasn't been enough to change the interpretation and implementation of the Genocide Convention, at least as of yet. In the long view, there are both long-term structural reasons—particularly the intertwined centuries-long history of colonialism and modernity—and lingering postwar circumstances—the continued suppression of the Global South from international governance—accounting for the odd present status quo.

The Color Line and Genocide Justice

While European states were struggling in Africa and elsewhere to minimize their colonial costs and liabilities, yet to maximize their colonial revenues and influence, the international law profession was organizing itself through the establishment of various liberal legal institutions. In this process that was initially dominated by the European imperial powers, the genesis of international law went hand in hand with the distinction between civilized and non-civilized communities—a euphemism for European and non-European—to deal with Europe's colonial world conquest. Typically, the rise of international law and its stated ideals reflected a kind of universalism that actually did not prevail. It was not the logic of civilization that dominated international law, but the myth of civilization, grounded by the logic of exclusion and inclusion. As the historian of international law, Martti Koskenniemi, has argued:

> It was a discourse of exclusion–inclusion; exclusion in terms of a cultural argument about the otherness of the non-European that made it impossible to extend European rights to the native, inclusion in terms of the native's similarity with the European, the native's otherness having been erased by a universal humanitarianism under which international lawyers sought to replace native institutions by European sovereignty.[30]

It is this Manichean opposition of exclusion-inclusion that extends from the great 16th century debate on the humanity of the indigenous, setting the *conquistadors* against Las Casas, up to the present and South Africa's case against Israel in January 2024, setting the the genocidists of the early 21st century against the Palestinians and their very humanity. And as we have seen, it is a similar discourse of exclusion-inclusion that overshadowed South Africa's original request in the actual Court judgement, through effective exclusion, dilution and erosion. Just as these filtering mechanisms had transformed Lemkin's full Genocide Convention into a torso.[31]

But there is an added split that characterizes this Manichean opposition, as it was defined by W.E.B. Du Bois:

> The problem of the twentieth century is the problem of the color line—the relation of the darker to the lighter races of men in Asia and Africa, in America and the islands of the sea.[32]

Du Bois, the legendary African-American civil rights activist, made his argument at the peak of the colonial conquest, the birth of international law and the segregation of Jews and Arabs in Palestine.[33] Before the 20th century, international law was predominantly written by and for the "civilized nations" of the white Global North. One of its critical effects was that it legitimized doctrines of racial inequality and effectively drew a color line that excluded citizens of the Global South and persons of African descent from participating in international law-making while subjecting them to colonialism and the slave trade. Despite its stated universalism, the result was international law that talked a lot about the Global South yet granted minimal voice and representation to the wide majority of the world's population. It was a hollow abstraction rather than an inclusive reality. Clauses pledged in the name of a rules-based order yet repeatedly cemented unwarranted bloodshed and death in the Global South. Internationalism in the name of legality disguised a brutal and merciless coercive power often manifested in the four major mass atrocity crimes: war crimes, crimes against humanity, ethnic cleansing and, ultimately, genocide, as defined by the 2005 UN World Summit.

In historical view, this divide can be tracked in the development of international regulation on racism and racial discrimination, particularly within the United Nations. These themes gained traction once the Global South gained more participation in international law-making after the First World War. This undermines the narrative that human rights are a creation of the Global North, as evidenced by the decisive contributions that countries of the Global South and people of color have made to anchor anti-racism in international law. These critical interventions go back to The League of Nations, the adoption and implementation of the International Convention on the Elimination of All Forms of Racial Discrimination, the debates within UNESCO on the notion of race itself, expansion of crimes against humanity to cover peacetime violations, as well as challenges to apartheid in South Africa.[34]

As we have seen in the case of the Genocide Convention, the history of human rights law is the story of the progressive efforts of the Global South to hold the white Global North fully accountable for the pledges the West has consistently and systematically violated. Certainly, the West doesn't have a monopoly on genocides, but the latter are inherent in its colonial legacies, its efforts to dilute the scope of the Genocide Convention in the late 1940s and the suppression of genocide prosecutions through the Cold War and the post-9/11 wars. Indeed, from the standpoint of the Global South, the appeal of the South African genocide case against Israel was, at least in part, in that it highlighted the role of colonial atrocities as a prelude to the killing of six million Jews in Europe and subsequent millions in the Middle East, Asia, Africa and elsewhere.

In the early 21st century, the real multipolar world economy is driven by the populous, once-colonized nations that hope to accelerate their economic development and to improve the living standards of their people. Realistically, the only long-term solution to ensure appropriate *inclusive* global governance is to accommodate the role of emerging and developing economies in the existing international regime—presently a relic of the 1945 victor's justice.

International Justice in a Multipolar World

The International Criminal Court's (ICC) track record in the past two decades suggests a substantial gap between its broad mandate and very limited resources and state support. As we have seen, there is a sharp difference between the activities of the ad hoc tribunals and the ICC.[35] In the case of the tribunals, influential governments, mainly the permanent members of the UN Security Council, while committing time and funds to backing what they perceive as international justice, have focused on selected conflicts based on their national interests. Led by the United States, the countries bankrolling these tribunals supported them politically and militarily. It wasn't a free lunch. It made the tribunals highly reliant on U.S. political support, intelligence and NATO-led forces. But it generated results. The Tribunal for the former Yugoslavia convicted nearly 90 individuals, including senior political and military officials. Similarly, the Rwanda Tribunal ultimately convicted more than 60 individuals, almost two-thirds of those charged with crimes.

Even though the ICC itself has extensive jurisdiction it has weak political support. For this reason, the Court seems to have moved cautiously when it began operations in 2003. It acted when the country in question explicitly requested court intervention (Congo DR, the Central African Republic, Uganda) or when the UN Security Council authorized the role of the court. This pattern changed around 2010, when the ICC Prosecutor launched an investigation in Kenya; the first undertaken without explicit state support. In the subsequent years, the ICC initiated several investigations that led it to be contested by several non-member states, including Russia (Georgia, Ukraine), Libya, Myanmar, U.S. (Afghanistan), and Israel (Gaza). In the process, the number of active investigations soared to 17, but the results, at least in terms of trials and convictions, were few. In over more than 20 years, the Court has secured convictions in just 4 cases, and most of its arrest warrants have been without effect. Compare that with the former Yugoslav Tribunal's track-record of 161 indictments, 90 convictions and sentences in less than seven years (Figure E-3).

**Figure E-3. Ad Hoc Tribunals and the ICC:
Indictments and Convictions**

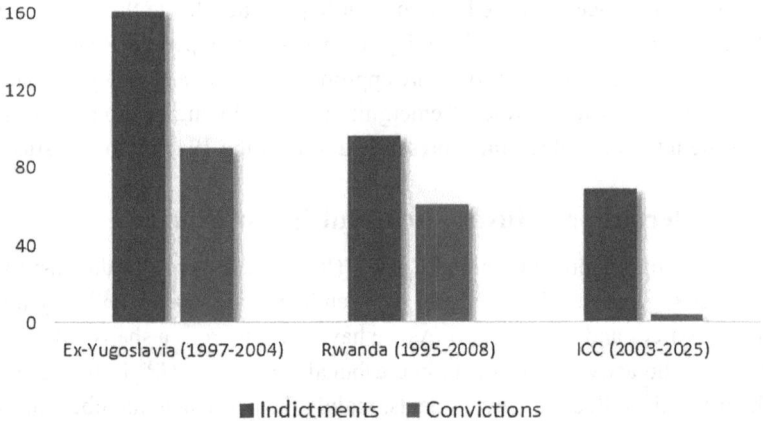

■ Indictments ■ Convictions

SOURCE: *ICTY, ICTR, ICC*

In several ICC cases, such as Sudan, Libya, Palestine, Burundi, Myanmar, and the Philippines, the prosecutor has lacked access to the territory in question or faced significant obstacles in taking investigative steps in the country. The ICC Kenya case, which occurred without explicit state support, is illustrative. After three years, the ICC charges were dropped in 2015 for lack of evidence.[36]

Yet, the track record of the ICC shows it can be quite effective when prosecution has strong political backing. When the primary funders of the ICC and most permanent members of the UN Security Council have been in consensus, the Court's implementation capacity has been boosted by abundant resources, as evidenced by the ICC arrest warrants for Russian leaders in 2023–24. The warrant against Russian President Putin was the first against the leader of a permanent member of the UN Security Council. Unsurprisingly, the ICC enjoyed maximum cooperation and resources in Ukraine.[37] Then again, as the Trump administration initiated its peace talks between Russia and Ukraine in spring 2025, the ICC's role was largely ignored.

Given its current trajectory, the ICC is likely to continue to go after a few high-profile cases. In those that are aligned with the interests of the West, the Court's ambitious rhetoric is more likely to be backed up with adequate resources and boosted implementation. In other cases, the colossal gap between stated objectives and actual achievements weakens the prospects of prosecution.

In principle, there are four possible ICC scenarios, based on state support and implementation capacity. When the Court has broad support and implementation is strong, it is truly empowered. Such an ICC has not existed yet and is unlikely to exist in the foreseeable future because the national interests of its constituent member-states tend to trump the Court's universalist predilections. When the ICC has narrow support but strong implementation capacity, it can be quite effective, as evidenced by the ad hoc tribunals (or the model the U.S. initially proposed to the Court). In this scenario, things get done but outcomes reflect self-interested policies vulnerable to allegations of politicization. The current ICC seems to represent a reverse scenario. When nominal broad support is coupled with weak implementation, the ICC is likely to prove ineffective; high on rhetoric, but weak in execution. The worst scenario would be a Court with both diminished state support and low execution capacity. Over time, it would translate to irrelevance. Distressingly, in the absence of major changes, this is where the current ICC may find itself, if the ongoing geoeconomic and -political divides continue to penalize global prospects (Figure E-4).

Figure E-4. The ICC Pathways: Four Scenarios

		Implementation Capacity	
		Weak	*Strong*
State Support	*Broad*	"Ineffective ICC"	"Empowered ICC"
	Narrow	"Irrelevant ICC"	"Effective ICC"

Obviously, great powers, particularly the permanent members of the UN Security Council, seek to influence such scenarios. As a result, the current ICC, overshadowed by its great ambitions but weak implementation capacity, is in an untenable position. The more it promotes universalistic objectives with narrow state support, the feebler it appears. Typically, instead of complying with the Court's warrants, countries downplay them, signaling they may not respect them in the future or openly defy them for domestic political reasons. After the warrants for PM Netanyahu and his ex-minister, Polish leaders welcomed Netanyahu's visit, as did their Hungarian peers. Germany hedged its bets. French officials stressed a state had "obligations under international law with respect to the immunities of States not party to the ICC."[38]

Typically, the ICC's four convictions have all been against citizens of member countries, whereas its cases against *non-member* state nationals have yielded almost nothing. Despite deposing indicted leaders, such as Sudan's Omar al-Bashir, their successors have pulled back from cooperating with the Court. Similarly, neither a post-Putin regime nor a post-Netanyahu cabinet is likely to send off its former officials for trial. In this regard, one test case may be the highly controversial deportation of the former President of the Philippines, Rodrigo Duterte, to the Hague by the Marcos Jr. government. Yet, this case is weakened by what the opposition calls Duterte's illegal arrest and deportation, and effective political persecution.[39]

Is there a way out? A potential though unlikely U.S.-led scenario would be for the UN Security Council, armed with the sparingly used Article 16 of the Rome Statute, to temporarily freeze court investigations into the conduct of non-member state individuals. But even those U.S. observers who regard it as a potential trajectory consider it unlikely.[40]

However, with the rise of China and the Global South, the above foundational conditions have dramatically changed in the past eight decades. In effect, the broadest state support and most effective implementation can only be actualized in a trajectory marked by multipolarity reflecting the existing global economic, political and military conditions—not those that prevailed 80 years ago.

In the multipolar scenario, the ICC trajectory would no longer be based on the West's unipolarity. The UN Security Council and its permanent members could retain their role, but it should be augmented by the new conditions of multipolarity; that is, the increasing role of the world's largest emerging and developing economies.

The *Duty* to Prevent Genocide

From the standpoint of the Genocide Convention, there has been little to no doubt about the commission of genocidal atrocities in Gaza ever since late 2023, as evidenced by massive documentation by the UN bodies, international media, a wide variety of NGOs and so on.[41] In this status quo of continuing genocidal atrocities, the old recipes of the *ex post facto* interpretions of the Convention seem outright absurd, particularly in light of the lethal combination of advanced technology and artificial intelligence.

As we have seen, the potential of alternative approaches is significant in the development of genocide indicators.[42] Yet, they are likely to remain ineffective as long as whatever enforcement mechanisms that may exist remain blocked by the politicization of their use. Since the turn of the 1950s, the Genocide Convention has provided instruments to identify and prosecute genocides. The fact that it has proved ineffective stems directly from the international status quo that is the net effect of World War II. The Gaza War is no exception. Whether seen in the light of war crimes, crimes against humanity or the Genocide Convention, these atrocities have caused each inditator, and almost all categories when scrutinized in detail, to blink red (Figure E-5).

Indeed, the very term, "Gaza War" is not just a misnomer but Orwellian.[43] Though widely used for more than two decades, it actually connotes ethnic cleansing aiming at forced population transfers and, in the case of determined opposition, extensive genocidal atrocities. It is slaughter of women and children in the name of war.[44] In the Gaza Strip, targeted killings of individuals had already begun in the early 2000s, then broadening to the destruction of entire buildings and settlement compounds in Beirut after the mid-2000s, as we have seen. And so, the stage was set for the genocidal atrocities following October 7, 2023. That is, after "the obligation to prevent genocide" had been ignored for almost quarter of a century. How could that happen?

"The missing piece here, the one that is relevant if genocide recurs," as William Schabas has noted, is "the view that humanitarian intervention to prevent genocide is not so much a 'right' as a duty."[45] The early signs of the impending changes include the rising resistance against the complicity of the West in genocides that take place in the Global South. What makes Nicaragua's effort to target German arms transfer to Israel in the International Court of Justice (ICJ) so important is that it "brings this trend of public interest litigation to another level by extending it—on the defendant side—to a state which is accused of supporting the alleged primary violation of international law."[46]

Though the ICJ was first established in 1945, its case load was relatively low through most of the Cold War, despite multiple genocidal atrocities, ethnic cleansing in the 1990s and the post-9/11 wars, which as we have seen cost some 1.1 million lives in Afghanistan, Iraq and elsewhere; that is, most prominently in the Global South. A substantial number of these cases centered on disputes relating to wars, not just the Gaza War and Ukraine's cases against Russia (2014, 2022–) but also, the mutual cases between Armenia and Azerbaijan, Gambia's case against Myanmar's Rohingya minority, and the case by Canada and the Netherlands against Syria.

Effectively, interstate litigation in the ICJ has become increasingly multilateral. The Gaza War is a case in point. South Africa and Nicaragua have invoked violations of legal rules that are owed to all states. Furthermore, *Nicaragua v. Germany* highlights the trend with states increasingly requesting provisional measures of the ICJ. As a final judgment takes years, this trend is seen is seen in the West to pose a risk of dragging the ICJ into rendering

Figure E-5. Triple Genocide Indicators

War Crimes	Crimes Against Humanity	Genocide Convention
1. Grave breaches of the Geneva Conventions of 12 August 1949, namely, any of the following acts against persons or property protected under the provisions of the relevant Geneva Convention: (a) Willful killing (b) Torture or inhuman treatment, including biological experiments (c) Willfully causing great suffering, or serious injury to body or health (d) Extensive destruction and appropriation of property, not justified by military necessity and carried out unlawfully and wantonly (e) Compelling a prisoner of war or other protected person to serve in the forces of a hostile Power (f) Willfully depriving a prisoner of war or other protected person of the rights of fair and regular trial (g) Unlawful deportation or transfer or unlawful confinement (h) Taking of hostages 2. Other serious violations of the laws and customs applicable in international armed conflict, within the established framework of international law... 3. In the case of an armed conflict not of an international character, serious violations of article 3 common to the four Geneva Conventions of 12 August 1949...[a] 4. Other serious violations of the laws and customs applicable in armed conflicts not of an international character, within the established framework of international law...	(a) Murder; (b) Extermination [including "the intentional infliction of conditions of life, inter alia the deprivation of access to food and medicine, calculated to bring about the destruction of part of a population"]; (c) Enslavement; (d) Deportation or forcible transfer of population; (e) Imprisonment or other severe deprivation of physical liberty in violation of fundamental rules of international law; (f) Torture; (g) Rape, sexual slavery, enforced prostitution, forced pregnancy, enforced sterilization, or any other form of sexual violence of comparable gravity (h) Persecution against any identifiable group or collectivity on political, racial, national, ethnic, cultural, religious, gender... (i) Enforced disappearance of persons; (j) The crime of apartheid; (k) Other inhumane acts of a similar character intentionally causing great suffering, or serious injury to body or to mental or physical health	*Article 2* (a) Killing members of the group; (b) Causing serious bodily or mental harm to members of the group; (c) Deliberately inflicting on the group conditions of life calculated to bring about its physical destruction in whole or in part; (d) Imposing measures intended to prevent births within the group; (e) Forcibly transferring children of the group to another group *Article 3* (a) Genocide; (b) Conspiracy to commit genocide; (c) Direct and public incitement to commit genocide; (d) Attempt to commit genocide; (e) Complicity in genocide

judgments on armed conflicts. On the other hand, from the standpoint of the Global South, applicant states seek to fast-track decisions, hoping to halt lethal military attacks by the offender state, typically representing the West, and forestall unwarranted deaths.[47]

In the past decade in particular, almost 40 cases—a fifth of all cases brought to the ICJ—have been filed, with dramatic acceleration since early 2023.[48] Importantly, many of these cases are brought by states from the Global South. In particular, the case of *Nicaragua v. Germany* could have had substantial implications for other states that were providing military support to Israel, reflected in Nicaragua's intention to bring similar cases against the UK, Canada, and the Netherlands at the ICJ. Such litigation prospects were paralleled by cases hoping to end weapons exports at domestic courts in several Anglo-Saxon countries and European states.

In January 2024, Blinne Ní Ghrálaigh gave a bold presentation in The Hague, Netherlands, of "the first live-streamed genocide" of the Palestinians in Gaza. Indeed, a number of countries supported South Africa's case in the Middle East (Algeria, Egypt, Iraq, Jordan, Lebanon, Libya, Palestine, Sahrawi, Syria) and Türkiye. It was also promoted in Latin America (Bolivia, Brazil, Chile, Colombia, Cuba, Mexico, Nicaragua, St. Vincent and the Grenadines, Venezuela), sub-Saharan Africa (Comoros, Djibouti, Namibia, Zimbabwe), Asia (Bangladesh, China, Indonesia, Malaysia), even Europe (Ireland, Slovenia, Spain). Yet, the case remained opposed by Israel, the United States, some of the largest Western economies and small countries with conservative governments relying on U.S. support in Europe and Latin America. If the supporters represented mainly the Global South, the opposers comprised Western states. The actual divergence between these two sets of countries would be even greater if the member states of international organizations—especially African Union and the Non-Aligned Movement—were included.

It is these initiatives that may offer an alternative path to the efforts that seek to "naturalize" the past record of the Convention as if it was pre-determined and inevitable.

From Victor's Justice to Victim's Justice

What is needed is not victor's justice but justice; and particularly justice of the victims, to set aside the cold disregard that has historically accompanied genocidal atrocities. Will the rise of the Global South and increasing multipolarity change the current status quo for the better? Until recently, global governance has been in the hands of those nations with largest per capita income, much of which originates from the period of colonialism that was excluded from the Genocide Convention (although, as previously noted, there is no explicit temporal limitation in the Genocide Convention to prevent it from having a *retroactive effect*, which could be seen as a potential, untapped legal venue).[49] As a result, "human rights" are effectively defined by economic gains with a questionable history. By shifting global governance to accord adequately with countries' population weight, the countries of the Global South would change the present status quo for the better. That is one scenario for the future. But another is that its emergence could be preempted, by undermining the rise of the large emerging economies, including China, India, Mexico, Indonesia, India and the emergence of major mid-sized powers.

As long as global governance remains dominated by a tenth of the world population, it is hardly surprising that genocide justice—that is, the quest for justice to the victims of the genocide—remains a mirage; and the more vulnerable emerging and developing nations, the likeliest victims. As long as global governance and world courts do not look or sound like the preponderance of humanity they proclaim to represent, theirs will remain a justice of the few, for the few and by the few.

Some argue that the devastation of Gaza might have been averted if the international community, groups of countries or individual states had intervened in the early weeks of the atrocities by issuing public rebukes, recalling diplomatic staff, and closing embassies. At the turn of 2023–2024, Brazilian President Luiz Inacio Lula da Silva likened the Israeli war against Hamas-led groups in Gaza to the Nazi genocide during World War II. "It's not a war between soldiers and soldiers, it's a war between a highly prepared army and women and children," President Lula said. The Israeli Foreign Ministry summoned the Brazilian ambassador for a reprimand over the remarks, which Israeli Prime Minister Benjamin Netanyahu described as "a trivialization of the Holocaust."[50]

If adequate international rebuke had emerged, critics argue it could have been supplemented by boycott and divestment by countries, companies and consumers. The impact of such opposition, in turn, could have been fostered by expanded sanctions in the trade, economic, political, cultural and social spheres, and particularly against the arms transfers and financing that enabled the mass atrocities. Also, to ensure global effectiveness, a long series of UN resolutions since the late 1940s should be implemented to ensure a fair and enduring solution in the Middle East.

Effectively, none of these broader and cumulative measures materialized in 2023–2025. Yet, somewhat similar measures had been influential in the case of South Africa, as the black resistance for equal rights was coupled with an effective international anti-apartheid movement that ultimately, though only after several popular uprisings, forced democratic change in South Africa. But despite efforts, similar outcomes have not materialized in Israel.[51] Though the United States, the UK, Israel and many other countries in the West did shun boycotts against South Africa for a long time, ultimately, they did change their policies. But that has not happened in the case of Israel, despite multiple wars, continuing hostilities, several Palestinian uprisings and Israel's enduring violations of international law.

What compounds the challenge is the extensive and institutionalized U.S. military aid to Israel since the 1970s. Despite these exceedingly dire, deplorable conditions suffered particularly by the Palestinians, the Netanyahu cabinets have been able to rely extensively on continuing American support, massive arms transfers and financing, even though its apartheid-style occupation has been condemned, not just internationally and by many leading human rights organizations, but by many former high-level officials of the Israeli military, Mossad and Shin Bet, the guardians of Israel's external and internal security.[52]

To be effective, adequate measures must address the issue of the Obliteration Doctrine, the Genocide Convention, its enforcement and genocide prevention. In this regard, there are lessons that can be drawn from our investigation of the realities of that doctrine and the failure of the genocide prevention, chapter by chapter.

Here is what must be done:

Contain abject devastation before it can proceed. In the absence of adequate containment, the devastation caused by the Obliteration Doctrine in the Gaza Strip is only a miniscule prelude for what might yet to come. It already offers a blueprint of sanctions, blockade and manufactured famine; information censure; and genocidal intent and acts.

Target war profiteering and "revolving door" practices. Genocides cannot be contained without adequate regulation of the U.S. industrial-military complex and its smaller international correlates that gain economic rents from mass atrocities and rely on military dominance. Such complexes feature revolving doors between the government, defense departments and military contractors. Ridden by monopolistic practices, they feature extraordinary moral hazards, conflicts of interest and ultimately harsh repression. Typically, the U.S. Pentagon alone has failed seven annual audits in a row.[53]

Prosecute genocide complicity. Along with genocidal intent and acts, genocide complicity must be effectively prosecuted, due to the great severity of the crime. As *Palestine et al. v. Biden et al.* has already evidenced in U.S. district courts and *Nicaragua v. Germany* at the ICC, legal venues to tackle complicity do exist but they must be used far more extensively to cover all major complicit parties. Furthermore, entities threatening and sanctioning ICC decisions by whatever means should themselves face legal action by international community.

Restore the original broad definition of Genocide Convention. Instead of building on Raphael Lemkin's original draft for the Genocide Convention, which was supported by much of the Global South, the major powers of the West excluded its broader definition by ejecting the notions of cultural genocide and political killings, and obfuscating ethnic cleansing. A torso of the original Convention is better than nothing but the original draft goals could be reincorporated; or addressed by adding an Optional Protocol, a legal instrument addressing issues that the parent treaty does not cover or does not cover sufficiently; or by consolidating international criminal courts' more inclusive definitions of the kinds of violent crime that can constitute genocide; or by any other means that a broad definition of the Convention can be realized.

Foster effective enforcement of the Genocide Convention. The postwar era saw the establishment of the International Criminal Tribunals in Nuremberg and Tokyo, yet genocide prosecution and its prevention were suppressed through the Cold War. The post-Cold War ad hoc tribunals have been selective and few, focusing mainly on wrongdoings in the Global South while largely shunning the wrongdoers in the West. The ICC decision to investigate Israel's conduct, coupled with a rising number of cases filed by the Global South, reflects a tacit trend to effective multipolarity that should be fostered—not undermined or sanctioned.

Focus on institutional changes precipitating genocide for timely prevention. Genocides should be prevented, not streamed in real-time. As long as the implementation of the Convention builds on *ex post facto* arguments, which identify the crime only after the bodies can no longer be revived and perpetrators have fled, genocides will prevail. What is needed is minute attention to institutional changes in military machines that herald mobilization for genocide so that it can be preempted in time.

Undermine proactively the uses of the Obliteration Doctrine. This doctrine is a lethal mix of scorched earth policy, civilian victimization and collective punishment, coupled with obliteration bombing, supremacy doctrines, states of emergency and the weaponization of artificial intelligence (AI). This doctrine didn't come out of the blue. It was developed and tested in two decades prior to the atrocities in Gaza. It could have been halted in time, but wasn't. Regard all these components of the Obliteration Doctrine as potential institutional drivers of genocide, as warning signals that require urgent intervention to ensure adequate genocide prevention.

Foster effective global consensus repudiating the Obliteration Doctrine. Unless contained, this doctrine, which now offers both a precedent and a template, is likely to result in new Gazas of far greater magnitude, particularly with nuclear proliferation. Furthermore, it is vital to see beyond the efforts to contain proliferation, which often serve as pretexts for certain great powers to impose constraints on proliferation but not on nuclear possession, war scenarios, devastating contingency simulations and so forth. The point is to curtain hegemonic ambitions and the instrument to do so is full and effective disarmament, in order to mitigate the presence of weapons of mass destruction that pose a threat to us all. Unsurprisingly, when Alva Myrdal, the Nobel Peace Prize-awarded Swedish sociologist, diplomat and politician, began her struggle for disarmament, she knew that its *driving* forces featured the countries of the Global South and non-state organizations and movements in the West, not the postwar great powers that remained stuck in the global arms race and financing.[54] Insofar as it plays a central role in these races, the Obliteration Doctrine must be nipped in the bud; not debated *ex post facto*. When the stakes are this high, if not existential, genocide prevention must be considered a binding *duty*, not just an obligation. In light of the rise of the Global South, and the fatal role of the color line in genocide justice, an effective global consensus is broadening to repudiate this doctrine. Nonetheless, investigations into a few individuals are grossly inadequate. In the case of the Gaza atrocities, Israel's war cabinet was the prime mover. Furthermore, complicity investigations must be broadened. As we have seen, Israel's war cabinet was willing to engage in mass atrocities, but it would not have been able to do so without continuing arms transfers and financing especially from the United States, but also from Germany, the UK, Italy and several other countries. In each case, the decisions to contribute to atrocities imply complicity, which must be challenged in all the aforementioned ways.

Additionally, no reconciliation is possible without the legal recognition of damages and the right of compensation. In the case of Israel/Palestine, these talks were first introduced in the aftermath of the ethnic expulsions of the 1948/49 War and briefly revived during the early days of the peace process, but without international pressure, they remain frozen.[55] Similarly, a true reconciliation cries for truth commissions to resolve conflicts left from the past. Internationally, such commissions have facilitated the dismantling of systems of repression and censure.

The path from victors' justice to victims' justice is not an easy one, but the alternatives are a lot worse.

* * *

The duty to prevent genocide is no longer just a moral prescription. In the era of massive global arms transfers and financing, and in the absence of effective disarmament, it is a matter of survival for humanity. Since alternatives are prohibitive, due to their excessive economic, political and moral costs, it should be regarded as a binding categorical imperative. Genocide justice—the quest for justice to the victims of the genocide—can no longer rest on victors' justice. It must *also* be predicated on the justice of the victims. This doesn't mean the exclusion of the Global North, despite the West's centuries of colonial atrocities. It means the effective inclusion of the Global South in global institutions, and the full implementation of the Genocide Convention, including both punishment for commission of genocide and further institutionalization of its prevention.

It is only with the full presence of the Global South in genocide justice that justice for the victims becomes a veritable possibility.

When and if genocides are no longer seen solely as gross moral regressions but also as situations giving rise to global legal, diplomatic, and economic penalties, the challenges of mass atrocities can be pursued on a more compelling track.

If, however, the lessons are not learned, the proliferation of ever new genocides will become largely technical and logistical issues over time, from the point of view of genocidists. At that point, the international community will look nostalgically toward the simple old days of Auschwitz and Hiroshima, when the lucrative business of mass destruction was still limited to just a few locations without regional, even global repercussions.

ENDNOTES

Preface

1 "The war in Gaza must end." Statement by Martin Griffiths, Under-Secretary-General for Humanitarian Affairs and Emergency Relief Coordinator, Jan. 5, 2024.

2 "World has failed Gaza in 'livestreamed genocide,' South Africa's delegation says at ICJ." *Guardian News,* Jan. 12, 2024. https://www.youtube.com/watch?v=y0t4aFLYry4

Prologue

1 Hauser Tov, Michael, with the AP. "'Israeli Gov't Is Intent on Destroying Palestinians in Gaza': South Africa Presents Genocide Case at ICJ." *Haaretz,* Jan. 11, 2024.

2 Ibid.

3 Statement by the Prime Minister of Israel on *X,* Jan. 11, 2024. https://twitter.com/IsraeliPM/status/1745186120109846710?lang=en

4 Statement by the Spokesperson of Israel's Foreign Ministry on *X,* Jan. 11, 2024. https://twitter.com/LiorHaiat/status/1745427037039280207?lang=en

5 Steinbock, Dan. 2025. *The Fall of Israel* (Atlanta, GA: Clarity Press), esp. Chapter 9.

6 "Gaza: ICJ ruling offers hope for protection of civilians enduring apocalyptic conditions, say UN experts." OHCHR, Jan. 31, 2024.

7 For journalistic accounts see Wintour, Patrick. "Israel appears to be in breach of ICJ orders on Gaza, senior UN official says." *The Guardian,* Feb. 10, 2024; "Here's a look at the 6 things the UN is ordering Israel to do about its operation in Gaza." *AP News,* Jan. 26, 2024; "South Africa welcomes 'landmark' ICJ ruling, Israel vows to continue war." *Washington Post,* Jan. 26, 2024.

8 "Israel Not Complying with World Court Order in Genocide Case." Human Rights Watch, Feb. 26, 2024; "Israel defying ICJ ruling to prevent genocide by failing to allow aid into Gaza." Amnesty International, Feb. 26, 2024.

9 "World court orders Israel to take action to address Gaza famine." *Reuters,* March 28, 2024.

10 On starvation as a method of war, see Chapter 1.

11 Quoted in Wilkins, Brett. "South Africa Files 750 Pages of 'Overwhelming' Evidence in ICJ Genocide Case Against Israel." *Common Dreams,* Oct. 28, 2024.

12 Albanese, Francesca. 2024. *Genocide as Colonial Erasure.* Report of the Special Rapporteur on the situation of human rights in the Palestinian territories occupied since 1967. UN General Assembly, A/79/384.

Chapter 1

1 Lemkin, Raphael. 1944. *Axis Rule in Occupied Europe: Laws of Occupation, Analysis of Government, and Proposals for Redress* (Washington, DC: Carnegie Endowment for International Peace), p. 79.

2 This progression draws from and updates Steinbock, Dan. 2025. *The Fall of Israel* (Atlanta, GA: Clarity Press), see esp. Chapters 1–3 and 9.

3 Compare Carapico, Sheila. "War and De-Development." In: *Politics, Governance, and Reconstruction in Yemen* (Project on Middle East Political Science, January 2018), pp. 58–81.

4 Benn, Aluf. "Israel: Censoring the past." *Bulletin of the Atomic Scientists,* July–Aug. 2001.

5 "Israel." Reporters Without Borders (retrieved on Jan. 11, 2025). https://rsf.org/en/country/israel

6 "Al Jazeera condemns Israeli government decision to shut down local offices." *Al Jazeera,* May 5, 2024.

7 Bandel, Netael. "Israel bureau of Al-Jazeera to be shut down for endangering national security." *Israel Hayom,* Oct. 20, 2023.

8 Sharon, Jeremy. "At Jerusalem conference, settler activists call for return to Jewish settlements in Gaza." *Jerusalem Post,* Jan. 28, 2024.

9 "Al Jazeera condemns Israeli government decision to shut down local offices." *Al Jazeera,* May 5, 2024.

10 "Journalist casualties in the Israel-Gaza war." The Committee to Protect Journalists, Jan. 27, 2024.

11 *Meta's Broken Promises: Systemic Censorship of Palestine Content on Instagram and Facebook.* Human Rights Watch, Dec. 2023.

12 Poulson, Jack, and Lee Fang. "Pro-Israel Group Censoring Social Media Led by Former Israeli Intelligence Officers." *All-Source Intelligence,* July 12, 2024.

13 Shellenberger, Michael. *The Censorship Industrial Complex: U.S. Government Support for Domestic Censorship And and Disinformation Campaigns, 2016–2022.* Testimony. The House Select Committee on the Weaponization of the Federal Government, March 9, 2023.

14 "Israel pushed Gaza to 'brink of collapse': WikiLeaks." *NBC News,* Jan. 5, 2011.

15 "Reader: 'Food Consumption in the Gaza Strip – Red Lines.'" Position Paper. Gisha – Legal Center for Freedom of Movement, Oct. 2012. According to defense ministry, "it was part of a research paper that came up in two discussions and that we never made use of."

16 The summary documents were released only in late 2012 after more than three years of legal battle. See "'Red Lines' presentation released after 3.5-year legal battle: Israel calculated the number of calories it would allow Gaza residents to consume." Gisha Legal Center, Oct. 17, 2012.

17 Steinbock 2025, *op. cit.,* see Chapter 2.

18 Based on a 15-slide presentation that was presented during the hearing before the Supreme Court dated January 27, 2008. See AAA 3300/11 *Ministry of Defense v. Gisha* "Food Consumption in the Gaza Strip – Red Lines" Presentation. Unofficial translation by Gisha.

19 Davis, Mike. 2001. *Late Victorian Holocausts El Nino Famines and the Making of the Third World* (New York: Verso), pp. 36–37. On the Temple wage, see Linden, Eugen. 2006. *The Winds of Change: Climate, Weather, and the Destruction of Civilizations* (New York: Simon & Schuster), p. 196.

20 "Israel Gaza blockade study calculated Palestinians' calories." *Reuters,* Oct. 17, 2012.

21 Defendant Gallant, ICC, Nov. 24, 2024. https://www.icc-cpi.int/defendant/gallant

22 Sachs, Jeffrey, and Mark Weisbrot. 2019. *Economic Sanctions as Collective Punishment: The Case of Venezuela.* Center for Economic and Policy Research, April 2019.

23 "Adopting Resolution 2417 (2018), Security Council Strongly Condemns Starving of Civilians, Unlawfully Denying Humanitarian Access as Warfare Tactics." UN, SC/13354, May 24, 2018.

24 Steinbock, Dan. 2022. "Great Powers and Globalization: Spotlight on the United States and China." In: *Schwerpunkt AuBenwirtschaft* (ONB/WKO, 2021/2022).

25 "Annual Country Report 2023: State of Palestine," World Food Programme (WFP); "Over one hundred days into the war, Israel destroying Gaza's food system and weaponizing food, say UN human rights experts." OHCHR, Jan. 16, 2024.

26 Steinbock 2025, *op. cit.,* Chapter 1.

27 Integrated Food Security Phase Classification (IPC) reports.

28 Summers, Charlie. "'No food shortage in Gaza,' says IDF official, dismissing UN claims to the contrary." *Times of Israel,* Jan. 11, 2024.

29 See e.g., "Gazans to IDF: Hamas steals UNRWA food, kills civilians who ask for aid." *The Jerusalem Post,* Jan. 8, 2024.

30 DeYoung, Karen, and John Hudson. "Despite U.S. pressure on Israel, casualty count in Gaza remains high." *Washington Post,* Jan. 15, 2024.

31 "Imminent famine in northern Gaza is 'entirely man-made disaster': Guterres." *UN News,* United Nations, March 18, 2024. See also "Manufacturing Famine: Israel Is Committing the War Crime of Starvation in the Gaza Strip." *B'Tselem,* April 4, 2024.

32 Hall, Richard, et al. "Biden is furious at allegations that Israel is using starvation as a weapon of war. But he is complicit in Gaza's famine." *The Independent,* May 14, 2024.

33 "Gaza Strip: acute food insecurity situation for 1 May–15 June and projection for 16 June–30 September 2024." Integrated Food Security Phase Classification, June 25, 2024.

34 Sharon, Jeremy. "New Gaza famine report reveals grim March predictions were vastly exaggerated." *Times of Israel,* July 2, 2024.

35 See Fliss-Isakov, Naomi, et al. 2024. *Food-aid supplied to Gaza during seven months of the Hamas-Israel war.* Working paper (pre-peer review preprint, June 2024).

36 Fliss-Isakov, Naomi, et al. 2024. "Food-aid supplied to Gaza during seven months of the Hamas-Israel war." Working Paper (pre-peer review preprint), June 2024.

37 *Report of the Special Committee to Investigate Israeli Practices Affecting the Human Rights of the Palestinian People and Other Arabs of the Occupied Territories.* UNGA, Sept. 20, 2024, p. 13.

38 "Giora Eiland outlines plan to get hostages back alive." *Globes,* Oct. 8, 2023.

39 "Health experts denounce retired general's claim to let Gaza be destroyed." *The Jerusalem Post,* Nov. 26, 2023; "Humanitarian catastrophe as policy." *B'Tselem,* Dec. 7, 2023.

40 Mahdi, Ibtisam. 2025. "Bombing plants, severing pipelines: Israel pushes Gaza water crisis to the brink." *+972 Magazine,* April 23, 2025.

41 Fliss-Isakov 2024, *op. cit.* The final version was released in February 2025: Fliss-Isakov, Naomi, et al. 2025. "Food supplied to Gaza during seven months of the Hamas-Israel war." *Israel Journal of Health Policy Research* 14, article no. 8.

42 Isaacson, Gila. "The ICC claimed Gazans were starving. They lied." *Jfeed,* March 10, 2025.

43 Compare Matar, Haggai. "Breaking new records, Israel sees unprecedented spike in media censorship." *+972 Magazine,* May 2, 2025.

44 "At least 60,000 children malnourished in Gaza as Israel keeps blocking aid." *Al Jazeera,* April 9, 2025; "'No Access to Life-saving Services' Gaza's Humanitarian Crisis at Its Worst Since War Began." *Haaretz,* April 17, 2025; Mordechai, Lee, and Liat Kozma. 2025. "Weaponizing starvation, Israel seeks full control over Gaza aid distribution." *+972 Magazine,* March 26, 2025.

45 "Palestinian children face starvation under Israel's total Gaza blockade." Al Jazeera, May 3, 2025; TOI Staff. 2025. "Netanyahu said to okay expanded Gaza op, with IDF readying for major reservist call-up." May 2, 2025.

46 *X/Twitter* tweet of April 23, 2025 [in Hebrew]. https://x.com/itamarbengvir/status/1914922576033337481?utm_source=substack&utm_medium=email

47 On the historical role of the Hunger Plan, see e.g., Tooze, A. 2006. *The Wages of Destruction* (London: Allen Lane), pp. 476–485, 538–549. See also Zimmerer, Jürgen. 2023. *From Windhoek to Auschwitz? Reflections on the Relationship between Colonialism and National Socialism* (Berlin, Germany: De Gruyter), pp. 141, 151.

48 Compare Kakel, C. 2011. *The American West and the Nazi East: A Comparative and Interpretive Perspective* (London: Palgrave).

49 Cox, Mary Elizabeth. 2014. "Hunger Games: or how the Allied blockade in the First World War deprived German children of nutrition, and Allied food aid subsequently saved them." *Economic History Review* 68, no. 2 (May 2015), pp. 600–631. See also Vincent, C. Paul. 1985. *The Politics of Hunger: The Allied Blockade of Germany, 1915–1919* (Ohio University Press).

50 See e.g., Harel, Amos. "The World Rejects Israel's 'Generals' Plan' for Gaza, So the Generals Work Around It." *Haaretz,* Nov. 22, 2024.

51 Donnison, Jon. "Israel has missed US deadline to boost Gaza aid, UN agency says." *BBC News,* Nov. 12, 2024.

52 IPC Global Initiative – Special Brief, Nov. 8, 2024, pp. 1–2.

53 Checchi, Francesco, et al. 2024. "Wartime food availability in the Gaza Strip, October 2023 to August 2024: a retrospective analysis." *medRxiv,* Oct. 21 [pre-print].

54 Lemkin, *Axis Rule in Occupied Europe,* p. 77.

55 On the context of the Gaza famine—Israel's ethnic cleansing since the 1940s, its occupation since 1967, and the Gaza War and its genocidal atrocities—see Steinbock 2025, *op.cit.,* esp. Chapters 1–2, 8–9.

56 Lemkin, Raphael. 1945. "Genocide – A Modern Crime." *Free World* 4 (April 1945), pp. 39–43.

57 That is, between Nov. 1941 and Feb. 1942. See Antonov, A. N. 1947. "Children born during the Siege of Leningrad in 1942." *Journal of Paediatrics* 30, pp. 250–259.

58 Winick, Myron. 2014. "Jewish medical resistance in the Warsaw Ghetto." In: Grodin, Michael A., Ed. 2014. *Jewish medical resistance in the Holocaust* (New York; Berghahn Books), pp. 93–105.

59 Ibid.

60 "People in northern Gaza forced to survive on 245 calories a day, less than a can of beans." Oxfam International, April 3, 2024.

61 Ibid. See also New York Post Editorial Board. "There is no Gaza famine, so why is the pro-Hamas media silent about this great news?" *New York Post,* June 20, 2024.

62 See Steinbock 2025, *op.cit.,* esp. Chapters 1–2, 5–6.

63 Rubinstein, W. D. 2004. *Genocide: A History* (London: Pearson Education), p. 308.

64 Compare Steinbock 2025, *op.cit.,* esp. Chapter 5.

65 Ibid., pp. 290–291.

66 "10,000 people feared buried under the rubble in Gaza." UN Office Geneva, May 3, 2024.

67 Jawad, Mohammed, et al. Estimating indirect mortality impacts of armed conflict in civilian populations: panel regression analyses of 193 countries, 1990–2017. *BMC Medicine* 18, article no. 266 (2020).

68 Khatib, Rashaa, et al. "Counting the Dead in Gaza: Difficult but Essential." *The Lancet,* July 5, 2024. Critics argued that the methodology deployed was implausible, while acknowledging the challenge of documenting mortality in Gaza amid genocide. See Spagat, Michael. "A critical analysis of The Lancet's letter 'Counting the Dead in Gaza: Difficult but Essential.'" AOAV, July 10, 2024. See also Steinbock 2025, *op. cit.,* esp. Chapter 8.

69 Attacks on hospitals during the escalation of hostilities in Gaza (7 October 2023–30 June 2024). UN Human Rights Office of the High Commissioner, Dec. 31, 2024.

70 Steinbock 2025, *op.cit.,* esp. Chapter 1.

71 Ibid., Chapter 9.

72 "'Domicide' must be recognised as an international crime: Un expert." OHCHR, Oct. 28, 2024.

73 Ibid. Dr Ziv Bohrer, an expert in international law at Bar-Ilan University quoted by Graham-Harrison.

74 Data from United Nations Development Programme (UNDP) and Palestinian Central Bureau of Statistics (PCBS) in May 2024.

75 *Impacts of the Conflict in the Middle East on the Palestinian Economy, December 2024 Update.* World Bank Economic Monitoring Report (International Bank for Reconstruction and Development/The World Bank, December 2024), p. 1.

76 Ibid. See also "Women and newborns bearing the brunt of the conflict in Gaza, UN agencies warn." Statement, World Health Organization, Nov. 3. 2023.

77 "The war in Gaza must end." Statement by Martin Griffiths, Under-Secretary-General for Humanitarian Affairs and Emergency Relief Coordinator, UN OCHA, Jan. 5, 2024.

78 "UN adds Israel to global list of offenders that harm children." *CNN,* June 7, 2024.

79 "Onslaught of violence against women and children in Gaza unacceptable: UN experts." UNHRO, May 6, 2024.

80 Defense for Children International (2003). *Kids Behind Bars: A Study on Children in Conflict with the Law* (Amsterdam: Defense for Children International), p. 2.

81 Ibid., pp. 2–3.

82 "Gaza's Missing Children." Save the Children, June 24, 2024.

83 Ibid. See also Qiblawi, Tamara, et al. "Anesthetics, crutches, dates. Inside Israel's ghost list of items arbitrarily denied entry into Gaza." *CNN,* March 2, 2024.

84 Sidhwa, Feroze. "65 Doctors, Nurses and Paramedics: What We Saw in Gaza." *New York Times,* October 9, 2024.

85 "'More than a human can bear': Israel's systematic use of sexual, reproductive and other forms of gender-based violence since 7 October 2023." Independent International Commission of Inquiry on the Occupied Palestinian Territory, including East Jerusalem, and Israel. UN Human Rights Council, A/HRC/58/CRP.6, March 13, 2025.

86 Rubinstein, *Genocide,* p. 308.

87 Holslag, Antonie. "Exposed Bodies: A Conceptual Approach to Sexual Violence during the Armenian Genocide." In: Randall, Amy E. 2015. *Genocide and Gender in the Twentieth Century: A Comparative Study* (New York: Bloomsbury), pp. 96–97. See also Ashraph, Sareta. "Beyond Killing: Gender, Genocide, & Obligations Under International Law." Global Justice Center, Dec. 2018.

88 See Lemkin, Raphael. 2013. *Totally Unofficial: The Autobiography of Raphael Lemkin,* edited by Donna-Lee Frieze (New Haven, CT: Yale University Press), p. 241, n1.

89 Guillaume, Alexia. 2022. *Cultural Apartheid: Israel's Erasure of Palestinian Heritage in Gaza* (Ramallah: Al-Haq, Jan. 2022), p. 7.

90 "#Gaza: Four Schools Hit in the Last Four Days." UNRWA, July 10, 2024.

91 "Israel kills dozens of academics, destroys every university in the Gaza Strip." *Euro-Med Human Rights Monitor,* Jan. 20, 2024.

92 "UN experts deeply concerned over 'scholasticide' in Gaza." UN Human Rights Office, April 18, 2024; "Education under Attack in Gaza, with Nearly 90% of School Buildings Damaged or Destroyed." Save the Children, April 16, 2024.

93 Herbicidal Warfare in Gaza. Forensic Architecture, July 19, 2019.

94 Sjursen, Daniel. 2021. *A True History of the United States: Indigenous Genocide, Racialized Slavery, Hyper-Capitalism, Militarist Imperialism and Other Overlooked Aspects of American Exceptionalism* (Steerforth Press / Truth to Power), p. 447.

95 See "Foreword" in Molawi, Shourideh C., and Eyal Weizman. 2024. *Environmental Warfare in Gaza: Colonial Violence and New Landscapes of Resistance* (New York: Pluto).

96 Ibid.

97 *West Bank and Gaza: Country Climate and Development Report.* World Bank Group, Sept. 2023, see Executive Summary.

98 Zwijnenburg, Wim, and Natasha Hall. *Uninhabitable? The reverberating public health and environmental risks from the war in Gaza* (PAX, December 2023), p. 20.

99 Based on estimates by Pehr Lodhammar, the former United Nationals Mine Action Service chief for Iraq. See Graham-Harrison, Emma. "Gaza's 37m tonnes of bomb-filled debris could take 14 years to clear, says expert." *The Guardian,* April 26, 2024.

100 Neimark, Benjamin, Patrick Bigger, Frederick Otu-Larbi, and Reuben Larbi. 2024. *A Multitemporal Snapshot of Greenhouse Gas Emissions from the Israel-Gaza Conflict* (Jan. 5, 2024). Available at SSRN: http://dx.doi.org/10.2139/ssrn.4684768.

101 Conversation between Elon Musk and Alice Weidel, co-chairwoman of Germany's far-right AfD party, posted on *X,* Jan. 10, 2025. See https://x.com/ElonClipsX/status/1877454219827098052

102 This section draws from Steinbock, Dan. 2025. "The Netanyahu Cabinet's War against Human Rights in Israel: B'Tselem in the Crosshairs." *Informed Comment,* March 3.

103 On the rise and background of these far-right leaders, see Steinbock 2025, *op.cit.,* esp. Chapters 1–2.

104 Ibid.

105 Peleg, Bar, Eden Solomon, Chen Maanit, and Yaniv Kubovich. "IDF Moves Troops to Base Where Violent Mob Protested Arrest of Soldiers for Abusing Gaza Detainee." *Haaretz,* July 30, 2024.

106 Leal, Iris. "Israel's Gov't Tender Souls Who Call for an Ethnic Cleansing of Gaza." *Haaretz,* Nov. 5, 2023.

107 Estrin, Daniel. 2024. "Israeli settlers in Gaza? Netanyahu's allies lay out a strategy." *NPR,* Oct. 25, 2024.

108 Hauser Tov, Michael. "'We're Rolling Out Nakba 2023,' Israeli Minister Says on Northern Gaza Strip Evacuation." *Haaretz,* Nov. 12, 2023.

109 Steinbock 2025, *op.cit.,* esp. Chapter 1 and 10.

110 Grim, Ryan. "Netanyahu's Goal for Gaza: 'Thin' Population 'to a Minimum.'" *The Intercept,* Dec. 3, 2023.

111 Steinbock, Dan. 2025. "The Netanyahu Cabinet's War against Human Rights in Israel: B'Tselem in the Crosshairs." *Informed Comment,* Mar. 3, 2025.

Chapter 2

1 Woodward, Bob. 2024. *War* (New York: Simon and Schuster), Chapter 46.

2 See Steinbock, Dan. 2025. *The Fall of Israel* (Atlanta, GA: Clarity Press), esp. Chapter 3.

3 Engelbrecht, H. C.; and Hanighen, F. C. 1934. *Merchants of Death* (Dodd, Mead & Co.).

4 Steinbock 2025, *op.cit.*, Chapter 3.

5 Ibid., on the evolution of U.S. aid to Israel, see Chapters 3 and 10.

6 Nicastro, Luke A., and Andrew Tilghman. *U.S. Overseas Basing: Background and Issues for Congress.* CRS, July 10, 2024.

7 Jacobs, Lawrence R., and Benjamin I. Page. "Who Influences U.S. Foreign Policy?" *American Political Science Review* 99, no. 1, February 2005.

8 Williams, Brooke, and Ken Silverstein. "Meet the Think Tank Scholars Who Are Also Beltway Lobbyists." *New Republic,* May 10, 2013; Beeton, Dan. "On Government Funding of Think Tanks." Washington, DC: Center for Economic and Policy Research, September 10, 2014; Lipton, Eric, and Brooke Williams. "How Think Tanks Amplify Corporate America's Influence." *New York Times,* August 7, 2016. On U.S.-Russian Cold War in this light, see Diesen, Glenn. 2023. *The Think Tank Racket: Managing the Information War with Russia* (Atlanta, GA: Clarity Press).

9 "The Military–Industrial Complex; The Farewell Address of President Eisenhower" (Basements Publications, 2006). See also Steinbock, Dan. 2014. "The Challenges for America's Defense Innovation." The Information Technology & Innovation Foundation, Nov. 2006, p. 6.

10 Freeman, Ben. "U.S. Government and Defense Contractor Funding of America's Top 50 Think Tanks." Foreign Influence Transparency Initiative, Center for International Policy, October 2020; Freeman, Ben. "Foreign Funding of Think Tanks in America," Foreign Influence Transparency Initiative, Center for International Policy, January 2020.

11 Arke, Raymond. "Pro-Israel Background." *OpenSecrets,* 2024 Election Cycle, Feb. 2019.

12 Freeman, Ben, and Nick Cleveland-Stout. "Big Ideas and Big Money: Think Tank Funding in America." *Quincy Brief* no. 68 (Jan. 2024).

13 Heinz, Brett, and Erica Jung. "The Military-Industrial-Think Tank Complex Conflicts of Interest at the Center for a New American Security." *POGO,* Feb. 2021.

14 Campbell, Kurt M., and Jake Sullivan. "Competition Without Catastrophe: How America Can Both Challenge and Coexist with China." *Foreign Affairs* (Sept./ Oct. 2019). On the pivot to Asia, see Campbell, Kurt M. 2016. *The Pivot: The Future of American Statecraft in Asia* (New York: Twelve).

15 Grazier, Dan. "The Troubling Business Connections of Biden's Asia Advisor Kurt Campbell." Project on Government Oversight, April 22, 2021. See also http://theasiagroup.com

16 Quotes from Pamuk, Humera. "Top Biden official doubts Israel can achieve 'total victory' in Gaza." *Reuters,* May 14, 2024.

17 "John O. Brennan, former Director of the Central Intelligence Agency, joins WestExec Advisors." WestExec Advisors, April 11, 2022.

18 Guyer, Jonathan. "How Biden's Foreign-Policy Team Got Rich." *The American Prospect,* July 6, 2020.

19 Hancock, Jay. "In Election Year, Drug Industry Spent Big to Temper Talk About High Drug Prices." *NPR,* Dec. 18, 2017; and "The Stealth Campaign to Kill Off Obamacare." *New York Times,* July 27, 2018.

20 Ackerman, Spencer. "She Helped Escalate an Endless War. Will She End It?" *The Daily Beast,* Nov. 13, 2020.

21 See https://www.westexec.com/

22 Fang, Lee. "Former Obama Officials Help Silicon Valley Pitch the Pentagon for Lucrative Defense Contracts." *The Intercept,* May 15, 2020.

23 Bender, Bryan, and Theodoric Meyer. "The secretive consulting firm that's become Biden's Cabinet in waiting." *Politico,* Nov. 23, 2020.

24 Guyer, Jonathan. "How Biden's Foreign-Policy Team Got Rich." *The American Prospect,* July 6, 2020.

25 See https://www.cnas.org/support-cnas/cnas-supporters

26 Thompson, Alex, and Theodoric Meyer. "Janet Yellen made millions in Wall Street, corporate speeches." *Politico,* Jan. 1, 2021.

27 Mosk, Matthew, and Mike Levine. "Watchdogs urge transparency as executives from powerful DC firm floated for Biden administration." *ABC News,* Nov. 12, 2020.

28 Lipton, Eric, and Kenneth P. Vogel. "Aides' Ties to Firms Present Biden With Early Ethics Test." *New York Times,* Nov. 28, 2020; Guyer, Jonathan. "How Biden's Foreign-Policy Team Got Rich." *The American Prospect,* July 6, 2020.

29 Steinbock 2025, *op.cit.,* Chapter 4.

30 For more, see the section "U.S. Case Against the Biden Administration" in the next chapter.

31 Tindera, Michela. "Here's How Much Joe Biden Was Worth In 2021." Forbes, Aug. 17, 2021. On the Bidens and the Ukraine entanglements, see Devalay, Arnaud. 2024. *Foreign Entanglements: Ukraine, Biden & the Fractured American Political Consensus* (Atlanta, GA: Clarity Press). See also Horton, Scott. 2024. *Provoked: How Washington Started the New Cold War with Russia and the Catastrophe in Ukraine* (The Libertarian Institute).

32 Remarks by President Biden on the Terrorist Attacks in Israel. Speech. The White House, Oct. 10, 2023.

33 Ibid.

34 OpenSecrets, 2024 Election Cycle. Retrieved on Nov. 16, 2024.

35 Guyer, "How Biden's Foreign-Policy Team Got Rich."

36 See https://act.uscpr.org/a/genocide-complicity

37 See e.g., Lipton, Eric, and Kenneth P. Vogel. "Biden Aides' Ties to Consulting and Investment Firms Pose Ethics Test." *New York Times,* December 15, 2020.

38 Compare Wisse, Ruth R. "A Tale of Five Blinkens." *Commentary,* Feb. 15, 2021; Simons, Marline. "Fresh Theories on Maxwell's Death." *New York Times,* Dec. 6, 1991; Webb, Whitney Alyse. 2022. *One Nation Under Blackmail: The Sordid Union Between Intelligence and Organized Crime that Gave Rise to Jeffrey Epstein* (Trine Day); Husseini, Sam. "Israel, Blackmail and the Presidents." Substack, Nov. 4, 2024.

39 See Alexander, Dan. "Inside The $10 Million Fortune Of Antony Blinken, Biden's Secretary Of State." *Forbes,* June 17, 2021. See also Vogel, Kenneth P., and Eric Lipton. "Washington Has Been Lucrative for Some on Biden's Team." *New York Times,* Jan. 2, 2021.

40 "Merrill Lynch CEO Thain Spent $1.22 Million On Office." *CNBC,* Jan. 22, 2009.

41 Compare Devalay, *Foreign Entanglements.*

42 "Lloyd Austin: Employment History." OpenSecrets, Revolving Doors, retrieved May 30, 2022. See https://www.opensecrets.org/revolving/rev_summary. php?id=82688

43 Hunnicutt, Trevor. "Biden's Defense nominee could get $1.7 million as he leaves Raytheon." *Reuters,* Jan. 10, 2021; "Secretary of Defense Lloyd Austin's Raytheon Controversy." Coalition for American Veterans, https://coalitionforamericanveterans. com/secretary-lloyd-austins-raytheon-controversy/

44 Alexander, Dan. "Here's How Much Secretary Of Defense Lloyd Austin Is Worth." *Forbes,* June 18, 2021.

45 "BP hires former MI6 boss John Sawers." *The Guardian,* May 14, 2015.

46 Report of the United Nations Fact-Finding Mission on the Gaza Conflict (the "Goldstone Report"). United Nations Office of the High Commissioner for Human Rights. Sept. 25, 2009. See also Slater, Jerome. "Just War Moral Philosophy and the 2008–09 Israeli Campaign in Gaza." *International Security* 37, no. 2 (Oct. 2012): 56–57.

47 The strategy was developed by the Bureau for Conflict Prevention and Stabilization, operating under the State Department.

48 *U.S. Strategy to Anticipate, Prevent, and Respond to Atrocities.* USAID, Aug. 17, 2023. https://www.usaid.gov/sites/default/files/2023-08/SAPRA_%20 August%202023_1_1.pdf

49 Quoted in Schwartz, Jon. "Samantha Power Calls on Samantha Power to Resign Over Gaza." *The Intercept,* Dec. 15, 2023. On the rise and fall of Samantha Power's humanitarian clout, see Guyer, Jonathan. "The Price of Power." *New York Magazine,* Oct. 4, 2024.

50 See https://samanthapower.com/about/ (retrieved on Jan. 8, 2024).

51 This section draws from Steinbock, Dan. "Trump 2.0 and Palestinians: from reversal to repression." *Informed Comments,* Jan. 24, 2025; and Steinbock 2025, *op.cit.,* esp. Chapter 3.

52 National Task Force to Combat Antisemitism, *Project Esther: A National Strategy to Combat Antisemitism.* Heritage Foundation, Oct. 7, 2024.

53 On the longstanding efforts at "imperial presidency" in America, see Steinbock, Dan. "US Executive Power and the 'State of Exception.'" *ConsortiumNews,* May 6, 2019.

54 National Task Force to Combat Antisemitism, *Project Esther.*

55 "Working Definition of Antisemitism," International Holocaust Remembrance Alliance (IHRA), May 16, 2016 (retrieved Feb. 1, 2025). See https://www. holocaustremembrance.com/news-archive/working-definition-antisemitism

56 Smith, Allan. "Trump to sign executive order targeting college anti-Semitism, Israel boycotts." *NBC News,* Dec. 11, 2019; "Anti-Semitism Awareness Act of 2018." ACLU. June 4, 2018; Concepcion, Summer. "Trump attacks American Jews, says they must 'get their act together' on Israel 'before it's too late.'" *NBC News,* Oct. 16, 2022.

57 Smith, Tovia. "Trump order cracks down on antisemitism and could deport foreign student protesters." *NPR,* Jan. 30, 2025. On the Khalil case, see Offenhartz, Jake. "Immigration agents arrest Palestinian activist who helped lead Columbia University protests." *Associated Press,* March 9, 2025. On the Öztürk case, see

Murray, Conor. "What We Know About Rumeysa Ozturk—Rubio Says Tufts Student Detained by ICE Had Visa Revoked." *Forbes,* March 27, 2025.

58 "Fact Sheet: President Donald J. Trump Takes Forceful and Unprecedented Steps to Combat Anti-Semitism." White House, Jan. 30, 2025.

59 Berman, Howard, Michèle Flournoy, Jane Harman, Leon Panetta, David Petraeus, Dennis Ross, and Robert Satloff. "Statement on Improving the Potential for a Diplomatic Resolution to the Iran Nuclear Challenge." Washington Institute, Dec. 17, 2021.

60 "'Obliteration' threat to Iran in case of nuclear attack." *The Guardian,* April 23, 2008.

61 Ignatius, Adi. "Raytheon CEO Gregory Hayes: How Ukraine Has Highlighted Gaps in US Defense Technologies." *Harvard Business Review,* March 25, 2022.

62 On Raytheon and AI, see Kahn, Jeremy. "A.I. is letting this company build a new kind of defense contractor." *Fortune,* July 28, 2021. On air travel malaise and Raytheon, see Aspan, Maria. "International air travel might not recover before 2024, Raytheon CEO warns." *Fortune Global Forum,* October 28, 2020. On Hayes's compensation, see Maffei, Lucia. "Raytheon's CEO pay rose 11% last year to $23.3M." *Boston Business Journal,* March 15, 2022.

63 Steinbock, Dan. "US Big Defense, the Only Winner of the Ukraine Proxy War: The Unwarranted Ukraine Proxy War: A Year Later." *The World Financial Review,* Jan. 2023. See also Steinbock, Dan. "The Unwarranted War: The avoidable war that will penalize severely Ukraine, Russia, the US and the NATO, Europe, developing countries and the global economy." *The World Financial Review,* March 2022.

64 Lillis, Katie Bo, and Oren Liebermann. "How Ukraine became a testbed for Western weapons and battlefield innovation." *CNN,* Jan. 16, 2023.

65 Smith, Elliott. "How Ukraine became a testbed for Western weapons and battlefield innovation." *CNBC,* Dec. 28, 2022.

66 Ebright, Katherine Yon. "Secret War: How the U.S. Uses Partnerships and Proxy Forces to Wage War Under the Radar." Brennan Center for Justice, NYU School of Law, Nov. 3, 2022.

67 Crawford, Neta C. *The U.S. Budgetary Costs of the Post-9/11 Wars.* A Costs of War Series. Watson Institute of International & Public Affairs, Brown University, Sept. 1, 2022.

68 On Novakovic's statement and Big Defense pivot to Asia Pacific, see Steinbock, Dan. "Shangri-La Arms Race: Or Follow the Money." *The Manila Times,* June 11, 2018; and Steinbock, Dan. "From peaceful, nuclear-free ASEAN to battle-ready Indo-Pacific?" *The Manila Times,* October 18, 2021.

Chapter 3

1 Woodward, Bob. 2024. *War* (New York: Simon and Schuster), see Chapters 42–43.

2 Ibid.

3 Pamuk, Humeyra. "Special Report: Emails show early US concerns over Gaza offensive, risk of Israeli war crimes." *Reuters,* Oct. 4, 2024.

4 See Black, Edwin. 2001. *IBM and the Holocaust: The Strategic Alliance Between Nazi Germany and America's Most Powerful Corporation* (New York: Crown).

5 Schabas, William. 2009. *Genocide in International Law: The Crime of Crimes,* 2nd Ed. (Cambridge University Press), p. 351.

6 Case Concerning the Application of the Convention on the Prevention and Punishment of the Crime of Genocide (*Bosnia and Herzegovina v. Serbia and Montenegro*), Feb. 26, 2007.

7 Ibid., para 431. Nonetheless, these sections of the ICJ ruling are in part diluted by the caveat that the obligation to prevent genocide is only breached if genocide is in fact committed. The genocide threshold can only be identified after the genocide has occurred.

8 Compare Steinbock, Dan. 2025. *The Fall of Israel* (Atlanta, GA: Clarity Press), esp. Chapter 5.

9 Woodward 2025, *op. cit.,* see Chapter 46.

10 Malsin, Jared, Nancy A. Youssef, and Carrie Keller-Lynn. "U.S. Plans $8 Billion Sale of Arms, Including Bombs, to Israel." *Wall Street Journal,* Jan. 4, 2025.

11 Scahill, Jeremy. "In Genocide Case Against Israel at The Hague, the U.S. Is the Unnamed Co-Conspirator." *The Intercept,* Jan. 11, 2024.

12 "Statement of Mourning for the Gazans and the World." Lemkin Institute, Oct 29, 2024.

13 "US 'not seeing acts of genocide' in Gaza, State Dept says." *Reuters,* Jan. 4, 2024.

14 See McGreal, Chris. "US rights group sues Biden for alleged 'failure to prevent genocide' in Gaza." *The Guardian,* Nov. 13, 2023; Pazanowski, Bernie, and Thomsen, Jacqueline. "Israeli Military Aid Package Not Reviewable by Federal Court." *Bloomberg Law,* Feb. 1, 2024.

15 *Defense for Children International – Palestine et al. v. Biden et al.* Justia Dockets & Filings. Retrieved Nov. 1, 2024.

16 Ibid.

17 Schabas, William. 2024. "Declaration of William A. Schabas." In: *Defense for Children International – Palestine et al v. Biden et al.* Justia Dockets & Filings. Retrieved Nov. 1, 2024.

18 *Ukraine v. Russian Federation,* Declaration of Intervention of the Government of the United States of America pursuant to article 63 of the Statute of the International Court of Justice, Sept. 6, 2022, para. 22.

19 Ibid.

20 Quoted in: Katty, Faisal. "A tale of two US court decisions, and the Palestine exception." *Al Jazeera,* March 13, 2024.

21 Raymond, Nate. "US judge allows lawsuit challenging aid to West Bank and Gaza to proceed." *Reuters,* Feb 6, 2024.

22 Compare O'Donnell, Michael J. 2004. "A Turn for the Worse: Foreign Relations, Corporate Human Rights Abuse, and the Courts." *Boston College Third World Law Journal* 24, no. 1 (Jan. 2004): 223–265.

23 Faisal, "A tale of two US court decisions, and the Palestine exception."

24 Communication Pursuant to Article 15 of the Rome Statute: Accessorial Liability of United States Officials." DAWN, Jan 19, 2025 [public version]. The submission centered on the U.S. military and political support, encouragement and

assistance to Israel; that is, the war crimes of starvation and intentionally directing attacks against the civilian population, and crimes against humanity, including murder, inhumane acts, and persecution, under the Rome Statute. It also included their role in the war crime of intentionally directing attacks against civilian objects under Article 8(2)(b)(ii) and the crime of genocide under Article 6.

25 Ibid.

26 Quoted in "ICC asked to investigate Biden and other former US officials for complicity in war crimes." Middle East Monitor, Feb 24, 2025.

27 Oamek, Paige. 2024. "Harris Refuses to Change Course on Israel in Alarming First Interview." New Republic. Aug 31.

28 Sillars, James. 2023. "Janet Yellen: America can 'certainly' afford to support Israel and Ukraine, US Treasury secretary says." Sky News, Oct 16; "Janet Yellen warns Iran that nothing is 'off the table' for sanctions." Financial Times. Oct 11, 2023.

29 Steinbock, Dan. 2019. "US Executive Power and the 'State of Exception'." Consortium News, May 6; and Steinbock, Dan. 2025. "The Imminent Consequences of Trump's Executive Orders." Modern Diplomacy, Jan 30.

30 Compare Tibon, Amir. "Netanyahu's New Gaza Plan Is Taken Straight Out of the Iraq War Playbook." Haaretz, May 5, 2025. See also Ravid, Barak. 2025. "U.S. and Israel near agreement on aid delivery to Gaza." Axios, May 2, 2025.

31 According to GIPRI, these charges of complicity rested on Article 25(3)(c) of the Rome Statute of the ICC. von der Leyen enjoyed no functional immunity before the ICC by virtue of Article 27 of the said Statute. See "Call to the International Criminal Court to investigate on Ursula von der Leyen for complicity in war crimes and genocide committed by Israel in the Occupied Palestinian Territories and in Gaza." Fondation GIPRI, Press Release, Geneva, May 27, 2024.

32 On these three developments, see Finn, Daniel. "The European Union Is Endorsing Israel's Attack on Gaza." Jacobin, March 2025; Inat, Kemal. "The European Union's Policy on the Genocide in Gaza: Josep Borrell vs. Ursula von der Leyen." Politics Today, March 26, 2024; Falk, Richard. "Gaza: Civil ICC case against Ursula von derLeyen raises stakes on genocide complicity." Middle East Eye, June 6, 2024.

33 See the comments of international genocide scholar William Schabas in Neslen, Arthur. "EU President Should Be Tried for Complicity in Israel's War Crimes." The Intercept, May 3, 2025.

34 Hansler, Jennifer, and Kylie Atwood. "US officials who resigned over Biden's Gaza policy are working together to put pressure on admin." CNN, June 9, 2024.

35 Report to Congress under Section 2 of the National Security Memorandum on Safeguards and Accountability with Respect to Transferred Defense Articles and Defense Services (NSM-20), May 10, 2024, pp. 18–32.

36 Ahmed, Akbar Shahid. "Exclusive: Veteran State Department Official Says She Quit Over Biden Administration 'Twisting The Facts' On Gaza." HuffPost, May 31, 2024.

37 Borger, Julian. "Two more US officials resign over Biden administration's position on Gaza war." The Guardian, May 30, 2024.

38 Singh, Kanishka. "US education official resigns over Biden's Israel-Gaza policy." Reuters, Jan. 4, 2024.

39 "South African Attorney Wikus Van Rensberg: Proceedings Against Israel In The ICJ Are Just A 'Precursor.'" *SABC*, Jan. 13, 2024.

40 "US and UK 'must be held accountable': South African attorney." *Global Times*, Jan. 30, 2024.

41 Sokol, Karen. 2024. Arms Transfers and International Law. Legal Sidebar, CRS, July 29. 2024.

42 Argüello Gómez, Carlos J. "Application instituting proceedings." International Court of Justice, March 1, 2024.

43 Saunders, Imogen. "Interventions and Inadmissibility: Nicaragua v Germany, the Monetary Gold principle, and the Genocide Convention at the International Court of Justice." ANU College of Law, March 6, 2024.

44 Ibid., p. 3.

45 "Convention on the Prevention and Punishment of the Crime of Genocide." OHCHR, Dec. 9, 1948.

46 Abrams, Elliott. "International Criminal Court Prosecutor Threatens United States Senators." Blog Post. Council on Foreign Relations, May 24, 2024.

47 "The massacre at El Mozote: the need to remember." Human Rights Watch, March 4, 1992; Walsh, Lawrence E. "Final Report of the Independent Counsel For Iran/Contra Matters Vol. I: Investigations and Prosecutions." Chapter 25. U.S. Court of Appeal for the District of Columbia, Aug. 4, 1993; Malkin, Elisabeth, "Trial on Guatemalan Civil War Carnage Leaves Out U.S. Role." *New York Times*, May 16, 2013.

48 Cotton, Tom, et al. "Letter to Mr. Khan." U.S. Senate, April 24. 2024.

49 Knoops, Geert-Jan. 2014. *An Introduction to the Law of International Criminal Tribunals* (Brill), p. 318.

50 That is, military personnel, elected or appointed officials, and other persons employed by or working on behalf of the government of a NATO member country, a major non-NATO ally including Australia, Egypt, Israel, Japan, Argentina, South Korea, and New Zealand. See "American Service-Members' Protection Act." US Department of State Archive. July 30, 2003.

51 Pace, William. "The Hague Invasion Act remains dangerous." Diplomatic Council, Feb. 12, 2019.

52 "Repeal Hague Invasion Act (2022 – H.R. 7523)." *GovTrack.us*. Retrieved Dec. 8, 2024.

53 2024 Report to Congress on Section 5 of the Elie Wiesel Genocide and Atrocities Prevention Act of 2018 (P.L. 115–441) [as amended], pp. 7–8.

54 Baumann, Nick. "The GOP Candidate Who Wants Journos Jailed." *Mother Jones*, Nov. 10, 2011; Manduley, Christina. "Sen. Tom Cotton: Waterboarding isn't torture." *CNN*, Nov. 9, 2016; Cotton, Tom. "Send in the Troops." *New York Times*, June 3, 2020.

55 McGreal, Chris. "US right heats up inflammatory rhetoric on Palestine as Muslim groups worry." *The Guardian*, Oct. 19, 2023.

56 Cotton, Tom. "The ICC is a kangaroo court and Karim Khan is a deranged fanatic." Post on *X*, Nov. 21, 2024.

57 "'Appalling': ICC president says threats, sanctions put court in jeopardy." *Al Jazeera*, Dec. 2, 2024.

58 Lacy, Akela. "GOP Representative Denies Existence of 'Innocent Palestinian Civilians' and Tries to Hobble Aid to Gaza." *The Intercept*, Nov. 1, 2023.

59 "Brian Mast." *OpenSecrets*, Dec. 24, 2024; Harb, Ali. "Brian Mast: Pro-Israel hawk set to lead US House foreign policy panel." *Al Jazeera*, Dec. 11, 2024. See also Steinbock 2025, *op.cit.*, esp. Chapter 5.

60 Wezeman, Pieter D., et al. *Trends in International Arms Transfers, 2023.* SIPRI, March 2024; Hussain, Zain. 2024. "How top arms exporters have responded to the war in Gaza." SIPRI, Oct. 3.

61 Exposing UK Arms Exports to Israel. Palestinian Youth Movement/Workers for a Free Palestine, Progressive International, May 7, 2025.

62 Steinbock 2025, *op.cit.*, Chapter 4.

63 "Biden at odds with allies as U.S. and Israel attack ICC over arrest warrants." NBC News. May 21, 2024; Whitson, Sarah Leah. 2024. "The White House's Defense of Israel Is Undermining International Law." Foreign Policy, Sept. 24; "Blinken says he'll work with US Congress on potential ICC sanctions." Reuters. May 22, 2024; Clare Foran; Haley Talbot. 2024. "House passes International Criminal Court sanctions bill after prosecutor seeks Netanyahu warrant." CNN, June 4.

64 "Reference: C.N.630.2014. TREATIES-XXVI.8 (Depositary Notification)." United Nations, Sept. 25, 2014; "Arms Trade Treaty: Treaty Status." United Nations, Nov. 6, 2024.

65 Ibid.

66 A joint statement written by Al-Haq, the International Service for Human Rights (ISHR), and the Women's International League for Peace and Freedom (WILPF)—and currently signed by 137 organizations after just one month of Israel's military response to October 7 in November 2023.

67 "Information Note by the UN Working Group on Business and Human Rights." UN Working Group on Business and Human Rights, Office of the United Nations High Commissioner for Human Rights. Retrieved on Nov. 6, 2024.

68 On UNRWA and U.S. aid, see Steinbock 2025, *op.cit.*, esp. Chapter 3.

69 Steinbock 2025, *op.cit.*, esp. Chapters 1 and 11.

70 Ibid, esp. Chapter 4.

71 Margesson, Rhoda, and Jim Zanotti. *UN Relief and Works Agency for Palestine Refugees in the Near East (UNRWA).* Congressional Research Service, Dec. 27, 2024.

72 Frank, BrieAnna J. "Jerusalem deputy mayor referred to Hamas militants as 'subhuman' in X post." *USA Today*, Dec. 14, 2023.

73 Smith, Alexander. 2025. "Trump's plans for a 'Riviera of the Middle East' in Gaza condemned." *NBC News*, Feb. 6.

74 Steinbock 2025, *op.cit.*, esp. Chapter 1.

Chapter 4

1 On this tension between Lemkin's published and unpublished works, his stated views and deeply-held beliefs, see esp. Fitzmaurice, Andrew. "Anticolonialism in Western Political Thought: The Colonial Origins of the Concept of Genocide," and Docker, John. "Are Settler-Colonies Inherently Genocidal? Re-reading Lemkin." In: Moses, A. Dirk. 2008. *Empire, Colony, Genocide: Conquest, Occupation, and Subaltern Resistance in World* (New York: Berghahn), Chapters 2–3, respectively.

2 Irvin-Erickson, Douglas. 2017. *Raphael Lemkin and the Concept of Genocide* (Philadelphia: PENN), p. 198.

3 See Himmerich y Valencia, Robert. 1996. *The Encomenderos of New Spain, 1521–1555* (Austin, TX: University of Texas Press).

4Bartolomé de las Casas. 1542/52. *A Short Account of the Destruction of the Indies* (London: Penguin), see Preface.

5 Reséndez, Andrés. 2016. *The Other Slavery: The Uncovered Story of Indian Enslavement in America* (New York: Houghton Mifflin Harcourt), see Chapter 1 and Appendix 1.

6 Juderías, Julián. 1914. *La leyenda negra y la verdad histórica* (Madrid, Tip. de la Revista de Archivos). While the atrocities were real, their subsequent portrayals, including this 16th century illustration by Theodor de Bry, remain distorted by the "Black Legend"; the demonization of the Spanish by the Dutch, the British, and the Americans, to foster *their* empires and colonial possessions.

7 On the debate, see Losada, Ángel. "Controversy between Sepúlveda and Las Casas." In Friede, Juan, and Benjamin Keen, Eds. 1971. *Bartolomé de las Casas in History: Toward an Understanding of the Man and his Work* (DeKalb: Northern Illinois University Press), pp. 279–309

8 Aristotle, *Politics*, Book 1, Section 1254, pp. 16–21. For a critical review of the inconsistencies of Aristotle's original argument, see Dobbs, Darrell. 1994. "Natural Right and the Problem of Aristotle's Defense of Slavery." *The Journal of Politics* 56 no. 1.

9 Fabian, Emanuel. "Defense minister announces 'complete siege' of Gaza: No power, food or fuel." *Times of Israel*, Oct. 9, 2023.

10 Pileggi, Tamar. 2015. "New deputy defense minister called Palestinians 'animals.'" *Times of Israel*, May 11.

11 On rabbi Meir Kahane and Jewish supremacy doctrines, see Steinbock 2025, *op.cit.*, Chapters 1–2, 5–6.

12 On the ongoing debate regarding the purported and actual function of *Encomienda*, see Yeager, Timothy J. 1995. "Encomienda or Slavery? The Spanish Crown's Choice of Labor Organization in Sixteenth-Century Spanish America." *The Journal of Economic History* 55, no. 4: 842–859. For the wider context, see Castro, Daniel. 2007. *Another Face of Empire: Bartolomé de Las Casas, Indigenous Rights, and Ecclesiastical Imperialism* (Duke University Press).

13 Squeezed between the Nazi extermination and the approaching Soviet forces amid World War II, he fled Europe and found asylum in the United States. Many of his relatives were not as lucky; 49 died in the Holocaust. See Bartrop, Paul R. 2014. *Modern Genocide: The Definitive Resource and Document Collection*, Vol. I (ABC-CLIO), pp. 1301–1302.

14 Lemkin, Raphael. 1944. *Axis Rule in Occupied Europe: Laws of Occupation, Analysis of Government, Proposals for Redress* (Clark, N.J: Lawbook Exchange), p. 79, footnote 1.

15 Lemkin, Raphael. 2013. *Totally Unofficial: The Autobiography of Raphael Lemkin*, ed. Donna-Lee Frieze. New Haven, CT: Yale University Press, p. 80.

16 Lemkin, Raphael. 1944. *Axis Rule in Occupied Europe: Laws of Occupation, Analysis of Government, and Proposals for Redress* (Washington, DC: Carnegie Endowment for International Peace; Cambridge University Press, 2013), p. 79.

17 Ibid., p. 79.

18 Sayapin, Sergey. 2014. *The Crime of Aggression in International Criminal Law: Historical Development, Comparative Analysis and Present State* (T.M.C. Asser Press), p. 148.

19 Lemkin 2013, *op. cit.*, p. 118.

20 Ibid., pp. 118–120.

21 "Convention on the Prevention and Punishment of the Crime of Genocide." United Nations Audiovisual Library of International Law. Retrieved Oct. 16, 2024.

22 "United Nations Treaty Collection." treaties.un.org. Retrieved Oct. 24, 2024.

23 Irvin-Erickson 2017, *op. cit.*, pp. 1–2.

24 Compare Schabas, William. 2009. *Genocide in International Law: The Crime of Crimes.* 2nd Ed. (Cambridge), p. 176.

25 See Docker 2008, *op. cit.*

26 Ibid.

27 For more, see the section on ethnic cleansing.

28 Quoted in Docker 2008, *op. cit.*

29 UN Doc. E/AC.25/12, Ad Hoc Committee Draft. Quoted in Irvin-Erickson 2017, *op. cit.*, pp. 182–183.

30 Lemkin 2013, *op. cit.*, p. 172.

31 Already in Nuremberg, Lemkin had been demanding, behind the scenes, that the judges include under the category of genocide acts of "forced sterilizations," "forced abortions," "the abduction of children," and the use of rape "to compel . . . women to bear children for your country"; that is, points that eventually became part of the Genocide Convention. See Lemkin, *Totally Unofficial*, pp. 123–126. On Lemkin's Nuremberg years 1946–1948, see also Irvin-Erickson 2017, *op. cit.*, esp. Chapter 6.

32 Irvin-Erickson 2017, *op. cit.*, p. 168.

33 Cooper, John. 2008. *Raphael Lemkin and the Struggle for the Genocide Convention* (London: Palgrave Macmillan), pp. 86–87.

34 For more, see the following section on "America's Black Genocide."

35 Compare Irvin-Erickson 2017, *op. cit.*, pp. 159–160.

36 Ibid., p. 176.

37 Staub, Ervin. 1989. *The Roots of Evil: The Origins of Genocide and Other Group Violence* (Cambridge, UK: Cambridge University Press), p. 8.

38 See https://www.un.org/en/observances/decade-people-african-descent/slave-trade. See Eltis, David, and David Richardson. 2019. *Atlas of the Transatlantic Slave Trade* (New Haven: Yale University Press); Stannard, David E. 1993. *American Holocaust: The Conquest of the New World,* Rev. Ed. (Oxford University Press).

39 Albanese, Francesca. *Report of the Special Rapporteur on the situation of human rights in the Palestinian territories occupied since 1967.* United Nations Human Rights Council, Oct. 1, 2024.

40 Compare Lemkin 2013, *op. cit.*, pp. 111–114.

41 Ibid., pp. 161–162. See also Irvin-Erickson 2017, *op. cit.*, p. 180.

42 On the Soviet side of the equation, see Weiss-Wendt, Anton. 2017. *The Soviet Union and the Gutting of the UN Genocide Convention* (Madison, WI: University of Wisconsin Press).

43 On genocidal atrocities in these histories, see for instance Cummings, Bruce. 2010. *The Korean War: A History* (Modern Library); Ganser, Daniele. 2005. *NATO's Secret Armies: Operation GLADIO and Terrorism in Western Europe* (Routledge); McSherry, J. Patrice. 2012. *Predatory States: Operation Condor and Covert War in Latin America* (Rowman & Littlefield); Valentine, Douglas. 1990. *The Phoenix Program: America's Use of Terror in Vietnam* (Open Road Media, 2014).

44 On Lemkin, the Cold War and the Civil Rights Movement, see Irvin-Erickson 2017, *op. cit.*, pp. 204–210

45 Quoted by Lewis, David Levering. 2009. *W. E. B. Du Bois: A Biography*. Updated (New York: Henry Holt and Co.), p. 192.

46 Civil Rights Congress. 1951. *We Charge Genocide: The Historic Petition to the United Nations for Relief from a Crime of the United States Government Against the Negro People* (New York: Civil Rights Congress).

47 Civil Rights Congress, *We Charge Genocide*, p. xiv.

48 Ibid., p. 6.

49 Martin, Charles H. 1997. "Internationalizing 'The American Dilemma': The Civil Rights Congress and the 1951 Genocide." *Journal of American Ethnic History* 16, no. 4 (Summer); "UN May Not Accept CRC Petition," *Atlanta Daily World*, Jan. 18, 1952; Docker, John. 2010. "Raphaël Lemkin, creator of the concept of genocide: a world history perspective," *Humanities Research* 16, no. 2.

50 Duberman, Martin B. 1989. *Paul Robeson* (Bodley Head), pp. 498–499, 563–564.

51 Irvin-Erickson 2017, *op. cit.*, p. 209.

52 Kramer, Mark, "Introduction," in Kramer, Mark, Ed. 2001. *Redrawing Nations: Ethnic Cleansing in East Central Europe* (Boulder: Rowman and Littlefield), p. 1.

53 Steinbock 2025, *op.cit.*, Chapter 1.

54 Schabas, William A. 2003/2004. "'Ethnic Cleansing' and Genocide: Similarities and Distinctions." *European Yearbook of Minority Issues*, Volume 3 (Brill), pp. 109–128..

55 Federal Ministry for Expellees, Refugees and War Victims. *Facts concerning the problem of the German expellees and refugees*, Bonn: 1967. See also Naimark, Norman M. 2001. *Fires of Hatred. Ethnic Cleansing in Twentieth–Century Europe*. Cambridge: Harvard University Press.

56 Zayas, Alfred De. 2006. *A Terrible Revenge: The Ethnic Cleansing of the East European Germans*, 2nd Ed. St. Martin's Griffin.

57 Douglas, R.M. 2012. *Orderly and Humane: The Expulsion of the Germans after the Second World War*. Yale University Press.

58 Talbot, Ian; Singh, Gurharpal. 2009. *The Partition of India*. Cambridge University Press.

59 See Steinbock 2025, *op.cit.* For the historical accounts, see Benny Morris. 1994. *1948 and After: Israel and the Palestinians* (Oxford); Pappe, Ilan. 2006. *The Ethnic Cleansing of Palestine* (London); Masakha, Nur. 2012. *Expulsion of the Palestinians: The Concept of "Transfer" in Zionist Political Thought, 1882–1948* (Institute for Palestine Studies).

60 Irvin-Erickson 2017, *op. cit.*, pp. 185–186.

61 Albert Einstein, Hannah Arendt, Sidney Hook, et.al., "New Palestine Party," Letter to *The New York Times*, Dec. 4, 1948.

62 Schabas 2009, *op.cit.*, p. 228.

63 International Convention on the Suppression and Punishment of the Crime of Apartheid, (1976) 1015 UNTS 243, art. II.

64 Compare Schabas 2009, *op. cit.*, p. 237, footnote 371.

65 See Steinbock 2025, *op.cit.*, esp. Chapter 2.

66 Anderton, Charles H., and Jurgen Brauer. 2016. *Economic Aspects of Genocides, Other Mass Atrocities, and Their Prevention* (New York: Oxford University Press), p. 25. For a legal analysis, see Pégorier, C. 2013. *Ethnic Cleansing: A Legal Qualification* (New York: Routledge).

67 International Criminal Court. 1998b. "Rome Statute of the International Criminal Court, Article 7." Nov. 10. See https://legal.un.org/icc/statute/99_corr/cstatute.htm, Accessed Nov. 25, 2024.

68 "The Situation in Bosnia and Herzegovina," UN Doc. A/RES/47/121. UN Doc. A/47/PV.91, 99 (102 in favor, with 57 abstentions, on a recorded vote). Yet, as Schabas notes, the abstentions concerned a provision in the resolution calling for an arms embargo to be lifted, and had nothing to do with the reference to genocide. Compare Schabas 2003/2004, *op. cit.*

69 "Interim report of the Commission of Experts Established Pursuant to Security Council Resolution 780 (1992)," UN Doc. S/35374 (1993), para. 56. See also Schabas 2003/2004, *op. cit*, p. 120.

70 *Prosecutor v. Milosevic et al.* (Case no. IT-99-37-I), Indictment, May 22, 1999.

71 Schabas 2003/2004, *op. cit*, pp. 109–128. See also *Prosecutor v. Jelisic* (Case no. IT-95-10-T), Judgment, 14 December 1999; *Prosecutor v. Sikirica et al.* (Case no. IT-95-8-1), Judgment on Defence Motions to Acquit, 3 September 2001; Prosecutor v. Stakic (Case No. IT-97-24-T), Judgment, 31 July 2003.

72 Schabas 2003/2004, *op. cit.*

73 Lemkin, *Axis Rule in Occupied Europe*, p. 79.

74 Lemkin, *Axis Rule in Occupied Europe*, p. 82.

75 This distinction between the physical act and the mental element feature in virtually all of the judgments of the international tribunals relating to charges of genocide, as genocide scholar William Schabas has noted. See Schabas 2009, *op.cit.*, p. 172.

76 Rubinstein, *Genocide*, p. 308.

77 "Convention on the Prevention and Punishment of the Crime of Genocide." OHCHR, December 9, 1948.

78 Ochab, Ewelina U., and David Alton. 2022. *State Responses to Crimes of Genocide: What Went Wrong and How to Change It* (Springer International Publishing), pp. 28, 30.

79 Bachman, Jeffrey S. 2022. *The Politics of Genocide: From the Genocide Convention to the Responsibility to Protect* (Rutgers University Press), pp. 47, 57.

80 On the debate, see e.g., Goldsmith, Katherine. 2010. "The Issue of Intent in the Genocide Convention and Its Effect on the Prevention and Punishment of the Crime of Genocide: Toward a Knowledge-Based Approach," *Genocide Studies and Prevention* 5, no. 3. See also Lewy, Guenter. 2007. "Can There Be Genocide Without Intent to Commit Genocide?" *Journal of Genocide Research* 9, no. 4, pp. 661–674.

81 Secretariat draft: UN Doc. E/447, pp. 5–13.

82 *Application of the Convention on the Prevention and Punishment of the Crime of Genocide (Croatia v Serbia)*, Preliminary Objections, Nov. 18, 2008, para. 123; *Application of the Convention on the Prevention and Punishment of the Crime of Genocide (Bosnia and Herzegovina v Serbia and Montenegro)*, Preliminary Objections [1996] ICJ Reports 617, para. 34.

83 Arendt, Hannah. 1951. *Origins of Totalitarianism* (Tel Aviv: Schocken Books), p. 289.

84 Klein, Shira. 2025. "The Growing Rift between Holocaust Scholars over Israel/ Palestine. *Journal of Genocide Research*, (Jan. 8, 2025): 1–21. For a historical and economic perspective, see Steinbock 2025, *op.cit.*, Chapter 9.

85 "History of the Optional Protocol" in the case of CEDAW from 1976 to 1979. See https://www.un.org/womenwatch/daw/cedaw/protocol/history.htm

86 Application of the Convention on the Prevention and Punishment of the Crime of Genocide (*The Gambia v. Myanmar*: 7 States intervening). Joint declaration of intervention of Canada, Denmark, France, Germany, the Netherlands and the United Kingdom. ICJ-CIJ, Nov. 15, 2023. See https://www.icj-cij.org/case/178/intervention

87 Carlson, Kerstin Bree, and Line Engbo Gissel. 2024. "What is genocide? Six Western countries want a broader application of the law – experts unpack why it matters." *The Conversation*, Jan. 19, 2024.

88 Bojang, Ousman Mamakeh. 2024. *History Of The Colonial Gambia: A historical review of British power and policies in the emergence of The Gambia, 1816–1965* (LAP Lambert Academic Publishing).

89 See e.g., "Myanmar/Bangladesh: Rohingyas – the Search for Safety." Amnesty International, September 1997; "UN calls for Myanmar generals to be tried for genocide, blames Facebook for incitement." *Reuters*, Aug. 27, 2018. For an analytical view, see Ibrahim, Azeem. 2016. *The Rohingyas: Inside Myanmar's Hidden Genocide* (Hurst); Wade, Francis. 2019. *Myanmar's Enemy Within: Buddhist Violence and the Making of a Muslim 'Other'* (Zed Books).

Chapter 5

1 Schabas, William. 2009. *Genocide in International Law: The Crime of Crimes.* 2nd Ed. (Cambridge), p. 642.

2 Sarkin, Jeremy. 2011. *Germany's Genocide of the Herero: Kaiser Wilhelm II, His General, His Settlers, His Soldiers* (Melton: James Currey).

3 Compare "The Ambassador in France (Sharp) to the Secretary of state, Paris, 28 May 1915," in *U.S. Foreign Relations, 1915*, Supplement, p. 981. See also United Nations War Crimes Commission. 1948. *History of the United Nations War Crimes Commission and the Development of the Laws of War* (London: His Majesty's Stationery Office), p. 35.

4 Compare Schabas, William. 2012. *Unimaginable Atrocities: Justice, Politics, and Rights at the War Crimes Tribunals* (Oxford: Oxford University Press), pp. 6–8. In an engaging work, the author later imagined such a trial, *if* it had happened. See Schabas, William. 2018. *The Trial of Kaiser* (Oxford: Oxford University Press).

5 *United Nations Documents 1941–1945* (Oxford University Press for the Royal Institute Of International Affairs. 1946).

6 Jackson, Robert H., Chief of Counsel for the United States. 1945. Opening Statement. The International Military Tribunal, Palace of Justice at Nuremberg, Germany, Nov. 21, 1945.

7 Sellars, Kirsten. 2013. *"Crimes Against Peace" and International Law* (Cambridge University Press), p. 165.

8 Heller, Kevin Jon. 2011. *The Trials. Introduction: the indictments, biographical information, and the verdicts* (Oxford University Press).

9 Lasby, Clarence G. 1971. *Project Paperclip: German Scientists and the Cold War* (New York: Atheneum); Jacobsen, Annie. 2014. *Operation Paperclip: The Secret Intelligence Program that Brought Nazi Scientists to America* (Little, Brown).

10 Simpson, Christopher. 2014. *Blowback: America's Recruitment of Nazis and Its Destructive Impact on Our Domestic and Foreign Policy* (Open Road Media); Crim, Brian E. 2018. *Our Germans: Project Paperclip and the National Security State* (JHU Press).

11 Compare Karstedt, Susanne. 1998. "Coming to Terms with the Past in Germany after 1945 and 1989: Public Judgments on Procedure and Justice." *Law and Policy* 20, p. 15.

12 Compare Steinbock, Dan. 2025. *The Fall of Israel* (Atlanta, GA: Clarity Press), esp. Chapter 7.

13 Karstedt, Susanne. 2008. "The Nuremberg Tribunal and German Society: International Justice and Local Judgment in Post-Conflict Reconstruction." In: Blumenthal, David A., and Timothy L. McCormack, Eds. 2008. *The Legacy of Nuremberg: Civilising Influence or Institutionalised Vengeance?* (Boston: Martinus Nijhoff), pp. 13–36. On the German-Israeli reconciliation, see Steinbock 2025, *op. cit.,* esp. Chapter 7.

14 Wolfgang Benz. "Ein Prozess, der die Republik veränderte." *Die Zeit,* Aug. 20, 2005.

15 "History of the Italian Rat Line" (10 April 1950), document signed by "IB Operating Officer" Paul E. Lyon, 430th Counter Intelligence Corps (CIC), Headquarters of the U.S. Forces in Austria, April 10, 1950. See also Breitman, et al. 2005. *U.S. Intelligence and the Nazis* (Cambridge University Press).

16 Aarons, Mark. "Justice Betrayed: Post-1945 Responses to Genocide." In Blumenthal and McCormack 2008, *op. cit.,* pp. 69–98.

17 Karstedt, "The Nuremberg Tribunal and German Society."

18 Dower, John W. 1986. *War Without Mercy* (New York: Pantheon Books), pp. 262–290.

19 Fellers, Bonner F. Memorandum to the Commander-in-chief. General Staff Corps, U.S. Army, Oct. 2, 1945. See also Bix, Herbert P. 2001. *Hirohito and the Making of Modern Japan* (New York: Perennial), p. 583.

20 Dower, John. 1999. *Embracing Defeat: Japan in the Wake of World War II* (New York: Norton & Norton), pp. 323–325.

21 Röling, B. V. A., and C. F. Rüter. 1977. *The Tokyo Judgment: The International Military Tribunal for the Far East (I.M.T.F.E), 29 April 1946 – 12 November 1948,* Vol. 1 (Amsterdam: APA-University Press), p. 478.

22 Driscoll, Mark. 2010. *Absolute Erotic, Absolute Grotesque: The Living, Dead, and Undead in Japan's Imperialism, 1895–1945* (Durham: Duke University Press), p. 266.

23 Kubica, Helena. 1994. "The Crimes of Josef Mengele." In Gutman, Yisrael, and Michael Berenbaum, Eds. *Anatomy of the Auschwitz Death Camp* (Bloomington, Indiana: Indiana University Press, 1998), pp. 317–337.

24 Nie, Jing Bao, et al. 2013. *Japan's Wartime Medical Atrocities: Comparative Inquiries in Science, History, and Ethics* (Routledge), p. 207.

25 Guillemin, Jeanne. 2017. *Hidden Atrocities: Japanese Germ Warfare and American Obstruction of Justice at the Tokyo Trial* (Columbia University Press).

26 Harris, Sheldon H. 1994. *Factories of Death: Japanese Biological Warfare 1932–45 and the American Cover-Up* (Routledge). See also Yan-Jun, Yang, and Tam Yue-Him. 2018. *Unit 731: Laboratory of the Devil, Auschwitz of the East: Japanese Biological Warfare in China 1933–45* (Fonthill Media). On the use of biowarfare and chemical weapons in the Korean War, see Endicott, Stephen, and Edward Hagerman. 1998. *The United States and Biological Warfare: Secrets from the Early Cold War and Korea* (Bloomington, IN: Indiana University Press).

27 Drayton, Richard. "An ethical blank cheque." *The Guardian*, May 10, 2005; Brody, Howard, et al. 2014. "United States Responses to Japanese Wartime Inhuman Experimentation after World War II: National Security and Wartime Exigency." *Camb Q Healthc Ethics* 23, no. 2 (April 2014): 220–230; Harris, S.H. 2002. *Factories of Death: Japanese Biological Warfare, 1932–1945, and the American Cover-up* (New York: Routledge).

28 Chrystal, Paul. 2023. *Bioterrorism and Biological Warfare: Disease as a Weapon of War* (Yorkshire: Pen and Sword), p. 198

29 Hornblum Allen M., et al. 2013. *Against Their Will: The Secret History of Medical Experimentation on Children in Cold War America* (Palgrave Macmillan). See also Lederer, Susan E. 1997. *Subjected to Science: Human Experimentation in America Before the Second World War* (JHU Press).

30 United States Congress Senate Select Committee on Intelligence. 1977. *Project Project MKULTRA, the CIA's Program of Research in Behavioral Modification* (U.S. Government Printing Office); McCoy, Alfred. 2007. *A Question of Torture: CIA Interrogation, from the Cold War to the War on Terror* (Macmillan).

31 Safferling, Christoph J. M. 2020. "German Participation in the Nuremberg Trials and Its Implications for Today." *The Nuremberg War Crimes Trial and its Policy Consequences Today* (Nomos), pp. 41–54 [in German]; Echternkamp, Jörg. 2020. *Postwar Soldiers: Historical Controversies and West German Democratization, 1945–1955* (Berghahn Books).

32 Heller, Kevin Jon. 2011. *The Nuremberg Military Tribunals and the Origins of International Criminal Law* (Oxford University Press), pp. 372–373.

33 Minear, Richard. 1971. *Victors' Justice: The Tokyo War Crimes Trial* (Princeton NJ: Princeton University Press).

34 See statement by Judge Röling, the last surviving member of the Tokyo Tribunal in Barenblatt, Daniel. 2004. *A Plague upon Humanity* (New York: Harper Collins), p. 222. See also Powell, John W. 1981. "A hidden chapter in history." *Bulletin of the Atomic Scientists* 37 (8): 44–52.

35 Carey, Henry F., and Stacey M. Mitchell, Eds. 2013. *Trials and Tribulations of International Prosecution* (Lexington Books), p. 169.

36 Minear, *Victors' Justice*, p. 3.

37 Compare Hoyt, Edwin P. 2001. *Warlord: Tojo Against the World* (Cooper Square Press).

38 Plato's *Republic*, transl. by Paul Shorey (1935), annotated and hyperlinked text at Perseus Project.

39 These members of the "free world" were at times ruled by military dictatorships (Turkey, Greece, Spain, and Portugal), while U.S. client states were often anti-Communist dictatorial regimes, particularly in South America, South Korea and Taiwan, South America, Asia, the Middle East and Africa.

40 Wilensky, Norman V. 1972. "Was the Cold War Necessary? The Revisionist Challenge to Consensus History." *American Studies* 13, no. 1 (Spring): 177–187. See also Williams, William Appleman. 1959. *The Tragedy of American Diplomacy* (New York: W.W. Norton, 2009); Gardner, Lloyd C. 1970. *Architects of Illusion: Men and Ideas in American Foreign Policy 1941–1949* (Chicago: Quadrangle).

41 May, Ernest R., Ed. 1993. *American Cold War Strategy: Interpreting NSC 68* (Bedford/St. Martin's).

42 NSC 68, April 14, 1950, Foreign Relations of the United States (FRUS), 1950, Vol. 1 (Washington, D.C: U.S. Government Printing Office, 1977), p. 245.

43 Cardwell, Curt. 2011. *NSC 68 and the Political Economy of the Early Cold War* (New York: Cambridge University Press), p. 14.

44 For more, see Chapter 3 on the doctrine and practice of obliteration.

45 Schabas, William. 2015. "The Special Adviser on the Prevention of Genocide and his Inscrutable Mandate." For publication in Roland Adjovi, Aatsa Atogho, Jean-Pelé Fomété and Charles R. Majinge, Eds., *Festschrift for Adama Dieng.*

46 Letter dated August 31, 2007 from the Secretary-General addressed to the President of the Security Council, UN Doc. S/2007/721.

47 Myre, Greg, and Steven Erlanger. "Israelis Enter Lebanon After Attacks." *New York Times,* July 13, 2006; Cody, Edward. "Lebanese Premier Seeks U.S. Help in Lifting Blockade." *Washington Post,* Aug. 24, 2006.

48 Hirst, David. 2010. *Beware of Small States: Lebanon, Battleground of the Middle East* (Faber and Faber), pp. 336–337.

49 Whitaker, Brian. "Beirut murder mystery." *The Guardian,* June 22, 2005; John Kifner, John, and Warren Hoge. "Top Syrian seen as prime suspect in assassination." *New York Times,* Oct. 21, 2005; "Hezbollah leader says Israel was behind Hariri killing." *CNN,* June 3, 2011; "Redacted Version of the Amended Consolidated Indictment." Special Tribunal for Lebanon, July 12, 2016; "Rafik Hariri tribunal: Guilty verdict over assassination of Lebanon ex-PM." *BBC News,* Aug. 18, 2020.

50 "Nasrallah: Israel Used Secret Agent to Turn Lebanon Gov't Against Hezbollah." *Haaretz,* Aug. 9, 2010; "Lebanon PM: UN Must Probe Claims of Israeli Complicity in Hariri Murder." *Haaretz,* Aug. 12, 2010.

51 Morley, Jefferson. "The Branding of Lebanon's 'Revolution.'" *Washington Post,* March 3, 2005.

52 "Rafik Hariri: Billionaire politician." *BBC News,* Sept. 4, 2000.

53 Al-Arshani, Sarah. "Two flight attendants have accused Lebanon's former prime minister Saad Hariri of 'brutal' sexual assault in a lawsuit filed in the US." *Business Insider,* April 3, 2023.

54 "Justice served: Lebanon's Special Tribunal closes." *UN News,* Dec. 31, 2023.

55 *Application of the Convention on the Prevention and Punishment of the Crime of Genocide (Croatia v Serbia)*, Preliminary Objections, 18 November 2008, para. 123; *Application of the Convention on the Prevention and Punishment of the Crime of Genocide (Bosnia and Herzegovina v Serbia and Montenegro)*, Preliminary Objections [1996] ICJ Reports 617, para. 34.

56 Schabas 2012, *op. cit.*, p. 77.

57 Ibid., p. 80.

58 This section draws from "Mossad's ICC Meltdown." In: Steinbock 2025, *op.cit.*, esp. Chapter 9.

59 Davies, Harry, Bethan McKernan, Yuval Abraham, and Meron Rapoport. "Spying, hacking and intimidation: Israel's nine-year 'war' on the ICC exposed." *The Guardian*, May 28, 2024. See also Abraham, Yuval, and Meron Rapoport. "Surveillance and Interference: Israel's covert war on the ICC exposed." *+972 Magazine*, May 28, 2024.

60 Megiddo, Gur. "How Israeli Security Nixed Haaretz's Report Into Alleged Mossad Extortion of International Court Prosecutor." *Haaretz*, May 30, 2022.

61 Melman, Yossi. "'Sounds Like Cosa Nostra Blackmail': Former Mossad Chief on Successor's Alleged Threats Against ICC Prosecutor." *Haaretz*, May 30, 2024.

62 "Application of the Convention on the Prevention and Punishment of the Crime of Genocide in the Gaza Strip (*South Africa v. Israel*) – Order." International Court of Justice, Jan. 26, 2024.

63 Ibid., see "Dissenting Opinion of Judge Sebutinde." https://www.icj-cij.org/sites/default/files/case-related/192/192-20240126-ord-01-02-en.pdf

64 Compare section "The Controversial Political Question Doctrine" in Chapter 3.

65 "Ugandan government distances itself from judge who cast sole dissenting vote in ICJ case." *Al Jazeera*, Jan. 27, 2024.

66 Feith, Douglas J. "The Forgotten History of the Term 'Palestine.'" *Mosaic Magazine*, Dec. 13, 2021. https://www.hudson.org/node/44363 On Netanyahu and Israel's neoconservative turn, see Steinbock 2025, *op.cit.*, esp. Chapter 6. On Feith and Iraq, see Hersh, Seymour M. "Selective Intelligence." *New Yorker*, May 5, 2003.

67 Lewis, Donald M. 2021. *A Short History of Christian Zionism from the Reformation to the Twenty-First Century* (InterVarsity Press). On the political alliances, see Chafets, Zeev. 2007. A *Match Made in Heaven: American Jews, Christian Zionists, and One Man's Exploration of the Weird and Wonderful Judeo-Evangelical Alliance* (New York: HarperCollins).

68 Blumenthal, Max. "Max Blumenthal: The Christian Zionist Leading the ICJ." *Consortium News*, Jan. 29, 2025.

69 On the U.S. stances toward the ICC, see Sokol, Karen. *The International Court of Justice and the International Criminal Court: A Primer.* Congressional Research Service, April 4, 2024; Rosen, Liana W. *U.S. Sanctions Policy in the 119th Congress: Recent Executive Actions and Legislative Implications.* Congressional Research Service, Feb. 3, 2025.

70 President Donald Trump. Imposing Sanctions on the International Criminal Court: Executive Order, Presidential Actions, White House, Feb. 6, 2025.

71 Edwards, Christian. "What is the ICC and why has Trump sanctioned it?" *CNN*, Feb. 7, 2025.

72 Implementing the Genocide Convention by Louise Arbour, United Nations High-Commissioner for Human Rights, UN Human Rights Office of the High Commissioner, April 4, 2008.

73 The following draws from "How the Court Works." International Criminal Court, see https://www.icc-cpi.int/about/how-the-court-works

74 Chapter VII of the UN Charter basically sets out the UN Security Council's powers to maintain peace. It allows the Council to "determine the existence of any threat to the peace, breach of the peace, or act of aggression" and to take military and nonmilitary action to "restore international peace and security." See https://www.un.org/en/about-us/un-charter/chapter-7. See also Johansson, Patrik. 2009. "The Humdrum Use of Ultimate Authority: Defining and Analysing Chapter VII Resolutions." *Nordic Journal of International Law* 78, no. 3 (2009): 309–342.

75 "The six men accused of inciting Kenya's post-election violence." *Christian Science Monitor,* Dec. 15, 2010.

76 "OSI Roundtable: Restoring American Leadership – The International Criminal Court." *Open Society Foundations,* Dec. 14, 2005.

77 Becker, Sven. "Ocampo's Offshore Companies." *Spiegel International,* Oct. 5, 2017.

78 "Uhuru: ICC is a toy of declining imperial powers." *Capital FM,* Oct. 12, 2013.

79 "Israel – International Criminal Court." Ministry of Foreign Affairs, France, Nov. 27, 2024.

80 Bosco, "Court in a Storm." See also Buchwald, Todd. "Part I: What Kinds of Situations and Cases Should the ICC Pursue? The Independent Expert Review of the ICC and the Question of Aperture." *Just Security,* Nov. 30, 2020.

81 Gaddis, John Lewis. 1972. *The United States and the Origins of the Cold War, 1941–1947* (Columbia University Press), p. 24. See also Hoopes, Townsend, and Douglas Brinkley. 1997. *FDR and the Creation of the United Nations* (Yale University Press), p. 178.

Chapter 6

1 Schabas, William. 2009. *Genocide in International Law: The Crime of Crimes.* 2nd Ed. (Cambridge), pp. 589–590, footnote 372.

2 Ibid., p. 592.

3 Breitman, Richard. 1998. *Official Secrets: What the Nazis Planned, What the British and Americans Knew* (New York: Hill & Wang). See also Aarons, Mark. "Justice Betrayed: Post-1945 Responses to Genocide." In: Blumenthal, David A., and Timothy L. H. McCormack. 2008. *The Legacy of Nuremberg: Civilizing Influence or Institutionalized Vengeance?* (Martinus Nijhoff), pp. 69–98.

4 See also Erdheim, Stuart. 1997. "Could The Allies Have Bombed Auschwitz-Birkenau?" *Holocaust and Genocide Studies,* pp. 129–170; Gilbert, Martin. 1981. *Auschwitz and the Allies* (Illinois: Holt, Rinehart, and Winston); Bird, Kai. 1992. *The Chairman: John J. McCloy & the Making of the American Establishment* (New York: Simon & Schuster).

5 Ibid, p. 5.

6 United Nations Press Release, SG/SM/9126.

7 UN Doc. S/RES/1366 (2001), p. 18.

8 Office of the UN Special Adviser on Genocide Prevention, www.un.org/preventgenocide/adviser

9 As stipulated in the Outcome Document of the 2005 United Nations World Summit.

10 Letter dated December 7, 2007 from the President of the Security Council addressed to the Secretary General, UN Doc. S/2007/722.

11 "Countries At Risk for Mass Killing 2023–24: Statistical Risk Assessment Results." Early Warning Project, Simon-Skjodt Center for the Prevention of Genocide, Jan. 2024, p. 3.

12 Lankford, Adam. 2016. "Public Mass Shooters and Firearms: A Cross-National Study of 171 Countries." Violence and Victims. 31 (2): 187–99; Fisher, Max; Keller, Josh. 2017. "Why Does the U.S. Have So Many Mass Shootings? Research Is Clear: Guns." New York Times, Nov. 7; Barnard, Leslie M., et al. 2023. "Characterization of Mass Shootings by State, 2014–2022." JAMA Network Open. 6 (7), July 26.

13 Simon-Skjodt Center 2024, op. cit., p. 13.

14 Salman, Abeer; Za'anoun, Khader Al. 2024. "Five-year-old Palestinian girl found dead after being trapped in car under Israeli fire." CNN, Feb. 10; Da Silva, Chantal. 2024. "'They killed her twice': Hind Rajab's mother mourns girl, 6, found killed days after being trapped under Israeli fire." NBC News, Feb. 11; "The Killing of Hind Rajab."

15 "US State Department Approves Sale of 120mm M830A1 HEAT MPAT Tank Cartridges to Israel." MilitaryLeak.com, Dec. 13, 2023.

16 Kelly, Meg, et al. "Palestinian paramedics said Israel gave them safe passage to save a 6-year-old girl in Gaza. They were all killed." Washington Post, April 16, 2024.

17 "Gaza: Initial findings show Israeli army purposefully kills a child, uses an American-made missile to target her rescue crew." Euro-Med Human Rights Monitor, Feb. 12, 2024. Clayton, Freddie. "Killing of 6-year-old Hind Rajab in Gaza may constitute a war crime, experts say." NBC News, July 22, 2024. See also Forensic Architecture. Retrieved on Jan. 11, 2025.

18 Nassrullah, Harun. "Pro-Palestine group launch legal action against European soldiers." Muslim News [UK], April 5, 2024; Czerny, Milan. "What is the Hind Rajab Foundation, which is making Israeli soldiers fear arrest abroad?" Shomrim, Haaretz, Jan. 10, 2025.

19 "War Crimes in Gaza: Al Jazeera Investigations," Oct. 7, 2024. For the documentary, see https://www.aljazeera.com/program/investigations/2024/10/7/war-crimes-in-gaza-i-al-jazeera-investigations

20 Compare Varble, Derek. 2003. The Suez Crisis (Osprey), p. 51; Lee, Sir David. 1989. Wings in the Sun: A History of the Royal Air Force in the Mediterranean 1945–1986 (Great Britain: RAF Air Historical Branch, HMSO Books), pp. 172–176; "RAF Akrotiri." Parliamentary Debates (Hansard), Vol. 174. UK Parliament: House of Commons. June 15, 1990; "British base on Cyprus attacked: Two wounded." New York Times, Aug. 5, 1986; "Second UK strike against Libyan defence assets." UK Ministry of Defence, March 21, 2011; "UK reportedly using Akrotiri for military flights to Tel Aviv since Gaza war." in-cyprus.philenews.com, Dec. 12, 2023.

21 TOI Staff. "12 complaints said filed against IDF soldiers abroad over alleged war crimes in Gaza." Times of Israel, Jan. 6, 2025.

22 Schabas 2009, *op. cit.,* p. 644. Schabas is referring to the conclusions of the first edition of his book, written in 1999. The implication is that a decade had not resulted in a real change in this matter.

23 Ibid.

24 UN Press release, New York, 15 October 2023.

25 UN Press release, New York, 29 October 2023.

26 For the definition of institutionalism, see the section on institutional changes.

27 Schabas 2009, *op. cit.*

28 Meyer, Peter J. *Organization of American States: In Brief.* Congressional Research Service R47230, May 2, 2023, pp. 5–6.

29 Pharatlhatlhe, Kesa, and Jan Vanheukelom. *Financing the African Union: On Mindsets and Money,* ECDPM Discussion Paper 240, Feb. 2019, pp. 3–7.

30 Schabas 2009, *op. cit.,* p. 649.

31 After all, "the use of mercenaries poses a rising threat to international peace and security, and like genocide, is a crime against humanity." See "Conflict prevention, early warning and security." UN/OHCHR: https://www.ohchr.org/en/topic/conflict-prevention-early-warning-and-security

32 Quoted in Netachin, Etan. "The Israeli Lawyer Filing a Landmark Incitement to Genocide Case Against Israel at the ICC." *Haaretz,* Jan. 24, 2025.

33 Schabas, William A. 2018. "Prevention of Crimes Against Humanity." *Journal of International Criminal Justice* 16, no. 4 (September 2018): 1–24.

34 On inflammatory speech, see Benesch, Susan. 2008. "Vile Crime or Inalienable Right: Defining Incitement to Genocide." *Virginia Journal of International Law* 48, no. 3; Benesch, Susan. "Countering Dangerous Speech: New Ideas for Genocide Prevention." Working Paper, Feb. 11, 2014.

35 Compare Steinbock 2025, *op. cit.,* esp. Chapter 2.

36 Timmermann, Wibke Kristin. 2006. "Incitement in international criminal law." *International Review of the Red Cross* 88, no. 864 (December 2006): 823–852. For the full statement, see Timmermann, Wibke Kristin. 2015. *Incitement in International Law.* London: Routledge.

37 Gordon, Gregory S. 2008. "From Incitement to Indictment – Prosecuting Iran's President for Advocating Israel's Destruction and Piecing Together Incitement Law's Emerging Analytical Framework." *Journal of Criminal Law & Criminology* 98, no. 3 (Spring): 853–920. For the full statement, see Gordon, Gregory S. 2017. *Atrocity Speech Law: Foundation, Fragmentation, Fruition* (Oxford University Press).

38 On these four conditions in pre-Gaza War legal debate, see Davies, Thomas E. 2009. "How the Rome Statute Weakens the International Prohibition on Incitement to Genocide." *Harvard Human Rights Journal* 22, no. 2 (Aug. 21, 2009): 245–270.

39 Quoted in Netachin, "The Israeli Lawyer Filing a Landmark Incitement to Genocide Case Against Israel at the ICC."

40 See e.g., Maanit, Chen. "Haaretz Exposé: AG Advises Against Investigating Remarks by Israeli Ministers, MKs on Suspicion of Inciting to Harm Gaza Civilians." *Haaretz,* Nov. 25, 2024.

41 The states parties to the Rome Statute could address this deficit by making a simple textual change so that the Rome Statute treats incitement in the same way as the statutes of international criminal tribunals in Rwanda and Yugoslavia do. See Davies 2009, *op. cit.*

42 Vazquez, Maegan. "Michigan lawmaker says Gaza should be approached 'like Nagasaki and Hiroshima.'" *Washington Post,* March 31, 2024.

43 Marquez, A. "Sen. Lindsey Graham Says Israel Should Do 'Whatever' it Has to While Comparing the War in Gaza to Hiroshima and Nagasaki." *NBC News,* May 12, 2024.

44 The Act provides for penalties to be imposed upon anyone who commits or attempts to commit any of such acts. It also provides for criminal penalties for directly and publicly inciting an act of genocide. S.1851 – *Genocide Convention Implementation Act of 1987* (the Proxmire Act), U.S. Congress, 1987.

45 President Ronald Reagan. Remarks on Signing the Genocide Convention Implementation Act of 1987 (the Proxmire Act). Chicago, Illinois, Nov. 4, 1988.

46 Gopalani, Ameer F. "The International Standard of Direct and Public Incitement to Commit Genocide: An Obstacle to U.S. Ratification of the International Criminal Court Statute." *California Western International Law Journal* 32, no. 1 (2001): 86–117. On the applications in the case of Gaza, see Intondi, Vincent. "The Threat of Nuclear Bombing and Incitement to Genocide." *Journal for Peace and Nuclear Disarmament 7, no. 2 (*Aug. 26, 2024): 528–535.

47 Gopalani, "The International Standard of Direct and Public Incitement to Commit Genocide," p. 102.

48 Steinbock 2025, *op.cit.,* see Chapter 1.

49 Gopalani, "The International Standard of Direct and Public Incitement to Commit Genocide," pp. 102–104.

50 Gonyea, Don. "Jesting, McCain Sings: 'Bomb, Bomb, Bomb' Iran." *NPR,* April 20, 2007.

51 McCullagh, Declan. "McCain's 'Bomb Iran' song was anti-Muslim?" *Cnet. com,* April 22, 2007.

52 Intondi 2024, *op. cit.,* p. 6.

53 DiMaggio, Paul. 1998. "The New Institutionalisms: Avenues of Collaboration." *Journal of Institutional and Theoretical Economics* (JITE) 154, no. 4 (December 1998): 696–705.

54 Seligman, Erwin R.A. 1903. *The Economic Interpretation of History,* 2nd Edition (New York: Columbia University Press), pp. 67, 162–163.

55 Barrow, Clyde W. 2000. *More Than a Historian: The Political and Economic Thought of Charles A. Beard* (New York: Routledge), esp. Chapter 2. See also Beard, Charles. 1913. *An Economic Interpretation of the Constitution of the United States* (New York: Macmillan).

56 See e.g., Commons, John R. 1924. *Legal Foundations of Capitalism* (New York: Macmillan); Commons, John R. 1934. *Institutional Economics* (New York: Macmillan).

57 Immergut, Ellen M. 1998. "The Theoretical Core of the New Institutionalism." *Politics & Society* 26, no. 1 (March 1998): 5–34.

58 Powell, Walter W., Eds.1991. *The New Institutionalism in Organizational Analysis.* Chicago: University of Chicago Press, pp. 1–38

59 See Oliver E. Williamson (2000). "The New Institutional Economics: Taking Stock, Looking Ahead," *Journal of Economic Literature* 38, no. 3 (September 2000): 595–613.

60 All these strands of institutionalism show how timing, sequences and path dependence affect institutions, and shape social, political, economic behavior and change. See Voeten, Erik. 2019. "Making Sense of the Design of International Institutions." *Annual Review of Political Science* 22 (January 2019): 147–163.

61 Chandler, Alfred D. Jr. 1962. *Strategy and Structure: Chapters in the History of the Industrial Enterprise* (Beard Books).

62 Ahmed, Akbar Shahid. "Stunning State Department Memo Warns Diplomats: No Gaza 'De-Escalation' Talk." *HuffPost*, Oct. 13, 2023. On the links of the Israeli ground assault with decades of ethnic cleansing and genocidal atrocities, see Steinbock 2025, *op.cit.,* esp. Chapter 1.

Chapter 7

1 Vaughan, Don. 2023. "Scorched-earth policy." *Encyclopedia Britannica.* Retrieved September 29, 2024.

2 This term is used by Mihesuah, Devon A. 1997. *American Indians: Stereotypes & Realities* (Atlanta, GA: Clarity Press).

3 Article 54 of Protocol I of the 1977 Geneva Conventions.

4 Common Article 33 of the Fourth Geneva Convention and Article 4 of the Additional Protocol II. See also Klocker, Cornelia. 2020. *Collective Punishment and Human Rights Law: Addressing Gaps in International Law* (London: Routledge).

5 Downes, Alexander B. 2008. *Targeting Civilians in War* (Cornell University Press), p. 15; Besaw, Clayton, Kellan Ritter, and Güneş Murat Tezcür. 2023. "Beyond Collateral Damage: The Politics of Civilian Victimization in a Civil War." *Global Studies Quarterly* 3, no. 3 (July 2023).

6 Kydd, Andrew H., and Barbara F. Walter. 2006. "The Strategies of Terrorism." *International Security* 31, no. 1 (Summer 2006): 49–80.

7 Balcells, Laia, and Jessica A. Stanton. 2021. "Violence Against Civilians During Armed Conflict: Moving Beyond the Macro- and Micro-Level Divide." *Annual Review of Political Science* 24, no. 1 (May 2021): 45–69.

8 Article 51(3) of the 1977 Additional Protocol I. See also Common Article 3 of the 1949 Geneva Conventions; and Article 13(3) of the 1977 Additional Protocol II.

9 Gómez, Javier Guisández. 1998. "The Law of Air Warfare." *International Review of the Red Cross (1961–1997)* 38, Special Issue 323 (June 1998): 347–363.

10 Patterson, Ian. 2007. *Guernica and Total War* (London: Profile).

11 While the estimate includes approved security assistance funding since October 7, 2023, supplemental funding for regional operations, and an estimated additional cost of operations, it does not include any other economic costs. It does not include commitments to future spending that were made this year. Nor does it include other broad categories of spending, such as increased U.S. security assistance to Egypt, Saudi Arabia or any other countries, and costs to the commercial airline industry and to U.S. consumers. See Bilmes, Linda J., et al. 2024. *United States Spending on Israel's Military Operations and Related U.S. Operations in the Region, October 7, 2023 – September 30, 2024.* Costs of War, Watson Institute for International & Public Affairs, Brown University, Oct. 7, 2024.

12 See Taylor, Frederick. 2005. *Dresden: Tuesday 13 February 1945* (London: Bloomsbury); Kershaw, Ian. 2012. *The End: Germany, 1944–45* (Penguin).

13 Overy, Richard. 2013. *The Bombing War, Europe 1939–45* (London: Penguin.

14 Ray, John. 2009. *The Battle of Britain: Dowding and the First Victory, 1940* (London: Cassel Military); Dear, I.C.B., and Foot, M.R.D. Editors. 2005. *Oxford Companion to World War II* (Oxford University Press), p. 109.

15 Pape, Robert A. "Hamas Is Winning: Why Israel's Failing Strategy Makes Its Enemy Stronger." *Foreign Affairs,* June 21, 2024.

16 Steinbock, Dan. 2025. *The Fall of Israel* (Atlanta, GA: Clarity Press), esp. Chapters 3–4.

17 Steinbock, Dan. "Netanyahu's Quest to Attack Iran with the Mother of All Bombs." *Informed Comment,* Feb. 16, 2025.

18 Evans, Richard J. 2003. *The Coming of the Third Reich* (New York: Penguin), p. 544. See also Whitman, James Q. 2017. *Hitler's American Model: The United States and the Making of Nazi Race Law* (Princeton University Press).

19 Rodogno, Davide. 2006. *Fascism's European Empire: Italian Occupation During the Second World War* (Cambridge, UK: Cambridge University Press), p. 46.

20 Morris-Suzuki, Tessa. 2000. Ethnic Engineering: Scientific Racism and Public Opinion Surveys in Midcentury Japan. *East Asia Cultures Critique* 8, no. 2 (Duke University Press, Fall 2000): 499–529. See also Dower, John W. 2012. *Ways of Forgetting, Ways of Remembering: Japan in the Modern World* (The New Press), pp. 58–60.

21 Smith, Woodruff D. 1980. "Friedrich Ratzel and the Origins of Lebensraum." *German Studies Review* 3, no. 1 (Feb. 1980): 51–68. See also Wanklyn, Harriet. 1961. *Friedrich Ratzel: A Biographical Memoir and Bibliography* (London: Cambridge University Press), pp. 36–40.

22 Fanon, Frantz. 1961. *The Wretched of the Earth* (New York: Grove Press, 1963), p. 42.

23 Armstrong, Charles K. 2010. "The Destruction and Reconstruction of North Korea, 1950–1960." *The Asia-Pacific Journal* 8, issue 51, no. 2 (December 20, 2010): 1.

24 Newsinger, John. 2016. *British counterinsurgency.* 2nd Ed. (London: Palgrave Macmillan); Hack, Karl. 2022. *The Malayan Emergency: Revolution and Counterinsurgency at the End of Empire* (Cambridge University Press

25 "France remembers the Algerian War, 50 years on." *France 24,* March 19, 2012. See also Horne, Alistair. 1977 (rev. ed. 2012). *A Savage War of Peace Algeria 1954–1962* (London: Pan Macmillan).

26 Fox, Diane N. 2003. "Chemical Politics and the Hazards of Modern Warfare: Agent Orange." In Monica, Casper, Ed. *Synthetic Planet: Chemical Politics and the Hazards of Modern Life* (Routledge Press).

27 Zierler, David. 2011. *The Invention of Ecocide: Agent Orange, Vietnam, and the Scientists Who Changed the Way We Think about the Environment* (Athens, Georgia: University of Georgia Press).

28 This section draws from Steinbock 2025, *op.cit.,* esp. Chapter 1.

29 Cited in John Quigley, John. 1994. "Israel's Forty-Five Year Emergency: Are There Time Limits to Derogations from Human Rights Obligations?" *Michigan Journal of International Law* 15, no. 2 (1994): 491.

30 Roberts, Christopher M. 2019. "From the State of Emergency to the Rule of Law: The Evolution of Repressive Legality in the Nineteenth Century British Empire." *Chicago Journal of International Law* 20, no. 1, article 1 (2019).

31 Hughes, Matthew. 2019. *Britain's Pacification of Palestine: The British Army, the Colonial State, and the Arab Revolt, 1936–1939* (New York: Cambridge University Press).

32 Burleigh, Michael. 2013. *Small Wars, Faraway Places: Global Insurrection and the Making of the Modern World 1945–1965* (New York: Viking), p. 164.

33 Bracha, Baruch. 1993. "Restriction of personal freedom without due process of law according to the Defence (Emergency) Regulations, 1945." *Israel Yearbook on Human Rights* 8 (1978): 296–323; Yaniv, Avner. 1993. *National Security and Democracy in Israel* (Boulder, CO: Lynne Riener), p. 175.

34 See e.g., Bull, Anna Cento. 2012. *Italian Neofascism: The Strategy of Tension and the Politics of Nonreconciliation* (Berghahn Books).

35 Ferraresi, Franco. 1997. *Threats to Democracy: The Radical Right in Italy after the War* (Princeton, N.J.: Princeton University Press); Ganser, Daniele. 2005. *NATO's Secret Armies: Operation Gladio and Terrorism in Western Europe* (London: Routledge).

36 Valdes, Juan Gabriel. 2008. *Pinochet's Economists: The Chicago School of Economics in Chile* (New York: Cambridge University Press).

37 Steinbock 2025, *op.cit.,* esp. Chapter 4.

38 Ibid.

39 Compare Jabotinsky, Ze'ev. "The Iron Wall." *Razsviet,* Nov. 4, 1923. Reprinted by the Jabotinsky Institute in Israel.

40 On the caveats of this purported deterrent, see Steinbock 2025, *op.cit.,* Chapter 4.

41 Ibid., esp. Chapter 8.

42 Ibid., esp. Chapters 4 and 11.

43 Ibid., esp. Chapters 9–10.

44 Woodward, Bob. 2024. *War* (New York: Simon and Schuster), Chapter 58.

45 "Country Report—Lebanon." *The Economist Intelligence Unit,* no. 4 (2006): 3–6; Katz, Yaakov, and Hendel, Yoaz. 2012. *Israel vs. Iran: The Shadow War* (New York: Potomac Books), p. 17.

46 Steinbock 2025, *op.cit.,* esp. Chapters 1–2, 8 and 10.

47 Hersh, Seymour. "Watching Lebanon." *New Yorker,* Aug. 21, 2006; Urquhart, Conal. "Israel planned for Lebanon war months in advance, PM says." *The Guardian,* March 10, 2007.

48 Kober, Avi. 2008. "The Israel Defense Forces in the Second Lebanon War: Why the Poor Performance?" *Journal of Strategic Studies* 31, no. 1: 3–40.

49 Justin Huggler and Mary Dejevsky. "Israeli Attack Ruins Deal to End Suicide Bombings." *The Independent,* July 25, 2002.

50 Steinbock 2025, *op.cit.,* esp. Chapter 8.

51 "The Pilots' Letter." Sept. 23, 2003. Archived in https://web.archive.org/web/20031011094058/http://www.jfjfp.org/BackgroundW/refusenik_pilots.htm

52 Ibid.

53 Steinbock 2025, *op.cit.,* Chapter 1.

54 "Israel's new defence minister." *The Economist,* May 20, 2016.

55 Keller-Lynn, Carrie. "At Tel Aviv protest, Ya'alon calls Netanyahu's government a 'dictatorship of criminals.'" *Times of Israel,* Jan. 21, 2023.

56 See "Chief of Staff Dumped His Stocks Three Hours After Soldiers' Abduction." *The Marker,* Aug. 15, 2006.

57 For more, see Chapter 2.

58 "Injunction Against Galant's Appointment: 'Suspected of War Crimes.'" *Walla,* Oct. 25, 2010; Harel, Amos, and Anshel Pfeffer. "IDF probes top officers on Gaza war strike that killed 21 family members." *Haaretz,* Oct. 22, 2010.

59 Kubovich, Yaniv. "Defense Minister Gallant Threatens to Send Lebanon Back to 'Stone Age' if Hezbollah Provokes Israel." Aug. 8, 2023; Fabian, Emanuel. "Defense minister announces 'complete siege' of Gaza: No power, food or fuel." *Times of Israel,* Oct. 9, 2023.

60 "Secretary of Defense Lloyd J. Austin III Joint Press Conference With Israeli Defense Minister Yoav Gallant in Tel Aviv, Israel." U.S. Department of Defense, Oct. 13, 2023.

61 "Gallant threatens Hezbollah: 'What we can do in Gaza, we can do in Beirut.'" *The Jerusalem Post,* Nov. 11, 2023.

62 Harris, William. 2014. *Lebanon: A History, 600–2011* (New York: Oxford University Press).

63 On Lebanon, the Civil War and the consequent population displacements, see esp. Saad-Ghorayeb, Amal. 2001. *Hizbu'llah: Politics and Religion* (London: Pluto Press).

64 Tveit, Odd Karsten. 2010. *Goodbye Lebanon. Israel's First Defeat* (Rimal Publication), pp. 163–164.

65 "Lebanon/Israel: Hezbollah Hit Israel with Cluster Munitions During Conflict." Human Rights Watch, Oct. 19, 2006.

66 "UN warning on Mid-East war crimes." *BBC News Online.* July 20, 2006. Although both were targeted, Hezbollah's resources were a fraction of those of Israel, which furthermore deployed its destructive assets against civilian infrastructure and non-combatants to a massive disproportionate effect.

67 McCarthy, Rory. 2006. "Israeli general quits over conduct of Lebanon war." *The Guardian,* Sept. 13, 2006.

68 Eisenkot, Gadi. 2010. A Changed Threat? The Response on the Northern Arena. Military and Strategic Affairs 2, no. 1 (June 2010): 29–40.

69 Quoted in Siboni, Gabi. *Disproportionate Force: Israel's Concept of Response in Light of the Second Lebanon War.* The *Institute for National Security Studies (INSS),* Oct. 2, 2008.

70 "UN appalled by Beirut devastation." *BBC News,* July 23, 2006. See also Israel/Lebanon: Deliberate destruction or "collateral damage"? Israeli attacks on civilian infrastructure. Amnesty International, Aug. 22, 2006.

71 Filiu, Jean-Pierre. 2014. *Gaza: A History* (Oxford), p. 318.

72 "Israel warns Hezbollah war would invite destruction." *Reuters,* Oct. 3, 2008.

73 This argument Is a variation of one by Israeli legal scholars on *de facto* and *de jure* annexation of the Palestinian occupied territories. See Levine-Schnur, Ronit, Tamar Megiddo, and Yael Berda. "A Theory of Annexation." SSRN, Feb. 5, 2023.

74 Siboni, Gadi. 2008. "Disproportionate Force: Israel's Concept of Response in Light of the Second Lebanon War." The Institute for National Security Studies (INSS), Oct. 2, 2008.

75 London, Y. "The Obliteration Strategy" [Interview with IDF Northern Command Chief Gadi Eisenkot], June 8, 2008.

76 Falk, Richard. "Dahiya Doctrine: Justifying Disproportionate Warfare—A Prelude to Genocide," April 1, 2024.

77 Ibid.

78 Quoted in "IDF general in bombshell speech: Israel today shows signs of 1930s Germany." *Jerusalem Post,* May 5, 2016.

79 "Netanyahu upbraids top general for 'outrageous' Shoah comparison." *Times of Israel,* May 8, 2016.

80 "Israeli official sparks firestorm by calling settlers 'despicable,' 'subhuman.'" *The Arab Weekly,* June 1, 2022.

81 Eisenkot, Gadi, and Gabi Siboni. 2019. *Guidelines for Israel's National Security Strategy.* The Washington Institute for Near East Policy, p. 37.

82 Bachner, Michael. "'Near-criminal behavior': Eisenkot claims disarray, indecision, politics in PM's war conduct." *Times of Israel,* Nov. 9, 2024.

83 "Israel is at a crossroads in Gaza." MISGAV/The Institute for National Security & Zionist Strategy, Nov. 4, 2024.

84 Eiland, Giora. "Let's not be intimidated by the world." Yedioth Ahronoth, Nov. 19, 2023.

85 Ibid.

86 On the consequent debate, see "Health experts denounce retired general's claim to let Gaza be destroyed." *The Jerusalem Post,* Nov. 26, 2023; "Humanitarian catastrophe as policy." *B'Tselem,* Dec. 7, 2023.

87 Horowitz, David. "A top ex-general's radical strategy for tackling Iran, saving the hostages, calming the north." *Times of Israel,* April 17, 2024.

Epilogue

1 Abraham, Yuval. "'A mass assassination factory': Inside Israel's calculated bombing of Gaza." *+972 Magazine,* Nov. 30, 2023. On the doctrines of mass devastation, see Steinbock, Dan. 2025. *The Fall of Israel* (Atlanta, GA: Clarity Press), esp. Chapter 4 .

2 "Emphasis is on damage, not accuracy': ground offensive into Gaza seems imminent." *The Guardian,* Oct. 10, 2023.

3 "Exclusive: Nearly half of the Israeli munitions dropped on Gaza are imprecise 'dumb bombs,' US intelligence assessment finds." *CNN,* Dec. 14, 2023.

4 Abraham, Yuval. "'Lavender': The AI machine directing Israel's bombing spree in Gaza." *+972 Magazine* in partnership with *Local Call,* April 3, 2024.

5 "'The smell of death is everywhere' in northern Gaza, UNRWA chief says." *UN News,* Oct. 22, 2024.

6 Mbembe, Achille. 2003. "Sign In." *Public Culture* 15, no. 1 (Winter 2003): 11–40; Mbembe, Achille. 2019. *Necropolitics* (Durham: Duke University Press).

7 On necrotization, see the section on "Varieties of Necrotization" in Steinbock 2025, *op. cit.*

8 Diamond, Jeremy. "At least 16 cemeteries in Gaza have been desecrated by Israeli forces, satellite imagery and videos reveal." *CNN,* Jan. 20, 2024; Kottasová, Ivana, et al. "Israel says it is exhuming bodies in Gaza to determine if they're hostages." CNN, Jan. 18, 2024; "100 bodies stolen by Israel reburied in mass grave in Rafah" *Al Jazeera,* Jan. 30, 2024.

9 Steinbock 2025, *op.cit.*

10 Mordowanec, Nick. "Israeli Official Calls for 'Doomsday' Nuclear Missile Option." *Newsweek,* Oct. 10, 2023.

11 Bachner, Michael. "Far-right minister says nuking Gaza an option, PM suspends him from cabinet meetings." *Times of Israel,* Nov. 5, 2023.

12 Steinbock 2025, *op.cit.,* see "The Begin Doctrine" in Chapter 10.

13 "Israel: The ICJ Orders Measure to Prevent Incitement to Genocide and Preserve Evidence." *Article 19,* Jan. 26, 2024.

14 This section draws from Steinbock, Dan. "Unveiling the Nuclear Threats: A Reality of Past and Present." *Antiwar.com,* Aug. 10, 2023. See also Ellsberg, Daniel. 1971. *The Pentagon Papers as published by the New York Times* (New York: Bantam Books). See also Sheinkin, Steve. 2015. *Most Dangerous: Daniel Ellsberg and the Secret History of the Vietnam War* (New York: Roaring Brook Press).

15 Weiner, Tim. "Robert Komer, 78, Figure in Vietnam, Dies." *New York Times,* April 12, 2000.

16 Compare Steinbock, Dan. "Making or Breaking Finland's Future: A Behind-the-Façade Look at Finland After the 2024 Election." *The World Financial Review,* Feb. 2024.

17 Ellsberg, Daniel. 2017. *The Doomsday Machine: Confessions of a Nuclear War Planner* (New York: Bloomsbury), see Prologue.

18 U.S. Nuclear War Plan Option Sought Destruction of China and Soviet Union as "Viable" Societies. Edited by William Burr. National Security Archive, Briefing Book # 638, Aug. 15, 2018.

19 Ellsberg, *The Doomsday Machine,* see Chapter 20.

20 Ibid, see Introduction.

21 Kristensen, Hans. "US Nuclear War Plan Updated Amidst Nuclear Policy Review." Federation of American Scientists, April 4, 2013.

22 2022 National Defense Strategy of the United States of America. Secretary of Defense, Pentagon, Washington, DC, Oct. 27, 2022.

23 Bennett, Michael, et al. *Projected Costs of U.S. Nuclear Forces, 2021 to 2030.* Congressional Budget Office, May 2021.

24 Reif, Kingston, and Alicia Sanders-Zakre. "U.S. Nuclear Excess: Understanding the Costs, Risks, and Alternatives," Arms Control Association, April 2019.

25 Hartung, William D. "Profiteers of Armageddon: Producers of the Next Generation of Nuclear Weapons." Center for International Policy, Oct. 2021. For more, see Chapter 2.

26 *Yearbook of the ILC, 1950,* Vol. I, pp. 131, 162.

27 90th Plenary Meeting of General Assembly: 49th Session. United Nations, Dec. 15, 1994, p. 35.

28 Quoted in: Ginger, Ann Fagan. 1998. *Nuclear Weapons Are Illegal* (New York: The Apex Press), pp. 75–76.

29 For the detailed legal analysis, see Bersagel, Annie Golden. "Use of nuclear weapons as an international crime and the Rome Statute of the International Criminal Court." In: Nystuen, Gro, et al. 2014. *Nuclear Weapons Under International Law* (New York: Cambridge University Press), pp. 221–243.

30 Koskenniemi, Martti. 2001. *The Gentle Civilizer of Nations: The Rise and Fall of International Law 1870–1960* (Cambridge: Cambridge University Press), p. 130.

31 On the exclusion, dilution and erosion, see Prologue. On the outcomes of these processes, see Chapters 1–3. On the undermining of the Genocide Convention, the repression of its enforcement and failure of prevention, see Chapters 4–6.

32 Du Bois, W.E.B. 1904. "Of the Dawn of Freedom." In Foner, Eric and Henry Louis Gates, Jr., Eds. 2021. *W.E.B. Du Bois, Black Reconstruction and Other Writings* (New York: Library of America), pp. 887–905. However, the phrase itself had been used since the time of reconstruction in the aftermath of the Civil War.

33 Steinbock 2025, *op. cit.,* esp. Chapters 1–4.

34 Schabas, William A. 2023. *The International Legal Order's Color Line: Racism, Racial Discrimination, and the Making of International Law* (Oxford: Oxford University Press).

35 Compare Chapter 5.

36 Steinbock, Dan. 2019. "The Uhuru blueprint." The World Financial Review, Mar. 25.

37 Bosco, David. 2022. "The ICC's Impact in Ukraine." Oct 27.

38 "Israel – International Criminal Court." *France Diplomacy,* Nov. 27, 2024, see https://www.diplomatie.gouv.fr/en/country-files/israel-palestinian-territories/news/2024/article/israel-international-criminal-court-27-11-24

39 Steinbock, Dan. 2025. "Duterte's rendition, PH political turmoil and the ICC's dilemma." The Manila Times, Mar. 24.

40 Bosco, David. 2025. "Court in a Storm: Israel, the ICC, and the Trump Administration." *Lawfare,* Feb 6.

41 Steinbock 2025, *op.cit.,* Chapters 1–2, 4 and 8.

42 Compare Chapter 2.

43 On the contested definitions of the term "Gaza War," see Prologue.

44 As trauma surgeon Feroze Sidhwa put it in the *New York Times:* "Nearly every day I was there, I saw a new young child who had been shot in the head or the chest, virtually all of whom went on to die." His statement has been supported by dozens of other remarkable medical volunteers in Gaza. Compare Sidhwa, Feroze. "65 Doctors, Nurses and Paramedics: What We Saw in Gaza." New York Times, Oct. 9, 2024. These testimonies, in turn, have been supported by many reports of multiple international NGOs and multilateral organizations that have been referenced throughout *The Obliteration Doctrine.*

45 Schabas, William. 2009. *Genocide in International Law: The Crime of Crimes.* 2nd Ed. (Cambridge), p. 645.

46 Wentker, Alexander. "More and more cases on war and genocide are being litigated at the ICJ." *Chatham House,* Sept. 4, 2024.

47 Ibid.

48 Data from ICJ.

49 For more on the possibility of "retroactive effect," see Chapter 4.

50 "Israel incensed after Brazil's Lula likens Gaza war to Holocaust." *Reuters,* Feb. 19, 2024.

51 On South African apartheid and Israel's ultra-apartheid, see Steinbock 2025, *op. cit.,* esp. Chapter 9. On similarities and differences between apartheid in Israel and South Africa, see Pappé, Ilan, et al. 2015. *Israel and South Africa: The Many Faces of Apartheid* (Zed Books). On the longstanding cooperation between Israel and apartheid South Africa, see Polakow-Suransky, Sasha. 2011. *The Unspoken Alliance: Israel's Secret Relationship with Apartheid South Africa* (Knopf Doubleday).

52 Steinbock 2025, *op. cit.,* esp. Chapters 1 and 9.

53 "Pentagon fails 7th audit in a row, eyes passing grade by 2028." *Breaking Defense,* Nov. 15, 2024.

54 See Myrdal, Alva. 1976. *The Game of Disarmament: How the United States and Russia Run the Arms Race* (New York: Pantheon).

55 For a discussion, see Steinbock 2025, *op. cit.,* esp. "Compensation Challenge" in Chapter 1.

INDEX